SAT Reading - Blue

Homework: Version 1.3

SAT Reading Blue: Table of Contents

B1HW: Homework and Extra Practice

SC TOPIC: Introduction / Review	RC TOPIC: Active Reading (Lesson B1b)

Homework Set 1

1. Byron had difficulty concentrating on his studies due to the ------ of the nearby construction crew, which included a jackhammer and two trucks with gratingly loud engines.

   (A) eulogy
   (B) accord
   (C) cacophony
   (D) ambivalence
   (E) apprehension

2. Thanks to a knack for making ------ maneuvers, Natasha became a highly successful chess player, eventually ------ the highest rank of "Grand Master."

   (A) prudent . . assailing
   (B) astute . . attaining
   (C) outmoded . . acquiring
   (D) shrewd . . impeding
   (E) moronic . . eradicating

3. At the end of Dickens' *A Christmas Carol*, Ebenezer Scrooge at last ------ his miserly ways and begins performing ------ acts instead.

   (A) retains . . philanthropic
   (B) amends . . vindictive
   (C) relinquishes . . sinister
   (D) endorses . . humanitarian
   (E) renounces . . benevolent

4. It is ------ that the Earth's average temperature is warmer than it was fifty years ago, although there is still some debate about the cause of the increase.

   (A) equitable
   (B) inexplicable
   (C) speculative
   (D) indubitable
   (E) precarious

5. Hugh hoped to ------ burglars by putting a home-security sign in front of his house, even though he did not install an actual security system.

   (A) collaborate with
   (B) entrust
   (C) concede to
   (D) entice
   (E) deter

6. Though it seemed ------ to Sofia that 2 + 2 could equal anything but 4, her teacher assured her that 2 + 2 could indeed equal either 0 or 1.

   (A) plausible
   (B) preposterous
   (C) credible
   (D) discreet
   (E) nominal

7. Leonora walked through the haunted house with great ------, shrieking fearfully at several sights; her anxiety did not ------ until after she exited the spooky abode.

   (A) timidity . . subside
   (B) trepidation . . escalate
   (C) veracity . . dwindle
   (D) spontaneity . . protract
   (E) audacity . . recede

8. After his parents left him alone for the weekend for the first time, Pablo ------ his newfound freedom by turning his music up very loud and dancing through the house.

   (A) dissented from
   (B) reveled in
   (C) derided
   (D) relegated
   (E) suppressed

Homework Set 2

9. Hak-ju reluctantly admitted that his claim that he could eat thirty hot dogs in ten minutes was ------; he could only eat five in that time. *false*

   (A) abundant
   (B) resolute
   (C) spurious ←
   (D) forthright
   (E) valid

10. Veronica was ------ to have won the card game, but her joy was ------; she lost the next ten games.

    (A) distressed . . detrimental
    (B) elated . . transitory ✓
    (C) ecstatic . . eternal
    (D) rueful . . fleeting
    (E) complacent . . perpetual

11. The servant walked around the ballroom with a plate of appetizers, ------ the food to the hungry guests.

    (A) refuting
    (B) withholding ✓
    (C) proffering
    (D) postponing
    (E) ascribing

12. When a police officer ------ *says* that you do something, it is in your best interest to *abide* ------; refusing to obey the police is punishable by probation, fines, and even imprisonment.

    (A) denounces . . abide
    (B) counsels . . antagonize
    (C) dictates . . elude
    (D) mandates . . comply ←
    (E) retracts . . quibble

13. When arguing a case before the Supreme Court, one should always try to ------ similar cases that reinforce your position.

    (A) invoke
    (B) indict
    (C) deplete
    (D) spurn
    (E) evade

14. After each grueling workday, Simone is ------ a debilitating ------ that prevents her from doing anything more active than watching television.

    (A) alleviated by . . fatigue
    (B) mitigated by . . fidelity
    (C) afflicted with . . lethargy
    (D) sustained by . . perplexity
    (E) irked by . . fervor

15. After he was late for class for the fifth time in one semester, Lonnie was *yelled at / punished* ------ by the principal for excessive tardiness and warned that one more offense would result in a suspension.

    (A) censured ← *criticized, found fault with*
    (B) lauded
    (C) acclaimed
    (D) salvaged
    (E) commended

16. Though many people doubted that the film would be successful, its director never ------ *lost* his belief that audiences and critics alike would enjoy the film.

    (A) persisted in
    (B) wavered in ←
    (C) circumvented
    (D) maintained
    (E) annihilated

Unauthorized copying or reuse of any part of this page is illegal.

Version 1.3

Homework Passage 1 (Short)

This passage was written by Henry Adams, the American scholar who was a descendant of the Presidents John Adams and John Quincy Adams.

I knew my grandfather John Quincy Adams only as an old man of seventy-five or eighty who was friendly and gentle with me, and except that I heard my
Line grandfather always called "the President" and my
(5) grandmother "the Madam," I had no reason to suppose that my Adams grandfather differed in character from my Brooks grandfather, who lived in Boston and was equally kind and benevolent. I liked the Adams side best, for no other reason than that it reminded me of the country, the
(10) summer, and the absence of restraint. Yet I felt also that Quincy was in a way inferior to Boston, and that socially Boston looked down on Quincy. The reason was clear enough even to a five year old child: Quincy had no Boston style. A simpler manner of life and thought could
(15) hardly exist short of cave dwelling. Bathrooms, water supplies, lighting, heating and the whole array of domestic comforts were unknown at Quincy. The superiority of Boston was evident but as a child, I liked it no better for that.

17. According to the passage, the narrator "liked the Adams side best" (line 8) primarily because

    (A) his Brooks grandfather was unfriendly.
    (B) he enjoyed the leisurely country lifestyle of Quincy.
    (C) he knew that Boston life was superior.
    (D) his Adams grandfather had been president.
    (E) he preferred to have a bathroom and other domestic comforts.

18. Based on the context of the passage, "simpler" (line 14) most nearly means

    (A) more effortless.
    (B) more austere.
    (C) more idiotic.
    (D) more unpleasant.
    (E) more straightforward.

Homework Passage 2 (Short)

We've learned a lot about living cells since Robert Hooke (1665) viewed cork through a crude microscope and likened the hollow chambers to the "cells" (bare
Line rooms) of a monastery. Now we know that living cells
(5) are not empty at all—they are dynamic micro-environments, complete with microtubule transport networks and protein motors.

With the development of cell theory in 1839, biology became a theoretical science, and with the publication of
(10) "Die Cellularpathologie" ("The Cellular Pathology") by Rudolf Virchow in 1858, modern clinical medicine gained a scientific foundation. Soon after, good health came to be viewed as an outward expression of healthy cells, with disease arising from the cells of a tissue.

19. The passage implies that which of the following is true regarding medicine before the mid-1800s?

    (A) It was not based on scientific principles.
    (B) It rejected folk remedies and superstitions.
    (C) It was largely theoretical.
    (D) It was a well-respected field.
    (E) It focused on the health of individual cells.

20. The primary purpose of the passage is most likely to

    (A) contrast 19th century cell theory with its modern counterpart.
    (B) describe the functions of microtubule transport networks.
    (C) explain the etymology of a common biological term.
    (D) list a few important achievements regarding our knowledge of human cells.
    (E) proclaim the genius of Robert Hooke.

Homework Passage 3 (Long)

This passage describes a new computer game that lets normal people help with actual scientific research.

When you're at home, chances are you're more likely to be folding laundry than folding proteins.

But that's changing with new developments from the
Line University of Washington. Rather than chasing bad guys
(5) and monsters, gamers can now spend screen time helping scientists figure out protein folding. And while the new program, Foldit, may seem like all fun and games to you, it's giving researchers insight into the structure of proteins and their roles in both diseases and treatments.
(10) Computational biologist David Baker created the game, which is free to download, to get more people involved in the important science of protein folding. Proteins, long strings of amino acids, fold up in different shapes that determine how each protein will act. If
(15) scientists can better understand protein folding, they may be able to figure out how to treat and even prevent diseases that stem from misfolded proteins.

Baker's idea for Foldit came from his distributed computing program called Rosetta@home. This program
(20) lets Baker and his colleagues run their software on home computers whose owners "donated" the processors' downtime. As the idle machines helped solve structures, owners watched animated proteins on their screen savers. Some told Baker that they wanted to manipulate the
(25) shape and orientation of the molecules.

Baker listened. With his colleagues Adrien Trehuille, Seth Cooper, and Zoran Popovic, he created Foldit to allow people to make their own moves. Within the first week of launching the program, around 30,000
(30) people worldwide had registered and were playing.

"Distributed computing projects like Rosetta@home tap into the computing power of people around the world, but the hope is with Foldit that we can tap into their brain power," says Baker.
(35) But don't worry. You don't have to know much about protein structures to play the game. In fact, Foldit's top scorer reports in his profile not knowing anything about proteins except that "you should eat them after exercising."
(40) "It's not clear that knowing things about proteins actually helps you do better. It's all about the spatial relationships," says Baker.

And while little knowledge of biology and proteins is necessary to start playing, users will walk away from
(45) the game with an enhanced understanding of these structures. "I think Foldit is a good way for people to learn about biomedical research, and I think that will be really neat because normally, in everyday life, you don't grapple with molecules," says Baker. "Now people have
(50) a much more vivid idea of what [proteins] are."

So how exactly does one play Foldit? It's quite simple. A protein structure will show up on your computer screen. Your job: Move it, shake it, and wiggle it into its most compact and stable form. You do this with
(55) the help of tools, such as "rubber bands" that pull pieces

of the protein together and the "lock tool" that keeps a piece in place. There are also red areas along the protein that represent "clashes," which must be cleared away to obtain the correct protein structure. Beginners even get
(60) tutorials provided by a Web cartoon of Baker himself.

Currently, gamers are working with known proteins. But Baker has plans to take the game where no protein has gone before. Soon, Foldit will offer players protein design problems that require them to develop new
(65) proteins that could disable the flu virus or break down a toxic compound, for example. "The ones that look the best," says Baker, "we can test in the lab experimentally."

The final results could hold a key to curing diseases such as HIV, cancer, and Alzheimer's disease. Baker also
(70) hopes that the program will reach out to people in third world countries who discover an interest and talent in protein folding and decide to pursue careers in structural biology.

So how good at the game is the man behind the
(75) molecule? Baker says he's played a little but is no protein-gaming genius. He says his 13-year-old son Benjamin, who has been involved in the project since early on, is "much better at the game."

21. In the second paragraph, "chasing bad guys and monsters" (lines 4-5) are given as examples of

(A) the types of jobs that David Baker wanted to have as a child.
(B) some of the capabilities of proteins.
(C) activities in typical computer games.
(D) pursuits that are less exciting than folding proteins.
(E) the goals of the computer game called Foldit.

22. According to the third paragraph (lines 10-17), why did David Baker create a video game about protein folding?

(A) because he wanted to make lots of money
(B) to give people a cheap way to spend their free time
(C) because protein is an important part of most people's diets
(D) to increase scientific knowledge by getting more people to understand and manipulate proteins
(E) so that Baker's son could do the same job that Baker does

23. In the context of the passage, the phrase "stem from" (line 17) most nearly means

   (A) originate with
   (B) obstruct
   (C) sail against a wind of
   (D) turn inward toward
   (E) stalk

24. What is one difference between the earlier "Rosetta@home" software and the newer "Foldit" program?

   (A) Foldit allows users to directly manipulate protein structures.
   (B) Foldit costs money to play.
   (C) Rosetta@home deals with sugars, not proteins.
   (D) Foldit runs during a computer's "downtime."
   (E) Rosetta@home was far more effective.

25. According to the passage, which skill is most important to achieving a good score at Foldit?

   (A) the ability to recognize spatial relationships
   (B) a knowledge of diseases such as HIV and Alzheimer's
   (C) the ability to create a computer program
   (D) a knowledge of protein structures
   (E) the ability to create new proteins in a laboratory setting

26. One can infer from the 10th parargraph (lines 51-60) that the most effective proteins are those that are

   (A) as large as possible.
   (B) small and durable.
   (C) the most complicated.
   (D) designed by biomedical experts.
   (E) composed of only a few amino acids.

27. According to the passage, which of the following is NOT a possible benefit of creating new protein structures?

   (A) discovering a cure for cancer
   (B) eliminating the need to test proteins in a lab
   (C) developing a method for disabling the flu virus
   (D) finding a way to prevent Alzheimer's disease
   (E) inventing a protein that breaks down hazardous chemicals

28. What is the most likely function of the last paragraph of the passage (lines 74-78)?

   (A) to identify the reason that Baker created the game
   (B) to prove that younger people are always the best Foldit players
   (C) to introduce a new concept
   (D) to contradict a point from earlier in the passage
   (E) to provide an anecdote that backs up the idea that anyone can play Foldit

29. The primary purpose of the passage is to

   (A) explain the structure of a particular protein.
   (B) describe an interesting new way of tackling a difficult problem.
   (C) summarize the career achievements of David Baker.
   (D) provide an overview of molecular biology.
   (E) argue that more people should play computer games.

Homework Passage 4 (Long)

A young American woman wrote this passage about her experiences living in a small South African village.

It's a Saturday afternoon in January in South Africa. When I begin the 45–minute walk to the shops for groceries, I can hear thunder cracking in the distance up
Line the mountain in Mageobaskloof. But at 4 p.m. the sky is
(5) still light and bright and I am sure—famous last words— I will be fine without an umbrella.

Just the basics: eggs, bread, Diet Coke in a bag slung into the crook of my elbow. Halfway from town, two black South African women—domestic workers in the
(10) homes of white Afrikaner families—stop me with wide smiles. They know me; I'm the only white person in town who walks everywhere, as they do. They chatter quickly in northern Sotho: "Missus, you must go fast. *Pula e tla na!* The rain, it comes!" They like me, and it feels very
(15) important to me that they do. *"Yebo, yebo, mma,"* I say— Yes, it's true—and I hurry along in flip-flops, quickening my pace, feeling good about our brief but neighborly conversation. These are Venda women.

My black South African friends tell me it's easy to
(20) tell a Venda from a Shangaan from a Xhosa from a Pedi. "These ones from Venda , they have wide across the nose and high in the cheekbones," they say. But I don't see it; I'm years away from being able to distinguish the nuances of ethnicity. Today, I know these women are
(25) Vendas simply because of their clothing: bright stripes of green and yellow and black fabric tied at one shoulder and hanging quite like a sack around their bodies. They've already extended a kindness to me by speaking in northern Sotho. It's not their language but they know I
(30) don't speak a word of Afrikaans (though they don't understand why; Afrikaans is the language of white people). They know I struggle with Sotho and they're trying to help me learn. So they speak Sotho to me and they're delighted and amused by my fumbling responses.
(35) And I am, quite simply, delighted by their delight.

The Venda ladies are right: the rain, it comes. Lightly at first, and by habit I begin trotting to hurry my way home. Just a little rain at first and there are plenty of us out in it. I can see others up ahead on the street and
(40) others still just leaving the shops to get back before the real rain begins.

The people who are walking along this swath of tar road are black. Black people don't live in this neighborhood—or in my town at all, for the most part.
(45) They work and board here as domestic workers, nannies, gardeners. Their families live in black townships and rural villages—some just outside of my town; others far away, in places like Venda.

Today, we're walking together in the rain, and I'm
(50) quickening my pace because—after all , *it's raining* . That's what you do in the rain. And even though it's coming down noticeably harder, it's 80 degrees and I'm not cold, I'm just wet. My hair is stuck to my forehead and my T-shirt is soaked... and I'm the only one running
(55) for cover. And I think: So what? It's just water and in the middle of the January summer, it's warm, refreshing water. Why run? Why do we run from the rain?

In my life back in the United States, I might run because I was carrying a leather handbag, or because I
(60) wore an outfit that shouldn't get wet. I would run because rain dishevels and messes things up. Mostly though, we run because we just do; it's a habit. I've done it a hundred times: running to my car or the subway station with a newspaper sheltering my head. I have never not
(65) quickened my pace in the rain until today.

It took all of my 27 years and a move to Africa, where I don't have a leather handbag to shelter or a pretty outfit to protect. I'm wearing an old cotton skirt and a T-shirt, and I'm drenched, and I love it. I learn things here
(70) in the most ordinary circumstances. And I feel like a smarter, better woman today because I got groceries in the rain.

30. Which of the following would make the best title for the passage?

   (A) How to Tell a Xhosa from a Pedi
   (B) Why I Miss My Leather Handbag and Pretty Outfit
   (C) Learning to Love the Rain
   (D) The Languages of South Africa
   (E) A History of Americans in Africa

31. In the first paragraph, the narrator describes "thunder cracking in the distance" in order to

   (A) provide an interesting but unimportant detail.
   (B) foreshadow an event that occurs later in the passage.
   (C) show that the rain will not come to her town.
   (D) hint that a battle is being fought in the nearby mountains.
   (E) use a metaphor to describe the relationship between blacks and whites in South Africa.

32. How does the narrator identify the ethnicity of the women that she talks to?

   (A) by listening to their accents
   (B) by asking them directly what village they are from
   (C) by determining which language they speak
   (D) by examining their facial features
   (E) by looking at the colors of their clothing

33. The passage implies that the narrator is different from the other white people in the town because she

   (A) does not speak Afrikaans.
   (B) does not speed up when it is about to rain.
   (C) does not drive a car.
   (D) has a leather handbag.
   (E) cannot distinguish between different ethnicities.

34. Why do the Venda women address the narrator in the language of northern Sotho?

   (A) That is their native tongue.
   (B) That is the narrator's native tongue.
   (C) The Venda women are trying to learn to speak Sotho.
   (D) They are helping the narrator learn the Sotho language.
   (E) They are trying to confuse the narrator.

35. The passage implies that most of the people on the road with the narrator are

   (A) black servants and other employees of the rich, white families in this neighborhood.
   (B) wealthy residents of the neighborhood.
   (C) poor citizens of the nearby slum.
   (D) tourists visiting from other countries.
   (E) American aid workers.

36. According to the author, why did she always run through the rain when she was in America?

   (A) She did not want to ruin her clothes and other belongings.
   (B) She was not carrying heavy objects like groceries.
   (C) She had running shoes on instead of flip-flops.
   (D) She was afraid of being hit by lightning.
   (E) She enjoyed playing in the refreshing water.

37. Why does the narrator feel like a "smarter, better woman" (line 71) after walking through the rain shower?

   (A) She has learned how to speak Sotho fluently.
   (B) She correctly predicted the arrival of the storm.
   (C) She is the only person in the town who realizes that rain will not damage a t-shirt.
   (D) She learned that rain does not have to be feared, and can even be pleasant to walk through.
   (E) She learned an important fact about the town in a conversation she had while in the rain.

38. Which of the following best expresses the main idea of the passage?

   (A) Black and white South Africans can learn to live together in harmony.
   (B) Weather forecasters are never correct.
   (C) Never leave home without an umbrella.
   (D) Not understanding the language of the locals can get you into trouble.
   (E) Sometimes, even ordinary events can teach you important lessons.

B2HW: Homework and Extra Practice

| SC Topic: Using the 5-Step Method (Lesson B2A) | RC Topic: Active Reading (Lesson B1b) |

Homework Set 1

1. The so-called "Pony Express"—a network of horses and riders that delivered mail in the 19th century—became ------ when railroads made mail delivery quicker and easier.

   (A) conventional
   (B) compulsory
   (C) outmoded
   (D) docile
   (E) congenial

2. Despite its advertising, which claimed that the product would help bald men have a full head of hair again, most users experienced only ------ hair re-growth.

   (A) pertinent
   (B) submissive
   (C) extravagant
   (D) marginal
   (E) egregious

3. Whereas Lillian's simple silver necklace was ------ and inexpensive, Jeanette's diamond-encrusted tiara was gaudy and ------.

   (A) abundant . . discreet
   (B) modest . . ostentatious
   (C) acerbic . . voracious
   (D) unadorned . . homely
   (E) inexplicable . . blatant

4. Miles has a gift for providing ------ and easy-to-follow explanations of even the most ------ phenomena.

   (A) comprehensible . . indubitable
   (B) timid . . covert
   (C) obsolete . . astute
   (D) discordant . . indistinct
   (E) lucid . . intricate

5. In some cultures, a funeral is not the ------ occasion that it is in America; for instance, the Maori celebrate the deceased by chanting and dancing around his or her grave.

   (A) auspicious
   (B) contentious
   (C) expansive
   (D) benign
   (E) somber

6. Ariel spoke with ------ voice, declaring that the world would end in 2012 because that is the end of the Mayan calendar.

   (A) a tranquil
   (B) a complacent
   (C) a portentous
   (D) a cordial
   (E) an incredulous

7. The suspect originally confessed to the crime, but later ------, saying that the police coerced his confession and that he was innocent of wrongdoing.

   (A) affirmed
   (B) recanted
   (C) conceded
   (D) elicited
   (E) attained

8. When writing an essay, it is better to be brief than ------, for a ------ argument will hold the reader's attention better than a long-winded one.

   (A) pliable . . contemptuous
   (B) verbose . . concise
   (C) economical . . superfluous
   (D) effusive . . desolate
   (E) eccentric . . terse

Homework Set 2

9. Preparing one's taxes can be a ------ process, requiring great patience and ------, which is why many people hire an accountant to relieve this burden.

   (A) rousing . . apprehension
   (B) laborious . . prominence
   (C) transitory . . perseverance
   (D) engrossing . . turmoil
   (E) tedious . . persistence

10. Ned was ------ to be a terrible dancer, but he proved his friends' perceptions wrong by performing an expert waltz at the school dance.

    (A) mandated
    (B) reputed
    (C) proffered
    (D) acclaimed
    (E) delegated

11. The ------ crowd cheered loudly and ------, not letting up until the band came out to perform an encore.

    (A) lethargic . . incessantly
    (B) dejected . . dubiously
    (C) vehement . . dormantly
    (D) fervent . . resolutely
    (E) indifferent . . protractedly

12. As her father tickled her belly, Moriko ------ on the bed, kicking her feet and giggling uncontrollably.

    (A) deplored
    (B) invoked
    (C) writhed
    (D) stifled
    (E) idled

13. The identical twins understood each other so well that they often communicated solely by ------ gestures, and rarely spoke out loud unless others were present.

    (A) implicit
    (B) assertive
    (C) emphatic
    (D) dissenting
    (E) derisive

14. Despite its many dangers, mountain climbing has a powerful ------ for many outdoors enthusiasts, who ------ the challenge of the climb and the reward of spectacular views.

    (A) repulsion . . denounce
    (B) glamour . . retract
    (C) allure . . savor
    (D) repugnance . . regard
    (E) contempt . . venerate

15. After over three hours of ------ exercise in the scorching summer heat, Linus was tired and drenched in sweat.

    (A) delinquent
    (B) negligible
    (C) strenuous
    (D) elusive
    (E) spurious

16. Zafar's friends watched in amazement as he ------ painted each tiny figurine with an even tinier brush, never making a mistake.

    (A) deftly
    (B) reclusively
    (C) adversely
    (D) spuriously
    (E) ineptly

Homework Passage 1 (Short Paired)

Passage 1:

When people think of taxes today, they often think first of the much-hated federal income tax, which requires each person to pay a portion of his or her *Line* earnings to the federal government each year. Yet the
(5) federal income tax is a relatively recent invention. The reason for this is that the Constitution specifically prohibited the federal government from collecting income taxes from citizens. Thus, the United States made do for more than 140 years with various forms of tariffs
(10) (taxes on imported goods) and excise taxes (taxes on the purchase of specific products, such as gasoline or tobacco). It was not until the ratification of the 16th Amendment in 1913 that the government gained the ability to impose a permanent income tax.

Passage 2:

(15) Nobody likes paying taxes; it is only human nature to want to hold on to as much of one's hard-earned income as possible, even if one knows the tax is being used for a good cause. The antipathy toward taxes is perhaps highest in America, with its individualist spirit
(20) and strong work ethic underscoring the value of a good day's work. The federal income tax, in particular, seems to have aroused the ire of the American populace, though some of this ire is misplaced.

For instance, anti-income tax protestors argue that
(25) the tax is overly progressive, in other words that it disproportionately affects the rich. These arguments seem at first to have some basis, as in 2007 over 50% of federal income tax collected was from the wealthiest 5% of earners. However, since these same 5% hold nearly
(30) 60% of the nation's wealth, the rich are perhaps paying slightly *less* than their fair share.

17. The primary purpose of Passage 1 is most likely to

(A) provide an overview of 20th century constitutional amendments.
(B) refute arguments against the federal income tax.
(C) recount a brief history of United States taxation.
(D) criticize rich Americans for not paying enough in taxes.
(E) discuss the reasoning behind arguments against the income tax.

18. Passage 2 implies that Americans are particularly susceptible to a dislike of taxes because

(A) the American tax system is quite unfair, compared to those of other countries.
(B) American culture is focused more on the individual than on the community.
(C) most people disagree with the ways in which the government uses its tax revenue.
(D) Americans, by and large, are greedy and selfish.
(E) America pays more in taxes than a less prosperous nation would.

19. The tones of the two passages' discussions regarding the United States federal income tax differ in that the tone of Passage 1 is more

(A) sympathetic.
(B) content.
(C) objective.
(D) sarcastic.
(E) prejudiced.

20. Both passages cite the income tax as being

(A) a uniquely American innovation.
(B) too harsh on rich taxpayers.
(C) more effective than tariffs and excise taxes.
(D) an institution that is commonly disliked.
(E) unconstitutional at the federal level prior to 1913.

Homework Passage 2 (Long)

The following passage examines the effects that electronic media have had on writing in an educational setting.

Hailed as a powerful educational resource, the e-medium has been found to encourage participation in writing activity. One reason for this is that e-mail and
Line online chats provide a non-threatening atmosphere in
(5) which writers feel less inhibited about expressing themselves, encouraging even timid students who usually refuse to speak in face-to-face discussions to actively participate in online chats. Another reason is that the Web provides an arena for writers to present their work
(10) to a real and larger audience that extends beyond classroom and school boundaries. When students realize that they are going to put their work on the Web for readers in the real world, they are motivated to write.

The online domain has also substantially increased
(15) opportunities for collaboration in writing. One recent study found that teachers are using the Internet to create complex partnerships among their students and posting the results online. Online collaborative tools allow students to exchange critiques synchronously or
(20) asynchronously. Students learn to reference each other's texts, thus developing "threading and synthesizing skills" as well as a heightened awareness of audience. This sense of audience motivates them to write carefully and to be more accountable for their writing.

(25) Collaborative writing activity has prompted researchers to compare the use of synchronous chats and asynchronous e-mail in providing peer response for aiding revision. While there was no difference in terms of the usefulness of comments, it was found that students
(30) made significantly greater use of e-mail for detailed reference to the contents and rhetoric, while they used chats for brainstorming and exploring the topic.

While the e-medium has been found to increase collaborative writing activity there are mixed views on
(35) whether it has had a similar effect on the quantity and quality of writing done by individual students. Because the e-medium reduces the intimidation factor and offers attractive features, it improves students' attitudes towards writing and practicing the target language and
(40) encourages students to produce more text. One study found that second-language learners using e-mail for their dialogue journals generated more language than those who used pencil and paper.

However, a second study, which addressed some of
(45) the limitations of the first, indicated that the e-mail group did not significantly out-perform the pen-and-pencil group in length of text, grammatical accuracy or vocabulary. Thus, there is no conclusive evidence that the use of e-mail has any advantages in terms of student
(50) performance. In addition, while some studies show that the amount of discourse increases when writing is done via e-mail, the length of "academic" writing does not seem to be affected.

Although some researchers claim that students
(55) proofread more given the ease with which revision can be carried out on-screen, one study found that many others rely only on software to check spelling and grammar. Students are also often unwilling to revisit words that have scrolled off their screen. Moreover,
(60) rewriting is a slow process and is in conflict with the computer culture that encourages speed. As a result, students are more accustomed to writing in the conversational style of e-mail discussions, but not in formal prose. Even if essays are longer and immaculately
(65) word-processed, they may be poorly structured and articulated. There is an "additive style" in the writing, similar to the structure of a small child's speech: "And this happened. And then that. And so then this." While this style is acceptable in online communication, it
(70) translates into poor structure in a formal essay.

Another study examined the texts of writers responding to writing prompts using different media: e-mail and word processing. While there were no obvious differences between e-mail and word-processed writing
(75) in the use of cohesive features, they differed in text length, with e-mail responses being significantly shorter than word-processed essays. In word-processed essays, writers make an effort to provide some kind of background information on the topic before responding
(80) to the essay prompt, while e-mail writers tend to begin right away by responding the prompt, doing away with contextualized information. This research reveals yet another example of how writing is being shaped by the e-medium.

21. Which of the following best describes the author's attitude toward electronic writing?

    (A) genuinely objective
    (B) highly critical
    (C) humorously disapproving
    (D) ironically cheerful
    (E) extremely complimentary

22. In context, the word "Hailed" (line 1) most nearly means

    (A) Spoken to
    (B) Praised
    (C) Summoned
    (D) Attacked
    (E) Sleeted

23. The passage states that one of the reasons electronic writing "has been found to encourage participation" (line 2) is that

(A) students can type faster than they can write by hand.
(B) teachers can easily grade electronic essays.
(C) students know that their essays will have better structure if they write electronically.
(D) electronic word processors improve students' grammar and spelling.
(E) students are more motivated to write when they know they will have an audience beyond their teacher.

24. What is the main effect of the "heightened awareness of audience" (line 22) that collaborative writing provides?

(A) It increases students' anxiety about pleasing their readers.
(B) It reduces students' inhibitions about sharing their thoughts.
(C) It encourages students to be more thoughtful and responsible in their writing.
(D) It makes it harder for them to synthesize the ideas in other writings.
(E) It allows students to share the credit for a successful paper.

25. The passage states that students are most likely to use online chats for what aspect of the collaborative writing process?

(A) brainstorming
(B) proofreading
(C) referencing other students' work
(D) detailed critique
(E) providing background information

26. According to the passage, why does the e-medium improve "students' attitudes towards writing" (lines 38-39)?

(A) The e-medium allows them to easily improve the structure of their essays.
(B) Students enjoy being able to surf the Internet while they write.
(C) The e-medium helps them to easily write grammatically correct essays.
(D) Computers allow for easy access to primary and secondary sources.
(E) The e-medium helps students feel more comfortable during the writing process.

27. The passage implies that the "second study" (line 44) to compare email writing to pen-and-paper writing

(A) was the first to show that email writing helps students to produce more language.
(B) was biased toward pen-and-paper writing.
(C) provides conclusive evidence that email writing helps students improve their grammatical accuracy.
(D) was better-designed that the earlier study.
(E) should be dismissed as flawed and inconclusive.

28. The primary function of the 6th paragraph (lines 54-70) is to

(A) praise the ease with which students can proofread using electronic word processors.
(B) provide an example of one of the advantages of writing essays through email.
(C) introduce the main idea of the passage.
(D) summarize several points made earlier in the passage.
(E) partially refute a claim made by others.

29. According to the passage, why are essays written in a word processor typically longer than those written through email?

(A) The email format encourages students to reduce the amount of cohesive features in an essay.
(B) Students using email use simpler grammatical structures.
(C) Students provide more background information when writing in a word processor.
(D) It is easier to collaborate on an essay using a word processor.
(E) Students use more of an "additive style" when writing in a word processor.

30. The primary purpose of the passage is to

(A) provide a short history of word processing software.
(B) contrast synchronous and asynchronous forms of communication.
(C) examine the effects of new technology on students' writing.
(D) praise teachers for replacing pen-and-paper essays with essays written on a computer.
(E) outline the proper structure for a formal essay.

Unauthorized copying or reuse of any part of this page is illegal.

Version 1.3

Homework Passage 3 (Long)

This excerpt from a popular science journal examines a few recent efforts to reduce damage caused by earthquakes.

The devastating effects of earthquakes are well known in Alaska. The great March 27, 1964 (Good Friday), Alaska earthquake shook the ground for more
Line than 4 minutes over a 50,000-square-mile zone of
(5) destruction and caused 131 deaths and as much as $500 million (1964 dollars) in property damage. This magnitude 9.2 event, the largest earthquake ever recorded in the Northern Hemisphere, left scars on the landscape that are still visible today.
(10) Much work has been done since 1964 to mitigate the damaging effects of earthquakes, both in Alaska and nationwide. For example, earthquake-monitoring networks have been established with real-time reporting capabilities, probabilistic seismic-hazard assessments
(15) have been performed, building-code seismic provisions have been updated and adopted, and emergency-response plans have been developed and practiced. The U.S. Geological Survey (USGS) and cooperating organizations have pursued extensive earthquake
(20) research in Alaska and elsewhere, but despite all these advances, further progress is needed, particularly in the area of earthquake engineering of structures.
Earthquake-resistant design is the first line of defense in reducing community losses from earthquakes.
(25) To improve building safety, better knowledge is needed of both the mechanics of ground shaking and the response of structures to that shaking. Seismologists are seeking to mathematically model how seismic waves propagate through the Earth, so that the strength and
(30) duration of future ground shaking at a site can be more accurately predicted. Additionally, engineers are working to understand how their designed structures respond to strong ground shaking, so that both existing and new buildings can be strengthened adequately to withstand
(35) projected earthquake shaking.
Study and analysis of how a structure responds to strong ground shaking is limited today by the scarcity of earthquake recordings from within buildings. Currently, only a few buildings in the United States have been
(40) extensively instrumented to record their performance during earthquakes. This scarcity of directly obtained data means that engineers must infer the characteristics of structural response to earthquakes when they design buildings.
(45) Recently, the Federal Government has provided funding for a pilot program to improve ground and structural recording of earthquake-induced shaking in high-risk urban areas. This effort, known as the Advanced National Seismic System (ANSS), has an
(50) eventual goal of placing 3,000 strongmotion recorders in buildings and other engineered structures around the United States, as well as 3,000 instruments at "free field" sites (that is, recordings on the ground free from the influence of engineered structures). Together, these
(55) structural monitoring systems will provide engineers with critical answers as to how particular building types respond to strong ground shaking.

31. What is the primary purpose of the first paragraph?

 (A) to argue that more buildings should be monitored for the effects of earthquakes
 (B) to give the reader and idea of the type of damage that a large earthquake can cause.
 (C) to describe some ways in which buildings can be made safer from earthquakes
 (D) to examine a problem with most current buildings
 (E) to list a few ways in which America has improved its earthquake readiness in recent years

32. Which of the following has the United States NOT done since 1964 to reduce the damage of earthquakes?

 (A) developed new plans for responding to disasters
 (B) gained a complete understanding of how buildings of all types respond to earthquakes
 (C) established networks to monitor earthquakes
 (D) revised building codes to require more earthquake protections
 (E) performed extensive research throughout the country

33. The passage implies that which of the following is the greatest cause of damage and loss of life in an earthquake?

 (A) an inadequate emergency response plan
 (B) falling rocks and other objects
 (C) unstable roads and bridges
 (D) gas leaks caused by broken pipes
 (E) damaged and collapsed buildings

34. What is the main limitation to scientists' current understanding of how buildings respond to earthquakes?

 (A) a lack of buildings fitted with instruments that measure movement during earthquakes
 (B) politicians' unwillingness to support the Advanced National Seismic System
 (C) there have been no major earthquakes in America in the last 15 years
 (D) an inability to extract meaningful data from the building sensors that are currently in place
 (E) developers' refusal to construct buildings that meet stricter building code standards

35. The passage implies that "strongmotion recorders" (line 50) are designed to

   (A) compute the cost needed to repair the damage caused by an earthquake
   (B) simulate the effects of a 9.2-magnitude earthquake
   (C) make note of how buildings move when the earth beneath them shakes
   (D) detect the epicenter of an earthquake
   (E) alert citizens that an earthquake is imminent

36. Which of the following best expresses the main idea of the passage?

   (A) The Good Friday earthquake caused more damage than any other American natural disaster.
   (B) Most structures built today are completely safe from earthquakes.
   (C) Efforts are underway to determine how to build structures that are more earthquake-resistant.
   (D) Building codes have changed little since the 1964 Alaska earthquake.
   (E) Most tall buildings in urban areas are now outfitted with strongmotion recorders.

B3HW: Homework and Extra Practice

SC TOPIC: Using the 5-Step Method (Lesson B2a)	RC TOPIC: Active Reading (Lesson B1b)

Homework Set 1

1. Though many people would consider a 600-square-foot apartment to be too cramped for 3 people, the Smith family prefers such a ------ existence.

   (A) marginal
   (B) expansive
   (C) malevolent
   (D) cozy
   (E) voluminous

2. One of the most ------ aspects of a college dean's job is the chance to ------ a favorite student a hard-earned degree during the graduation ceremony.

   (A) repugnant . . begrudge
   (B) exasperating . . impart to
   (C) alluring . . evade from
   (D) disquieting . . retract from
   (E) gratifying . . bestow upon

3. Though Helena was talkative around her friends, she was not ------; her ------ disappeared when she was forced to interact with strangers.

   (A) reclusive . . eloquence
   (B) congenial . . frigidity
   (C) evocative . . terseness
   (D) gregarious . . effusiveness
   (E) equivocal . . apprehension

4. Bernard was generally quite easygoing and willing to compromise, but he could be quite ------ when he desperately wanted something.

   (A) pertinent
   (B) astute
   (C) cordial
   (D) obstinate
   (E) proficient

5. Advertising has increasingly come to ------ not just radio and television, but all other aspects of our lives, as ------ by the logos on many sports team uniforms.

   (A) perplex . . embodied
   (B) pervade . . exemplified
   (C) reconcile . . mandated
   (D) permeate . . relinquished
   (E) repudiate . . endorsed

6. To Vladimir, the ------ reason to pay off his credit card at the end of each month is to avoid paying interest on his purchases; he hates paying more than necessary.

   (A) dubious
   (B) resilient
   (C) predominant
   (D) superfluous
   (E) negligible

7. Amelie would have loved to attend all of the World Cup soccer matches, but she could not, because many of them were held ------ at different venues.

   (A) ambivalently
   (B) tentatively
   (C) preposterously
   (D) concurrently
   (E) voraciously

8. After patiently scanning the forest for over 12 hours, the scientist was rewarded for her ------ when a magnificent blue bird-of-paradise emerged and performed a mating dance.

   (A) prosperity
   (B) antagonism
   (C) censure
   (D) contempt
   (E) vigilance

Homework Set 2

9. Bart paid ten dollars extra to ------ the delivery of his textbook, for he needed to have it as soon as possible.

    (A) impede
    (B) circumvent
    (C) curtail
    (D) deplete
    (E) expedite

10. Whenever she is ------, Kyung-yoon's friends take her out to a happy movie to try to ------ her misery.

    (A) elated . . provoke
    (B) dejected . . comply with
    (C) auspicious . . mitigate
    (D) cognizant . . revel in
    (E) despondent . . alleviate

11. During the debate, Arnold skillfully ------ all of his opponent's arguments using ample evidence and ------ logic.

    (A) contradicted . . erroneous
    (B) ascribed . . spurious
    (C) placated . . abundant
    (D) refuted . . impeccable
    (E) recanted . . scant

12. The charity program provides both ------ benefits, such as food and shelter, and less noticeable ones, like hope.

    (A) tangible
    (B) averse
    (C) implicit
    (D) equitable
    (E) destitute

13. The condition of the mountain cabin slowly ------ over the decades until the walls finally fell over.

    (A) cultivated
    (B) deteriorated
    (C) protracted
    (D) recuperated
    (E) revoked

14. The tone of the conversation quickly turned ------ when Christina ------ Brittany's outfit as cheap and ugly.

    (A) placid . . mocked
    (B) contentious . . commended
    (C) laudatory . . invoked
    (D) conducive . . attained
    (E) acerbic . . derided

15. To be a successful inventor, one must possess both persistence and the ------ to challenge old ways of thinking.

    (A) timidity
    (B) audacity
    (C) lenience
    (D) indifference
    (E) frailty

16. Marco lives ------ life, with only one set of clothes and few other possessions.

    (A) an extravagant
    (B) a compulsory
    (C) an ascetic
    (D) a lavish
    (E) a fervent

Homework Passage 1 (Short Paired)

Passage 1:

All air conditioners work using the same basic chemical processes. A fan blows warm air across pipes that contain a cold fluid, cooling the air inside a building,
Line car, or other space. The fluid, which is now warm, then
(5) flows outside the building, taking its warmth with it. To enhance the cooling power of the fluid, the pipes are bent into lots of small coils. This maximizes the surface area of cold pipe that is exposed to the airflow from the fan.

Early air conditioners used water as the fluid, but its
(10) relatively high freezing point of 32º F (0º C) limited the amount of cooling power it could provide (frozen water can't flow through pipes, after all). One common modern coolant, by contrast, freezes at -247º F (-155º C) and *boils* at -55º F (-49º C). This allows modern air
(15) conditioners to cool the air far more efficiently and effectively than older models.

Passage 2:

You may think of air conditioning as a fairly recent invention, and indeed the *modern* air conditioner was
Line only invented (by Willis Haviland Carrier) in 1902. The
(20) basic process of blowing air across a cool fluid to lower a room's temperature, though, dates back almost two thousand years. The Chinese inventor Ding Huan devised a rotary fan in the year 180 that blew water across fountains to cool the imperial palace. His invention
(25) remained popular for over 1,000 years in China but never spread to other countries.

In the 17ᵗʰ and 18ᵗʰ centuries, Western scientists began to develop more advanced systems, using salt water, alcohol, and ether as the cooling fluids. With the
(30) many important discoveries in chemistry in the 19ᵗʰ century, coolants that could achieve even lower temperatures were developed, leading to the first modern air conditioners starting in the early 20ᵗʰ century. One downside to these improvements is that the new coolants
(35) have the potential to cause enormous amounts of environmental damage by contributing to global warming effects. Today's most common coolants are thousands of times more damaging by volume than the most common "greenhouse gas," carbon dioxide.

17. Passage 1 implies that the most important factor in determining the best coolant is

(A) the temperatures at which it freezes and boils.
(B) its density.
(C) its potential to contribute to global warming.
(D) how much it costs.
(E) the degree to which it is poisonous to humans.

18. The author of Passage 2 most likely italicizes the word *"modern"* in line 18 in order to

(A) indicate that the word is a slang term.
(B) introduce an English word that has a Chinese origin.
(C) show that the author considers the word to be outdated.
(D) emphasize a distinction between a current technology and its ancestors.
(E) specify that the term is being used ironically.

19. Both passages mention which improvement in air conditioning technology?

(A) using closed pipes rather than open pipes to reduce energy loss
(B) developing coolants that can reach drastically lower temperatures
(C) using rotary fans instead of hand-powered fans
(D) bending pipes into dense coils with greater surface area
(E) identifying coolants that are less environmentally destructive

20. The tones of the two passages differ in that Passage 1's tone is more

(A) informal.
(B) reflective.
(C) pessimistic.
(D) sympathetic.
(E) technical.

Homework Passage 2 (Long)

This passage analyzes the effects of long summer breaks on students' ability to retain knowledge.

In the early years of formal schooling in America, school calendars were designed to fit the needs of each particular community. Some communities had long
Line summer breaks that released children from school in
(5) spring to help with planting and in fall to help with the harvest, while urban schools sometimes operated on 11- or 12-month schedules. By 1900, migration from the farm to the city and an increase in family mobility created a need to standardize the time children spent in
(10) school. The present 9-month calendar emerged when 85% of Americans were involved in agriculture and when climate control in school buildings was limited. Today, about 3% of Americans' livelihoods are tied to the agricultural cycle, and air-conditioning makes it
(15) possible for schools to provide comfortable learning environments year-round. Nevertheless, the 9-month school year remains the standard.

In 1993, the National Education Commission on Time and Learning urged school districts to develop
(20) school calendars that acknowledged differences in student learning and major changes taking place in American society. The report reflected a growing concern about school calendar issues, especially for students at risk for academic failure.
(25) Educators and parents often voice three concerns about the possible negative impact of summer vacation on student learning. One concern is that children learn best when instruction is continuous. The long summer vacation breaks the rhythm of instruction, leads to
(30) forgetting, and requires a significant amount of review of material when students return to school in the fall. Also, the long summer break can have a greater negative effect on the learning of children with special educational needs. For example, children who speak a language at
(35) home other than English may have their English language skills set back by an extended period without practice, although there currently is little evidence related to this issue. Children with some disabilities may also profit from summer programs. While there is little
(40) evidence that a student's IQ is related to the impact of summer break at least one study has provided some evidence that children with learning disabilities may need extra summer learning opportunities. Many states mandate extended-year programs for students with
(45) learning disabilities because they recognize these children's need for continuous instruction. And finally, tying summer vacation to equity issues, one study noted that "Higher SES students may return to school in the fall with a considerable educational advantage over their less
(50) advantaged peers as a result of either additional school-related learning, or lower levels of forgetting, over the summer months."

A summary of recent research integrated 39 studies examining the effects of summer vacation on
(55) standardized achievement test scores. The 39 studies included 13 that could be included in a meta-analysis (a statistical integration) of the results. The meta-analysis indicated that summer learning loss equaled at least one month of instruction as measured by grade level
(60) equivalents on standardized test scores. On average, children's tests scores were at least one month lower when they returned to school in fall than scores were when students left in spring.

The meta-analysis also found differences in the
(65) effect of summer vacation on different skill areas. Summer loss was more pronounced for math facts and spelling than for other tested skill areas. The explanation of this result was based on the observation that both math computation and spelling skills involve the acquisition of
(70) factual and procedural knowledge, whereas other skill areas, especially math concepts, problem solving, and reading comprehension, are conceptually based. Findings in cognitive psychology suggest that without practice, facts and procedural skills are most susceptible to
(75) forgetting. Summer loss was more pronounced for math overall than for reading overall. The authors speculated that children's home environments might provide more opportunities to practice reading skills than to practice mathematics. Parents may be more attuned to the
(80) importance of reading, so they pay attention to keeping their children reading over summer.

21. The passage implies that American schools in the 1800s

(A) mostly took only a short summer break.
(B) were predominantly located in urban areas.
(C) relied on air conditioning in the summers.
(D) had varying schedules depending on the needs of the community.
(E) were rigidly standardized.

22. According to the passage, "the 9-month calendar" (line 10) became the standard because

(A) most students needed to take the summer months off to work on farms.
(B) educators thought that students needed a long break from learning.
(C) cash-strapped school districts could not afford to stay open all year.
(D) air conditioning allowed students to stay cool at home in the summer months.
(E) only 3% of students lived in rural areas.

23. The passage implies that which types of students are most harmed by long summer breaks?

    (A) those who have learned the most during the school year
    (B) those who speak English as their native language
    (C) those who are at risk of failing
    (D) those who live in rural areas
    (E) those with high IQs

24. Which of the following is NOT a concern about the 9-month schedule voiced by parents and educators?

    (A) Students with learning disabilities do not have a chance to catch up to their peers.
    (B) The long break interrupts the rhythm of instruction.
    (C) Much of the beginning of each school year is devoted to re-learning previously learned material.
    (D) Parents are unable to afford childcare for the summer months.
    (E) Children who speak a language other than English at home may have very high levels of forgetting.

25. What is the "meta-analysis" (line 56) that the author refers to in the last 2 paragraphs?

    (A) a computer simulation of expected results
    (B) an argument that the author disagrees with
    (C) a survey of parents that gauges their support for year-round school
    (D) a study that incorporates the results of many other studies
    (E) research that produced no conclusive results

26. As it is used in the passage, the word "pronounced" (line 66) most nearly means

    (A) expressed with symbols
    (B) noticeable
    (C) officially approved
    (D) spoken aloud
    (E) replaceable

27. The passage implies that reading skills decline less over the summer than math skills because

    (A) there are many opportunities for reading instruction at home.
    (B) the brain remembers words more easily than numbers.
    (C) reading requires only factual and procedural skills.
    (D) parents do not recognize the importance of mathematics.
    (E) students who struggle with math tend to be poorer than average.

28. What is the function of the last two paragraphs of the passage?

    (A) to claim that extra summer reading instruction should be educators' first priority
    (B) to refute the arguments of certain researchers
    (C) to introduce the primary argument of the passage
    (D) to show that the summer break has only a negligible effect on most students' learning
    (E) to use research to outline the extent of a problem

29. Which of the following best describes the author's attitude toward year-round schooling?

    (A) worshipful
    (B) dismissive
    (C) favorable
    (D) unsympathetic
    (E) indifferent

30. The primary purpose of the passage is to

    (A) outline some of the evidence against long summer vacations for students
    (B) argue that students' IQs decrease during summer breaks
    (C) compare summer learning loss of math and verbal skills
    (D) argue that students do not get enough vacation time
    (E) point out the importance of the agricultural cycle in modern American life

Homework Passage 3 (Long)

The following passage is an excerpt from a short story written by George Matten Martin about life in a poor New York neighborhood called "the Tenement."

The ladies of the Tenement felt that it was a matter concerning the reputation of the house. Therefore on this particular hot July morning they were gathered in the
Line apartment of Miss Mary Carew and Miss Norma
(5) Bonkowski, if one small and dingy room may be so designated, and were putting the matter under discussion.

Miss Carew, tall, bony, and more commonly known to the Tenement as Miss C'rew, of somewhat tart and acrid temper, being pressed for her version of the story,
(10) paused in her awkward and intent efforts at soothing the beautiful, fair-haired child upon her lap and explained that she was stepping out her door that morning with her water-bucket, thinking to get breakfast ready before Miss Bonkowski awoke, when a child's frightened crying
(15) startled her, coming from a room across the hall which for some weeks had been for rent.

"At that," continued Miss Carew, moved to unusual loquacity, and patting the child industriously while she addressed the circle of listening ladies, "at that, 'sure as
(20) life!' says I, and stepped across and opened the door, an' there, sittin' on this shawl, its eyes big like it had jus' waked up, an' cryin' like to break its heart, was this here baby. I picked her right up an' come an' woke Norma, but it's nothin' we can make out, 'ceptin' she's been in that
(25) there room all night."

Many were the murmurs and cries of surprise from the circle of wondering ladies, while Miss Bonkowski, a frowzy-headed lady in soiled shirt waist and shabby skirt, with a small waist and shoulders disproportionately
(30) broad; and with, moreover, a dab of paint upon each high-boned cheek—nothing daunted by previous failures, leaned forward and putting a somewhat soiled finger beneath the child's pretty chin, inquired persuasively, "And isn't the darling going to tell its Norma its name?"
(35) Miss Bonkowski spoke airily and as if delivering a part. But this the good ladies forgave, for was not this same Miss Norma the flower who shed an odor of distinction over the social blossoming of the whole Tenement? Was not Miss Bonkowski a chorus lady at
(40) The Garden Opera House?

So her audience looked on approvingly while Miss Norma snapped her fingers and chirruped to the baby encouragingly. "And what is the darling's name?" she repeated.
(45) The little one, her pitiful sobbing momentarily arrested, regarded Miss Bonkowski with grave wonder. "Didn't ya know I are Angel?" she returned in egotistical surprise.

31. The passage implies that the ladies of the house are gathered together because

(A) they are hoping to hear some interesting gossip.
(B) they were cleaning the apartment together.
(C) the way they resolve this problem will affect how all of them are seen in the community.
(D) they are trying to soothe the fierce temper of Miss Carew.
(E) the electric power is out in the house and this is the only room with candles.

32. How does Miss Carew discover the abandoned child?

(A) She sees the child sitting alone on the front step.
(B) The child comes knocking on her door.
(C) She trips over the child's sleeping body in the hallway.
(D) She hears the child's cries as she is heading out to get water.
(E) Her neighbors tell her that there is a child in the apartment across the hall.

33. In the third paragraph, why does the author uses abbreviated words such as "sittin'" and "jus'" (line 21)?

(A) to give the reader a sense of the unique accent and diction of Miss Carew
(B) because the author himself talks in that way
(C) because the author was writing for people who spoke in that manner
(D) to show that Miss Carew is uneducated and unintelligent
(E) because the author is quoting from another work

34. Why do the ladies forgive Miss Bonkowski for speaking "airily as if delivering a part" (lines 35-36)?

(A) The ladies are very religious.
(B) Miss Bonkowski is socially important in the neighborhood.
(C) They are afraid of Miss Bonkowski.
(D) Miss Bonkowski had just apologized.
(E) The ladies are rehearsing a play.

35. What is the meaning of the word "arrested" as it is used in line 46?

(A) stopped
(B) attracted
(C) captured
(D) taken into custody
(E) slept

Unauthorized copying or reuse of any part of this page is illegal.

Version 1.3

36. Which of the following would make the best title for the passage?

(A) Discovering the Angel of the Tenements
(B) The Story of Miss Carew
(C) Miss Norma the Flower
(D) The Garden Opera House
(E) Unhealthy Conditions in New York Neighborhoods

Version 1.3

Unauthorized copying or reuse of any part of this page is illegal.

B4HW: Homework and Extra Practice

SC Topic: Using the 5-Step Method (Lesson B2a)	**RC Topic**: Finding Evidence (Lesson B4b)

Homework Set 1

1. Not wanting to seem ------, Maurice always took time to ------ each course of action before making a decision.

   (A) deliberate . . repudiate
   (B) docile . . meditate
   (C) capricious . . ponder
   (D) impulsive . . disregard
   (E) calculated . . omit

2. The escaped prisoner attempted to ------ his captors by fleeing through a sewer pipe, but he was caught anyway.

   (A) attain
   (B) acclaim
   (C) recollect
   (D) elude
   (E) converge on

3. The feuding couple agreed to a ------ only after each agreed to refrain from yelling at or insulting the other.

   (A) rupture
   (B) reconciliation
   (C) malice
   (D) discord
   (E) desolation

4. Leo apologized for making a ------ reply to his friend's seemingly ------ question and promised to try to be gentler in the future.

   (A) caustic . . innocuous
   (B) gregarious . . ambivalent
   (C) mitigating . . sarcastic
   (D) astute . . conventional
   (E) acerbic . . tedious

5. To Faroukh, the only ------ explanation for his bag's disappearance was that someone had stolen it; any other possibility seemed extremely dubious.

   (A) credulous
   (B) preposterous
   (C) paltry
   (D) absurd
   (E) plausible

6. After the fire, Maureen had feared that all of her possessions had been destroyed, so she was grateful to be able to ------ a few family photos.

   (A) revert
   (B) detract
   (C) salvage
   (D) placate
   (E) assail

7. Sanjay received a perfect score on his essay because his professor was immediately won over by the essay's ------ argument and its wealth of ------ evidence.

   (A) coherent . . pertinent
   (B) articulate . . covert
   (C) pliable . . trivial
   (D) spurious . . legitimate
   (E) chaotic . . relevant

8. Adlai felt a strong sense of ------, and even shame, after he neglected to pick up his daughter from school.

   (A) proficiency
   (B) allure
   (C) perplexity
   (D) predominance
   (E) reproach

Homework Set 2

9. While some bosses prefer underlings who are ------ and do whatever they are told to do, others prefer their employees to act more independently and ------.

   (A) subservient . . assertively
   (B) diligent . . dejectedly
   (C) tentative . . provincially
   (D) benign . . implicitly
   (E) incessant . . resiliently

10. The famous rapper loved to ------ his wealth by wearing gaudy jewelry and driving ------ expensive cars.

    (A) flaunt . . ostentatiously
    (B) cloak . . discreetly
    (C) stifle . . conspicuously
    (D) flourish . . temperately
    (E) denounce . . flamboyantly

11. Linnette is an excellent climber in part because she has a grip that is both ------ and strong, allowing her to cling to tiny cracks in a cliff face and not let go.

    (A) outmoded
    (B) feeble
    (C) contemptuous
    (D) tenacious
    (E) timid

12. When Peter added up all the calories from the food he had eaten that day, he was delighted to find that the ------ was almost exactly equal to the total he had targeted.

    (A) antecedent
    (B) impediment
    (C) remnant
    (D) detriment
    (E) aggregate

13. To her surprise, Edna found her neighbors to be ------ company; she had expected them to be more reserved.

    (A) amiable
    (B) smug
    (C) secluded
    (D) indifferent
    (E) repulsive

14. The motel room was ------ decorated, containing only a bed, a small nightstand, and ------ television, which looked like it had not been turned on in twenty years.

    (A) portentously . . an obsolete
    (B) austerely . . an antiquated
    (C) lavishly . . a contemporary
    (D) ascetically . . a prevalent
    (E) elegantly . . a cordial

15. The columnist known as "Miss Manners" gives advice to those who are unsure of the rules of ------ or are faced with social situations that require great delicacy.

    (A) audacity
    (B) belligerence
    (C) obstinacy
    (D) decorum
    (E) disdain

16. Roy was quite ------ his piano recital until he heard the cheers of the crowd, at which point his anxiety disappeared.

    (A) evocative of
    (B) elated about
    (C) apprehensive about
    (D) conducive to
    (E) complacent about

Homework Passage 1 (Short)

This passage is taken from a travel memoir written by the famed American humorist Mark Twain.

The captain, with his gentle nature, his polish, his sweetness, his moral and verbal purity, seemed pathetically out of place in his rude and autocratic
Line vocation. It seemed another instance of the irony of fate.
(5)   He was going home under a cloud. The passengers knew about his trouble, and were sorry for him. Approaching Vancouver through a narrow and difficult passage densely befogged with smoke from the forest fires, he had had the ill luck to lose his bearings and get
(10) his ship on the rocks. A matter like this would rank merely as an error with you and me; it ranks as a crime with the directors of steamship companies. The captain had been tried by the Admiralty Court at Vancouver, and its verdict had acquitted him of blame. But that was
(15) insufficient comfort. A sterner court would examine the case in Sydney—the Court of Directors, the lords of a company in whose ships the captain had served as mate a number of years. This was his first voyage as captain.

17. In what way is the captain "out of place" (line 3)?

   (A) He has extremely bad luck.
   (B) He is kind and good, whereas most captains are harsh and amoral.
   (C) He is a working-class person who is surrounded by the wealthy.
   (D) He will soon be tried for a crime.
   (E) He is an Australian on a ship full of Americans.

18. The author's attitude toward the captain's "crime" (line 11) can best be described as

   (A) heartless.
   (B) infuriated.
   (C) indifferent.
   (D) compassionate.
   (E) elated.

Homework Passage 2 (Short)

Many Americans have never heard of Horace Greeley, but in his day, he was one of the most influential men in America. From the 1841 founding of
Line his newspaper *The New York Tribune* until his death in
(5) 1872, Greeley helped to shape the opinion of his large readership. Generally, he advocated for progressive causes such as abolition of slavery and workers' rights, though he was also known for eccentric fascinations with pseudo-scientific beliefs.
(10)   After years of crusading for Whig and Republican political candidates, most notably for Abraham Lincoln, Greeley chose to run for President in 1872. He was dissatisfied with the corruption of Ulysses S. Grant's Republican administration, so he joined the new Liberal
(15) Republican Party. Surprisingly, the Democratic Party (which Greeley had vociferously opposed for his entire career) also nominated him to oppose Grant. Despite this alliance, Greeley won only 6 of the 37 states. He died just a few weeks after the election, not even living to see
(20) the allocation of the electoral votes (he would have won 66, far short of the required total).

19. The primary purpose of the passage is most likely to

   (A) inform the reader about a relatively unfamiliar historical figure.
   (B) criticize President Grant for running a corrupt administration.
   (C) compare mid-19th century newspapers to more modern media.
   (D) describe the 1872 U.S. presidential election.
   (E) explain the electoral process for presidential elections.

20. In retrospect, Greeley's decision "to run for President in 1872" (line 11) can best be classified as

   (A) devastating.
   (B) triumphant.
   (C) sensible.
   (D) rousing.
   (E) malicious.

Homework Passage 3 (Long)

The following passage describes the coffee-growing industry in the Honduran town of Corquín and its effects on the surrounding environment.

January is the "mero mero," or height, of coffee season in Corquín. Everything I had heard about the coffee season is true: The world revolves around the
Line harvest; it is cold and wet; there are a lot of new people,
(5) cars, and businesses. Corquín is full of workers from many other towns, workers who live and work in extremely poor conditions for little pay. It was a bad year for a lot of people. Prices were low, about 30 or 40 cents a pound! This year's harvest was about half as big as last
(10) year's. The cold weather made it hard to find enough willing workers, and the coffee berries began to fall off the trees, threatening the health of the trees for next year's harvest. Despite all this, harvesting and processing coffee is the most excitement Corquín sees all year.
(15) People who manage the farms work from before sunup until 9 or 10 at night driving workers, washing, depulping, drying, bagging, and selling the coffee. The people who stay home cook all day for many new people.

The process of cultivating and harvesting coffee
(20) leads to a huge contamination of Corquín's streams and rivers, as well as all the water that runs downhill from us. This year, the environmental arm of the mayor's office and a local nonprofit tried to diminish the environmental impact with several new ordinances and training. One
(25) obvious problem is that people chop down forests to plant farms. Another major problem is the *aguas mieles*, or honey water, that comes from washing the pulpy sweet part of the fruit. Still another problem comes from the thousands of workers. The living conditions consist of
(30) several families, plus other individuals, living on the farms in makeshift shacks, sleeping on the ground, cooking where they can, and (here comes the contamination) going to the bathroom where there are no bathrooms. Some farms have latrines, but a lot of them
(35) don't, and even if the farms do, coffee cutters don't have latrines at their homes, and so they aren't used to the latrines and don't necessarily like using them. If you don't grow up with a toilet, it is not that easy to use one.

These are big, complicated problems. Most of us are
(40) not visionaries and do not think long-term or worldwide. It is hard to convince someone that deforestation is bad when his family needs firewood to cook every day. Coffee is the only source of income for the majority; they are concerned with getting paid for the biggest harvest
(45) possible today, not with the illnesses they or their neighbors might develop later from contaminated water. And most of us do not make the connection between our everyday actions and the fact that there are no longer fish in the river or that the fresh, cool breeze that used to
(50) blow where there were trees no longer does.

The mayor's office said that all coffee farm owners needed to have a certain number of latrines for their workers, and that they had to build lagoons to treat the water from the coffee-washing process. And they are
(55) trying to do a good job with follow-up. A lot of people got angry with the news, or just ignored it. The authorities needed to guarantee anonymity to anyone willing to denounce a neighbor. I am not confident that anonymity exists in Corquín. Everyone is family! Who
(60) will denounce his or her cousin to the police? I am hopeful that the program will make a difference, but I will not be surprised if the impact is small.

A positive change is that there are several model farms in our area, where the farmers are using organic
(65) fertilizers and pesticides and soil conservation techniques. They receive training in how to grow and process coffee safely, and in how to grow other important plants and trees in their coffee farms. They work as ideal educators in their communities.

(70) I have hope for our environmental problems. I can't do much about the contamination from harvesting coffee; instead, I focus on a more visible problem—trash. During the coffee season, I invited a group of kids over to make environmental signs to hang in convenience stores. The
(75) kids drew pictures, and I wrote messages like, "Please don't throw your trash in the river," "I love Corquín. Do you?" and "A Clean Corquín Is a Pretty Corquín." Then the kids asked store owners to hang up the signs. Later we made art projects out of junk food wrappers found in
(80) the street. In the last few months, we have gone on hikes to our water sources, seen the effects of forest fires, and continued with our environmental poster campaign. It's a small start!

21. All of the following contributed to the "bad year" (line 7) that Corquin experienced EXCEPT

(A) there were not enough workers.
(B) the coffee prices were very low.
(C) the harvest was very small.
(D) the farm workers did not work long enough hours.
(E) the weather was very cold.

22. As it is used in line 22, the word "arm" most nearly means

(A) limb.
(B) weapon.
(C) sleeve.
(D) division.
(E) support.

Version 1.3

Unauthorized copying or reuse of any part of this page is illegal.

23. The passage implies that some farm workers may not use latrines at the farms because

(A) they suspect that the toilets are contaminating the river.
(B) the latrines are too far from the fields.
(C) they prefer to use the toilets at their homes.
(D) the toilets are filthy.
(E) they are not comfortable using toilets.

24. According to the passage, why do many people "not think long-term or worldwide" (line 40)?

(A) They do not make their homes in Corquin and so they care little about its environment.
(B) They would rather have fun and make art projects than worry about consequences.
(C) They are too concerned with survival to consider the broader effects of their actions.
(D) They are ignorant and uneducated about the environment.
(E) They are actively trying to destroy the environment.

25. Why is the latrine-regulation program (described in lines 51-54) unlikely to have a large effect?

(A) The lack of latrines is not a large or important problem.
(B) The mayor's office is not following up on the new rules.
(C) The coffee farms are all moving away from Corquin.
(D) The standards are extremely lenient and easy to meet.
(E) The townsfolk are unlikely to turn each other in for violating the rules.

26. In the context of the passage, the 5th paragraph (lines 63-69) primarily serves

(A) to contradict a statement made in the previous paragraph.
(B) as a diversion from the main idea of the essay.
(C) to provide an example of a beneficial program.
(D) as a metaphor for a real-world problem.
(E) to summarize the main points of the passage.

27. Why does the author encourage children to make "art projects out of junk food wrappers" (line 79)?

(A) He wants to show that trash can be used for good purposes instead of being thrown in the street
(B) Junk food wrappers are the only available material for art projects.
(C) He is trying to bring out the children's inner creativity so that they will become artists.
(D) He wants the children to buy less junk food so that they will have a healthier diet.
(E) The children can then enter an art contest that has a large cash prize.

28. As described in the last paragraph (lines 70-83), the author chooses to focus on reducing trash because

(A) the residents urge him to focus on trash instead of contamination.
(B) it is a simple problem that can be eliminated by posting a few signs.
(C) the problem of trash is more obvious than other environmental problems.
(D) the other environmental problems have already been brought under control.
(E) it is the biggest problem facing Corquin.

29. The author's attitude toward the programs intended to improve the environmental conditions in Corquin can best be described as

(A) apathetic.
(B) ecstatic.
(C) angry.
(D) resigned.
(E) hopeful.

30. The primary purpose of the passage is to

(A) denounce people who are not aware of the environmental hazards of growing coffee.
(B) tell the history of a small town in Honduras.
(C) compare coffee farming to tea farming.
(D) illuminate a few of the environmental issues facing a particular community.
(E) describe a global initiative for reducing deforestation.

Unauthorized copying or reuse of any part of this page is illegal.

Version 1.3

Homework Passage 4 (Long)

The following passage analyzes the depiction of heroes and heroines in children's literature from around the world.

If anything has universal appeal among children, it is a good story with heroes and heroines. Stories with rich descriptions of the lives and personalities of inspiring
Line individuals (mythical or real, contemporary or historical)
(5) entertain as well as serve as role models for children. Through heroes and heroines of different cultures, children develop an understanding of societal expectations and norms in various parts of the world, and what it can mean to live in a particular region, or time
(10) period, or to be male or female.

Heroes and heroines often stand out because they have distinctive strengths or personality traits. However, many stories may present an ordinary person leading an ordinary life, who in drawing upon "ordinary" character
(15) traits can stand out as being special. Heroes and heroines in good literature are portrayed as complex individuals, so it is necessary to analyze them in a holistic manner by paying special attention to the interplay of both positive and negative traits. Many main characters are strong role
(20) models because they rise above their own negative traits or weaknesses and overcome personal challenges. We often find protagonists inspiring because they demonstrate the need for individuals to be resilient and to respond proactively to challenging circumstances.
(25) Discussing heroes and heroines with children presents countless opportunities for considering how character traits are expressed in others, and how children can develop positive character traits in themselves.

A content analysis of award-winning children's
(30) books from around the world indicates some character traits are universally appreciated. These include: personal courage, caring for others, perseverance, resourcefulness, a belief in oneself, and optimism. Through books, children can see heroes and heroines in different regions
(35) respond to issues such as racial, ethnic, and religious strife in ways that demonstrate courage and resilience. While different societies may value similar character traits, how these traits are expressed can vary in different regions. Descriptions indicating cultural variations in
(40) how character traits are manifested help children gain a sensitive understanding of how universal traits can also be unique. By using heroes and heroines to explore the different impact societal issues have on people around the world we can delve into examining issues
(45) surrounding expressions of individuality, identification with social groups, and strategies for dealing with various forms of discrimination.

Heroes and heroines are best understood and appreciated when viewed within the social contexts in
(50) which their lives played out. Just as every cultural and ethnic group has its own distinctive system of values and beliefs, which reflect unique ways of thinking, behaving, and living, so, too, character traits considered desirable are a unique reflection of a group's value and belief
(55) system. Accordingly, it is important to foster non-judgmental discussions among students about how some cultures may view certain character traits to be positive while others may consider these traits in a negative light.

Actively considering the dynamic nature of social,
(60) economic, and political contexts contributes to a thoughtful analysis of the thoughts, emotions, and actions of individual heroes and heroines. We must be careful when making connections between valued character traits in societies in the present and those from different
(65) historical periods. At the same time, ever-changing present day realities also require us to be cautious in understanding contemporary heroes and their societies. Certain character traits we viewed positively just a few years ago may now be offensive within our societies.
(70) Certain attitudes heroes and heroines took for granted just a short time span ago may now be sources of conflict. On the whole, we must take care to analyze each hero or heroine's character traits and actions first within the context in which they have been presented, and only
(75) then attempt to make meaning of these character traits in a manner that transcends contextual boundaries.

31. In the context of the passage, the first paragraph (lines 1-10) serves to

(A) foreshadow the events described later in the passage.
(B) outline the main ideas of the passage.
(C) describe the setting of the passage.
(D) introduce several specific events that will be tied together in the rest of the passage.
(E) compare two seemingly unrelated ideas.

32. According to the passage, heroes "in good literature" (line 16) are depicted as

(A) flawless and universally admired.
(B) unable to rise above their personal flaws.
(C) the same in every culture.
(D) engaged in a fight against discrimination.
(E) having both positive and negative traits.

33. "Discussing heroes and heroines with children" (line 25) can have which of the following effects, according to the author?

(A) The children may want to buy video games and action figures of the heroes and heroines.
(B) Some children may become arrogant because they see themselves as heroes.
(C) The children can lose confidence if they do not possess the same traits as the heroes.
(D) The children may become jealous of the heroes.
(E) Examining the heroes' positive traits can help bring out those traits in the children.

34. The passage lists all of the following as universally appreciated traits EXCEPT

(A) hopefulness
(B) fighting skill ←
(C) self-confidence
(D) resiliency
(E) bravery

35. As it is used in line 41, "sensitive" most nearly means

(A) insightful
(B) volatile
(C) embarrassing
(D) vulnerable
(E) secret

36. The author implies that children may be judgmental about

(A) authors who do not include enough heroes in their stories.
(B) heroes who have negative traits.
(C) cultures that have different value systems from their own.
(D) teachers who do not understand the stories they read.
(E) heroes who share many traits with the children.

37. In the last paragraph, the author warns that

(A) boys often have difficulty recognizing the positive traits of heroines in stories they read.
(B) positive character traits from other eras may not be seen as positive today.
(C) heroes showing "ordinary" character traits are not as interesting.
(D) examining villains can be much more helpful than examining heroes.
(E) reading about racial or religious strife can be traumatic for young children.

38. The primary purpose of the passage is to

(A) illustrate the difference in how heroines are depicted over time.
(B) show how children can learn about their own and other cultures by examining heroes and heroines.
(C) encourage children to act more like heroes and heroines.
(D) criticize authors who use discrimination in their children's stories.
(E) explain how to write an award-winning children's book.

39. The overall tone of the passage can best be described as

(A) laudatory.
(B) indifferent.
(C) harsh.
(D) analytical.
(E) contradictory.

Unauthorized copying or reuse of any part of this page is illegal.

Version 1.3

B5HW: Homework and Extra Practice

| **SC Topic**: Circling Structure Words (Lesson B5a) | **RC Topic**: Finding Evidence (Lesson B4b) |

Homework Set 1

1. Catarina avoids eating broccoli, a vegetable that she finds utterly ------; she would ------ the world's supply if possible.

   (A) exquisite . . annihilate
   (B) repulsive . . augment
   (C) divine . . reconcile
   (D) detestable . . eradicate
   (E) repugnant . . bolster

2. The events of the past few days had been so surreal that Robert wondered if they had only been a ------ or a figment of his overactive imagination.

   (A) veracity
   (B) predominance
   (C) devotion
   (D) delusion
   (E) censure

3. After her son became sick, Marla had him drink a special herbal tea that would help to ------ his symptoms.

   (A) acclaim
   (B) ameliorate
   (C) proffer
   (D) delegate
   (E) equivocate

4. Several students tried to ------ the school's strict dress code by wearing their neckties as bandanas, but the principal was not fooled and ordered them to wear the ties correctly.

   (A) circumvent
   (B) concede to
   (C) mandate
   (D) invoke
   (E) flaunt

5. The congresswoman was ------ that the police could listen in on her phone calls without her ------ and vowed to sue the city for the violation of her privacy.

   (A) fervent . . dissent
   (B) sympathetic . . discretion
   (C) incensed . . consent
   (D) placated . . compliance
   (E) effusive . . austerity

6. Michelle has a ------ smile that brightens the day of anyone who sees it.

   (A) gloomy
   (B) malevolent
   (C) deplorable
   (D) radiant
   (E) despondent

7. To many people, studying a broad array of topics might seem ------ or even counter-productive, but a librarian must have ------ knowledge of many different subjects.

   (A) trivial . . provincial
   (B) astute . . expansive
   (C) diligent . . detrimental
   (D) superfluous . . voluminous
   (E) indubitable . . abundant

8. Despite spending over 20 years in prison, Giorgio always maintained his innocence, until finally, he was ------ by DNA tests that showed he was not guilty.

   (A) refuted
   (B) vindicated
   (C) recanted
   (D) venerated
   (E) assailed

Homework Set 2

9. During the early part of the opera, the star's voice ------ several times, but it seemed to gain strength as the show went on, and the final solo was flawless.

   (A) faltered
   (B) asserted
   (C) forbade
   (D) commended
   (E) confronted

10. The volcano lay ------ for thousands of years before suddenly erupting and destroying several nearby towns.

    (A) resolute
    (B) industrious
    (C) evocative
    (D) cognizant
    (E) dormant

11. Despite Angelo's attempts to ------ the meeting by eliminating a few discussion points, the meeting actually lasted even longer than usual.

    (A) elaborate
    (B) attain
    (C) revoke
    (D) protract
    (E) expedite

12. The protest was quite peaceful until a few people ------ a riot by ------ police officers and hurling bottles at them.

    (A) instigated . . deriding
    (B) persisted . . relinquishing
    (C) incited . . alleviating
    (D) impeded . . reproaching
    (E) deterred . . abiding by

13. Horses were once ------ in cities as well as in the country; before the industrial revolution, the horse was the primary mode of transporting people and goods.

    (A) voracious
    (B) omnipresent
    (C) negligible
    (D) capricious
    (E) marginal

14. The ------ of modern life is a ------ theme of the novels of Don DeLillo, which often feature protagonists who feel alienated from even their friends and family.

    (A) ambivalence . . verbose
    (B) dejection . . dubious
    (C) benevolence . . concise
    (D) desolation . . recurrent
    (E) concord . . conventional

15. Sacha had an excellent opportunity to score a goal but was ------ when the goalkeeper made an amazing save.

    (A) ascribed
    (B) mitigated
    (C) sustained
    (D) thwarted
    (E) indulged

16. Normally ------ individual, Clint was uncharacteristically ------ around Leann; he always followed her orders without question.

    (A) an obstinate . . auspicious
    (B) a headstrong . . docile
    (C) an imprudent . . audacious
    (D) a pliable . . submissive
    (E) an eccentric . . contrary

Unauthorized copying or reuse of any part of this page is illegal.

Version 1.3

Homework Passage 1 (Short)

Stress is a necessary and unavoidable concomitant of daily living—necessary because without some stress we would be listless and apathetic creatures, and
Line unavoidable because it relates to any external event, be it
(5) pleasurable or anxiety-producing. Severe stress has been correlated with coronary disease, respiratory problems, backaches, high blood pressure, and other illnesses. Many of these illnesses are psychosomatic (influenced by one's mind), to the extent that for most people stress is a
(10) loaded term that connotes unhealthy or harmful conditions, such as disease or illness. In truth, however, stress can also motivate and invigorate and enable people to achieve far more than they thought themselves capable of doing.

17. The passage implies that stress

   (A) is always a beneficial, motivating force.
   (B) can be avoided with careful planning.
   (C) can aggravate certain dangerous health conditions.
   (D) is pointless in our modern, convenient lifestyle.
   (E) inevitably leads to illness and disease.

18. The author's attitude toward stress can best be characterized as

   (A) disgusted.
   (B) apprehensive.
   (C) humorous.
   (D) ambivalent.
   (E) grateful.

Homework Passage 2 (Short)

In early 1898, a new battle cry reverberated throughout the United States: "Remember the *Maine*, to hell with Spain!" This call was used as part of the
Line campaign to start what became known as the Spanish-
(5) American War. The origins of the phrase lie in the destruction of the battleship *U.S.S. Maine*, which suddenly exploded in the harbor of Havana, Cuba on February, 15, 1898, killing 266 U.S. servicemen.

At the time, Spain controlled Cuba, though America
(10) had long had an interest in that territory. Some Americans had been agitating to start a war with Spain over the Cuba issue for years, and they seized upon the Maine's destruction as a means of promoting their anti-Spanish agenda.
(15) Despite the common perception (fostered by the anti-Spain contingent) that a Spanish mine or missile sank the *Maine*, there was—and is—no evidence of Spanish involvement in the disaster. Though the ultimate cause of the ship's sinking remains unclear, the most
(20) likely explanation is that a fire started in a coal bunker and spread to the ship's large cache of ammunitions, which then exploded, sinking the ship.

19. The passage implies that the "common perception" (line 15) was reinforced by

   (A) Spain's antagonism toward America in the Cuba region.
   (B) evidence that indicated a missile had destroyed the *Maine*.
   (C) widespread racism against the Hispanic people of Cuba.
   (D) testimonials from American survivors of the *Maine* tragedy.
   (E) Americans who were searching for an excuse to start a war with Spain.

20. The primary purpose of the passage is most likely to

   (A) criticize America for starting the Spanish-American War.
   (B) memorialize the heroic servicemen who died in the *U.S.S. Maine* disaster.
   (C) discuss the causes and effects of a historical event.
   (D) give a brief history of U.S.-Spain relations.
   (E) promote an anti-Spain agenda.

Homework Passage 3 (Long)

This passage examines the benefits and drawbacks of using rewards to convince children to change behaviors.

Studies over many years have found that behavior modification programs are rarely successful at producing lasting changes in attitudes or even behavior. When the
Line rewards stop, people usually return to the way they acted
(5) before the program began. More disturbingly, researchers have recently discovered that children whose parents make frequent use of rewards tend to be less generous than their peers.

Indeed, extrinsic motivators do not alter the
(10) emotional or cognitive *commitments* that underlie behavior—at least not in a desirable direction. A child promised a treat for learning or acting responsibly has been given every reason to stop doing so when there is no longer a reward to be gained.

(15) Research and logic suggest that punishment and rewards are not really opposites, but two sides of the same coin. Both strategies amount to ways of trying to manipulate someone's behavior—in one case, prompting the question, "What do they want me to do, and what
(20) happens to me if I don't do it?", and in the other instance, leading a child to ask, "What do they want me to do, and what do I get for doing it?" Neither strategy helps children to grapple with the question, "What kind of person do I want to be?"

(25) Rewards are no more helpful at enhancing achievement than they are at fostering good values. At least two dozen studies have shown that people expecting to receive a reward for completing a task (or for doing it successfully) simply do not perform as well as those who
(30) expect nothing. This effect is robust for young children, older children, and adults; for males and females; for rewards of all kinds; and for tasks ranging from memorizing facts to designing collages to solving problems. In general, the more cognitive sophistication
(35) and open-ended thinking that is required for a task, the worse people tend to do when they have been led to perform that task for a reward.

There are several plausible explanations for this puzzling but remarkably consistent finding. The most
(40) compelling of these is that *rewards cause people to lose interest in whatever they were rewarded for doing*. This phenomenon, which has been demonstrated in scores of studies, makes sense given that "motivation" is not a single characteristic that an individual possesses to a
(45) greater or lesser degree. Rather, intrinsic motivation (an interest in the task for its own sake) is qualitatively different from extrinsic motivation (in which completion of the task is seen chiefly as a prerequisite for obtaining something else). Therefore, the question educators need
(50) to ask is not how motivated their students are, but how their students are motivated.

In one representative study, young children were introduced to an unfamiliar beverage called kefir. Some were just asked to drink it; others were praised lavishly
(55) for doing so; a third group was promised treats if they drank enough. Those children who received either verbal or tangible rewards consumed more of the beverage than other children, as one might predict. But a week later these children found it significantly less appealing than
(60) they did before, whereas children who were offered no rewards liked it just as much as, if not more than, they had earlier. If we substitute reading or doing math or acting generously for drinking kefir, we begin to glimpse the destructive power of rewards. The data suggest that
(65) the more we want children to *want* to do something, the more counterproductive it will be to reward them for doing it.

Another study describes the use of rewards as "control through seduction." Control, whether by threats
(70) or bribes, amounts to doing things *to* children rather than working *with* them. This ultimately frays relationships, both among students (leading to reduced interest in working with peers) and between students and adults (insofar as asking for help may reduce the probability of
(75) receiving a reward).

Moreover, students who are encouraged to think about grades, stickers, or other "goodies" become less inclined to explore ideas, think creatively, and take chances. At least ten studies have shown that people
(80) offered a reward generally choose the easiest possible task. In the absence of rewards, by contrast, children are inclined to pick tasks that are just beyond their current level of ability.

21. According to the passage, "punishment and rewards" (lines 15-16) are

(A) completely different concepts.
(B) similar psychologically, though rewards are much more beneficial.
(C) two different ways of achieving the same goal.
(D) similarly ineffective at altering behavior.
(E) subjects in need of further research.

22. Based on evidence in the passage, one can infer that the author considers which of the following skills to be most beneficial?

(A) self-evaluation
(B) the ability to avoid punishments
(C) the ability to recognize rewards
(D) manipulating others' behavior
(E) the ability to complete uninteresting tasks

23. Which groups of people improve their performance on open-ended problems when offered a reward?

(A) men only
(B) young children only
(C) older children only
(D) No group improves when a reward is offered.
(E) All groups improve with rewards.

24. As used in the passage, "sophistication" (line 34) most nearly means

(A) stylishness
(B) superiority
(C) deception
(D) defectiveness
(E) complexity

25. The author states that the "most compelling" (lines 39-40) explanation for the ineffectiveness of rewards is that

(A) many of the studies of reward systems are flawed.
(B) adults often use the wrong type of rewards.
(C) reward systems are more effective outside of a laboratory setting.
(D) rewards do not help people to motivate themselves.
(E) rewards are too much of an intrinsic motivator.

26. The example of the "kefir" study (in lines 52-62) is used to

(A) prove that doing math is different from drinking a beverage.
(B) describe an argument that supports the effectiveness of reward systems.
(C) provide further evidence that the positive impacts of rewards quickly fade.
(D) counter an argument made in the previous paragraph.
(E) demonstrate that rewards have no effect whatsoever on behavior, even in the short term.

27. The passage implies that the ideal way for adults to interact with children is to

(A) threaten them frequently.
(B) work with them to solve problems and enhance their curiosity and sense of self.
(C) encourage them to work alone rather than ask for help.
(D) ignore them and let them fend for themselves.
(E) use bribes to convince children to change their behavior.

28. Based on the evidence presented in the passage, why might "children whose parents make frequent use of rewards" (lines 6-7) be less generous than other children?

(A) Rewards encourage children to be selfish and discourage permanent behavioral changes.
(B) The rewards helped the children to become better students but did not improve their behavior.
(C) The parents stopped rewarding the children too soon.
(D) Rewards can be beneficial, but only when used in moderation.
(E) The rewarded children were not punished for being selfish.

29. The primary purpose of the passage is to

(A) argue that children should receive more rewards for getting good grades.
(B) offer an in-depth history of behavioral science.
(C) claim that rewards are far less effective at producing changed behavior than punishments are.
(D) compare the effectiveness of rewards for children and adults.
(E) highlight some of the flaws of behavior modification programs.

30. The author's attitude toward using rewards to change children's behavior can best be described as

(A) approving.
(B) ambivalent.
(C) balanced.
(D) ironic.
(E) skeptical.

Homework Passage 4 (Long)

The following is an excerpt from James Joyce's short story "Evangeline," about a young woman who leaves her depressing department-store job to move to a new town.

She sat at the window watching the evening invade the avenue. Her head was leaned against the window curtains and in her nostrils was the odour of dusty fabric.
Line She was tired.
(5) Few people passed. The man out of the last house passed on his way home; she heard his footsteps clacking along the concrete pavement and afterwards crunching on the cinder path before the new red houses. One time there used to be a field there in which they used to play
(10) every evening with other people's children. Then a man from Belfast bought the field and built houses in it—not like their little brown houses but bright brick houses with shining roofs. The children of the avenue used to play together in that field—the Devines, the Waters, the
(15) Dunns, little Keogh the cripple, she and her brothers and sisters. Ernest, however, never played: he was too grown up. Her father used often to hunt them in out of the field with his blackthorn stick; but usually little Keogh used to keep watch and call out when he saw her father coming.
(20) Still they seemed to have been rather happy then. Her father was not so bad then; and besides, her mother was alive. That was a long time ago; she and her brothers and sisters were all grown up her mother was dead. Tizzie Dunn was dead, too, and the Waters had gone back to
(25) England. Everything changes. Now she was going to go away like the others, to leave her home.

Home! She looked round the room, reviewing all its familiar objects which she had dusted once a week for so many years, wondering where on earth all the dust came
(30) from. Perhaps she would never see again those familiar objects from which she had never dreamed of being divided. And yet during all those years she had never found out the name of the priest whose yellowing photograph hung on the wall above the broken
(35) harmonium beside the coloured print of the promises made to Blessed Margaret Mary Alacoque. He had been a school friend of her father. Whenever he showed the photograph to a visitor her father used to pass it with a casual word:
(40) "He is in Melbourne now."

She had consented to go away, to leave her home. Was that wise? She tried to weigh each side of the question. In her home anyway she had shelter and food; she had those whom she had known all her life about her.
(45) Of course she had to work hard, both in the house and at business. What would they say of her in the Stores when they found out that she had run away with a fellow? Say she was a fool, perhaps; and her place would be filled up by advertisement. Miss Gavan would be glad. She had
(50) always had an edge on her, especially whenever there were people listening.

"Miss Hill, don't you see these ladies are waiting?"
"Look lively, Miss Hill, please."
She would not cry many tears at leaving the Stores.

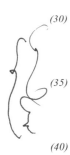

31. Which of the following would be the best title for the passage?

(A) All About the Stores
(B) The Children of the Avenue
(C) The Many Loves of Evangeline
(D) Preparing to Leave Home
(E) Promises to Blessed Margaret Mary Alacoque

32. For Miss Hill, the "man out of the last house" (line 5) triggers memories of

(A) a friend of her father's who now lives in Melbourne.
(B) Miss Gavan and her other co-workers.
(C) the children she used to play with.
(D) dusting the objects in her room.
(E) the man she is engaged to marry.

33. In the context of the passage as a whole, the function of the last two sentences of the second paragraph ("Everything … her home.") is to show that the main character

(A) wishes her old neighbors would move back to the neighborhood.
(B) realizes that she cannot recapture the past and must move forward.
(C) is going to her job at the Stores for the first time.
(D) no longer loves her father.
(E) has never dreamed of parting with her possessions.

34. The "photograph" described in lines 32-40 serves

(A) to remind the main character that she is leaving home soon.
(B) as a comparison between the nameless priest and Miss Hill's father.
(C) to distinguish between the place Miss Hill is leaving and the place she will be moving.
(D) to reveal the main character's faulty memory.
(E) to exaggerate the strangeness of the main character's home.

Unauthorized copying or reuse of any part of this page is illegal.

Version 1.3

35. The main character considers one of the benefits of staying at home to be that

    (A) she is surrounded by people she has known for a long time.
    (B) she will miss her co-workers if she leaves.
    (C) she does not have to work much at home.
    (D) she does not want to end up like her father.
    (E) that the man she loves will not be leaving with her.

36. The passage implies that Miss Gavan is

    (A) the main character's mother.
    (B) the main character's superior at work.
    (C) one of the children the main character grew up with.
    (D) a customer at the Stores.
    (E) a nun whose picture is on the wall at the main character's house.

37. The overall tone of the passage can best be described as

    (A) fearful.
    (B) nostalgic.
    (C) wild.
    (D) callous.
    (E) light-hearted.

B6HW: Homework and Extra Practice

SC TOPIC: Circling Structure Words (Lesson B5a)	RC TOPIC: Eliminating Answers (Lesson B6b)

Homework Set 1

1. During his difficult final semester of college, Gautam had to ------ both ------ course load and the death of his father.

    (A) detract from . . a rigorous
    (B) instigate . . a grueling
    (C) cope with . . an arduous
    (D) confront . . a conducive
    (E) grapple with . . a negligible

2. Etymology—the study of word origins—may seem ------, but it is quite useful in many everyday scenarios, such as trying to understand unfamiliar vocabulary.

    (A) prevalent
    (B) austere
    (C) esoteric
    (D) pertinent
    (E) fruitful

3. Leonora is perhaps a bit too idealistic; her ideas are always interesting and creative, but they are rarely ------.

    (A) futile
    (B) feasible
    (C) oppressive
    (D) wretched
    (E) contemptible

4. The famous billionaire Bill Gates is now primarily concerned with ------ pursuits, such as improving education in America and ------ disease in Africa.

    (A) philanthropic . . devising
    (B) compulsory . . mitigating
    (C) magnanimous . . eradicating
    (D) humanitarian . . upholding
    (E) detrimental . . salvaging

5. The governor stated that she could not ------ any plan that could potentially damage the state's schools.

    (A) repudiate
    (B) evade
    (C) sanction
    (D) renounce
    (E) impair

6. Hye-sang's pleasure at receiving a car for her birthday was ------, for she quickly realized that the car did not run and needed extensive repairs.

    (A) implicit
    (B) persistent
    (C) resilient
    (D) portentous
    (E) transitory

7. Speaking in ------ tone can help reduce the sting of criticism; on the other hand, speaking in ------ tone can make even praise seem hurtful.

    (A) a fervent . . an acerbic
    (B) an obsolete . . a cordial
    (C) a contentious . . a belligerent
    (D) an amiable . . a benevolent
    (E) a genial . . a caustic

8. The skyscraper was seemingly being constructed at a ------ pace; some observers wondered if it would be finished within the next century.

    (A) nimble
    (B) glacial
    (C) proficient
    (D) diligent
    (E) brisk

Homework Set 2

9. The robber ------ snatched the woman's purse despite the fact that several policemen were standing nearby ready to ------ the criminal.

   (A) audaciously . . succumb to
   (B) tentatively . . seize
   (C) hastily . . cede
   (D) brashly . . apprehend
   (E) frugally . . squander

10. Sunan thought that it would be ------ to tell his parents about the surprise party that his sister was planning for them.

    (A) ostentatious
    (B) prudent
    (C) indiscreet
    (D) plausible
    (E) astute

11. In the hopes of acting on more complete information, Anne held off on making a decision until she had a chance to ------ both plans.

    (A) indict
    (B) laud
    (C) scrutinize
    (D) thwart
    (E) compel

12. The dog's ------ barking woke Lydia up at 4 A.M., and she could not ------ the continual noise long enough to fall back asleep.

    (A) effusive . . incite
    (B) obsolete . . stifle
    (C) elated . . amplify
    (D) incessant . . suppress
    (E) voracious . . flaunt

13. Just as one should not ------ a victory, one should also react to a loss with graciousness.

    (A) gloat about
    (B) deter from
    (C) endorse
    (D) commend
    (E) comply with

14. Emilia had hoped to be able to fly her kite today, but the ------ rain prevented her from even going outside.

    (A) sporadic
    (B) pliable
    (C) incidental
    (D) inconsequential
    (E) unrelenting

15. Unlike his friends, who eagerly jumped into the lake, Rasheed waded slowly and ------ as if afraid of what might be ------ beneath the water.

    (A) capriciously . . veiled
    (B) timidly . . benign
    (C) obstinately . . conspicuous
    (D) warily . . lurking
    (E) perceptively . . arid

16. Despite her softball team's poor record, Federica's ------ for the game was undiminished; she enjoyed playing whether she was winning or losing.

    (A) lethargy
    (B) zeal
    (C) indifference
    (D) decorum
    (E) complacency

Homework Passage 1 (Short Paired)

Passage 1:

The history of presidential campaign slogans is a long and varied one. From William Henry Harrison's legendary "Tippecanoe and Tyler Too" (referring to
Line Harrison's victory at the 1811 Battle of Tippecanoe and
(5) his vice-presidential nominee, John Tyler), used in the campaign of 1840, to Barack Obama's ubiquitous "Yes We Can" from the 2008 campaign, nearly every successful presidential run has featured a memorable slogan. Other noteworthy successes include Ronald
(10) Reagan's 1984 slogan, "It's Morning Again in America," and Dwight D. Eisenhower's 1952 mantra, "I Like Ike."

Not all slogans are so successful, however. For instance, Herbert Hoover's 1932 slogan, "We Are Turning the Corner," only served to remind voters of the
(15) dreadful economic situation (the Great Depression) that Hoover's policies had contributed to. Franklin D. Roosevelt defeated Hoover in a historic landslide. The next candidate to run against FDR did even worse: Alf Landon's 1936 slogan, "Let's Make It a Landon-slide,"
(20) tried to be prophetic but ended up just being ironic. Roosevelt won re-election by 523 electoral votes to Landon's 8—not exactly the type of "Landon-slide" implied by the slogan.

Passage 2:

Line In 1840, an unknown Zanesville, Ohio, barber
(25) named Alexander Coffman Ross created perhaps the most influential bit of political sloganeering in history. Ross adapted the score of an older song for use in the presidential election of that year, which pitted William Henry Harrison, the general who made his fame with a
(30) rout of Native American forces at the Battle of Tippecanoe in 1811, against incumbent president Martin Van Buren. Ross sought to establish Harrison's military valor (with the references to Tippecanoe), mock Van Buren as ineffectual (by referring to him as "Little Van"
(35) and "Little Matty"), and create a sense that Harrison's victory was inevitable (as with the lyric "And swift the ball is rolling on / for Tippecanoe and Tyler too").

By all accounts, the result of Ross' work, called "Tippecanoe and Tyler Too," was supremely effective.
(40) The new song (and its lyrics) spread like wildfire, and Ross' vision of a Harrison landslide was fulfilled. Today, little else is remembered about the 1840 election but Ross' song and the slogan it produced.

17. The reason that "Herbert Hoover's 1932 slogan" (line 13 of Passage 1) failed is most likely that it

(A) was not associated with a popular song.
(B) emphasized the traumatic events of Hoover's presidency.
(C) seemed to be ironic.
(D) was excessively optimistic.
(E) contained too many words.

18. Based on the information in Passage 2, one can conclude that all of the following statements about the song "Tippecanoe and Tyler Too" are true EXCEPT that it

(A) was composed by a famous songwriter.
(B) used metaphors to make General Harrison's election seem certain.
(C) is still remembered today.
(D) poked fun at Martin Van Buren.
(E) glorified General Harrison and his accomplishments.

19. The focus of the two passages differs in that only Passage 1 discusses

(A) the outcome of the 1840 presidential election.
(B) the lyrics of the "Tippecanoe and Tyler Too" song.
(C) the reason that William Henry Harrison was nicknamed "Tippecanoe."
(D) some examples of failed slogans.
(E) the man who coined William Henry Harrison's slogan.

20. The authors of both passages would most likely agree that

(A) William Henry Harrison would have won the 1840 election regardless of which slogan he used.
(B) every candidate who has a good slogan wins the election in a landslide.
(C) William Henry Harrison was a better president than Martin Van Buren.
(D) the "Battle of Tippecanoe" was actually a massacre of a defenseless Native American tribe.
(E) a good campaign slogan can improve a candidate's chances of winning an election.

Homework Passage 2 (Long)

This excerpt was written by William H. Holtclaw, and describes his efforts to start a school for African-American children in rural Mississippi in the late 1800s.

At the end of the first year's work I was able to make to the trustees a creditable report, from which the following is taken:

Line
(5) As soon as we secured a cabin to teach in, the young people came in great numbers. We soon had an attendance of 200. One teacher after another was employed to assist, until seven teachers were daily at work. After three months in our temporary quarters conditions were very trying. There was no money to pay
(10) teachers or to meet the grocery bills for teachers' board. The winter was well on, and the structure in which we were located was little protection against it. The rain easily came through the roof, and water was often two inches deep on certain parts of the floor. Several teachers
(15) and students were suffering with pneumonia or kindred disorders, as a result of all this exposure. I confess that during this dark period only a carefully planned system and much determination prevented despair.

During all this time I was trying to secure the
(20) interest of the people. I went from door to door, explaining our efforts; then I made a tour of the churches; after riding or walking five or ten miles at night I would return, and then teach the next day. After a protracted struggle of this kind, and after visiting almost everybody
(25) for many miles, I found that I had secured about $600. This greatly relieved us. Forty acres of land were purchased, and a part of the lumber for a good, comfortable building was put upon the grounds. Some of our trustees in New York city and Boston now came to
(30) our assistance, and with this, and contributions from a few other friends, we were able to get through the year. Although it was a great struggle, I found in it some pleasure. To know that you were doing the work that the world needs, and must have done, is a pleasure even
(35) under trying difficulties.

Starting last October without a cent, in the open air, we have succeeded in establishing a regularly organized institution incorporated under the laws of the State of Mississippi, with 225 students and seven teachers, and
(40) with property valued at $4,000. Forty acres of good farm-land about a mile from town have been secured. A model crop is now growing on this farm. We have erected a building—a two-story frame—at a cost of something over $2,000.

(45) I hope you will not get, from what I have said, an idea that I am measuring the success of my efforts by material advancement. I am not. There are forces that our labors have set to work here, the results of which cannot be measured in facts and figures. One year ago religious
(50) services were held once a month, at which time the day was spent in singing, praying, and shouting. The way some of the people lived for the next twenty-nine days would shock a sensitive individual to read about it. Young people would gamble with the dice, etc., in a most
(55) despicable way, within a short distance of the church, during services; others would discharge revolvers at the church door during services; ignorance, superstition, vice, and immorality were everywhere present, notwithstanding the handful of determined Christian men
(60) and women who were trying to overcome these evil tendencies. I do not maintain that these evils have been crushed out. They have not. But what I do maintain is that the general current has been checked. The revolution is on; and if we continue the work here, as we surely will,
(65) these evil tendencies will soon be crushed out.

21. As it is used in line 9, "trying" most nearly means

(A) making an effort.
(B) extremely difficult.
(C) experimenting.
(D) prejudicial.
(E) related to a legal case.

22. According to the author, what helped him get through the first winter in the school's "temporary quarters" (line 8)?

(A) faith and prayer
(B) perseverance and preparation
(C) money and a comfortable lifestyle
(D) fame and recognition
(E) laughter and song

23. The process that the author went through to secure the funds to build a new school can best be described as

(A) brief but dangerous.
(B) surprisingly simple.
(C) lengthy and arduous.
(D) pleasant and worry-free.
(E) doomed to failure.

24. What is the most likely reason that the author lists the value of the school's "property" line 40?

(A) to show how far the school has come from its humble beginnings
(B) to illustrate how poor his school still is
(C) to offer a comparison to modern-day schools
(D) to argue that readers should support his efforts
(E) to brag about the incredible profits of the school

Version 1.3

Unauthorized copying or reuse of any part of this page is illegal.

25. The author implies that financial success is far less important to him than

   (A) the amount of crops grown on the farm.
   (B) the number of teachers at the school.
   (C) the opinions of his trustees.
   (D) the quality of his reports.
   (E) the progress made against immorality.

26. According to the author, what is the current status of the fight against ignorance and vice?

   (A) Sinful behavior has not been wiped out, but it has become less common.
   (B) There is no longer any immorality in the town.
   (C) People are just as evil as they have always been.
   (D) Many people are losing their way and becoming ignorant.
   (E) Superstition is at an all-time high.

27. In the context of the passage, what is the main function of the last paragraph (lines 45-65)?

   (A) to show that the author has been working to achieve moral as well as educational goals
   (B) to refute a common misconception
   (C) to compare two different types of people
   (D) to influence others to donate to his cause
   (E) to summarize the main points of his argument.

28. The author's primary purpose in writing the passage is to

   (A) criticize those who have been overcome by evil tendencies.
   (B) describe both his achievements and the obstacles he had to overcome.
   (C) illustrate the terrible conditions at several Mississippi schools.
   (D) brag about his many amazing accomplishments and how much money he made.
   (E) argue for the integration of public schools.

29. Throughout the passage, the author's tone is one of

   (A) skeptical discouragement
   (B) determined optimism
   (C) selfish pride
   (D) unrivalled joy
   (E) callous indifference

Unauthorized copying or reuse of any part of this page is illegal.

Version 1.3

Homework Passage 3 (Long)

This essay, written in 2005, describes how life in Romania differs from life in America in one small but crucial way.

Romania has turned me into a pack rat. Not that I didn't collect things in the past. Once I cried for three hours when my father made me throw away a childhood
Line collection of wrapping paper and bows that filled up my
(5) closet. Living in Romania has reawakened this pack rat impulse inside me. Here, every food item I buy is not judged by its caloric content or nutritional value, but by its food storage potential. My eyes glisten at the thought of empty water bottles lying useless in the trash. My
(10) heart skips a beat when I mistakenly get an extra plastic bag at the market. Every container is useful in ways that I had never envisioned. Juice bottles make perfect milk containers when you buy milk in a bag. Three-liter bottles are great jugs. An empty yogurt cup makes an
(15) excellent glass, tomato-sauce jars make great mugs, and sour cream "buckets" are quite the prize because they come complete with lids perfect for leftovers. Everything has a use and nothing is wasted.

Romanians are extremely resourceful. As my friend
(20) Mirela says, "We have to be." When you make an average of a hundred dollars a month, you learn to stretch your money until the last leu. (The leu is the official Romanian currency.) Before the fall of the Iron Curtain and the onslaught of capitalism and creative packaging,
(25) Romanian recycling was not a mere choice but a necessity. Who knew when and what the shortages would be? Survival meant collecting. A roll of toilet paper was worth its weight in gold when none was to be found for months in the market. Plastic bags, foodstuffs, jars,
(30) buttons, thread, material—everything was useful when nothing else was available. Recycling thus evolved as a necessity, not a choice. Plastic bags still remain golden items; they cost extra at the grocery stores.

Though informal, or personal, recycling is integral to
(35) the Romanian lifestyle today, organized recycling has only recently come back into vogue. For years, recycling was anything but voluntary. Under the regime of Ceausescu—the former communist dictator who ran the country from the mid '60s till Romania's revolution in
(40) 1989—recycling was mandatory. Children were required to bring a quota of paper from home to school to be recycled. Forced recycling left a bad taste in the mouths of many Romanians. So bitter was this taste that after the fall of communism, not recycling became an act of
(45) asserting one's freedom. It is hard to fathom just how controlling the state of communism must have been, when freedom boiled down to the right to do what you wished with your own trash.

The question is, how do you disassociate memories
(50) of a formerly oppressive act—recycling by decree—from the importance of the act itself? How do you get people to recycle of their own volition, not because they have to, but because it's the right thing to do? The answer is kids!

Since being here, I have thought a lot more about the
(55) things that I throw away. In fact, my trash haunts me. I dream about the mountain of waste that I have nonchalantly tossed: plastic bottles, glass jars, soda cans, paper towels, foam plates, mounds and mounds of formerly useful things sitting stagnant in the ground,
(60) waiting uncounted years to decompose. I feel sick.

I discussed my guilty conscience with my students. They too confessed to feeling guilty about the amount of paper that lay wasting in school trash cans failing to be recycled. We talked and talked and finally decided to do
(65) something about our garbage guilt together. We formed a coalition called the Green Marshals and initiated a recycling competition between classes. The Green Marshals' leader, Mihaela, made contact with a company outside of town that offered to pay us for the paper. We
(70) gave each class a cardboard recycling box that we salvaged from market garbage bins.

Thus the project began, and it was a big hit. The winning class recycled over a hundred kilos [220 pounds] of paper in under two months, but more important, we
(75) got people to think about what they were throwing away. The kids were pleased, and together we hope to continue the good recycling karma this school year. "The best thing," Mihaela explained, "is changing the way people think." Romania has definitely changed the way I think
(80) about trash. Truly I have learned that one person's trash may be another person's treasure.

30. The first paragraph primarily serves

(A) to identify several items that everyone should recycle.
(B) to introduce the topic of the essay using the author's personal experiences.
(C) as a light-hearted digression from the passage's main idea.
(D) to compare Romania's economy with that of the United States.
(E) as a scathing criticism of her father's cruelty.

31. In the first paragraph, the author lists all of the following as examples of packaging that can be re-used EXCEPT

(A) yogurt cups.
(B) juice bottles.
(C) sour cream buckets.
(D) toilet paper rolls.
(E) plastic bags.

Version 1.3

Unauthorized copying or reuse of any part of this page is illegal.

32. The author implies that many Romanians recycle everyday objects because

(A) they cannot afford to buy many new household items.
(B) they feel guilty for not recycling in the past.
(C) the communist government requires them to.
(D) they are asserting their own freedom.
(E) their children enjoy reusing food containers.

33. One can infer from the passage that shopping in Romania before "the fall of the Iron Curtain" (line 23) was

(A) much more convenient than it is now.
(B) similar to the way Americans shopped at the time.
(C) expensive but rewarding.
(D) a difficult and frustrating process.
(E) more of a hobby than a necessity.

34. The primary purpose of the third paragraph (lines 34-48) is to

(A) use historical evidence to provide a contrast with the previous two paragraphs.
(B) examine why Romanians are so much more likely to engage in organized recycling than Americans are.
(C) detail the history of the communist movement.
(D) contrast the author's own behaviors with those of most other Romanians.
(E) provide another example that supports the arguments made earlier in the essay.

35. What does the author mean when she says that "The answer is kids!" (line 53)?

(A) Children should be forced to recycle a quota of paper each week.
(B) By appealing to adults using cute children, pro-recycling advertisements will be more effective.
(C) Children are more open to recycling than adults who lived through communist oppression.
(D) Children are the only Romanians who do not recycle.
(E) Children should be employed at the nation's recycling plants.

36. Why does the author feel "sick" (line 60)?

(A) She has wasted many useful objects by throwing them away.
(B) Romania's government has banned many forms of recycling.
(C) She cannot bear to hear about the brutality of the Ceausescu regime.
(D) She has contracted a disease from handling too much trash.
(E) Children in her class do not feel an urge to recycle.

37. The author implies that the most important aspect of the "Green Marshals" program is that

(A) a small amount of paper was recycled.
(B) the coalition made a lot of money selling its paper.
(C) the children learned how to communicate with businesses.
(D) the author's class won the competition.
(E) it has helped to change people's attitudes.

38. Throughout the passage, the author's attitude toward Romanians can best be described as

(A) condescending.
(B) unconcerned.
(C) ironic.
(D) derogatory.
(E) sympathetic.

39. The primary purpose of the passage is to

(A) argue that people should not be forced to recycle.
(B) detail an exciting new project at the author's school.
(C) inspire others to become "pack rats."
(D) compare several different types of recycling.
(E) describe the complex attitudes that Romanians have toward recycling.

B7HW: Homework and Extra Practice

| **SC TOPIC:** Circling Structure Words (Lesson B5a) | **RC TOPIC:** Eliminating Answers (Lesson B6b) |

Homework Set 1

1. Malik liked to study in the ------ corner of the library because there were few distractions.

   (A) bustling
   (B) extravagant
   (C) secluded
   (D) condensed
   (E) resonant

2. As their food supplies ------, the stranded adventurers restricted themselves to an increasingly ------ amount of food at each meal.

   (A) flourished . . sparse
   (B) subsided . . abundant
   (C) dwindled . . scanty
   (D) persisted . . ample
   (E) accumulated . . meager

3. The ------ children ran screaming through the house until an adult stopped them and ------ them for making too much noise.

   (A) submissive . . acclaimed
   (B) mute . . scolded
   (C) boisterous . . reproached
   (D) rowdy . . vindicated
   (E) subdued . . yielded to

4. After hearing that there were "canals" on Mars, many people ------ that human-like life forms had built the canals, though they are now known to be natural formations.

   (A) censured
   (B) refuted
   (C) exempted
   (D) despised
   (E) posited

5. When he was caught trespassing in his neighbor's house, the teenager offered only the ------ excuse that he mistakenly thought it was his own house.

   (A) plausible
   (B) compelling
   (C) credible
   (D) astute
   (E) flimsy

6. After discovering that the "juice" actually contained only water, high fructose corn syrup, and food coloring, Klaus decided to ------ the product, and never bought it again.

   (A) acclaim
   (B) placate
   (C) boycott
   (D) consolidate
   (E) redeem

7. Mona managed to climb to the top of the hill despite being ------ by a backpack full of heavy scientific instruments.

   (A) alleviated
   (B) instigated
   (C) encumbered
   (D) elucidated
   (E) expedited

8. The weather in Chicago is quite extreme: ------ heat in the summer and ------ cold in the winter.

   (A) stifling . . brash
   (B) unrelenting . . benign
   (C) placid . . glacial
   (D) oppressive . . frigid
   (E) austere . . tepid

Homework Set 2

9. During his ------, the park director angrily ranted about the inconsiderate people who threw their trash on the ground instead of into a trashcan.

    (A) hymn
    (B) eulogy
    (C) reconciliation
    (D) equivocation
    (E) tirade

10. Ileana was feeling quite ------ and alone in her new house until she met her ------ neighbors, whose warmth cheered her up very quickly.

    (A) despondent . . genial
    (B) spurious . . virulent
    (C) dismal . . malevolent
    (D) covert . . amiable
    (E) glum . . adverse

11. Though it is not native to the Americas, the "kudzu" vine has ------ since its arrival there, and now is perhaps the most recognized plant in the Southeast.

    (A) vacillated
    (B) proliferated
    (C) proffered
    (D) impeded
    (E) retracted

12. The speaker at the charity fundraiser ------ the guests to help the earthquake-ravaged country, and pledged that their ------ would be put to good use to help the victims recover.

    (A) invoked . . frugality
    (B) implored . . benevolence
    (C) assailed . . magnanimity
    (D) appealed to . . stinginess
    (E) thwarted . . wariness

13. As ------ for ruining his mother's Christmas party, Roland offered to send notes of apology to all those who attended.

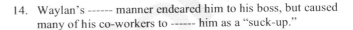

    (A) predominance
    (B) repute
    (C) deterrence
    (D) abundance
    (E) penance

14. Waylan's ------ manner endeared him to his boss, but caused many of his co-workers to ------ him as a "suck-up."

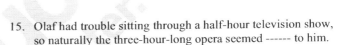

    (A) gregarious . . elicit
    (B) ambivalent . . commend
    (C) obsequious . . deride
    (D) obstinate . . indict
    (E) subservient . . tout

15. Olaf had trouble sitting through a half-hour television show, so naturally the three-hour-long opera seemed ------ to him.

    (A) inexplicable
    (B) incredulous
    (C) interminable
    (D) indifferent
    (E) indubitable

16. The ------ of the neighborhood full of mansions stands in stark contrast to the poverty of the nearby slums.

    (A) affluence
    (B) eccentricity
    (C) destitution
    (D) perplexity
    (E) contentiousness

Unauthorized copying or reuse of any part of this page is illegal.

Version 1.3

Homework Passage 1 (Short)

This passage is adapted from Our Mutual Friend, *a novel written by Charles Dickens. It describes a newly rich couple who are moving into a new home.*

Mr. and Mrs. Veneering were brand-new people in a brand-new house in a brand-new quarter of London. Everything about the Veneerings was spick-and-span
Line new. All their furniture was new, all their friends were
(5) new, all their servants were new, their dishes were new, their carriage was new, their harness was new, their horses were new, their pictures were new, they themselves were new, they were as newly married as was lawfully compatible with their having a brand-new baby,
(10) and if they had a great-grandfather, he would have come home in packaging from the moving van, without a scratch upon him, polished to the crown of his head.

For, in the Veneering establishment, from the hall-chairs with the new coat of arms, to the grand pianoforte
(15) with the new action, and upstairs again to the new fire-escape, all things were in a state of high varnish and polish. And what was observable in the furniture was observable in the Veneerings—the surface still smelt a little too much of the workshop.

17. The reference to the Veneerings' great-grandfather in lines 10-12 ("if they had … of his head") is most likely meant to

(A) imply that the Veneerings use strange means of transportation.
(B) indicate that the Veneerings order their relatives from a store.
(C) ridicule the great-grandfather for being completely bald.
(D) playfully emphasize the freshness of the Veneerings.
(E) praise the great-grandfather's youth and vitality.

18. The primary purpose of the passage is to

(A) promote the use of antique, sturdy furniture.
(B) establish the most noteworthy characteristic of two characters.
(C) describe mid-19th-century London.
(D) contrast the innocence of a couple with the weary boredom of those around them.
(E) provide information about the Veneerings' life before they moved to London.

Homework Passage 2 (Short)

For scholars and policy-makers, national security has at least two levels of commonly accepted meaning. First, in its most basic sense national security means protection
Line of a nation's borders and territories against invasion or
(5) control by foreign powers. In a world where the nation-state remains the basic unit having principal control of physical force, such protection is so important that no other goals can be realized without it.

Second, the broader view of national security
(10) involves the promotion of national values, interests, and institutions and the protection of them from various threats. Today, political events in seemingly remote parts of the world and various kinds of problems (monetary instability, world-wide inflation and unemployment,
(15) ecological disturbances, etc.) can directly affect a nation's well-being.

19. In what way does "the broader view of national security" (line 9) differ from the more basic view?

(A) The basic view's subjects are ultimately less critical to a nation's interests than those of the broader view.
(B) The broader view concerns issues that are non-military in nature.
(C) The broader view focuses mostly on local or regional events, as opposed to global ones.
(D) The basic view deals only with financial and monetary problems.
(E) The broader view requires more frequent use of physical force.

20. The passage implies that at some point in the past

(A) all scholars considered the promotion of national values around the world to be crucial.
(B) the phrase "national security" had many more levels of meaning.
(C) events from distant lands had less bearing on the welfare of a country.
(D) most foreign countries were too primitive to accept the institutions of a more advanced culture.
(E) global institutions made national armies unnecessary.

Homework Passage 3 (Long)

The following excerpt from an educational journal describes some of the problems faced by Asian American students.

In 1995, 268,000 of the 720,000 new immigrants that came to the United States were from Asia and the Pacific Islands. The Asian American population doubled between 1980 and 1990, and it will double again between (5) 1990 and 2020. "Asian American" as a racial group represents 29 distinct ethnic categories. Further, there is considerable social and economic variation between recent Asian immigrants and Asian-American communities that have been in the United States for (10) generations. The number of Asian-American school-age children and youth increased from 212,900 in 1980 to almost 1.3 million in 1990, creating a significant influx in many of the nation's public school systems, especially cities along the East and West coasts.

(15) The various stereotypes assigned to Asian American students cause them emotional distress and create conflicts with their peers, both those of different races and those in their own racial group. Even more important, stereotyping limits students' opportunities and (20) access to resources. Indeed, one study found higher levels of distress from peer discrimination (being threatened, called racially insulting names, and excluded from activities) in Chinese and Korean students than in African Americans, Hispanics, and whites.

(25) A recent report showed that high- and low-achieving Asian-identified students experienced anxiety to uphold the expectations of the model minority stereotypes. The students who were unable to perform well academically felt depressed and were embarrassed to seek help. (30) Moreover, dispelling the Asian-American universal academic success myth, the Educational Testing Service found that twelfth grade students from six major ethnic groups (Chinese, Japanese, Korean, Filipino, South Asian, and Southeast Asian) had significant variations in (35) their educational backgrounds and achievement. ETS also demonstrated how stereotyping has led to the neglect of the development of student services and support for the many Asian American students who are undereducated and have low socioeconomic status.

(40) The model minority stereotypes attribute educational and economic success to all Asian Americans, with the danger that they ignore the between- and within-group differences of assimilation/acculturation, social, political, economic, and education backgrounds. By focusing on (45) exceptional "success stories" and generalizing to all Asian Americans, the model minority myth does not take into consideration the large number of Asian-American students and their families who suffer from poverty and illiteracy. For example, while only 5.6 percent of (50) Japanese Americans have only an elementary education or less, 61 percent of the Hmong Americans fall into this category. Further, although the poverty rates for Japanese and Filipino Americans are 3.4 percent and 5.2 percent respectively, 24 percent of Vietnamese, 42 percent of (55) Cambodians, and 62 percent of Hmong Americans live below the poverty line.

The model minority stereotype that Asian American students are "whiz kids" and immune from behavioral or psychological distresses prevents them from (60) acknowledging academic and emotional problems and seeking help.

Whether the Asian-American students are excelling academically or having problems, it is essential to recognize and acknowledge that they experience school, (65) social, and familial stresses to uphold their "model minority" image. In fact, a study found that although Asian American students did better academically and had fewer delinquent behaviors than Caucasian Americans, the Asian-American youth reported more depressive (70) symptoms, withdrawn behavior, and social problems. They also had poorer self-images and reported more dissatisfaction with their social support.

In addition, Asian American students have reported experiencing racial and ethnic discrimination by their (75) peers. A recent study of literate Asian-American students at risk demonstrates the social and psychological struggles resulting from the model minority stereotypes that foster discrimination and anti-Asian sentiments from their peers. The review found that a large proportion (63 (80) percent) of Vietnamese, Hmong, and Korean elementary and secondary students reported that American students were "mean" to them. Being insulted or laughed at by classmates were cited as reasons for not liking school and lacking friends. In addition, commonly mentioned (85) concerns of Vietnamese, Chinese, and Cambodian refugee school age children were physical altercations with peers in school and in social interactions.

The increase in the number of Asian-American students in schools highlights the importance of (90) understanding how Asian-American stereotypes are reinforced in the school context and contribute to a biased and limited perspective of Asian Americans that does not reflect their within-group heterogeneity.

21. The main function of the first paragraph (lines 1-14) is to

(A) describe the author's motivations in writing the passage.
(B) compare several different ethnic groups.
(C) provide important background information for the rest of the passage.
(D) list the main points of the essay.
(E) use a humorous anecdote to introduce the passage's topic.

22. According to the passage, stereotypes of Asian Americans cause all of the following harmful effects EXCEPT

  (A) increasing the dropout rate.
  (B) restricting access to new opportunities.
  (C) creating discord within minority communities.
  (D) inciting conflict between minorities and other groups.
  (E) causing anxiety due to peer discrimination.

23. One can infer that a pervasive myth regarding Asian American students is that they are universally

  (A) friendly and outgoing.
  (B) very religious.
  (C) less intelligent than Caucasian Americans.
  (D) excellent academic performers.
  (E) unable to speak English fluently.

24. The passage implies that the "model minority myth" (line 46) is particularly unfair when applied to which group(s)?

  (A) Japanese and Filipino Americans
  (B) Cambodian and Hmong Americans
  (C) African Americans
  (D) Hispanics
  (E) Caucasians

25. According to the fifth paragraph (lines 62-72), even those students who meet the academic expectations of the model minority myth often

  (A) receive poor grades.
  (B) become egotistical and selfish.
  (C) become involved in criminal behavior.
  (D) experience stress-induced emotional problems.
  (E) lose sight of their cultural heritage.

26. The author implies that Asian-American students are often "insulted or laughed at" (line 82) by their peers because

  (A) everyone is made fun of at some point in his or her childhood.
  (B) Asian Americans often do poorly in school.
  (C) teachers and principals actively encourage discrimination against Asian Americans.
  (D) other students are jealous of Asian-Americans' "model minority" status.
  (E) Asian Americans have different-sounding names. ???

27. The last paragraph primarily serves to

  (A) disprove the arguments advanced earlier in the essay.
  (B) conclude the passage on a light-hearted note.
  (C) use the data from the first paragraph to accentuate the main ideas of the passage.
  (D) expand the subject of the essay to include other minority groups.
  (E) indicate a few ways in which readers can take action to correct a problem.

28. The author of the passage would most likely argue that

  (A) Asian Americans should not be treated as a uniform group.
  (B) All Asian Americans are high achievers.
  (C) Asian Americans are smarter than other students but more fragile emotionally.
  (D) Hmong students are the only group that faces significant discrimination.
  (E) Stereotypes have little effect on the mental wellbeing of Asian-American students.

29. Throughout the passage, the author's tone can best be described as

  (A) cynical
  (B) biased.
  (C) objective
  (D) humorous
  (E) digressive

30. The primary purpose of the passage is to

  (A) contrast the cultures of Korea, China, and Vietnam.
  (B) use experimental evidence to show that Asian-American students get higher test scores than other students.
  (C) analyze recent trends in the sources of immigration to the United States.
  (D) discuss the harmful effects that stereotypes and discrimination have on a particular minority group.
  (E) argue that Asian-Americans face more discrimination than any other group.

Version 1.3

Unauthorized copying or reuse of any part of this page is illegal.

Homework Passage 4 (Long)

This magazine article describes a new type of medicine with an unusual basis—the poison of a certain type of sea snail.

Now, people who suffer from severe pain that is unresponsive even to morphine may find relief from an unlikely source: the venom of a poisonous sea snail. The
Line Food and Drug Administration approved a new drug
(5) derived from this venom in 2005. It is the culmination of decades of research supported by the National Institute of General Medical Sciences (NIGMS).

The new medicine, called ziconotide, has its roots in a boy's curiosity about the deadly poisons inside the
(10) beautiful shells he collected in his native Philippines. Now a professor of biology at the University of Utah in Salt Lake City, Baldomero Olivera, Ph.D., analyzes the highly toxic venoms of these cone snails. His research is backed by 25 years of NIGMS funding.

(15) Ziconotide is 1,000 times more powerful than morphine, but, unlike morphine, it is not believed to be addictive. The FDA approved its use for chronic, intractable pain, such as that suffered by people with cancer, AIDS, or certain neurological disorders. It is
(20) delivered directly into fluid surrounding the spinal cord by external or implanted pumps.

The new drug is a synthetic compound identical to a toxin in the venom of the *Conus magus* snail. This is remarkable in itself, because natural compounds are
(25) almost always chemically modified to make them work better as drugs. In this case, nature perfected the compound on its own.

Also noteworthy is that the toxin was discovered by a teenager named J. Michael McIntosh, who, just days
(30) after graduating from high school, began assisting Olivera with his research. Now, 25 years and an M.D. degree later, McIntosh is a research psychiatrist at the University of Utah. He still collaborates with Olivera on the cone snail research.

(35) Ziconotide may be just the first of many new medicines derived from cone snail venom. There are about 500 different types of cone snails, and each one typically produces about 100 different toxins in its venom. According to Olivera's research, the toxins affect
(40) the nervous system in different ways—some instantly shock the snail's prey, as does the sting of an electric eel, scorpion, or sea anemone. Others cause paralysis, like the venoms of cobras and Japanese puffer fish.

Olivera's investigations further revealed that each
(45) toxin targets a certain type of molecule, usually a "channel" protein that helps pass messages in the nervous system. For example, the ziconotide molecule blocks calcium channels in specific nerve cells, preventing certain pain signals from reaching the brain. The toxins
(50) are so accurate at pinpointing their targets that researchers now use them to identify and study specific brain proteins.

The extreme specificity of the compounds—a characteristic highly prized in drug molecules—has not
(55) escaped the notice of pharmaceutical companies.

Already, they are testing the potential of dozens of cone snail toxins to treat epilepsy, cardiovascular disease, and other disorders.

Olivera continues to study and synthesize toxins
(60) produced by cone snails. He believes—and his research supports—that the snails are a treasure trove of novel chemical compounds with the potential to be useful in the clinic or the laboratory. Eventually, Olivera hopes to harness the molecules to treat Alzheimer's disease,
(65) Parkinson's disease, schizophrenia, and depression.

31. Which of the following would make the most appropriate title for the passage?

(A) The Life Cycle of the Cone Snail
(B) How to Treat Extreme Pain
(C) Making Medicine from Poison
(D) Great Discoveries Made by Teenagers
(E) The Deadly Poisons of the Phillipines

32. The tone of the passage can best be described as

(A) fervent.
(B) informative.
(C) sarcastic.
(D) apathetic.
(E) conversational.

33. In relation to morphine, ziconotide is

(A) more powerful but less addictive.
(B) much easier to administer to patients.
(C) less proven in experimental settings.
(D) more expensive but less effective.
(E) more dangerous and better-known.

34. As it is used in line 20, "delivered" most nearly means

(A) released from captivity.
(B) sent through the mail.
(C) fulfilled a promise.
(D) born.
(E) injected.

35. What is particularly notable about the chemical structure of the *Conus magus* snail's venom?

    (A) It is created to send pain signals directly to the brain.
    (B) It helps the venom to shock the snail's prey with an electrical charge.
    → (C) It did not have to be modified at all to become an effective medicine.
    (D) It targets many different types of proteins instead of just one.
    (E) It was nearly identical to that of a medicine that was already on the market.

36. The passage implies that because there are so many different kinds of cone snail venoms,

    (A) scientists will be unable to fully understand what effect each venom has.
    (B) no two venoms will have the same effect.
    (C) future medicines based on cone snail venoms are quite likely.
    (D) research into new medicines will be too expensive for Olivera and McIntosh to pursue.
    (E) one of the venoms will be even more effective at treating pain than ziconotide is.

37. Why do scientists use cone snail toxins "to identify and study specific brain proteins" (lines 51-52)?

    (A) Many brain proteins function more efficiently when the body is paralyzed.
    (B) Because the toxins affect many different brain proteins, researchers can study many proteins at once.
    (C) The "shocking" effect of some toxins is used to stimulate brain activity.
    (D) The toxins facilitate communication between the brain and the rest of the nervous system.
    (E) Each toxin targets only one protein, which allows scientists to easily study each protein.

38. The last paragraph of the passage serves to

    (A) describe several ways in which ziconotide is currently being used.
    (B) summarize the evidence used in the article.
    (C) refute an assumption stated in the previous paragraph.
    (D) provide a glimpse into the potential uses of cone snail toxins.
    (E) compare two different types of toxin.

Version 1.3

Unauthorized copying or reuse of any part of this page is illegal.

B8HW: Homework and Extra Practice

| **SC TOPIC**: Underline Meaning Words (Lesson B8a) | **RC TOPIC**: Eliminating Answers (Lesson B6b) |

Homework Set 1

1. As ------ checkers player, Herbert's goal was not so much to win each game as to learn and become a better player.

    (A) a novice
    (B) an adept
    (C) a perpetual
    (D) a competent
    (E) a vintage

2. The teacher cannot ------ papers that contain ------ remarks or off-topic arguments, so she gives a failing grade to any essay that deviates even slightly from its thesis.

    (A) concede to . . compelling
    (B) withstand . . momentous
    (C) repulse . . superficial
    (D) abide . . tangential
    (E) persist . . predominant

3. Devoted to ------ lifestyle, Natalia ------ shopping malls and restaurants, preferring to grow her own food and make what few possessions she owns.

    (A) a lavish . . despises
    (B) an ascetic . . shuns
    (C) an austere . . relishes
    (D) a voracious . . spurns
    (E) a magnanimous . . accedes to

4. The reviews of the new ballet were decidedly mixed, with some ------ its playful score and inventive set design and others mocking its inept choreography.

    (A) deriding
    (B) deploring
    (C) expediting
    (D) extolling
    (E) recanting

5. Every successful entrepreneur must overcome obstacles; DeJuan's main ------ was ------ amount of money that prevented him from hiring experienced workers.

    (A) asset . . a meager
    (B) encumbrance . . an ample
    (C) cognizance . . a luscious
    (D) affluence . . an exquisite
    (E) hindrance . . a scanty

6. The ------ author J.D. Salinger made no public appearances and gave only a few short interviews in the last forty years of his life.

    (A) communal
    (B) detestable
    (C) delusional
    (D) congenial
    (E) reclusive

7. While it is usually beneficial to follow standard procedures, sometimes the ------ choice requires a bit more creativity.

    (A) imprudent
    (B) conventional
    (C) brash
    (D) judicious
    (E) sociable

8. Seemingly unable to make a decision, Miku would ------ for twenty minutes over minor choices like what kind of cheese to put on a sandwich.

    (A) thwart
    (B) decree
    (C) resolve
    (D) revel
    (E) vacillate

Homework Set 2

9. Archibald ------ interrupted the funeral to tell the ------ mourners to cheer up, for he had just won $10 in the lottery.

(A) congenially . . elated
(B) discreetly . . sorrowful
(C) warily . . dismal
(D) ruthlessly . . auspicious
(E) callously . . despondent

10. Mrs. Cavanagh did not need to ------ her students to show the proper ------ to the war hero; they sat respectfully through his speech without any urging.

(A) invoke . . belligerence
(B) implore . . deference
(C) deplete . . decorum
(D) reproach . . penance
(E) evade . . debris

11. The novel was so difficult to follow that Daniel had to ask his mother to ------ nearly every chapter for him.

(A) perplex
(B) fluster
(C) revert
(D) commend
(E) elucidate

12. At over 6 feet, 10 inches, tall and with a fierce expression permanently etched on his face, the pitcher Randy Johnson was an ------ figure on the mound.

(A) innocuous
(B) imposing
(C) obsolete
(D) incredulous
(E) obsequious

13. Even though his parents had expressly forbidden him to go out alone at night, Noah decided to risk their ------ to sneak out to see a midnight showing of his favorite movie.

(A) gregariousness
(B) vindication
(C) zeal
(D) submissiveness
(E) wrath

14. So as not to ------ the discussion, Jiang limited herself to a few ------ comments and let others have some input.

(A) yield . . recurrent
(B) squander . . incessant
(C) allot . . pervasive
(D) monopolize . . intermittent
(E) accumulate . . unrelenting

15. In order to reach the South Pole on foot, the explorer had to ------ hundreds of miles of barren rock and glacier.

(A) circumvent
(B) flaunt
(C) dwell on
(D) sanction
(E) trek over

16. After only a few hours of negotiations, the two countries were able to reach ------ to share the costs of a new scientific project that would benefit both nations.

(A) a denunciation
(B) a portent
(C) an accord
(D) a censure
(E) an impasse

Homework Passage 1 (Short)

Theirs not to reason why, / Theirs but to do and die: / Into the valley of Death / Rode the six hundred.

These words may sound familiar; they are from "The
Line Charge of the Light Brigade," by Alfred, Lord Tennyson,
(5) which is one of the most well known poems in the English language. The poem memorializes the doomed charge of 600 (or so) mounted British soldiers during the Battle of Balaclava, in the Crimean War. British officers mistakenly ordered the soldiers to charge into a far
(10) superior Russian force; nearly half were killed or injured.

Tennyson was the poet laureate of England at the time and felt an obligation to present a patriotic tone in his work. As such, he sought to balance the inherent horror of the event with praise for the bravery of the
(15) soldiers. The resulting poem became hugely popular among both the royalty and the general populace. Even today, schoolchildren are regularly taught the poem, which will continue to "Honour the charge they made! / Honour the Light Brigade, / Noble six hundred!"

17. The author's tone when describing Tennyson can best be described as

(A) nationalistic.
(B) menacing.
(C) remorseful.
(D) courteous.
(E) scolding.

18. According to the passage, Tennyson's "patriotic tone" (line 12) was mainly due to

(A) ignorance of war's ability to cause suffering.
(B) a belief that Russian soldiers were cruel and stupid.
(C) fervor over the British victory at the Battle of Balaclava.
(D) admiration for the officers who ordered the charge.
(E) a sense of duty he felt as a representative of the country.

Homework Passage 2 (Short)

The appendix is a small tract in the human digestive system, located near the meeting of the large intestine and the small intestine. For hundreds of years, scientists
Line were unable to determine if this tiny organ had a
(5) function. Indeed, patients who have had their appendixes removed experienced no negative side effects. Based on analysis of the organs of other species, some anatomists concluded that the appendix was formerly used to digest leaves and other vegetation, but as humans evolved to
(10) consume a more easily digested diet, the appendix shrank until it lost that ability.

Recently, scientists have discovered that the appendix does still have at least two minor functions. Research shows that the appendix can both help the body
(15) to fight infections and also serve as a sort of storehouse for beneficial bacteria.

19. In context, "meeting" (line 2) most nearly means

(A) appointment.
(B) junction.
(C) appropriateness.
(D) gathering.
(E) acquaintance.

20. The second paragraph (lines 12-16) primarily serves to

(A) provide historical background for a theory.
(B) refute evidence from the previous paragraph.
(C) define a key term used throughout the passage.
(D) summarize two conflicting explanations of a phenomenon.
(E) reveal information that may clear up a mystery.

Homework Passage 3 (Long)

This passage is a first-person account of what life was like in Poland in the years after the end of the Soviet Union.

I am talking with Kasia, a woman I met a couple of years ago. Kasia works for a Western firm, at a salary lower than that of an American but still quite generous by
Line Polish standards. She's a bit younger than I am, slender,
(5) with finely etched features, blue-gray eyes. There's a quiet voice, a certain reserve in her manner: what I think of as the "Polish aristocrat" look. We are in her office, drinking tea. She is amazed at the number of Americans who have returned to Poland after a brief stay in the
(10) United States.

"But the same thing happened to me, years ago," she says thoughtfully. "I thought that the West would be wonderful, and then I lived there for a year; I started thinking about Poland, and something inside me wanted
(15) to come back. And you know, when I came back it seemed that Poland was perfect." She looks at me. "But now I think it is time for me to leave again."

"Is it because you've changed, or Poland has changed?"

(20) "I think both." She pauses, glances out the window. Across the street, the renovations on the Sezam department store are under way, and the new McDonald's next to it is doing a brisk business.

"I will tell you about something that happened a few
(25) months ago. It was Wigilia—Christmas Eve—and my husband and I were in our apartment. We heard someone at the door. Not our apartment door, but the door to the outside, downstairs."

"On the intercom," I say. The existence of an
(30) intercom system in a building is a definite plus in security-conscious Warsaw.

"Yes, on the intercom. I asked who it was. We were not expecting anyone at just that time, but my husband's family—his mother, his brother and wife and children—
(35) were coming over later for dinner. My daughter was putting the plates on the table, and my husband was helping me with the dinner. I remember when I heard the intercom, I said to him: 'This is your mother, I know it, and she will be coming in the kitchen and telling me
(40) how to fix the dinner.'

"But it was a man, a stranger. He was a refugee from Yugoslavia, he said, and he was looking for someplace where he could spend the night. He had no money; he had no place to go. He didn't know anyone in Warsaw.
(45) Before I could say anything, my husband told him that we were sorry. We couldn't help him."

"That seems the reasonable thing to do," I tell her. "After all, you didn't know who it was."

She shakes her head. "You know, we have a
(50) tradition here, on Christmas, to set an extra place for the stranger who might come. I looked at our table and I remembered the extra place. I wanted to ask the man in, and I told my husband, 'Let him in, it's Christmas.'

"'No,' he said, 'how do we know that this person does
(55) not have two others behind him with guns?'

"'Marek,' I said, 'it's Christmas! There is the extra place!' But he still said no. So we quarreled a little bit— yes, I quarreled with my husband on Christmas. I was angry, but I knew that he was right. And we didn't open
(60) the door.

"So I am thinking now that maybe I do not want to live in Poland for a while. I know that the old system was bad, but I think now that we are losing our soul, and that the problem we have in Poland is not just the inflation
(65) that people complain about. It is something else, and I don't know what to call it. But we are losing ... a part of ourselves."

She pauses. "I don't want to live in this country if we are so afraid that we do not even open our door on
(70) Christmas to a stranger. If we are so busy that we forget what it means, the extra place."

We sit for a moment, not speaking. What can I tell her? I remember last winter; I was living in an American city, in the Northeast, where an elderly woman locked
(75) herself out of her house and froze to death on her neighbor's porch. The neighbor was afraid to answer the knock on the door. I think about the millions of dollars in aid, the hundreds of advisors sent here to help the Poles change their system, and I wonder if we ever thought to
(80) warn them of the losses that come with the gains, of the extra places that are only empty plates.

21. Which of the following would be the best title for the passage?

(A) A History of Post-Soviet Poland
(B) Using Intercoms to Enhance Home Security
(C) The Meaning of the Empty Place
(D) A Family Gathering at Christmastime
(E) Americans in Warsaw

22. The author and Kasia seem to share what type of attitude toward post-Soviet Poland?

(A) joy
(B) despair
(C) cynicism
(D) ambivalence
(E) jealousy

Version 1.3

Unauthorized copying or reuse of any part of this page is illegal.

23. The passage implies that, compared to Americans, Polish workers

   (A) are more qualified.
   (B) are more generous with their co-workers.
   (C) have a more aristocratic attitude.
   (D) receive less compensation for the same work.
   (E) receive less education and job training.

24. As it is used in the passage, "reserve" (line 6) most nearly means

   (A) emotional restraint
   (B) emergency supply
   (C) natural resource
   (D) contract stipulation
   (E) back-up team member

25. Why did Kasia leave America after she "lived there for a year" (line 13)?

   (A) She was afraid of America's rampant crime.
   (B) She lost her job at the American company.
   (C) She worried that America had lost its soul.
   (D) She felt that Poland would fill a void inside her.
   (E) She realized that she could make more money in Poland.

26. The "renovations on the Sezam department store" and "the new McDonald's" (lines 21-22) are representative of what aspect of modern Poland?

   (A) its increasing Westernization
   (B) its improving economy
   (C) its high crime rates
   (D) its unhealthy diet
   (E) its generosity toward strangers

27. According to the passage, having an intercom system is "a definite plus" (line 30) because

   (A) it serves as a symbol of wealth and social status.
   (B) it is extremely convenient.
   (C) it is cheaper than having phone service.
   (D) it allows for a greater degree of safety from strangers.
   (E) Polish children dream of having an intercom when they grow up.

28. The passage implies that Kasia considers her mother-in-law to be

   (A) dangerous.
   (B) domineering.
   (C) helpful.
   (D) jovial.
   (E) reasonable.

29. Kasia would probably describe her husband's decision to turn away the stranger as

   (A) kind but reckless.
   (B) cruel and stupid.
   (C) unfortunate but sensible.
   (D) humorous and uplifting.
   (E) alarming and unjustified.

30. According to Kasia, "the problem that we have in Poland" (line 64) is

   (A) a loss of traditional Polish values.
   (B) an inability to listen to the advice of foreigners.
   (C) a high rate of inflation.
   (D) an insufficient concern with security.
   (E) a lack of effective gun control laws.

31. The last paragraph (lines 72-81) serves to

   (A) justify the actions of Kasia and her husband.
   (B) support the idea that safety is more important than generosity.
   (C) summarize the arguments made in the passage.
   (D) advocate for Poland to be more like the United States.
   (E) draw a connection between the problems of Poland and those of the United States.

Unauthorized copying or reuse of any part of this page is illegal.

Version 1.3

Homework Passage 4 (Long)

The following passage examines the impact of geography on sailing during the Age of Exploration (~1400 – 1600 AD).

Five hundred years ago most of the people who lived in Europe thought that the earth was flat. They knew only the land that was near them. They knew the continent of
Line Europe, a small part of Asia, and a strip along the
(5) northern shore of Africa.

They thought this known land was surrounded by a vast body of water that was like a broad river. Sailors were afraid to venture far upon this water, for they feared they would fall over the edge of the earth.

(10) Other seafaring men believed that if they should sail too far out upon this water their vessels would be lost in a fog, or that they would suddenly begin to slide downhill, and would never be able to return. Wind gods and storm gods, too, were supposed to dwell upon this mysterious
(15) sea. Men believed that these wind and storm gods would be very angry with anyone who dared to enter their domain, and that in their wrath they would hurl the ships over the edge of the earth, or keep them wandering round and round in a circle, in the mist and fog.

(20) It is no wonder that the name "Sea of Darkness" was given to this great body of water, which we now know to be the Atlantic Ocean; nor is it surprising that the sailors feared to venture far out upon it.

These sailors had no dread at all of a sea called the
(25) Mediterranean. This sea was named the Mediterranean because it was supposed to be in the middle of the land that was then known. On this body of water the sailors were very bold, fighting, robbing, and plundering strangers and foes, without any thought of fear.

(30) They sailed through this sea eastward to Constantinople, their ships being loaded with metals, woods, and pitch. These they traded for silks, cashmeres, dyewoods, spices, perfumes, precious stones, ivory, and pearls. Caravans brought all of these things from the far
(35) Eastern countries, such as India, China, and Japan, to the cities on the east coast of the Mediterranean.

This caravan journey was a very long and tiresome one. Worse than this, the Turks, through whose country the caravans passed, began to see how valuable this trade
(40) was, and they sent bands of robbers to prevent the caravans from reaching the coast.

As time went on, these land journeys grew more difficult and more dangerous, until the traders saw that the day would soon come when they would be entirely
(45) cut off from traffic with India and the rich Eastern countries. The Turks would secure all their profitable business. So the leaders of that time tried to think of some other way of reaching the East.

Among those who wished to find a short route to
(50) India was Prince Henry of Portugal, a bold navigator as well as a studious and thoughtful man. He was desirous of securing the rich Indian trade for his own country. So he established a school for navigators at Lisbon, and gathered around him many men who wanted to study
(55) about the sea.

Here they made maps and charts, and talked with one another about the strange lands that they thought might be found far out in that mysterious body of water that they so dreaded. It is probable that they had heard
(60) some accounts of the voyages of other navigators on this wonderful sea, and the beliefs about land beyond.

32. What is the primary function of the third paragraph (lines 10-19)?

   (A) to use a fable from an earlier era to explain a modern phenomenon
   (B) to describe the map-making process
   (C) to make fun of the naïveté of early sailors
   (D) to contradict a statement made in the previous paragraph
   (E) to help the reader understand the mystery of the Atlantic Ocean during one era

33. Why did sailors have "no dread at all" (line 24) of the Mediterranean?

   (A) They were unaware of the dangers of sailing through Turkish waters.
   (B) They believed that the wind and storm gods of this sea would protect them.
   (C) It was a shallow sea, so the sailors had no fear of drowning.
   (D) They were familiar with all of the surrounding lands.
   (E) There was no fighting on those waters.

34. The passage implies that the Far East generally lacked which of the following resources?

   (A) perfumes
   (B) ivory
   (C) metals
   (D) silk
   (E) precious stones

35. What prompted some people to "think of some other way of reaching the East" (lines 47-48)?

   (A) a fear of being lost in fog at the edge of the world
   (B) strange tales of a land beyond the mysterious sea
   (C) an earthquake that blocked the road to India
   (D) a decrease in the value of precious stones and silks
   (E) the increasing dangers of the overland route

Version 1.3

Unauthorized copying or reuse of any part of this page is illegal.

36. The author mentions "Prince Henry of Portugal" (line 50) because he is one of the first people to

(A) believe that wind and storm gods dwelled in the Sea of Darkness.
(B) rely on evidence rather than superstition when mapping the unknown oceans.
(C) dread sailing beyond the familiar seas of the Mediterranean.
(D) sail eastward to Constantinople.
(E) recognize the value of the Indian trade routes.

37. As it is used in line 60, "accounts" most nearly means

(A) stories.
(B) customers.
(C) business arrangements.
(D) monetary investments.
(E) tables of figures.

38. The author's attitude toward the sailors of the Age of Exploration can best be described as

(A) cruel.
(B) understanding.
(C) surprised.
(D) fearful.
(E) patronizing.

39. The primary purpose of the passage is to

(A) criticize the Turks for interfering with trade routes.
(B) compare Prince Henry of Portugal to other famous navigators.
(C) describe the geography of the Mediterranean region.
(D) poke fun at those who believed in the "Sea of Darkness."
(E) describe the impact that geographical perceptions had on a particular era.

Unauthorized copying or reuse of any part of this page is illegal.

Version 1.3

B9HW: Homework and Extra Practice

| SC TOPIC: Underline Meaning Words (Lesson B8a) | RC TOPIC: Paired Passages (Lesson B9b) |

Homework Set 1

1. Rather than ------ his position and admit that he was wrong, Lester chose to ------ himself further, even proclaiming that he would never give up.

   (A) proliferate . . evoke
   (B) concede . . defer
   (C) acclaim . . vacillate
   (D) relinquish . . entrench
   (E) sustain . . confront

2. In order to ------ the project's success, Wook-sung took charge and ------ individual tasks to each group member based on their strengths.

   (A) expedite . . purged
   (B) hinder . . mandated
   (C) impede . . appointed
   (D) facilitate . . delegated
   (E) detract from . . aggregated

3. Pedro used ------ to deal with difficult situations even though he knew that lightheartedness was not always appropriate.

   (A) decorum
   (B) levity
   (C) allure
   (D) severity
   (E) penance

4. The ------ of Jacques' comment was somewhat shocking to his colleagues, who had considered Jacques to be wise and knowledgeable.

   (A) hypocrisy
   (B) apprehension
   (C) strife
   (D) naïveté
   (E) propriety

5. Louisa sought to ------ the damage she had done to her friendship with Natasha and end their ------ by buying Natasha a new photo album.

   (A) estrange . . amiability
   (B) venerate . . contentiousness
   (C) placate . . mitigation
   (D) attain . . tumult
   (E) ameliorate . . quarrel

6. The principal declared that it would be ------ for the science class to visit two different water-treatment plants on field trips, saying that one trip would more than suffice.

   (A) intermittent
   (B) compulsory
   (C) plausible
   (D) prudent
   (E) redundant

7. Stuck in the middle of a bookshelf full of immense technical manuals, the slim children's book seemed very ------.

   (A) incongruous
   (B) abundant
   (C) pertinent
   (D) resilient
   (E) tedious

8. The police officer did not want to ------ the domestic dispute, but he was forced to separate the couple when they started throwing objects at each other.

   (A) intervene in
   (B) elucidate
   (C) elude
   (D) retract
   (E) posit

Homework Set 2

9. The candidate impressed some observers with his smooth manner and eloquent language, but others found fault with his ------ arguments and lack of evidence.

(A) rigorous
(B) spurious
(C) voluminous
(D) judicious
(E) feasible

10. Marion recognized that he was not ------, but still wished that he could learn to make fewer mistakes.

(A) infallible
(B) intrusive
(C) intangible
(D) incensed
(E) incredulous

11. English is becoming increasingly ------ in world affairs as citizens of many ------ cultures seek a common language to help ease diplomatic relations.

(A) omnipresent . . malevolent
(B) prevalent . . disparate
(C) desolate . . distinctive
(D) predominant . . analogous
(E) provincial . . antecedent

12. Once a world leader in developing new technologies, the company is now relying on ------, overused ideas rather than focusing on creating ------ new ones.

(A) verbose . . ingenious
(B) dormant . . callous
(C) compelling . . conventional
(D) stagnant . . innovative
(E) inciting . . trite

13. Detective Benson doubted the witness' ------ after discovering that his story differed greatly from that of the other witnesses.

(A) veracity
(B) capriciousness
(C) adversity
(D) equivocation
(E) timidity

14. The lawyer always prepared diligently and vowed never to be ------ in her responsibility to her client.

(A) voracious
(B) industrious
(C) obstinate
(D) meticulous
(E) remiss

15. Though he had not even glanced at the details of his supervisor's plan, the ------ employee frequently ------ its virtues and even declared the supervisor a genius.

(A) obsequious . . ridiculed
(B) brash . . overlooked
(C) sycophantic . . extolled
(D) preposterous . . scorned
(E) assertive . . deluded

16. Marissa felt the need to ------ happiness when she attended the formal dance, for she did not want to let her sadness interfere with other people's pleasure.

(A) feign
(B) parody
(C) amplify
(D) assail
(E) refute

Homework Passage 1 (Short Paired)

Passage 1:

      Psychiatry, a medical field that studies mental disorders and attempts to treat them with medication, psychotherapy, and a variety of other techniques, has
Line always had its share of detractors. In the 18th century,
(5) before the term "psychiatry" was even coined, the author Daniel Defoe (author of *Robinson Crusoe*) noted that concern over patients' mental health was being abused, in particular by husbands who had their disobedient—but sane—wives committed to insane asylums.
(10)   Today, critics of psychiatry point out that the definitions of mental disorders are extremely vague and contain a high degree of overlap, meaning that many patients are diagnosed with (and treated for) multiple similar conditions. Another concern relates to the overuse
(15) of psychiatric medications, many of which have harmful side effects. Many former psychiatric patients, as well as some doctors, have joined a movement to limit the use of these dangerous psychiatric medications.

Passage 2:

Line   Early psychiatry dealt almost exclusively with the
(20) individual. Psychiatrists examined, treated, and medicated a patient as if each disorder were entirely contained within the patient's mind. In the last half of the 20th century, some psychiatrists began advocating a broader view. The field they created, called social
(25) psychiatry, focuses on the interplay of people and society in the cause and remediation of a mental disorder.
      A good example may be a child who begins developing signs of depression as a result of environmental triggers such as bullying. A social
(30) psychiatrist would typically discuss these social traumas with the patient during therapy to try to develop flexible coping strategies. The psychiatrist may then try to enact guidelines (in concert with parents, school authorities, and others) that will allow for a less stressful social
(35) environment for the patient. Using these techniques, social psychiatrists contribute to the improved mental health of tens of thousands of patients each year.

17. One can infer from Passage 1 that which of the following statements is true regarding 18th century psychiatry?

    (A) Doctors who treated mental disorders were universally respected.
    (B) Doctors treated patients by helping them cope with their existing social environment.
    (C) Women were treated less fairly than men.
    (D) The definitions of mental disorders were far less murky than they are today.
    (E) Psychiatric medications were widespread and overused.

18. According to Passage 2, the key innovation in "social psychiatry" (lines 24-25) is to

    (A) treat each disorder as if it is contained entirely within the patient's mind.
    (B) increase the usage of psychiatric medications.
    (C) diagnose the patient with only one disorder.
    (D) work with people who know the patient to encourage healthier social interactions.
    (E) require the patient to undergo an intensive program of psychotherapy.

19. How would the author of Passage 2 most likely respond to the concern in Passage 1 that many "psychiatric medications … have harmful side effects" (lines 13-14)?

    (A) No effective treatment plan can be accomplished without medication.
    (B) Such medications, even when they do not cause side effects, are detrimental to the patient's mental health.
    (C) Many psychiatric issues can be treated without medication, by using therapy and coping strategies.
    (D) There is no scientific evidence that psychiatric medications cause harmful side effects.
    (E) Side effects can be effectively treated with additional medications.

20. Which of the following statements most accurately describes the tones of the two passages when describing psychiatry?

    (A) Both passages are quite sympathetic.
    (B) Both passages are reverential, though Passage 1 is slightly more so than Passage 2.
    (C) Passage 1 is mostly pessimistic while Passage 2 is much more favorable.
    (D) Passage 1 is ambivalent whereas Passage 2 is indifferent.
    (E) Both passages express profound distrust.

Homework Passage 2 (Long Paired)

The following passages, written by Peace Corps volunteers, describe how water is a central aspect of village life. The first passage takes place in the African nation of Mali; the second concerns the Caribbean nation of the Dominican Republic.

Passage 1:

When a woman carries water on her head, you see her neck bend outward behind her like a crossbow. Ten liters of water weighs 22 pounds, a fifth of a woman's
Line body weight, and I've seen women carry at least 20 liters
(5) in aluminum pots large enough to hold a television set.

To get the water from the cement floor surrounding the outdoor hand pump to the top of your head, you need help from the other women. You and another woman grab the pot's edges and lift it straight up between you.
(10) When you get it to the head height, you duck underneath the pot and place it on the wad of rolled-up cloth. This is the cushion between your skull and the metal pot full of water. Then your friend lets go. You spend a few seconds finding your balance. Then with one hand steadying the
(15) load, turn around and start your way home. It might be a 20-minute walk through mud huts and donkey manure. All of this is done without words.

It is an action repeated so many times during the day that even though I have never carried water on my head, I
(20) know exactly how it is done.

Do not worry that no one will be at the pump to help you. The pump is the only source of clean drinking water for the village of 3,000 people. Your family—your husband and children—rely on the water on your head;
(25) maybe 10 people will drink the water you carry. Pump water, everyone knows, is clean. Drinking well water will make you sick. Every month, people here die from diarrhea and dehydration. The pump is also where you hear gossip from the women who live on the other side of
(30) the village. Your trip to the pump may be your only excuse for going outside of your family's home alone.

When a woman finds her balance under 40 pounds of water, I see her eyes roll to the corners in concentration. Her head makes the small movements of
(35) the hands of someone driving a car: constant correction. The biggest challenge is to turn all the way around from the pump to go home again. The load is a small portion of the ocean, and it swirls and lurches on her head with long movements.
(40) It looks painful and complicated and horrible for the posture and unhealthy for the vertebrae, but I wish I could do it. I have lived in this West African village for two years, but cannot even balance something solid, like a mango, on my head, let alone a pot filled with liquid.
(45) When I lug my 10-liter plastic jug of water to my house by hand, it is only a hundred meters, but the container is heavy and unwieldy. Changing the jug from one hand to the other helps, but it is a change necessary every 20 meters. Handles do not balance. Because my life has
(50) never depended on it, I have never learned to balance.

Passage 2:

Strange and subtle sometimes are the habits of courtesy. Water is a precious commodity out here in the *campo* (countryside). So there is a whole culture built
Line around its acquisition and usage. If you go to any store or
(55) wait for *aguagua* (water bus), the custom, usually, is to push or shove your way to the front. When it comes to water, at least in my community, the rules are different. I spent the morning collecting water for myself at the communal tap. The *samedoñas* who elbowed me aside in
(60) the *colmado* (corner store) last night made sure I got my water when it was my turn—first come, first served.

Water is one of the first things you offer a visiting Volunteer, water to drink and to wash off the dusty road. A good host is not stingy with his water, even if he has to
(65) go to great effort to get it. A good guest notices how difficult it is to get the water and limits her usage accordingly. Even better, the guest helps replace the water used.

Volunteers from water-poor communities are often
(70) quick to notice the lavish habits of Volunteers from water-rich communities. "I can't believe she used three full gallons to take a bath. You'd think she were washing an elephant." On the other hand, Volunteers from water-rich communities are struck by the stinginess of the water
(75) poor. "He hoarded water like it was gold at Fort Knox, rationing it out drop by drop."

I consider myself a decent host in this area. I keep about 15 gallons in my house almost all the time. Since the average Volunteer uses about three to four gallons a
(80) day, that's a pretty good quantity.

I never tire of marveling at the combinations of strength and grace displayed by the women and girls, who carry five gallons on their heads, with a gallon in each hand. My favorite is when they casually turn to chat
(85) with a neighbor, blithely ignoring the burden with which they are laden. I once watched a woman gracefully bend down and pluck a peso without spilling a precious drop!

I carry the water on my shoulder. I've assumed that the wide berth the folks give me is not due to unpleasant
(90) body odor, but because of the constant splashes that leap forth from my bucket. But I'm improving. Now, people rarely ask me if I've recently gone swimming after I've actually been carrying water. And the water source is one of the best places to catch the latest gossip. I have
(95) concluded that *chesmes* (rumors) are flying due to the occasional, "No me digas!" ("Don't tell me!") and "Adquerosa!" ("Gross!") that escapes from their mouths while they are huddled over the tap.

I suppose that's what I like best about the water
(100) collection process. It's one of the places where I fit into the community best. My Spanish is what it is, and I do remain the *gringo*. Yet, I understand the rules at the tap and even some of the subtleties. The community sees I am on even ground with them and ask no privileges. It is
(105) a calm and orderly place. Maybe I will fondly remember the communal tap when I am reaching for the hot water faucet in the shower. Then again, maybe not…

21. The author of Passage 1 describes the process of balancing the water jug on a person's head as being

    (A) quiet and complex.
    (B) painful and pointless.
    (C) rushed and noisy.
    (D) quick and easy.
    (E) unhealthy and disorderly.

22. Why does the author of Passage 1 tell the reader, "Do not worry that no one will be at the pump to help" (line 21)?

    (A) to alert the reader that helpers can be hired nearby
    (B) to give the reader a sense of the bustling activity around the water pump
    (C) to encourage others to lift the 10-liter jugs by themselves
    (D) to promise that she will be at the pump when the reader needs help
    (E) to introduce a new device that allows a person to carry water more easily

23. According to the author of Passage 1, a trip to the water pump has all of the following benefits EXCEPT

    (A) it helps prevent death and disease.
    (B) it improves the posture of the women who carry water.
    (C) it provides an opportunity to hear the news of the community.
    (D) it ensures that one's whole family has water to drink.
    (E) it allows a woman to leave her home for a while.

24. What is the most likely reason that the author of Passage 1 states, "I wish I could [carry water on my head]" (lines 41-42)?

    (A) She respects the strength and poise of the women who can do so.
    (B) She is jealous of the women who carry water, who are wealthier and more influential than she is.
    (C) She wishes to prove herself superior to the villagers who have mistreated her.
    (D) She considers water-carrying to be excellent exercise.
    (E) Her life, and the life of her family, depends on her learning to carry water.

25. According to the author of Passage 2, what is the biggest difference between shopping at the *colmado* and getting water at the communal tap?

    (A) The people at the *colmado* are more likely to engage in gossip.
    (B) The Volunteers are not allowed to shop at the *colmado*.
    (C) The *colmado* is closer to the author's home.
    (D) The villagers are pushier and more selfish at the *colmado*.
    (E) The owner of the *colmado* sells water at a cheaper price.

26. A "good guest" (line 66) would most likely offer to do which of the following?

    (A) Elbow his way to the front of the line at the *colmado*.
    (B) Wash the host's dishes with water from the communal tap.
    (C) Help the host to fetch water to replace the water he has used.
    (D) Tell the host all the gossip he has heard.
    (E) Teach the host a few phrases of Spanish.

27. The author of Passage 2 would probably describe his water-carrying ability as

    (A) masterful.
    (B) completely inept.
    (C) graceful and stylish.
    (D) casual but ignorant.
    (E) unimpressive but improving.

28. The final sentence of Passage 2 ("Then again, maybe not…") most likely is intended to convey that the author

    (A) is unsure which method of acquiring water that he prefers.
    (B) yearns to return to America.
    (C) enjoys using the communal tap but does not prefer it to having running hot water.
    (D) hopes to introduce modern running water systems to his village in the near future.
    (E) cannot explain why he enjoys being around the communal water source.

Version 1.3

Unauthorized copying or reuse of any part of this page is illegal.

29. Both passages describe the villagers at the communal water source as being

    (A) rushed.
    (B) stingy.
    (C) disdainful.
    (D) unselfish.
    (E) quiet.

30. The authors of both passages share what attitude when observing the villagers who carry large amounts of water?

    (A) respect
    (B) confusion.
    (C) indifference.
    (D) joviality
    (E) scorn.

31. Both passages describe the communal water source as having what function in addition to providing water?

    (A) a swimming area for the townsfolk
    (B) a center for gossip and social interaction
    (C) a place for volunteers to bathe
    (D) a store for buying food and other goods
    (E) a clinic for the sick and dehydrated to be treated

32. The tone of Passage 2, in comparison to the tone of Passage 1, is more

    (A) playful.
    (B) wistful.
    (C) admiring.
    (D) objective.
    (E) subtle.

Homework Passage 3 (Long)

This excerpt from Harold Brighouse's story "Once a Hero" describes an encounter between a rich man and his employee at the opening of a war memorial funded by the rich man.

Standing in a sheltered doorway a homeless man, with a slouch hat crammed low over a notably unwashed face, watched the outside of the new cafeteria of the Sir
Line William Rumbold Ltd., Engineering Company. Perhaps
(5) because they were workers while he was unemployed, he had an air of compassionate cynicism as the audience assembled and thronged into the building, which, as prodigally advertised throughout Calderside, was to be opened that night by Sir William in person.

(10) There being no one to observe him, the homeless man could be frank with his cynicism; but inside the building, in the platform ante-room, Mr. Edward Fosdike, who was Sir William's locally resident secretary, had to discipline his private feelings to a suave
(15) concurrence in his employer's florid enthusiasm. Fosdike served Sir William well, but no man is a hero to his (male) secretary.

"I hope you will find the arrangements satisfactory," Fosdike was saying, tugging nervously at his maltreated
(20) moustache. "You speak at seven and declare the memorial open. Then there's a meal." He hesitated. "Perhaps I should have warned you to dine before you came."

Sir William was aware of being a very gallant
(25) gentleman. "Not at all," he said heroically, "not at all. I have not spared my purse over this War Memorial. Why should I spare my feelings? Well, now, you've seen about the Press?"

"Oh, yes. The reporters are coming. There'll be
(30) flashlight photographs. Everything quite as usual when you make a public appearance, sir."

Sir William wondered if this resident secretary of his were quite adequate. Busy in London, he had left all arrangements in his local factotum's hands, and he was
(35) doubting whether those hands had grasped the situation competently. "Only as usual?" he said sharply. "This War Memorial has cost me ten thousand pounds."

"The amount," Fosdike hastened to assure him, "has been circulated, with appropriate tribute to your
(40) generosity."

"Generosity," criticised Rumbold. "I hope you didn't use that word."

Mr. Fosdike referred to his notebook. "We said," he read, "'the cost, though amounting to ten thousand
(45) pounds, is entirely beside the point. Sir William felt that no expense was excessive that would result in a fitting and permanent expression of our gratitude to the glorious dead.'"

"Thank you, Fosdike. That is exactly my feeling,"
(50) said the gratified Sir William, paying Fosdike the unspoken compliment of thinking him less of a fool than he looked.

33. The author most likely draws a comparison between the "homeless man" (lines 10-11) and Fosdike in order to

    (A) accuse Fosdike of being incompetent.
    (B) describe how both of them display the same attitude toward Sir William.
    (C) imply that the homeless man is trying to sabotage the event.
    (D) show how people in different positions react in different ways to the event.
    (E) illustrate how both characters are subservient to Sir William's desires.

34. Fosdike's attitude toward Sir William can best be described as

    (A) worshipful.
    (B) loyal but realistic.
    (C) compassionate.
    (D) openly cynical.
    (E) ungrateful.

35. What "gallant" (line 24) action does Sir William take?

    (A) He compliments Fosdike on being highly competent.
    (B) He volunteers to eat the same food as the commoners at the cafeteria.
    (C) He signs up to serve in the Army.
    (D) He gives money to the homeless man.
    (E) He refuses to be publicly praised for his generosity.

36. As it is used in line 26, "purse" most nearly means

    (A) prize.
    (B) tightening.
    (C) wealth.
    (D) kiss.
    (E) handbag.

37. The passage implies that Sir William is concerned that the press reports might make him seem to be

    (A) uncaring toward the common man.
    (B) stingy in his spending habits.
    (C) nervous at speaking in front of a crowd.
    (D) overly critical toward Fosdike.
    (E) bragging about how much he spent on the memorial.

38. Throughout the passage, Sir William is described as being

    (A) generous and compassionate.
    (B) quietly enthusiastic.
    (C) honest and open.
    (D) arrogant and self-centered.
    (E) light-hearted and friendly.

SC Topic: Underline Meaning Words (Lesson B8a)	**RC Topic**: Paired Passages (Lesson B9b)

Homework Set 1

1. Hans did not want to fight with Greta any longer, so he adopted a ------ tone in their conversation.

    (A) contemptuous
    (B) conventional
    (C) contentious
    (D) condescending
    (E) conciliatory

2. The principal did her best to remain ------ from her students; in her mind, friendly relations between students and faculty were to be avoided because they only ------ discipline.

    (A) aloof . . hindered
    (B) congenial . . ameliorated
    (C) hospitable . . encumbered
    (D) disdainful . . entrenched
    (E) acerbic . . instigated

3. Roy wanted his bosses to respect him for his ideas and not because he was ------, so he never ------ his opinions around his bosses, even when he disagreed with them.

    (A) sycophantic . . averred
    (B) unrelenting . . stifled
    (C) subservient . . suppressed
    (D) submissive . . asserted
    (E) indubitable . . thwarted

4. A true scientist should never be ------, but should instead be willing to change his or her opinions when new evidence comes to light.

    (A) capricious
    (B) audacious
    (C) fallible
    (D) dogmatic
    (E) intermittent

5. The novel's plot is so ------ and its prose so ------ that most readers are unable to follow the events of the book.

    (A) intricate . . lucid
    (B) transparent . . eloquent
    (C) amiable . . incomprehensible
    (D) elaborate . . incoherent
    (E) austere . . dubious

6. Milly wanted to go to the concert, but she was unable to ------ herself from her obligation to babysit her sister that night.

    (A) ascribe
    (B) extricate
    (C) incite
    (D) immerse
    (E) perplex

7. Many people use the word "radar," but few know that it is actually an acronym ------ "RAdio Detection And Ranging."

    (A) refuting
    (B) quarreling
    (C) complying
    (D) denoting
    (E) disquieting

8. As the villagers' food shortage became more and more ------, many adults began going without food altogether so that they could feed their children.

    (A) negligible
    (B) superfluous
    (C) minute
    (D) acute
    (E) conducive

Unauthorized copying or reuse of any part of this page is illegal.

Version 1.3

Homework Set 2

9. In 1848, Mexico ------ much of the present-day American Southwest to the United States after losing the Mexican-American War.

(A) aggregated
(B) eluded
(C) ceded
(D) protracted
(E) amassed

10. After numerous attempts to photograph the "Bigfoot" proved ------, Arlen was forced to admit that perhaps "Bigfoot" was a mythical creature, as others claimed.

(A) portentous
(B) serene
(C) futile
(D) potent
(E) triumphant

11. The police officers had ------ that the suspect was guilty of the robbery, but despite this hunch they were unable to ------ him in the crime and he was released.

(A) a foreboding . . vindicate
(B) a fallacy . . insinuate
(C) a delusion . . acquit
(D) an intuition . . implicate
(E) an uproar . . exonerate

12. Among astronomers, there is much ------ over exactly what ------ a planet, and especially whether Pluto is large enough and its orbit regular enough to qualify.

(A) controversy . . constitutes
(B) accord . . designates
(C) deliberation . . contradicts
(D) conformity . . embodies
(E) recurrence . . eradicates

13. Although we could walk to the store instead of driving there, it would not be ------ to do so, and we cannot afford any delays.

(A) preposterous
(B) callous
(C) lethargic
(D) expedient
(E) stagnant

14. To relieve the ------ of driving through the flat, featureless landscape, the family began singing traveling songs.

(A) levity
(B) bustle
(C) monotony
(D) tenacity
(E) zeal

15. The ------ family moved several times a year to wherever there was available work picking crops on a farm.

(A) alluring
(B) itinerant
(C) dormant
(D) caustic
(E) static

16. In the film, the hero befriends ------ but skilled martial arts master whose brief bits of wisdom help the hero to become ------ at karate.

(A) a loquacious . . adept
(B) a concise . . inauspicious
(C) a verbose . . diligent
(D) an effusive . . naïve
(E) a terse . . proficient

Homework Passage 1 (Short Paired)

Passage 1:

The first prominent female film director, Leni
Riefenstahl, may be both the most admired and the most
vilified director of the 20th century. She is respected for
Line her innovative uses of new techniques, from unusual
(5) camera angles and tracking shots to smash cuts and
extreme close-ups. However, the context of her
groundbreaking films cannot be forgotten, for
Riefenstahl's films were made during the Nazi era of
Germany, and some explicitly glorify Adolf Hitler and
(10) his regime. Her most famous work, *Triumph of the Will*,
documents the huge Nuremberg Nazi rally of 1934; it can
rightly be called the most consequential piece of
propaganda ever put to film. While much of her other
work, such as *Olympia*, a stylized chronicle of the 1936
(15) Berlin Olympic Games, is not explicitly political, it does
contain themes that glorify Nazism and its leaders.

Riefenstahl lived to be 101, and she accomplished
much in her long life (including becoming the oldest
scuba diver in the world), but she would never direct a
(20) feature film after the fall of the Nazi regime. Some
crimes outweigh even great achievements.

Passage 2:

Athletic competitions are normally a mere diversion,
a way of entertaining audiences with the amazing
Line capabilities of the human body. Sometimes, however,
(25) they rise above this and become something more
consequential. Often, this transformation occurs at the
quadrennial event known as the Olympics, which brings
together thousands of the world's best athletes in a show
of global solidarity. The eyes of the entire world watch
(30) each event with interest. Great performances at the
Olympics gain a sense of grandeur and importance that
similar deeds on lesser stages simply lack.

Perhaps the most impressive performance in
Olympic history occurred during the 1936 Berlin games,
(35) which were hosted by Adolf Hitler's virulently racist
government. At these games, the American track star
Jesse Owens (who was black) won gold medals in four
events (the 100 meters, 200 meters, long jump, and 100
meter relay). Film of Owens' marvelous performance,
(40) captured by the Nazi filmmaker Leni Riefenstahl in
Olympia, drew the admiration of people around the
globe, and more importantly, served as a vivid rebuke to
the Nazis' racist beliefs. Not even Riefenstahl, the
notorious propagandist, could blunt the damage to the
(45) Nazi agenda caused by Owens' triumph.

17. The attitude of the author of Passage 1 toward Leni
Riefenstahl can best be described as

(A) flattering.
(B) absolving.
(C) ambivalent.
(D) unfeeling.
(E) scornful.

18. According to Passage 2 events at the Olympics "gain a sense
of grandeur" (line 31) from

(A) the games' global scale.
(B) their ability to entertain and distract the public.
(C) the use of innovative techniques to record the events.
(D) the artistic films that chronicle the performances.
(E) an undercurrent of political conflict.

19. In the context of both passages, the word "consequential"
(lines 12 and 26) most nearly means

(A) following after.
(B) conclusive.
(C) arrogant.
(D) momentous.
(E) detrimental.

20. Both passages imply that an underlying purpose of
Riefenstahl's film *Olympia* was to

(A) glorify the athletic achievements of Jesse Owens.
(B) record athletic events in a modern, stylized manner.
(C) censure Hitler's racist beliefs.
(D) advance the cause of Nazism.
(E) show global solidarity.

Homework Passage 2 (Long Paired)

These passages describe two areas in which the American education system may be lacking.

Passage 1:

For most of history, the concept of character formation—the duty of the older generation to form the character of the young—has been a basic principle
Line structuring moral education. For example, Aristotle wrote
(5) about the development of excellence, stating that to become excellent at any craft, including becoming virtuous, we have to exercise (practice) those behaviors. He stated: "We become just by the practice of just actions, self-controlled by exercising self-control, and
(10) courageous by performing acts of courage. Hence, it is no small matter whether one habit or another is inculcated in us from early childhood; on the contrary, it makes... all the difference."

Clearly, the business world expects a basic
(15) understanding and practice of ethical behavior from its workers as they enter the workforce. David Berliner and Bruce Biddle, in their book *The Manufactured Crisis*, report data collected from personnel directors of major industries. These employers were asked to list the five
(20) most important and the five least important skills needed by their employees. The surveys suggest that the habits and motivation of workers are more important to employers than the technical skills workers bring to their jobs. The authors conclude, "if schools are truly to serve
(25) the needs of business, it appears they should concentrate...more on the values that students will need when they enter the workplace.

Professionals in education need objective knowledge about how children form a basic sense of right and wrong
(30) and what schools can do to reinforce appropriate development. William Damon, author of *Greater Expectations*, provides that foundation. He describes research that children thrive on accomplishment, not on empty self-esteem message. They do not become
(35) overburdened by reasonable pressures related to worthwhile activities, including difficult homework. They are tough and resilient and are motivated to learn. But they need the guidance that can best be provided by able, caring, concerned adults.

(40) Daniel Goleman, author of the highly acclaimed book *Emotional Intelligence*, has documented the effects of positive and counter-productive child-rearing practices that result in either positive or anti-social behaviors. Many of these practices are related to teaching. Such at-
(45) risk behaviors as impulsiveness and belligerency, stubbornness and indecisiveness, overreaction to irritation, and inability to put off gratification are learned. These behaviors interfere with social and educational success, which Goleman calls "mental clarity." Other
(50) dispositions, equally learned, are much more conducive to optimism and full maturity. These include a strong cultural work ethic, temperance, the ability to cope with frustrations, optimism, and empathy.

Passage 2:

Line "What I want in a new worker, no high school can
(55) supply—a twenty-six-year-old with three previous employers." This statement reflects the views of many employers who are discouraged with the work ethic and skills of young adults. In focus groups of large and small employers in eight cities across the country, "employer
(60) laments incorporated the perennial concerns of older people for a generation that must inevitably replace them: young people lack discipline; they expect to be catered to; they don't want to do the dirty jobs; they don't respect authority... they are neither numerate nor literate; they
(65) can't make change; they don't understand the importance of providing customer service." In a Business and Industry Forum conducted by the South Carolina Council on Vocational Technical Education, one employer representative from the E. I. DuPont de Nemours & Co.
(70) stated that he has to interview 1,500 people for every 10 qualified employees he hires. A skills gap between employer needs and worker skills was also perceived by 69.4% of employers in a North Carolina study who were asked to evaluate the skills possessed by graduates of the
(75) state's educational institutions. Of the surveyed employers, 46.1% believe that high school graduates have inadequate reading skills. Other skills reported to be inadequate were writing (51.8%), math (48.2%), thinking (40%), and communication (51.2%).

(80) These criticisms of today's youth are especially significant as they reflect absence of the very skills employers want and expect schools to provide in their students. They also give substance to employers' attraction to applicants who have work experience, who
(85) have demonstrated through their employment history that they have good job performance skills, verbal and math skills, and interpersonal skills. In the currently tight labor market, these practices are resulting in a declining number of good jobs for first-time workers.

(90) One researcher notes the "chilling effect that the current absence of labor demand" had on the focus group discussions of large and small employers in the National Center on the Educational Quality of the Workforce study. "Among the participants from large firms,
(95) particularly in the older cities experiencing the greatest downsizing of large-scale manufacturing enterprises, there was a note of gallows humor—firms that had not hired since 2005; enterprises that had halved their work forces in the last five years; established companies on the
(100) verge of bankruptcy." Employers in the focus groups indicated their focus is on retraining their remaining employees or in recruiting skilled and otherwise qualified workers who were laid off because of other organizations' downsizing efforts.

(105) The increased competition for jobs, which has extended the school-to-work transition time of teenaged youth, necessitates that high school students be prepared to meet employer demands if they hope to become employed. The question is "Does vocational education
(110) prepare students with these skills valued by employers?"

21. The first paragraph of Passage 1 serves to

    (A) distract the reader from the main idea of the passage.
    (B) introduce an argument that is refuted later in the essay.
    (C) present the topic of the essay in a historical context.
    (D) describe a foundation that can be used to solve a key problem.
    (E) provide real-world data in support of the essay's main idea.

22. According to "William Damon" (line 31), children are

    (A) responsive to challenges but in need of emotional guidance.
    (B) unable to handle difficult homework without mental breakdowns.
    (C) unmotivated by the attitudes of the adults who teach and care for them.
    (D) in constant need of messages that raise their self-esteem.
    (E) fragile and unwilling to learn.

23. "Daniel Goleman" (line 40) would most likely argue that children with positive values and work habits

    (A) are born with those attributes.
    (B) will not lapse into stubbornness or indecisiveness even if poorly taught.
    (C) will still not be able to get work unless they can show technical skills.
    (D) learn those habits from adult role models.
    (E) are likely to have inadequate writing and math abilities.

24. The "employer laments" (lines 59-60) listed in the first paragraph of Passage 2 show that

    (A) no high school student is capable of thinking or communicating clearly in a work setting.
    (B) vocational education programs prepare students well for the realities of the workplace.
    (C) employers do not recognize the value of a good education.
    (D) most high school graduates possess technical skills but are immature and anti-social.
    (E) established workers perceive recent high school graduates to be lacking in a variety of areas.

25. Why is the perception that teenagers lack technical skills "especially significant" (lines 80-81)?

    (A) Research shows these perceptions to be largely untrue.
    (B) Most employers are willing to overlook a lack of skills if a worker is mature and optimistic.
    (C) Because the demand for workers is so high, many unskilled teenagers are being hired for critical positions.
    (D) It proves that educators should focus more on teaching values than on teaching skills.
    (E) Employers prefer established workers who already possess these skills to untested teenagers.

26. In context of the passage, the term "gallows humor" (line 97) refers to

    (A) stories that provide humor by making a bad situation seem even worse than it is.
    (B) a collection of jokes about hangings.
    (C) jokes that compare certain employers to executioners.
    (D) the implication that if these young people do not get jobs, they will likely become criminals.
    (E) laughing in an inappropriate situation

27. The authors of both passages would most likely agree that the American education system should

    (A) ignore technical skills in favor of moral and ethical education.
    (B) place more emphasis on fostering a strong work ethic in students.
    (C) require every student to take vocational courses.
    (D) increase its emphasis on standardized testing, especially in writing and math.
    (E) avoid assigning children a large amount of homework so as not to burden them.

28. Which of the following best sums up the two passages' concerns regarding the technical skills of students?

   (A) Both passages lament the precipitous decline in students' technical skills.
   (B) Whereas Passage 1 states that technical skills are less important than work habits, Passage 2 states that many students possess inadequate technical skills.
   (C) Both passages argue that other aspects of education are more important than technical skills.
   (D) While Passage 1 argues that technical skills do not matter, Passage 2 argues that they are the most important aspect of job performance.
   (E) Whereas Passage 1 notes that technical skills are in great demand from employers, Passage 2 claims that employers prefer other attributes.

29. What advice would the author of Passage 1 most likely give to the "high school students" (line 54) mentioned in Passage 2?

   (A) When applying for a job, focus on conveying positive habits and motivations.
   (B) Drop out of school, because you will not learn anything there that will help you find a job.
   (C) Take extra classes so as to acquire technical skills.
   (D) Try being less even-tempered and more impulsive; employers value such quick decision-making.
   (E) Lie about having previous job experience.

30. Which statement regarding the tone of the two passages is most accurate?

   (A) Neither passage provides much evidence to support its argument.
   (B) Though both passages argue in favor of revolutionizing the education system, Passage 2 does so more strongly.
   (C) Though both passages provide evidence to identify a problem, only Passage 1 provides a solution.
   (D) Both passages are predominantly light-hearted in tone.
   (E) While Passage 1 is serious and straightforward, Passage 2 is ironic and sarcastic.

Homework Passage 4 (Long)

The following passage describes the unusual behavior of a particular species of ant.

The Ecitons, or foraging ants, are very numerous throughout Central America. While the leaf-cutting ants are entirely vegetable feeders, the foraging ants are
Line hunters, and live solely on insects or other prey; and it is
(5) a curious analogy that, like the hunting races of mankind, they have to change their hunting-grounds when one is exhausted, and move on to another. In Nicaragua they are generally called "Army Ants." One of the smaller species (Eciton predator) used occasionally to visit our house,
(10) swarm over the floors and walls, searching every cranny, and driving out the cockroaches and spiders, many of which were caught, pulled or bitten to pieces, and carried off. The individuals of this species are of various sizes; the smallest measuring an eighth of an inch, and the
(15) largest a quarter of an inch.

I saw many large armies of this, or a closely allied species, in the forest. My attention was generally first called to them by the twittering of some small birds, belonging to several different species, that follow the
(20) ants in the woods. On approaching to ascertain the cause of this disturbance, a dense body of the ants, three or four yards wide, and so numerous as to blacken the ground, would be seen moving rapidly in one direction, examining every cranny, and underneath every fallen
(25) leaf. On the flanks, and in advance of the main body, smaller columns would be pushed out. These smaller columns would generally first flush out the cockroaches, grasshoppers, and spiders.

The pursued insects would rapidly run off, but many,
(30) in their confusion and terror, would bound right into the midst of the main body of ants. A grasshopper, finding itself in the midst of its enemies, would give vigorous leaps, with perhaps two or three of the ants clinging to its legs. Then it would stop a moment to rest, and that
(35) moment would be fatal, for the tiny foes would swarm over the prey, and after a few more ineffectual struggles it would succumb to its fate, and soon be bitten to pieces and carried off to the rear. The greatest catch of the ants was, however, when they got amongst some fallen
(40) brushwood. The cockroaches, spiders, and other insects, instead of running right away, would ascend the fallen branches and remain there, whilst the host of ants were occupying all the ground below. By and by, up would come some of the ants, following every branch, and
(45) driving before them their prey to the ends of the small twigs, when nothing remained for them but to leap, and they would alight in the very throng of their foes, with the result of being certainly caught and pulled to pieces. Many of the spiders would escape by hanging suspended
(50) by a thread of silk from the branches, safe from the foes that swarmed both above and below.

I noticed that spiders were generally most intelligent in escaping, and did not, like the cockroaches and other insects, take shelter in the first hiding-place they found,
(55) only to be driven out again, or perhaps caught by the advancing army of ants. I have often seen large spiders making off many yards in advance, and apparently determined to put a good distance between themselves and their foe. I once saw one of the false spiders, or
(60) harvest-men (Phalangidae), standing in the midst of an army of ants, and with the greatest circumspection and coolness lifting, one after the other, its long legs, which supported its body above their reach. Sometimes as many as five out of its eight legs would be lifted at once, and
(65) whenever an ant approached one of those on which it stood, there was always a clear space within reach to put down another, so as to be able to hold up the threatened one out of danger.

31. The author most likely mentions "leaf-cutting ants" (line 2) in order to

 (A) show a key similarity between two species of ant.
 (B) debunk a common myth about Ecitons.
 (C) introduce the main topic of the essay.
 (D) contrast the behavior of these ants with that of Ecitons.
 (E) offer an example that supports the main argument of the passage.

32. The "curious analogy" (line 5) implies that

 (A) foraging ants use strategies and tools reminiscent of human hunters.
 (B) Ecitons are easily tired and must rest often.
 (C) foraging ants must move from place to place to avoid predators.
 (D) the Ecitons are so voracious that they eat all of the available food in a given area.
 (E) foraging ants are poor hunters, and must also eat plants in order to survive.

33. Which of the following best describes the hunting strategy of the Ecitons?

 (A) Solitary ants track and kill prey with no help from other individuals.
 (B) Individual ants create crude traps to capture prey.
 (C) Small groups surround individual insects one at a time.
 (D) A few quick ants chase down and immobilize prey using poison.
 (E) Many individuals cover every available surface so that no prey can hide.

Unauthorized copying or reuse of any part of this page is illegal.

Version 1.3

34. As it is used in line 30, "bound" most nearly means

   (A) compel.
   (B) move quickly.
   (C) tangle.
   (D) make certain.
   (E) border.

35. Based on the descriptions given in the third paragraph (lines 29-51), which of the following methods of escape would most likely be effective for an insect encountering a swarm of Ecitons?

   (A) to climb up onto a branch
   (B) to immediately try to outrun the ant swarm
   (C) to charge right toward the ants in the hopes of confusing them
   (D) to hop intermittently
   (E) to hide in the first available cranny on the ground

36. What key advantage do the "spiders" (line 49) have over cockroaches and other insects?

   (A) their ability to create a strand of silk
   (B) their ability to leap very high
   (C) their ability to climb branches
   (D) their ability to hide under leaves
   (E) their large size, which helps to intimidate the Ecitons

37. The author most likely includes several stories about spiders escaping from Ecitons in order to

   (A) prove that spiders are more fascinating than ants.
   (B) brag about his observational skills.
   (C) show the limitations of the ants' hunting abilities.
   (D) offer a humorous digression from the essay's main point.
   (E) explain why Ecitons are now endangered.

38. When describing the various ways in which spiders escaped from the Ecitons, the author's tone is most nearly

   (A) admiring.
   (B) circumspect.
   (C) mocking.
   (D) unimpressed.
   (E) obstinate.

39. The primary purpose of the passage is to

   (A) argue that spiders are smarter than cockroaches.
   (B) use personal recollections to illustrate a fascinating natural phenomenon.
   (C) contrast the behaviors of two different varieties of ant.
   (D) offer an extensive analysis of the biology of the foraging ant.
   (E) relate a harrowing anecdote about a house overrun with ants.

SC Topic: Making Predictions (Lesson B11a)	RC Topic: Paired Passages (Lesson B9b)

Homework Set 1

1. Though it is not an official rule of poker, it is ------ understood by most players that one should not needlessly ------ a decision or otherwise delay the game.

    (A) tacitly . . protract
    (B) implicitly . . expedite
    (C) unequivocally . . circumvent
    (D) marginally . . prolong
    (E) indubitably . . curtail

2. After Abdul had paid his rent, car payment, and utility bills, he only had enough money left over to afford ------ meals of beans and rice.

    (A) meager
    (B) abundant
    (C) elaborate
    (D) expansive
    (E) astute

3. Rather than be ------ or despondent after finding out she did not get the job, Rosita remained optimistic, and ------ continued to apply for available positions.

    (A) sullen . . persistently
    (B) dogmatic . . malevolently
    (C) deferent . . tentatively
    (D) dejected . . implausibly
    (E) congenial . . obstinately

4. The water in the lake slowly ------ over the course of the year-long drought until the lake was nothing more than a few puddles.

    (A) dissented
    (B) dwindled
    (C) abounded
    (D) flourished
    (E) delegated

5. As he was installing the fence around his yard, Hak-ju was careful not to ------ his neighbors' property or otherwise disturb the harmony of the community.

    (A) comply with
    (B) proffer
    (C) recant
    (D) infringe on
    (E) elude

6. Fiercely independent and uncompromising, Henrietta ------ those who try to tell her what to do.

    (A) extols
    (B) extricates
    (C) revels in
    (D) lauds
    (E) reviles

7. Cesar was extremely relieved when the woman returned his lost cat, and offered her ------ thanks in addition to the small monetary reward.

    (A) timid
    (B) sparse
    (C) profuse
    (D) terse
    (E) reclusive

8. Although many animals in the forest were on the ------ of extinction, the deer population was ------ due to a lack of predators and a plentiful food supply.

    (A) verge . . desolate
    (B) mandate . . bountiful
    (C) affluence . . voluminous
    (D) ascent . . scanty
    (E) precipice . . abounding

Unauthorized copying or reuse of any part of this page is illegal.

Version 1.3

Homework Set 2

9. The animal-rights activist was concerned about the poor living conditions of livestock and ------ more ------ treatment of cows, pigs, and chickens.

   (A) touted . . callous
   (B) incited . . vulgar
   (C) advocated for . . humane
   (D) endorsed . . voracious
   (E) assailed . . benevolent

10. The judge was normally lenient to first-time offenders, but in this case the crime was so ------ that he handed down a very harsh sentence.

    (A) flagrant
    (B) placid
    (C) benign
    (D) inconspicuous
    (E) dormant

11. As a reporter, Jennifer respected the talents of the famous actor, but did not ------ him; she could criticize him when necessary.

    (A) exalt
    (B) denounce
    (C) assail
    (D) implicate
    (E) posit

12. Vipul won his classmates over with his ------ nature, though they soon discovered that he was also ------, with little substance underneath his friendly exterior.

    (A) amiable . . vacuous
    (B) brash . . audacious
    (C) genial . . judicious
    (D) astute . . proficient
    (E) aloof . . equivocal

13. The poet hopes to ------ the language in his latest work before publishing it, for it seems far too ------ in its current, unornamented form.

    (A) embellish . . drab
    (B) elaborate on . . vigorous
    (C) elucidate . . ostentatious
    (D) impair . . tedious
    (E) abridge . . desolate

14. Georgia did not want to go to the art gallery alone, so she ------ her friends until one agreed to go with her.

    (A) despised
    (B) prodded
    (C) evaded
    (D) repulsed
    (E) bolstered

15. The class' discussion today was even more ------ than usual; the supposed topic was modernist literature, but much of the discussion was about ancient mythology.

    (A) infallible
    (B) evocative
    (C) commendable
    (D) digressive
    (E) feasible

16. When caught up in ------ mood, Manuel is so focused on his own thoughts as to be almost oblivious to the outside world.

    (A) a miserly
    (B) a transitory
    (C) a gregarious
    (D) an omnipresent
    (E) an introspective

Homework Passage 1 (Short Paired)

Passage 1:

The city of Jerusalem has been continuously inhabited for perhaps 5,000 years, making it one of the oldest inhabited cities in the world. Today, despite its
Line ancientness, the city is still growing, and now covers an
(5) area of nearly 50 square miles. By way of comparison, the "Old City" of Jerusalem, which for thousands of years formed the boundary of the city, measures only 0.35 square miles in area. The population of the city has been growing rapidly as well; in 1931, only about 90,000
(10) people lived there, but today more than 750,000 call Jerusalem home.

These people are quite varied, since many cultures have a historical basis in or near Jerusalem, and three major religions (Judaism, Islam, and Christianity)
(15) consider the city a holy place. About two-thirds of Jerusalem's residents are Jewish; most of the rest are Muslim, with about 2% being Christians. This religious diversity has led to centuries of conflict (much of it violent), but this conflict has not restrained the continued
(20) growth of this venerated city.

Passage 2:

Conflict between religions is perhaps inevitable, given the deeply held differences of opinion about fundamental matters that occur between different faiths.
Line This conflict is exacerbated when religions revere the
(25) same people or places. It is a difficult task to convince a religion to share control of a site with those of another faith. At some point in any such negotiation, at least one party is apt to take offense. Frequently, negotiation is dispensed with entirely in favor of armed conflict.
(30) It is no surprise then that the city of Jerusalem, which is claimed by three of the world's major religions, has been subject to much strife over its five-thousand-year history. Rarely has the city experienced a century— or even a decade—without some sort of violent, religion-
(35) fueled outburst. Sites such as the Temple Mount and the Cave of the Patriarchs have been the source of particularly heated dispute. While the city is predominantly governed by a Jewish authority today, a sizable Muslim minority resides there as well. Jerusalem's future depends on these opposing groups
(40) reaching an agreement that allows each to have access to its most holy sites.

17. Based on information in Passage 1, Jerusalem can be fairly described as all of the following EXCEPT

(A) expanding.
(B) diverse.
(C) sacred.
(D) tranquil.
(E) historic.

18. One can infer from Passage 2 that "the Temple Mount and the Cave of the Patriarchs" (lines 35-36) are

(A) located in the Muslim Quarter of the Old City.
(B) shrines built since 1931.
(C) Christian holy sites that were destroyed by other religions.
(D) peacefully shared by Jewish and Muslim authorities.
(E) locations that hold significance for more than one religion.

19. Both passages indicate that Jerusalem

(A) is the capital of Israel.
(B) has had a long and turbulent history.
(C) is less important to Christians than it is to Jews or Muslims.
(D) is the holiest city in Islam.
(E) was once a much smaller and less important city.

20. How would the author of Passage 1 most likely respond to Passage 2's concern that "Jerusalem's future depends on" (line 39) achieving religious harmony?

(A) Religious conflict has not prevented the city from flourishing in the past.
(B) Without significant concessions from the three main religious groups, the city is surely doomed.
(C) The Islamic minority is willing to work for peace, but the Jewish majority is too stubborn to negotiate.
(D) The people of Jerusalem have increasingly shown an ability to set aside differences in the name of peace.
(E) Religious conflict is an unsolvable problem, so the city should be divided along religious lines.

Homework Passage 2 (Long Paired)

South Africa has been hit particularly hard by the AIDS epidemic. These passages describe some of the effects that AIDS has had on South African culture.

Passage 1:

The strangest thing about my adopted home community in South Africa is the number of establishments selling tombstones in town. It seems the
Line shop names are meant to be optimistic: Paradise
(5) Tombstones; Eternal Flame Tombstones. The sign "Town Tombstones" looms large over the main drag, Danie Joubert Street. The billboard is hand-painted, an enormous gray elephant's head stretching the length of the sign, with red, green, and yellow lettering: African-
(10) style death. The town boasts a three-story building calling itself a mall, and just in the center, on the second floor, is Perpetuity Tombstones. Its window displays are like any other store's, but instead of half-price sneakers or polyester pants, Perpetuity Tombstones displays—
(15) what else?—demo tombstones. Eerily enough, the window displays read: "Buy Now! Pay Later!"

I find myself living in a country with the largest HIV/AIDS population in the world. In the rural villages, where the disease is spreading like wildfire, people know
(20) of AIDS, but they don't speak of it. They don't want to know their status because a positive diagnosis may bring rejection and ostracism. Family members in the advanced stages of the disease may be relegated to the fringes of the community, if they are not chased from the village.
(25) Those who are allowed to stay are often neglected at home because of the stigma or simply because the enormous burden of caring for an AIDS patient cripples the family's already meager resources. Most people won't get proper, if any, medical treatment. Just the word—
(30) AIDS—causes family and community members feelings of shame. A loved one's death is euphemistically called "natural," and village people attend to the burial ceremonies as though nothing were unusual about a 30-year-old man or woman dying of "natural causes." And
(35) that's the crux of the crisis: There's nothing unusual about it anymore.

The rural poor of South Africa's villages attend more funerals in a single weekend than I've attended in my entire 27 years. I know. I live here. And on weekends,
(40) I've tied a scarf around my hair to stand in the cemetery with my African friends, the only white face among hundreds. The life departed may be recognized and celebrated. But to me, something feels deeply wrong about celebrating a life so short.
(45) One in every four people I meet is likely to die of AIDS before the decade is out. Those who don't die will be left behind: children without parents, mothers burying adult children—lives that might have been long and full, but were unrealized.
(50) This is not the grief I experienced when my grandfather died. His death caused an aching absence, but one that aligned with what I know to be right and normal in life. I grieved and I accepted it. But I simply do not accept the impending death of 5.3 million HIV-
(55) positive South Africans. These people may not have names to us. But they have names, and stories, and families, and they might—in another world—have had a granddaughter to write about their lives. But they are dying too young for that, and they are leaving their own
(60) babies behind, not grandchildren. There is nothing normal or right about it.

Passage 2:

Queen Nthuli begins the ritual of calling her ancestors by burning dried herbs in an earthenware pot
Line beside her. She breathes in the smoke from the herbs to
(65) take the spirits of the ancestors into her body, where she can communicate with them. Next she throws her shells. They scatter on the reed mat in front of her in a unique pattern—one that is different every time she throws them. She asks the ancestors to reveal the messages
(70) found in that arrangement of shells so that she may answer the questions of her client. "What is causing the pain in my leg?" "Is my daughter's baby going to be boy or a girl?" "Has someone cast a spell on me that caused my crops to die?" The ancestors will have the answers to
(75) all of these inquiries—if only they decide to share their knowledge with Queen and her client.

Based on what the ancestors have identified as the source of the client's problem, Queen will prescribe the most effective solution. For physical ailments she will
(80) use her extensive knowledge of herbs, many of which are stored in the jars that line the walls inside her home, to create a *muti*, or medicine, to be taken as a cure. Or she may instruct the client to participate in a ritual to cleanse the body of impurities believed to be causing the pain. If
(85) the source of the trouble is spiritual—supernatural or otherwise—Queen may order the sacrifice of a chicken, goat—or even a cow—to appease angry spirits or placate ancestors to whom thanks are due.

Such things are all in a day's work for a traditional
(90) healer in South Africa. Also known as *sangomas* or traditional medical practitioners, people such as Queen Nthuli act as doctor, herbalist, counselor, and spiritual advisor to thousands of people all over the country. Her practices might seem a bit strange to Americans who are
(95) used to going to a doctor right down the road—at least that was the reaction of my friends and family when I told them my stories about traditional healers. In South Africa, however, many people don't have any other choice; for them, traditional healers provide the only
(100) medical care that is accessible and affordable.

The majority of South Africans first go to a traditional healer for help with their medical problems—including HIV/AIDS. But most traditional healers know much more about herbal medicines than they know about
(105) new *muti* like anti-retroviral drugs (ARVs). Because of their lack of access to health information, traditional healers sometimes prescribe remedies for patients with

Version 1.3

Unauthorized copying or reuse of any part of this page is illegal.

AIDS that cause them more harm than good. For example, a few herbs that typically ease the symptoms of
(50) common illnesses, when taken with ARVs, cause the ARVs not to work and patients to develop resistance—in the same way as if they had missed a dose.

The AIDS Foundation of South Africa has been working with traditional healers for more than 10 years—
(55) trying to help them increase their knowledge of HIV/AIDS. Queen Nthuli has learned a lot from the AIDS Foundation and is now a master trainer, which means she passes on her knowledge of HIV/AIDS and ARVs to other traditional healers. But our work is far
(60) from over. There are still other traditional healers all over South Africa who need to know about HIV/AIDS and the new *muti* out there that fights the disease.

21. What is the purpose of the first paragraph of Passage 1 (lines 1-16)?

(A) to outline an argument that will be refuted later in the passage.
(B) to explain the source of a troublesome trend.
(C) to arouse the reader's curiosity by highlighting an unusual aspect of a foreign culture.
(D) to introduce the main figure of the article and her occupation.
(E) to contrast American and South African advertising.

22. The author of Passage 1 implies that South Africans refer to AIDS-related deaths as "natural" (line 32) because

(A) most South Africans are unaware that such a disease exists.
(B) admitting that a family member had the disease causes a great deal of shame.
(C) they do not believe that AIDS is a preventable disease.
(D) they are distinguishing between death from disease and death from violence or accidents.
(E) it is not caused be evil spirits, unlike many other diseases.

23. The author of Passage 1 mentions the death of her grandfather in order to

(A) describe how AIDS-related deaths are handled in America.
(B) stimulate the sympathies of the reader.
(C) draw a sharp contrast between two causes of death.
(D) prove that she has suffered through as much grief as most South Africans.
(E) shift the focus of her essay to a completely new topic.

24. Based on the entirety of Passage 1, what is the most likely reason that there are so many "establishments selling tombstones" (line 3) in South Africa?

(A) The AIDS epidemic has caused a tremendous rise in the death rate.
(B) Family members replace their ancestor's tombstones periodically as a sign of respect.
(C) South Africans enjoy preparing for their own deaths while still young and healthy.
(D) Americans and other foreigners prize South African tombstones for their quality and affordability.
(E) Tombstones are seen as a status symbol in South African culture.

25. The author of Passage 2 describes the "ritual" (line 62) of calling ancestors for advice in order to

(A) lament that Queen Nthuli does not take her job more seriously.
(B) poke fun at South Africans for engaging in such unscientific acts.
(C) familiarize the reader with the typical practices of a traditional South African healer.
(D) analyze all the flaws of such an approach to medicine.
(E) convince Americans to consult with their ancestors in a similar fashion.

26. As it is used in line 65, the word "spirits" most nearly means

(A) alcoholic beverages.
(B) attitudes.
(C) feelings of loyalty and belonging.
(D) determination.
(E) souls.

27. According to Passage 2, what is the greatest danger in treating an HIV/AIDS patient with traditional medicine?

   (A) The patient's ancestors may become angered and seek vengeance.
   (B) Traditional healers are incompetent and unable to cure any illness.
   (C) Other villagers will think the patient is strange for not using more modern medicines.
   (D) Traditional medicine is often extremely expensive.
   (E) Some traditional herbal cures can interfere with modern AIDS drugs.

28. Throughout Passage 2, the author's tone when describing Queen Nthuli is one of

   (A) contempt.
   (B) grief.
   (C) hilarity.
   (D) respect.
   (E) skepticism.

29. The author of Passage 2 would most likely respond to the statement in Passage 1 that "most people won't get proper… medical treatment" (lines 28-29) by saying that

   (A) most citizens of South Africa have no interest in receiving modern medical care.
   (B) those people likely have no access to any medical care except for traditional healers.
   (C) herbal remedies are more effective than ARVs and other Western treatments.
   (D) only a few unfortunate people do not receive excellent care.
   (E) such a characterization is insulting to Queen Nthuli and others like her.

30. Both passages describe South African culture as being

   (A) unusual from an American perspective.
   (B) obsessed with folk remedies and mysticism.
   (C) locked in a constant struggle for racial equality.
   (D) fixated on death and dying.
   (E) extremely excited about soccer, rugby, and other sports.

31. In comparison to Passage 1, Passage 2 is focused more on

   (A) the social ramifications of an HIV diagnosis.
   (B) the plight of the families of HIV victims.
   (C) statistics outlining the enormity of the HIV/AIDS epidemic.
   (D) the methods used to fight HIV/AIDS.
   (E) the omnipresence of death in South African society.

32. Which of the following best expresses the difference in the authors' attitudes toward the current state of the fight against HIV/AIDS in South Africa?

   (A) Both authors are horrified that no progress has been made in the last 10 years.
   (B) Both authors are pleased with the cultural attitude of South Africans toward the disease.
   (C) Both authors are resigned to the fact that the disease is unstoppable.
   (D) While the author of Passage 1 largely ignores the disease's impact, the author of Passage 2 exaggerates its effects.
   (E) While the author of Passage 1 is appalled, the author of Passage 2 is cautiously encouraged.

Homework Passage 4 (Long)

The following is an excerpt from Memoir of Old Elizabeth, *published in 1863, which tells the true story of Elizabeth, a 97-year-old woman who was born into slavery. This excerpt describes her early childhood.*

I was born in Maryland in the year 1766. My parents were slaves. Both my father and mother were religious people, and belonged to the Methodist Society. It was my
Line father's practice to read in the Bible aloud to his children
(5) every Sabbath morning. At these seasons, when I was but five years old, I often felt the overshadowing of the Lord's Spirit, without at all understanding what it meant; and these incomes and influences continued to attend me until I was eleven years old, particularly when I was
(10) alone, by which I was preserved from doing anything that I thought was wrong.

In the eleventh year of my age, my master sent me to another farm, several miles from my parents, brothers, and sisters, which was a great trouble to me. At last I
(15) grew so lonely and sad I thought I should die, if I did not see my mother. I asked the overseer if I might go, but being positively denied, I concluded to go without his knowledge. When I reached home my mother was away. I set off and walked twenty miles before I found her. I
(20) stayed with her for several days, and we returned together. Next day I was sent back to my new place, which renewed my sorrow. At parting, my mother told me that I had "nobody in the wide world to look to but God." These words fell upon my heart with ponderous
(25) weight, and seemed to add to my grief. I went back repeating as I went, "none but God in the wide world." On reaching the farm, I found the overseer was displeased at me for going without his liberty. He tied me with a rope, and gave me some stripes of which I carried
(30) the marks for weeks.

After this time, finding as my mother said, I had none in the world to look to but God, I betook myself to prayer, and in every lonely place I found an altar. I mourned sore like a dove and chattered forth my sorrow,
(35) moaning in the corners of the field, and under the fences.

33. When the narrator was a very young child, religion

(A) had little influence on her attitude.
(B) was forbidden by her master.
(C) helped prevent her from misbehaving.
(D) was easy for her to understand.
(E) caused her to become embittered toward her family.

34. The passage implies that the "stripes" given to the narrator are

(A) scars from a whip or lash.
(B) poor grades on her report card.
(C) warnings from the overseer.
(D) new articles of clothing to replace the ones she had lost.
(E) a reward for returning home so promptly.

35. As it is used in line 28, "liberty" most nearly means

(A) independence.
(B) stubbornness.
(C) permission.
(D) impoliteness.
(E) freedom of speech and religion.

36. After returning to her new master's farm, what happened to the narrator's religious practices?

(A) She worshipped less frequently.
(B) She began to pray whenever and wherever she could.
(C) She worshipped only in her master's church.
(D) She vowed to pray only when she was reunited with her family.
(E) She chose a different religion.

37. The childhood of "Old Elizabeth" can best be described as

(A) sorrowful.
(B) atheistic.
(C) carefree.
(D) jubilant.
(E) wealthy.

38. Throughout the passage, the narrator's tone can best be described as

(A) pious.
(B) exuberant.
(C) amiable.
(D) ironic.
(E) wicked.

C2 education
be smarter.

Unauthorized copying or reuse of any part of this page is illegal.

Version 1.3

B12HW: Homework and Extra Practice

SC TOPIC: Predicting Answers (Lesson B11a) | **RC TOPIC:** Tone Questions (Lesson B12b)

Homework Set 1

1. The controversial athlete argued that most of the unflattering stories told about him were ------ and were likely concocted by jealous rivals hoping to ------ his reputation.

   (A) infallible . . exalt
   (B) spurious . . sully
   (C) veracious . . tarnish
   (D) dubious . . laud
   (E) bogus . . ameliorate

2. The social worker was shocked by the ------ conditions that the children were living in, with spoiled food and other filth everywhere.

   (A) esoteric
   (B) reputable
   (C) pristine
   (D) squalid
   (E) ascetic

3. As an ------ chess player, Jamie knows that sometimes it is wise to ------ a piece if the future advantage in position outweighs the immediate loss of the piece.

   (A) absurd . . cede
   (B) adverse . . cherish
   (C) indifferent . . denounce
   (D) adept . . relinquish
   (E) inexplicable . . retain

4. Contrary to the frequent firefights that police engage in on television, shooting at a suspect is always a ------ event in an officer's career, and many never fire their weapons at all.

   (A) recurrent
   (B) pliable
   (C) singular
   (D) prevalent
   (E) redundant

5. The politician refuted the assertion that his plan was ------ and countered by ------ that he could prove the effectiveness of every single aspect of the plan.

   (A) preposterous . . shunning
   (B) infeasible . . contending
   (C) unrelenting . . circumventing
   (D) judicious . . retracting
   (E) viable . . espousing

6. In a last-minute attempt to ------ a flood, the townsfolk frantically piled sandbags atop the banks of the river.

   (A) impose
   (B) avert
   (C) attain
   (D) endeavor
   (E) acclaim

7. The student's efforts in English class were not terrible, but they were more ------ than exceptional.

   (A) profuse
   (B) magnanimous
   (C) pedestrian
   (D) prominent
   (E) malevolent

8. Lisa was so ------ that her friends did not believe that she could ever become excited or angry.

   (A) itinerant
   (B) flagrant
   (C) zealous
   (D) temperate
   (E) acerbic

Homework Set 2

9. Xavier was ------ enough that he believed his friends when they told him they had seen a pink rhinoceros behind his house, and was disappointed that they had not.

   (A) complacent
   (B) cerebral
   (C) discreet
   (D) dogmatic
   (E) credulous

10. Olivia only became aware of her ------ talent for painting when a friend encouraged her to sign up for her first art class.

    (A) overt
    (B) flaunted
    (C) voluminous
    (D) latent
    (E) obstinate

11. When both of his daughters claimed the last cookie, Greg came up with an ------ solution: each daughter would get half the cookie.

    (A) equitable
    (B) austere
    (C) unjust
    (D) implicit
    (E) arbitrary

12. In order to become a champion gymnast one must be not only ------ enough to attempt the flips and twists, but also ------ to train over 30 hours per week.

    (A) bulky . . heedless
    (B) agile . . lethargic
    (C) frail . . compulsory
    (D) provincial . . diligent
    (E) nimble . . industrious

13. The doctor opted to ------ the patient's treatment because he feared that starting too soon would only ------ the patient's symptoms.

    (A) expedite . . aggravate
    (B) endorse . . alleviate
    (C) extricate . . mitigate
    (D) entrench . . abide
    (E) defer . . exacerbate

14. Sonja may have been despondent today, but that was only an ------, for she is usually quite cheerful.

    (A) allegiance
    (B) antecedent
    (C) acquiescence
    (D) audacity
    (E) aberration

15. Justine was fortunate to have such ------ grandchildren, who came by every Saturday to perform household chores that she found difficult in her old age.

    (A) imprudent
    (B) conscientious
    (C) wary
    (D) remiss
    (E) apathetic

16. Wherever he went, Sung-hwan spread ------ and laughter, for his ------ personality was quite infectious.

    (A) severity . . resilient
    (B) sternness . . congenial
    (C) plausibility . . sullen
    (D) levity . . jovial
    (E) hilarity . . dejected

Unauthorized copying or reuse of any part of this page is illegal.

Version 1.3

Homework Passage 1 (Short)

The main currents of nineteenth-century science have produced more and higher specialization than ever before. Descartes was philosopher, scientist, and
Line mathematician; some of the great men of the eighteenth
(5) century were hardly less so. Even through a large part of the nineteenth century many of the greater men ranged widely over the field of science and mathematics. Today the force of circumstances has unfortunately changed all that. The chemist is likely to look upon the physicist, or
(10) even the physical chemist, with suspicion on account of his mathematical interests. On the other hand, the mathematician, unlike Newton, Euler, and Gauss, is commonly no longer a physicist at all. There are today very few people who possess even a superficial
(15) acquaintance with all the principal departments of science, and between the work of the astronomer, on the one hand, and that of the anatomist, on the other, there is perhaps no closer relationship than the fact that both employ optical instruments in their researches.

17. The author of the passage most likely has what attitude toward the changes brought about by the "main currents of nineteenth-century science" (line 1)?

(A) grateful celebration.
(B) moderate distaste
(C) barely restrained fury
(D) warm encouragement
(E) utter anguish

18. One can infer that "Newton, Euler, and Gauss" (line 12) were

(A) the first mathematicians who were not also physicists.
(B) 19th-century scientists.
(C) rivals of Descartes.
(D) chemists who disdained physicists.
(E) mathematicians who studied other fields as well.

Homework Passage 2 (Short)

While there is no doubt that a new era (for better and for worse) began when Christopher Columbus first "discovered" the Americas in the late 15th century, he
Line was certainly not the first Western explorer to find these
(5) lands. Archaeologists have confirmed, based on both Norse histories and artifacts uncovered in Canada, that the Norse (or Vikings) had a short-lived colony in the Americas. The site of this colony, now known as L'anse aux Meadows, in Newfoundland, features indisputable
(10) evidence of Norse settlement. The evidence includes houses, tools, and other objects. The colony apparently died out or fled to Greenland after only a few years.
Some archaeologists claim to have found evidence of other cultures interacting with Native Americans
(15) before Columbus. For instance, the remains of a chicken found in Chile have been radiocarbon dated to around 100 years before Columbus' arrival. This is surprising because chickens are generally considered to have been a European introduction to the Americas. Also, the sweet
(20) potato (an American crop) was widespread in Polynesia by the time Europeans first reached the area, suggesting pre-Columbian contact.

19. The passage implies that the "Norse settlement" (line 10) in the Americas is less famous than those begun by Christopher Columbus mainly because

(A) Columbus found gold and other treasures, but the Norse did not.
(B) the Norse settlement did not last long enough to influence history.
(C) many scientists and historians doubt the authenticity of the Norse artifacts from Newfoundland.
(D) the Norse did not record the extent of their voyages.
(E) the Norse intermarried with the Native Americans rather than conquer them.

20. The author's tone when describing the "evidence of other cultures" (lines 13-14) in the second paragraph can best be described as

(A) mostly uninterested.
(B) purely mocking.
(C) cautious but curious.
(D) rigidly displeased.
(E) credulously accepting.

Homework Passage 3 (Long)

This passage describes the circumstances and accomplishments of the 1848 Seneca Falls Convention for Women's Rights, led by Elizabeth Cady Stanton.

America in the 1840s was in the throes of cultural and economic change. In the years since the Revolution and the Constitutional Convention, the nation's
Line geographic boundaries and population had more than
(5) doubled, the population had shifted significantly westward, and many Americans' daily lives had drifted away from Jefferson's vision of a nation composed of independent farmers. Instead, farmers, artisans, and manufacturers existed in a world built around cash crops,
(10) manufactured goods, banks, and distant markets. Not all Americans welcomed these changes, which often left them feeling isolated and cut off from traditional sources of community and comfort.

In an effort to regain a sense of community and
(15) control over their nation's future, Americans, especially women, formed and joined reform societies. These groups attacked what they perceived as the various wrongs in their society, including the lack of free public school education for both boys and girls, the inhumane
(20) treatment of mentally ill patients and criminals, the evil of slavery, the widespread use of alcohol, and the "rights and wrongs" of American women's legal position. The Seneca Falls Convention is a part of this larger period of social reform movements, a time when concern about the
(25) rights of various groups percolated to the surface.

What brought three hundred men and women to this small upstate New York town in July 1848? Women of the Revolutionary era such as Abigail Adams and Judith Sargent Murray raised questions about what the
(30) Declaration of Independence would mean to them, but there had never been a large-scale public meeting to discuss this topic until Seneca Falls. Many women participated in reform organizations whose goals were to improve the lives of others and to fight for the rights of
(35) those who could not speak for themselves, such as schoolchildren and the mentally ill, so the air was ripe for a close examination of women's rights as well. A consciousness-raising experience, however, was necessary to turn these women's thoughts to their own
(40) condition.

The triggering incident was a direct result of participation in anti-slavery organizations by Elizabeth Cady Stanton and Lucretia Mott. Anti-slavery societies proliferated in the Northeast region of the United States
(45) and in some parts of what today we call the Midwest. Many of these organizations had female members. In 1840 the World Anti-Slavery Convention met in London; some of the American groups elected women as their representatives to this meeting. Once in London, after a
(50) lengthy debate, the female representatives were denied their rightful seats and consigned to the balcony. It was at this meeting, while sitting in the balcony and walking through the streets of London, that Elizabeth Cady Stanton and Lucretia Mott met. Eight years later, Stanton

(55) and Mott called a convention to discuss women's rights.

On July 14, 1848, the *Seneca County Courier* announced that on the following Wednesday and Thursday a "convention to discuss the social, civil, and religious condition and rights of women" would be held.
(60) The Convention issued a document titled the Declaration of Sentiments, a statement written by Stanton and modeled on the Declaration of Independence.

In adapting the Declaration of Independence, Stanton replaced "King George" with "all men" as the
(65) agent of women's oppressed condition and compiled a suitable list of grievances, just as the colonists did in the Declaration of Independence. These grievances reflected the severe limitations on women's legal rights in America at this time: women could not vote; they could not
(70) participate in the creation of laws that they had to obey; their property was taxed; and a married woman's property and wages legally belonged to her husband. Further, in the relatively unusual case of a divorce, custody of children was virtually automatically awarded
(75) to the father; access to the professions and higher education generally was closed to women; and most churches barred women from participating publicly in the ministry or other positions of authority.

Stanton's Declaration of Sentiments proclaimed that
(80) "all men and women were created equal" and that the undersigned would employ all methods at their disposal to right these wrongs. In the 1840s and even today, the language of Thomas Jefferson resonates through American life. Americans from every background
(85) believe that the ideals of the Revolution are alive and well, and applicable to life in the present, just as the women of the 1848 Seneca Falls Convention felt those ideals spoke to them.

21. Throughout the passage, the author's attitude toward Cady Stanton and other activists can best be described as

   (A) angry.
   (B) respectful.
   (C) amused.
   (D) worshipful.
   (E) sarcastic.

22. Which of the following is NOT identified as a change that occurred between the Revolution and the 1840s?

   (A) The new country expanded to twice its original size.
   (B) America's population increased dramatically.
   (C) Many people's lives became less community-oriented.
   (D) The nation became less dependent on farming.
   (E) Women gained many new legal and social freedoms.

Unauthorized copying or reuse of any part of this page is illegal.

Version 1.3

23. The first paragraph (lines 1-13) primarily serves to

   (A) describe the early life of an important historical figure.
   (B) set the scene for the events discussed in the rest of the passage.
   (C) bring up a common misconception that is refuted later in the passage.
   (D) introduce the main idea of the passage.
   (E) explain why the events described in the rest of the passage were so surprising.

24. In lines 21-22, "rights and wrongs" most likely refers to

   (A) a list of demands made by women's-rights activists.
   (B) the freedoms women hoped to achieve and the injustices of their current situation.
   (C) the author's ambivalent opinion toward 19th-century reform societies.
   (D) the positive and negative aspects of the fact that women could not vote.
   (E) the inconsistent views of Abigail Adams and Judith Sargent Murray.

25. The passage implies that, for many female activists, the issue of women's rights

   (A) was the only important social issue.
   (B) was not a major cause for concern.
   (C) was best left to male activists, who had more influence.
   (D) was not the first injustice that they had rallied against.
   (E) was much less important than the rights of mentally-ill patients.

26. As it is used in line 40, "condition" most nearly means

   (A) illness.
   (B) training.
   (C) social situation.
   (D) clause.
   (E) physical fitness.

27. According to the passage, why did the "World Anti-Slavery Convention" (line 47) serve as a catalyst for the women's rights movement?

   (A) It was so successful that activists were able to move on to other issues.
   (B) Most people at the convention were women.
   (C) It reminded important activists that discrimination against women was widespread and harmful.
   (D) Its focus on equality for all inspired activists to expand the rights movement to include women.
   (E) Attendees at the convention realized that women faced far worse hardships in America than slaves did.

28. As described in the passage, the tone of Cady Stanton's "Declaration of Sentiments" (lines 60-61) can best be described as

   (A) justifiably aggrieved.
   (B) unexpectedly crude.
   (C) unfortunately plagiarized.
   (D) unfairly limited.
   (E) utterly ecstatic.

29. According to the passage, Cady Stanton drew on the form and language of the Declaration of Independence because

   (A) she hoped to parody the misogynistic attitudes of Jefferson and the other founding fathers.
   (B) she was not original enough to come up with her own style.
   (C) she considered its ideals to be particularly applicable to the plight of women.
   (D) she hoped that her document would replace the Declaration of Independence.
   (E) Thomas Jefferson was her childhood hero.

30. The primary purpose of the passage is to

   (A) describe the circumstances surrounding an influential event in American history.
   (B) provide a detailed biography of a pioneering figure in women's rights.
   (C) critique the effectiveness of the women's rights movement of the 19th century.
   (D) compare and contrast two important historical documents.
   (E) analyze the role of women in the Revolutionary era.

Version 1.3

Unauthorized copying or reuse of any part of this page is illegal.

Homework Passage 4 (Long)

This passage, taken from a 1912 biography of Mark Twain, describes an interesting period in the life of the acclaimed author.

It must have seemed to many who knew him that Mark Twain at forty had reached the pinnacle of his fame and achievement. His name was on every lip; in whatever
Line environment observation and argument were likely to be
(5) pointed with some saying or anecdote attributed, rightly or otherwise, to Mark Twain. "As Mark Twain says," or, "You know that story of Mark Twain's," were universal and daily events. It was dazzling, towering fame, not of the best or most enduring kind as yet, but holding
(10) somewhere within it the structure of immortality.

He was in a constant state of siege from all varieties of humanity for favors such as only human need and ingenuity can invent. His ever-increasing mail presented a marvelous exhibition of the human species. True, there
(15) were hundreds of appreciative tributes from readers who spoke only out of a heart's gratitude; but there were nearly as great a number who came with a compliment, and added a petition, or a demand, or a suggestion, usually unwarranted, often impertinent. Politicians,
(20) public speakers, aspiring writers, actors, singers, and inventors (most of them he had never seen nor heard of) cheerfully asked him to endorse their abilities and projects.

Young men wrote requesting verses or sentiments to
(25) be inscribed in young ladies' autograph albums. Young girls wrote asking him to write the story of his life, to be used as a school composition. Men starting obscure newspapers coolly invited him to lend them his name as editor, assuring him that he would be put to no trouble,
(30) and that it would help advertise his books. A humorist wrote that he had invented some five thousand puns, and invited Mark Twain to lend his name to them in book form for a share of the returns. But the list is endless. He said once:

(35) "The symbol of the race ought to be a human being carrying an ax, for every human being has one concealed about him somewhere, and is always seeking the opportunity to grind it."

Then there was a report which came now and then
(40) from an English castle—the minutes of a certain "Mark Twain Club," all neatly and elaborately written out, with the speech of each member and the discussions that had followed—the work, he found out later, of another eccentric; for there was no Mark Twain Club, the reports
(45) being just the mental diversion of a rich young man with nothing else to do.

Letters came oddly addressed. There is one envelope still in existence that bears Twain's name in elaborate design and a very good silhouette likeness, the work of
(50) some talented artist. "Mark Twain, United States," was a common address; "Mark Twain, The World," was also used; "Mark Twain, Somewhere," mailed in a foreign country, reached him promptly, and "Mark Twain, Anywhere," found its way to Hartford in due season.

(55) Then there was a letter (though this was later; he was abroad at the time), mailed by Brander Matthews and Francis Wilson, addressed, "Mark Twain, God Knows Where." It found him after traveling half around the world on its errand, and in his answer he said, "He did."
(60) Then someone sent a letter addressed, "The Devil Knows Where." Which also reached him, and he answered, "He did, too."

Surely this was the farthest horizon of fame.

31. Throughout the passage, the author's tone is predominantly

(A) analytical.
(B) disparaging.
(C) dispassionate.
(D) gloomy.
(E) humorous.

32. The passage implies that Mark Twain's fame reached such heights that

(A) he was assumed to be the source of other people's stories and sayings.
(B) he became frustrated with public life and retired to become an ax-grinder.
(C) most people respected his desire to live a quiet, private life.
(D) hundreds of people joined a "Mark Twain Club" at an English castle.
(E) he decided to use his fame to raise money for some of his favorite charities.

33. According to the passage, much of Twain's "ever-increasing mail" (line 13) consisted of

(A) excellent business opportunities.
(B) unreasonable demands and suggestions.
(C) verses from ladies' autograph albums.
(D) hateful letters from jealous rivals.
(E) letters with no address on them.

34. The author implies that the writers of the letters listed in the third paragraph (lines 24-34) were

(A) eccentrics with nothing better to do.
(B) attempting to use Twain's fame for their own benefit.
(C) journalists hoping to write articles about Twain.
(D) fans writing to Twain out of heartfelt gratitude.
(E) friends and relatives in dire need of financial assistance.

education
be smarter.

Unauthorized copying or reuse of any part of this page is illegal.

Version 1.3

35. The tone of the Twain quotation in lines 35-38 ("The symbol … grind it.") can best be described as

    (A) optimistic.
    (B) indifferent.
    (C) buoyant.
    (D) cynical.
    (E) admiring.

36. As used in line 40, "minutes" most nearly means

    (A) tiny objects.
    (B) short distances.
    (C) units of time.
    (D) transcript.
    (E) angle divisions.

37. In the 6th paragraph (lines 47-62), the examples of unusual addresses on letters delivered to Twain serve to

    (A) prove that the United States Postal Service is the best and most efficient in the world.
    (B) further reinforce the notion of Twain's immense worldwide fame.
    (C) provide an interesting insight into Twain's personality.
    (D) refute the idea that everyone knew who Twain was.
    (E) provide a contrast to the wacky letters described earlier in the passage.

38. The primary purpose of the passage is to

    (A) describe the American mail system of the late 1800's.
    (B) analyze the writings of a noted author.
    (C) illustrate some of the unusual effects that fame had on the life of a legendary figure.
    (D) offer advice to those who wish to become famous.
    (E) compare Mark Twain to other famous authors of his era.

SC Topic: Predicting Answers (Lesson B11a)	RC Topic: Tone Questions (Lesson B12b)

Homework Set 1

1. Since she was a little girl, Mary Lou has ------ to be an astronaut, but the closest she has ever come is a trip to Space Camp.

   (A) detested
   (B) averted
   (C) deterred
   (D) recanted
   (E) yearned

2. A ------ person is much better suited to being a teacher than a librarian, since the former job requires lots of talking and the latter job ------ noise in most situations.

   (A) verbose . . instigates
   (B) loquacious . . repudiates
   (C) latent . . spurns
   (D) terse . . exalts
   (E) tacit . . disdains

3. The pedestrians paid no attention to the warnings and ------ of the man shouting on the street corner, thinking there was no way such a man could see the future.

   (A) austerities
   (B) penances
   (C) vindications
   (D) premonitions
   (E) concessions

4. His friends could not ------ Shariq's philanthropy and his ------ demeanor; he seemed to be two completely different people: one generous and one arrogant.

   (A) mitigate . . magnanimous
   (B) correlate . . contentious
   (C) reconcile . . smug
   (D) discriminate between . . aloof
   (E) extricate . . jolly

5. The ------ author was respected throughout the country for the wisdom he had imparted in his numerous essays and books.

   (A) pedestrian
   (B) sycophantic
   (C) venerable
   (D) naïve
   (E) moronic

6. As yet, no one had come forward to take credit for the anonymous donation to the school, though some people have ------ that a local businessman is the secret ------.

   (A) reviled . . rascal
   (B) implicated . . bandit
   (C) placated . . humanitarian
   (D) posited . . antagonist
   (E) insinuated . . benefactor

7. A wildlife photographer must often be ------, for many animals are wary of humans and will flee as soon as they notice that one is nearby.

   (A) expansive
   (B) flagrant
   (C) oafish
   (D) belligerent
   (E) stealthy

8. The Japanese garden was utterly ------: there was no evidence that humans had ever set foot in, much less tended, the garden.

   (A) frenzied
   (B) repugnant
   (C) capricious
   (D) embellished
   (E) pristine

Unauthorized copying or reuse of any part of this page is illegal.

Version 1.3

Homework Set 2

9. Because Adrian became quite ------ whenever the apartment was even the slightest bit dirty, his roommate took great care to ensure that each room remained ------.

   (A) agitated . . immaculate
   (B) obsequious . . destitute
   (C) amiable . . impeccable
   (D) pacified . . exemplary
   (E) restless . . squalid

10. Loni's goal was to become a ------ person, so she spent as much time as possible performing kind or charitable acts.

    (A) submissive
    (B) apprehensive
    (C) credulous
    (D) righteous
    (E) vindictive

11. As a book lover, Tobias would have loved to have stayed at the library and read every single book, but he only had enough time to ------ a few volumes.

    (A) peruse
    (B) ascribe
    (C) eradicate
    (D) encumber
    (E) despise

12. Svetlana, a ------ person, would rather be immoral on occasion than be so ------ that she could not have fun.

    (A) malicious . . negligent
    (B) cognizant . . conscientious
    (C) jovial . . petty
    (D) dejected . . painstaking
    (E) carefree . . scrupulous

13. In a desperate attempt to be ready for the final exam, Phineas took ------ notes during the review session.

    (A) implicit
    (B) miniscule
    (C) copious
    (D) guarded
    (E) marginal

14. Carla had not expected the famous movie star to be so ------; she had always thought of him as being much more sociable.

    (A) cordial
    (B) reserved
    (C) transitory
    (D) gregarious
    (E) portentous

15. In order to determine exactly what had ------, the detective interviewed dozens of witnesses and consulted several security tapes of the events in question.

    (A) abounded
    (B) transpired
    (C) abstained
    (D) augmented
    (E) transcended

16. His fortune almost totally ------ by his excessive spending, the former singer was left with only a small ------ of his former wealth.

    (A) squandered . . aggregate
    (B) depleted . . vestige
    (C) exhausted . . ensemble
    (D) proliferated . . remnant
    (E) compiled . . decorum

Homework Passage 1 (Short Paired)

These passages are taken from the autobiographies of two prominent 19th-century writers, Edward Bok and Charles Darwin. Passage 1 describes Bok's childhood; Passage 2 describes Darwin's college years.

Passage 1:

One day it occurred to him to test the accuracy of the biographies he was reading. James A. Garfield was then spoken of for the presidency; Edward wondered whether
Line it was true that the man who was likely to be President of
(5) the United States had once been a boy on the tow-path, and with a simple directness characteristic of his Dutch training, wrote to General Garfield, asking whether the boyhood episode was true, and explaining why he asked. Of course any public man, no matter how large his
(10) correspondence, is pleased to receive an earnest letter from an information-seeking boy. General Garfield answered warmly and fully. Edward showed the letter to his father, who told the boy that it was valuable and he should keep it. This was a new idea. He followed it
(15) further: if one such letter was valuable, how much more valuable would be a hundred! If General Garfield answered him, would not other famous men? Why not begin a collection of autograph letters? Everybody collected something.

Passage 2:

(20) But no pursuit at Cambridge was followed with nearly so much eagerness or gave me so much pleasure as collecting beetles. It was the mere passion for collecting, for I did not dissect them, and rarely compared their external characters with published
(25) descriptions, but got them named anyhow. I will give a proof of my zeal: one day, on tearing off some old bark, I saw two rare beetles, and seized one in each hand; then I saw a third and new kind, which I could not bear to lose, so that I popped the one which I held in my right hand
(30) into my mouth. Alas! it ejected some intensely acrid fluid, which burnt my tongue so that I was forced to spit the beetle out, which was lost, as was the third one.

17. Passage 1 implies that "any public man" (line 9) would have responded to Edward's letter with

(A) fanaticism.
(B) brutality.
(C) indulgence.
(D) deception.
(E) stinginess.

18. The narrator of Passage 2 collected beetles primarily in order to

(A) amass as complete an assortment of species as possible.
(B) study the biology of the insects by dissecting them.
(C) satisfy his thirst for adventure.
(D) discover and classify new species.
(E) make money by selling them.

19. After the events described in each passage, the emotions of the authors most likely differed in that the author of Passage 2 was more

(A) soothed.
(B) dismayed.
(C) inquisitive.
(D) exhilarated.
(E) fatigued.

20. The authors of both passages describe the act of collecting with what sort of tone?

(A) reluctance
(B) abhorrence
(C) apathy
(D) resentment
(E) fondness

Homework Passage 2 (Long)

This passage explores so-called "pulp" magazines, which featured fantastic stories of air and space travel, and their influence on popular culture.

Almost a half-century before humans would invent the airplane, the editors of some popular publications understood the appeal and excitement of flight and
Line incorporated the burgeoning field of flight into their
(5) adventure fiction magazines. Filled with futuristic ideas, these publications were never meant to be educational or sophisticated. They were entertainment aimed primarily at young males, simply written and filled with illustrations. Printed on cheaply produced, wood-pulp
(10) paper, they were given the derogatory name "pulps." Despite their lowbrow appeal, however, pulps gave birth to the way we imagine air and space travel.

The parent of the 20th-century pulp was the story papers of the mid- and late-1800s. Titles like *The Boys of*
(15) *New York* and even the still-publishing *The Atlantic Monthly* featured a combination of short and serialized fiction, non-fiction, and commentaries. Transportation was always a favorite subject, offering escapism, adventure, romantic destinations, and the opportunity to
(20) spotlight the latest gizmo. Decades before the Wright brothers' first successful flight in 1903, the heroes of story papers took to the air in a bizarre assortment of airships. Frank Reade, a character who originally appeared in *The Boys of New York* but was later re-
(25) created as Frank Reade, Jr., in the *Frank Reade Weekly Magazine*, traveled the prairies in a steam-powered air vehicle that looked like a ship held aloft by several oversized umbrellas and a large propeller. By the early 20th century, Frank Reade, Jr., also flew a helicopter and
(30) an Earth-orbiting satellite. The character was very successful and whetted the public's appetite for more air adventure. Airplanes could give a story a creative spin without pulling it too far away from conventional fiction. A hero could use his airplane to fight exotic enemies,
(35) visit foreign countries, or impress young women.

Two notable writers, Jules Verne and H.G. Wells, inspired readers to dream about adventure beyond Earth, and the pulps took notice. A few of the early pulps regularly printed science fiction, but it was publisher
(40) Hugo Gernsback who created the first all-science-fiction pulp. He began with "invention" magazines that featured a mixture of articles on futuristic (and occasionally preposterous) technologies and science fiction stories. In 1929, he launched *Amazing Stories*, the all-science
(45) fiction pulp that would make him famous. Although *Amazing Stories* cost 25 cents, a high price when compared to other magazines of the time, it was a thick publication and featured reprints of stories by famous authors like Verne and Wells, while developing
(50) its own stable of good writers who transformed space travel from a Victorian novelty into a 20th-century possibility. *Amazing Stories* gave us the first space hero, Anthony "Buck Rogers", featured in the story "Armageddon, 2419", who would become the model for

(55) space travelers up through the early 1960s. Rocket ships would become the transportation of choice among pulp readers. Raymond Palmer, the editor for *Amazing Stories* from 1946 to 1949, launched a pulp called *Air Adventures*, but it ran only six issues before folding.
(60) *Air Ace* and *Airboy* lasted longer than the war, but tastes would soon shift back to science fiction, with the help of a real pilot. On June 25, 1947, the Pendleton, Oregon, paper, *East Oregonian*, ran an article about a "flying saucer" seen the day before by pilot Kenneth
(65) Arnold. From that small article started an enormous flying saucer craze and a new public passion for anything space-related. Pulp science fiction experienced an explosion in popularity, with a number of new titles, including *Startling Stories*, *The Magazine of Fantasy*
(70) *and Science Fiction*, *If*, *Galaxy*, and many others that entered the market in the late 1940s and early 1950s. The pulps of this era attracted good authors like Arthur C. Clarke, Robert Heinlein, and Poul Anderson, who created believable tales of space travel that even, occasionally,
(75) adhered to the laws of physics. They also attracted skilled artists, who brought the stories to colorful life. Together, the pulp authors and artists created the popular look and feel of futuristic human space travel: long, tapered, V-2-like rockets, diving gear-like helmets and pressure suits,
(80) ringed space stations, and even the aliens and flying saucers that astronauts could expect to meet during their trip.

Pulps continue to take readers to the new frontier, pushing the limits of human space exploration, and
(85) leaving the bonds of Earth behind. They are also leaving paper behind. More and more pulp-style magazines are finding a home on the Internet. The future of space travel may only be a mouse click away, a fitting transition for a medium that has always celebrated futuristic
(90) technologies.

21. Based on the description of "adventure fiction magazines" (line 5), one can infer that the tone of these publications could generally be described as

    (A) sophisticated.
    (B) tedious.
    (C) educational.
    (D) derogatory.
    (E) lively.

Version 1.3

Unauthorized copying or reuse of any part of this page is illegal.

22. According to the passage, "pulps" got their name from

    (A) early airplanes that were built from wood pulp.
    (B) the fact that their stories were gruesome and violent.
    (C) a story that was set in a wood mill.
    (D) the cheap paper they were printed on.
    (E) the product of one of the futuristic inventions described in an early magazine.

23. The passage implies that early air travel stories were popular among readers because

    (A) many readers had pleasant memories of their trips on fantastic airships.
    (B) airplanes were a traditional part of conventional fiction.
    (C) they were extremely well written.
    (D) the technologies described in the stories were always very realistic.
    (E) it allowed readers to imagine distant, exotic places.

24. *The Frank Reade Weekly* was an example of

    (A) an early space-travel periodical.
    (B) a well-respected but unsuccessful story paper.
    (C) popular escapist air-travel literature.
    (D) an "invention" magazine.
    (E) a failed attempt at creating an airplane-based pulp after World War II.

25. As it is used in line 32, "spin" most nearly means

    (A) variation.
    (B) confusion.
    (C) quick, rotating movement.
    (D) brief car trip.
    (E) biased interpretation.

26. The passage implies that *Amazing Stories* was able to charge more than other pulps because it

    (A) was printed on better paper.
    (B) had articles about futuristic technologies.
    (C) contained more stories and was written by higher-quality authors.
    (D) was the first periodical to publish science fiction.
    (E) was a Victorian-era novelty.

27. According to the passage, what happened to airplane-based pulps midway through the 20th century?

    (A) They continued to be as popular as ever, thanks to characters such as Frank Reade.
    (B) They began using more artistic illustrations.
    (C) They gained respect in the literary community.
    (D) They experienced a resurgence due to the exploits of a pilot named Kenneth Arnold.
    (E) They were eclipsed in popularity by stories of rocket ships and space travel.

28. "Arthur C. Clarke, Robert Heinlein, and Poul Anderson" (lines 72-73) are cited as examples of

    (A) artists who illustrated many stories in the late 1940s.
    (B) fictional space heroes.
    (C) real-life astronauts who read science fiction.
    (D) editors of pulp magazines.
    (E) talented writers who created relatively realistic stories.

29. What is the purpose of the final paragraph (lines 83-90)?

    (A) to contrast modern science fiction with early pulps
    (B) to offer more examples of famous pulp magazines
    (C) to criticize pulps for not realistically depicting the laws of physics
    (D) to analyze the effect that pulps had on serious literature
    (E) to describe the current state of pulp-style literature

30. Which of the following best expresses the main idea of the passage?

    (A) Stories about air travel remain as popular today as they ever have been.
    (B) Even a low-class art form can have a large impact.
    (C) Frank Reade is the most interesting character in adventure fiction.
    (D) Science fiction writers are not as skilled as writers of other genres.
    (E) Though futuristic technology was once a popular subject, it likely will not be in the future.

31. Based on the passage as a whole, one can infer that the author's attitude toward "pulps" is one of

    (A) mockery.
    (B) fury.
    (C) apathy.
    (D) misery.
    (E) enjoyment.

Unauthorized copying or reuse of any part of this page is illegal.

Version 1.3

Homework Passage 4 (Long)

The following excerpt from a popular science article describes how scientists have managed to make bacteria perform an unusual feat.

Synthetic biologists dream of reproducing life's basic processes from the ground up. Borrowing concepts from physics and engineering, some of them want to start by
Line designing tiny genetic circuits inside cells so the cells
(5) behave like the switches and amplifiers in your radio or car.

So far, they've made bits and pieces like cellular toggle switches, counters and edge detectors. But until recently, their circuit-building toolbox lacked a basic
(10) instrument: an oscillator.

Oscillators switch back and forth between two states. You've seen simple oscillators if you've ever encountered a swinging pendulum, a weight on a spring or alternating current in a power outlet. Your body is filled with natural
(15) oscillators, too, such as the daily light/dark cycling of circadian rhythms.

Synthetic biologists made their first primitive cellular oscillator in 2000. Building one that was more stable and strong seemed just around the corner.
(20) However, "it's been harder than we thought," says Jeff Hasty, a bioengineer at the University of California, San Diego.

Nine years later, Hasty and his team transformed cells—in this case, pill-shaped *E. coli* bacteria—into the
(25) robust oscillators biologists had envisioned. He did it by inserting two genes that take turns switching on and off. When there's too much of the "on" gene, the "off" gene activates and shuts it down. As the genes continue to switch on and off at intervals, they also turn a fluorescent
(30) protein called GFP on and off so the researchers can see what's happening.

Hasty still had work to do, though. Each cell oscillated on its own. The cells were "a bunch of guys doing their own thing" with no coordination, he says.
(35) Now, Hasty's team has tweaked the oscillator to work in synchrony. One of the two circuit genes now sends out small signaling molecules that tell cells when other cells are nearby. As the cells sense a big enough community, they start to oscillate together. Researchers
(40) call this coordinated behavior "quorum sensing."

Hasty's synchronized oscillator represents the first big step toward developing a blink-based sensor that could detect pollutants or release drugs into the body when they're needed. That's because the engineered
(45) bacteria react to subtle environmental changes by blinking faster or slower, or dimming or brightening.

While ten years may seem like a long time to develop an oscillator that shows bacterial sensors are possible, it would have taken even longer without the
(50) help of computer modeling.

"We use computers to see if we're in the right ballpark," says Hasty. "We're not at a point where we can make precise predictions, but we can get a sense of what we might want to change to get the circuit to work."

(55) For instance, computer models showed his team that they needed to continually flush away some of the signaling molecule in their experiment. Otherwise, the bacteria would stay on instead of blinking.

Although modeling let Hasty and others work
(60) through complex questions ahead of time, it didn't reveal everything. Hasty says the bacteria behaved in ways he hadn't expected.

"Every time we build something and it surprises us, we're reminded that we don't understand [these
(65) phenomena] all that well," he adds. "By designing circuits with parts whose properties we think we understand, we find out what we don't understand. Then we adjust what we know. So synthetic biology both requires and contributes to fundamental knowledge."

32. According to the passage, what is the predominant underlying motivation behind cellular oscillator research?

(A) to use computers to simulate life
(B) to explain the laws of physics using biological tools
(C) to re-create biological processes in a laboratory
(D) to engineer electronic devices from living cells
(E) to determine how to detect pollutants in water

33. What is the function of the 5th paragraph (lines 20-22)?

(A) to introduce an unexpected development
(B) to explain an important concept
(C) to provide evidence to support a claim made in the previous paragraph
(D) to compare several types of oscillators
(E) to describe a key breakthrough in the research

34. Which of the following provides the best definition of the term "quorum sensing" (line 40)?

(A) the ability of cells to oscillate in unison when enough cells are nearby
(B) a phenomenon in which bacteria behave differently than a computer model predicts
(C) the process of transforming *E. coli* bacteria into oscillators
(D) the daily light/dark oscillations of the human body
(E) the design of tiny genetic circuits inside cells

35. Which of the following best states the effects that "computer models" (line 55) have had on the research described in the passage?

    (A) They have largely been ineffective.
    (B) They have slowed the research down but have increased scientists' understanding.
    (C) They have solved every problem presented by the research.
    (D) They have added to the researchers' confusion by misrepresenting the behavior of bacteria.
    (E) They have been very helpful, though they have limited uses.

36. Which of the following words from the passage is NOT an example of figurative language?

    (A) "toolbox" (line 9)
    (B) "corner" (line 19)
    (C) "guys" (line 34)
    (D) "pollutants" (line 43)
    (E) "ballpark" (line 52)

37. The research performed on cellular oscillators can best be described as

    (A) a waste of time and effort.
    (B) a protracted but successful process.
    (C) following a natural rhythm.
    (D) a fleeting success followed by repeated failures.
    (E) a series of impressive discoveries in rapid succession.

38. The primary purpose of the passage is to

    (A) condemn researchers for wasting time on an important project.
    (B) predict future innovations in the field of synthetic biology.
    (C) detail the development of a new biological tool.
    (D) explain the difference between genetic circuits and electrical circuits.
    (E) describe the many functions of the *E. coli* bacteria.

39. What is the author's attitude toward the fact that the cellular oscillator research has not gone as quickly as hoped?

    (A) ironic
    (B) critical
    (C) understanding
    (D) intimidated
    (E) startled

B14HW: Homework and Extra Practice

| **SC Topic**: Eliminating Answers (Lesson B14a) | **RC Topic**: Tone Questions (Lesson B12b) |

Homework Set 1

1. Thanks to the ------ weather, Simon was not sure whether he would need to wear his raincoat or his sunglasses—or both.

   (A) stagnant
   (B) pristine
   (C) abiding
   (D) erratic
   (E) resolute

2. In order to ensure the ------ of his articles, the reporter always found ------ evidence for any information he received before he published it.

   (A) spuriousness . . substantiating
   (B) plausibility . . contradictory
   (C) infallibility . . refuting
   (D) veracity . . corroborating
   (E) insinuation . . negligible

3. Nathaniel's decision to purchase the lottery ticket proved to be ------ when he won $50.

   (A) inauspicious
   (B) preposterous
   (C) derisive
   (D) fortuitous
   (E) dreadful

4. The community safety advisor wrote a report in which he ------ adding crossing guards to all busy intersections so as to make pedestrians safer.

   (A) equivocated on
   (B) reviled
   (C) deplored
   (D) advocated
   (E) extricated

5. Life's most important decisions should not be made ------; often, careful consideration will reveal a better course of action.

   (A) pertinently
   (B) recurrently
   (C) judiciously
   (D) portentously
   (E) impetuously

6. Though he was ------ at first, Juan quickly warmed up to his new classmates, and soon began talking so much that he could be described as ------.

   (A) reserved . . terse
   (B) amiable . . candid
   (C) reticent . . loquacious
   (D) brash . . verbose
   (E) timid . . succinct

7. Though her former employer had offered her ------ raise if she would stay, Zhou did not ------ in her determination to change jobs.

   (A) a repulsive . . avert
   (B) an ample . . waver
   (C) a scanty . . relent
   (D) a hefty . . persist
   (E) a diminutive . . elaborate

8. The Cathedral of St. John the Divine in New York is an impressive ------, with an interior height of over 120 feet.

   (A) edifice
   (B) compulsion
   (C) detriment
   (D) premonition
   (E) precipice

Homework Set 2

9. The reviewer ------ the film for being overly ------, saying that it did not paint a realistic picture of the era because it focused too much on the events that we remember fondly.

    (A) commended . . foreboding
    (B) reproached . . nostalgic
    (C) reprimanded . . cynical
    (D) exalted . . evocative
    (E) censured . . oblivious

10. Donnell's report was completed in ------ way; his teacher could tell that he did not spend much time examining the data.

    (A) an adept
    (B) a cursory
    (C) a scrupulous
    (D) a painstaking
    (E) a profuse

11. The sweet old couple who ran the bed and breakfast were so ------ that many visitors wished that they could live there regularly instead of just on vacation.

    (A) aloof
    (B) itinerant
    (C) caustic
    (D) malevolent
    (E) accommodating

12. After he was told that pink unicorns grazed in his front yard at night, the ------ young boy watched ------ from his window until the sun rose and he realized he'd been tricked.

    (A) gullible . . hastily
    (B) indubitable . . lethargically
    (C) credulous . . vigilantly
    (D) skeptical . . acutely
    (E) wary . . capriciously

13. Unlike most of her classmates, who were too shy or quiet to talk in class, Laetitia had no ------ about speaking up whenever she knew an answer.

    (A) audacity
    (B) intuition
    (C) inhibition
    (D) tenacity
    (E) gregariousness

14. The farmer considered insects to be solely responsible for his failed crops and sought to ------ the ------ from his lands with vast amounts of insecticide.

    (A) entrench . . concession
    (B) exacerbate . . plague
    (C) eradicate . . prestige
    (D) obliterate . . scourge
    (E) instigate . . prominence

15. Sven was quite ------ by the huge selection of cereals at the American supermarket; he did not see the need for more than a few choices.

    (A) elated
    (B) bewildered
    (C) denounced
    (D) embellished
    (E) enlivened

16. The town's enthusiasm for its new minor league baseball team began to ------ when the team lost its first 25 games.

    (A) ameliorate
    (B) mount
    (C) wane
    (D) pervade
    (E) transpire

Homework Passage 1 (Short Paired)

Passage 1:

Why are weather forecasters so bad at predicting the weather? This question has a deceptively difficult answer. It's not just that weather forecasters have limited
Line information or flawed judgment (though they surely have
(5) both). It is actually a much more fundamental problem.

Because we live in a scientific society, we often believe that, if we have sufficient information about what is happening now, we should be able to predict what will happen in the near future. The weather, however, does
(10) not work like this: even though we know the current state of the weather, and even though current conditions determine future conditions, those future conditions are unpredictable. There are just far too many interrelated factors. This counterintuitive idea is one of the
(15) conclusions of chaos theory, an important new scientific field. (Chaos theory also gave us the "butterfly effect," in which tiny events can come to have huge consequences.) So don't blame your weatherman the next time it rains unexpectedly. His job is literally impossible.

Passage 2:

(20) "Red sky at night, sailor's delight / Red sky in morning, sailors take warning."

This rhyme has been used to successfully predict storms for centuries. In fact, the knowledge communicated in the rhyme has been around at least
(25) since the times of Jesus; a similar saying is expressed in the Bible (Matthew 16:2-3). Modern science has confirmed the basics of this particular piece of lore.

At sunrise and sunset, the sun's light must pass through much more of the Earth's atmosphere than at
(30) other times of day. Because of this, the blues, greens, and violets are scattered, leaving only reddish hues. The reddish hues are illuminated against the bottoms of clouds. Red light at sunrise shines on clouds to the west; at sunset, it shines on clouds to the east. Since storm
(35) fronts generally move from west to east, the red clouds in the west (at sunrise) indicate that rain is coming. Conversely, the red clouds in the east (at sunset) are unlikely to pose a threat.

17. The author of Passage 1 describes the failures of "weather forecasters" (line 1) with an attitude of

(A) compassion.
(B) censure.
(C) condescension.
(D) antipathy.
(E) remorse.

18. When describing the simple weather-forecasting rhyme in lines 20-21 ("Red sky ... take warning"), the tone of the author of Passage 2 can best be described as

(A) pious.
(B) dubious.
(C) ambivalent.
(D) affirming.
(E) arrogant.

19. The primary purpose of Passage 2 is most likely to

(A) argue that predicting storms is ultimately impossible.
(B) trace the origins of various weather-related sayings.
(C) criticize those who refuse to take advantage of modern technology.
(D) explain the physics of storm formation.
(E) validate a traditional method using modern science.

20. How would the author of Passage 2 most likely respond to the statement in Passage 1 that weather conditions "are unpredictable" (lines 12-13)?

(A) The Bible provides guidelines that allow anyone to accurately predict the weather in any situation.
(B) Such failures are entirely due to errors made by incompetent weather forecasters.
(C) The prevailing scientific theories indicate that weather will one day be completely foreseeable.
(D) It may be impossible to predict all weather events, but some simple rules are very often correct.
(E) Ancient weather lore is generally more precise than even the most advanced scientific predictions.

Homework Passage 2 (Long)

This passage, taken from a short story written by Maurice Baring, describes an encounter between two women on a train during the Russian Revolution.

Sitting opposite me in the second-class carriage of the express train that was crawling at a leisurely pace from Moscow to the south was a little girl who looked as

Line if she were about twelve years old, with her mother. The
(5) mother was a large fair-haired person, with a good-natured expression. They had a dog with them, and the little girl, whose whole face twitched every now and then from St. Vitus' dance*, got out at nearly every station to buy food for the dog.

(10) On the same side of the carriage, in the opposite corner, another lady (thin and fair) was reading the newspaper. She and the mother of the child soon made friends over the dog. That is to say, the dog made friends with the strange lady and was admonished by its
(15) mistress, and the strange lady said: "Please don't scold him. He is not in the least in my way, and I like dogs." They then began to talk.

In the course of the conversation the stout lady mentioned her husband, who, it turned out, was the head
(20) of the local militia in a town in Siberia. This seemed to interest the thin lady immensely. She at once asked what were his political views, and what she herself thought about politics.

The large lady seemed to be reluctant to talk politics
(25) and evaded the questions for some time, but after much desultory conversation, which always came back to the same point, she said:

"My husband is a Conservative; he is a very good man and very just. He has his own opinions and he is
(30) sincere. He does not believe in the revolution or in the revolutionaries. He took the oath to serve the Emperor when everything went quietly and well, and now, although I have often begged him to leave the military, he says it would be very wrong to leave just because it is
(35) dangerous. 'I have taken the oath,' he says, 'and I must keep it.'"

Here she stopped, but after some further questions on the part of the thin lady, she said: "I never had time or leisure to think of these questions. I was married when I
(40) was sixteen. I have had eight children, and they all died one after the other except this one, who was the eldest. I used to see political exiles and prisoners, and I used to feel sympathy for them. I used to hear about people being sent here and there, and sometimes I used to go down on
(45) my knees to my husband to ask what he could do for them, but I never thought about there being any particular idea at the back of all this."

Then after a short pause she added: "It first dawned on me at Moscow. I had been staying with some friends
(50) in the country, and I happened by chance to see the funeral of that man Bauman, the doctor, who was killed. I was very much impressed when I saw that huge procession go past, all the men singing the funeral march, and I understood that Bauman himself had nothing to do

(55) with it. Who cared about Bauman? But I understood that he was a symbol. I saw that there must be a big idea that moves all these people to give up everything, to go to prison, to kill, and be killed. I understood this for the first time at that funeral. I cried when the crowd went past. I
(60) understood there was a big idea, a great cause behind it all. Then I went home."

* St. Vitus' dance—a neurological disease that causes involuntary shaking of the body

21. Which of the following would make the best title for the passage?

(A) How My Daughter Got St. Vitus' Dance
(B) Traveling through the Russian Countryside
(C) Discussing a Big Idea with a Stranger
(D) Bauman's Funeral
(E) The Local Militia of Siberia

22. As it is used in lines 5 and 11, "fair" most nearly means

(A) sunny and calm
(B) equitable
(C) somewhat large
(D) adequate
(E) light in color

23. The first two paragraphs primarily serve which of the following functions?

(A) to introduce the main characters of the passage
(B) to explain the meaning of "St. Vitus' dance"
(C) to describe the surrounding landscape
(D) to compare two people's political views
(E) to state the main idea of the passage

24. Based on evidence from the passage, the "strange lady" (line 14) can best be described as

(A) friendly and curious.
(B) sorrowful and quiet.
(C) conservative and sincere.
(D) shy and terse.
(E) caring and apolitical.

Unauthorized copying or reuse of any part of this page is illegal.

Version 1.3

25. The passage implies that the "stout lady" (line 18) has what sort of attitude about discussing politics?

    (A) humorous
    (B) unenthusiastic
    (C) disgusted
    (D) eager
    (E) sympathetic

26. In response to the fact that the "large lady seemed to be reluctant to talk politics," (line 24) the passage suggests that the other woman did what?

    (A) dropped the subject immediately
    (B) returned to her seat
    (C) apologized profusely
    (D) periodically repeated her queries
    (E) became angry and bitter

27. The passage describes the husband of the large lady as being

    (A) harsh
    (B) hypocritical
    (C) radical
    (D) fearful
    (E) honorable

28. According to the passage, why had the large lady not given much thought to questions of politics early in her life?

    (A) She preferred less controversial subjects, such as art and medicine.
    (B) She was too focused on caring for her family to think much about politics.
    (C) Her village received no political news worth thinking about.
    (D) Her husband actively forbade her from discussing such matters.
    (E) She was sick of politics because her father was so involved in the subject.

29. According to the passage, why did so many people attend the funeral of Bauman?

    (A) He had committed a terrible crime.
    (B) He was a symbol of a political struggle.
    (C) He had been close friends with many people.
    (D) He was a much-admired figure in Moscow.
    (E) They were forced to by the government.

Homework Passage 4 (Long)

This article examines some of Americans' changing attitudes toward their careers.

Several years ago, a Wall Street Journal/ABC News poll reported that nearly 50% of all those working in the United States would choose a new type of work if they
Line had the chance. Why do so many people feel dissatisfied
(5) with their work? The answer is complex and multifaceted. We live in an age in which work has become more personal than ever—when who you are is what you do—a deeper source of personal satisfaction than ever. Many are reexamining their careers in light of
(10) the growing realization that work should be more than a job. Instead of listening to internal signals, many individuals make choices about work and careers on the basis of external criteria such as income potential, status, and the opinions of others. Although they may achieve
(15) success in these careers, they may be unhappy and dissatisfied because their work is not aligned with who they are—their "core self." Others may select careers based on their aptitudes—things they are good at doing— but just like external criteria these aptitudes may not
(20) reflect their "deep interests," that is, the things that really make them happy.
According to Timothy Butler and James Waldroop, examining the terminology used to describe work can help unravel some of the questions about choosing work
(25) that is meaningful. Although the term "career" is used most frequently, the term "vocation" is more profound because it has to do with doing work that makes a difference and that has meaning. The Latin word *vocare*, which means "to call," is the root of the word "vocation."
(30) A vocation is a calling that one has to listen for. It is not immediately recognizable and one has to be attuned to the message for it to be heard. Finding meaningful work, therefore, involves listening for those internal signals that signify "deep interests" and then allowing the interests to
(35) lead to work that is aligned with a "core self."
Traditional vocational or career guidance grew out of the needs of the modern industrial era and focused on measuring individual differences or traits and then using this information to match people to occupations. Part of
(40) this tradition was measuring job satisfaction through a positive evaluation of individuals' attitudes toward their jobs. Career satisfaction measures concentrated on correlating external job factors with global measures of satisfaction. Job satisfaction also depended on an
(45) individual's ability to recognize and follow his or her interests. According to Henderson, when "the popular literature began suggesting deeper meaning in work... these traditional studies and assessment techniques began to have an empty ring" for both individuals and career
(50) development professionals.
In response to the need to address the evolving concept of meaningful work, a new construct known as career happiness has emerged. As defined by Henderson and a number of colleagues, career happiness results
(55) when individuals find or develop careers that allow them

to express their core identities and values, careers that tap into their true essence. According to Henderson, "Career happiness appears to have emerged more from philosophy, mythology, and psychology, than from the
(60) existing job satisfaction literature."
Career happiness is connected to human development and is influenced by developmental processes. Career happiness may result "when career activities, challenges, and environments support, gently
(65) challenge, and resonate with fundamental developmental tasks," but as an individual grows and changes, activities that once resulted in career happiness may not continue to be meaningful.

30. The author begins the passage by citing "a Wall Street Journal/ABC News poll" (lines 1-2) in order to

   (A) start the article on a light-hearted note.
   (B) criticize the conclusion of the poll.
   (C) refute a common misconception.
   (D) provide background information for the discussion that follows.
   (E) praise the honesty of those who answered the poll.

31. All of the following are "external criteria" (line 13) EXCEPT

   (A) whether work is aligned with a person's core self.
   (B) how much a job pays.
   (C) what a guidance counselor recommends.
   (D) the amount of prestige associated with a career.
   (E) where a job is located.

32. In the second paragraph, the author discusses the etymology of the word "vocation" in order to

   (A) explain why this word is inappropriate for use in the modern world.
   (B) provide an interesting anecdote that is unrelated to the passage's main theme.
   (C) argue that a "career" is more likely to make a worker happy than a "vocation."
   (D) change the essay's focus from career happiness to word origins.
   (E) draw a distinction between two words used to describe a person's work.

education
be smarter.

Unauthorized copying or reuse of any part of this page is illegal.

Version 1.3

33. "Traditional vocational or career guidance" (line 36) eventually was seen to have which of the following flaws?

(A) it did not account for external factors such as salary and status.
(B) it could not be used to match people to their ideal occupations.
(C) it did not account for the possibility that people would find a deep satisfaction from their work.
(D) it used faulty terminology.
(E) it evaluated people's attitudes towards their jobs.

34. As it is used in line 49, "ring" most nearly means

(A) chiming sound
(B) group of people
(C) circle
(D) piece of jewelry
(E) meaning

35. Which of the following is NOT true a true statement regarding "career happiness"?

(A) It involves finding a career that suits one's core identity and values.
(B) It is not closely related to traditional career guidance literature.
(C) It is influenced by developmental processes.
(D) A person's salary has little effect on his or her career happiness.
(E) Once found, activities that lead to career happiness will always do so.

36. Which of the following best states the main idea of the article?

(A) Career guidance during the industrial era was short-sighted.
(B) As work becomes more important, some people are changing the way they think about their careers.
(C) Most Americans are unhappy with their current jobs.
(D) The word "vocation" comes from a Latin word that means "to call."
(E) Success in one's career usually leads to happiness and personal fulfillment.

37. The tone of the article is predominantly

(A) humorous.
(B) perplexed.
(C) sardonic.
(D) informative.
(E) outraged.

SC TOPIC: Eliminating Answers (Lesson B14a)	**RC TOPIC**: Analysis Questions (Lesson B15b)

Homework Set 1

1. When Anatoly heard that his favorite television show had been canceled, he felt a ------ sense of sadness that could only be ------ by watching old episodes on DVD.

   (A) tedious . . vacillated
   (B) keen . . alleviated
   (C) pointed . . proliferated
   (D) caustic . . despised
   (E) scanty . . mitigated

2. Carla was so short and skinny that people assumed she was ------, but her wiry frame gave her a significant amount of physical strength.

   (A) feeble
   (B) tenacious
   (C) hearty
   (D) obstinate
   (E) expansive

3. The only sound Nasir heard as he fell asleep was the ------ rumble of the train moving forward unceasingly.

   (A) transitory
   (B) redundant
   (C) wavering
   (D) provocative
   (E) monotonous

4. Though the ------ attitude of the students in Ms. Sims' class was one of joviality, Abel seemed to be perpetually ------.

   (A) ambivalent . . bewildered
   (B) predominant . . morose
   (C) pedestrian . . zealous
   (D) singular . . sullen
   (E) prevailing . . congenial

5. The guest speaker was extremely focused on his subject and refused to ------ when asked about other topics.

   (A) sanction
   (B) flaunt
   (C) retract
   (D) persist
   (E) digress

6. The art teacher was amazed that ------ could paint such a marvelous landscape without the benefit of any instruction.

   (A) a neophyte
   (B) a patriarch
   (C) a benefactor
   (D) a sycophant
   (E) an advocate

7. During their ------ training, the new army recruits were forced to march 50 miles without being allowed a ------ of longer than twenty minutes.

   (A) rigorous . . succession
   (B) cursory . . remission
   (C) succinct . . inauguration
   (D) grueling . . respite
   (E) apparent . . sustenance

8. Thanks to a booming oil industry and other natural resources, the state of Alaska has become ------.

   (A) dogmatic
   (B) outmoded
   (C) prosperous
   (D) despondent
   (E) destitute

Unauthorized copying or reuse of any part of this page is illegal.

Version 1.3

Homework Set 2

9. The charity aimed to reduce ------ in education by providing free textbooks, tutoring, and test preparation to the disadvantaged.

(A) immaculateness
(B) affluence
(C) righteousness
(D) inequity
(E) symmetry

10. The suspect ------ that he was not a criminal and that he would soon be ------ by the facts of the case.

(A) asserted . . indicted
(B) averred . . exonerated
(C) averted . . implicated
(D) attested . . alleged
(E) absolved . . vindicated

11. Hannah was quite pleased with her guests' ------ behavior until one of them belched loudly without apologizing for his rudeness.

(A) decorous
(B) impertinent
(C) dormant
(D) voracious
(E) primal

12. When bad things happen, you should not ------ your misfortune, but rather work ------ to reverse your luck.

(A) bemoan . . intermittently
(B) extol . . ascetically
(C) lament . . diligently
(D) posit . . unrelentingly
(E) relinquish . . industriously

13. After the ledge she was standing on began to collapse, Vera was in ------ position: clinging to a cliff face with no rope or harness to prevent her from falling.

(A) a reticent
(B) an unassailable
(C) a precarious
(D) a gregarious
(E) a latent

14. While the subject of quantum gravity is ------, the author's ------ observations and coherent explanations make the book accessible to any reasonably well-educated reader.

(A) inexplicable . . belligerent
(B) conventional . . adept
(C) intricate . . perplexing
(D) transparent . . secluded
(E) esoteric . . astute

15. Jacques was so ------ about his writing that he would not turn in an essay until every sentence was precisely how he wanted it to be.

(A) indifferent
(B) fastidious
(C) callous
(D) lethargic
(E) scornful

16. Neda had difficulty flying her kite in the ------ winds, which were constantly shifting in direction and intensity.

(A) submissive
(B) fickle
(C) omnipresent
(D) steadfast
(E) resilient

Homework Passage 1 (Short)

This passage, which is from an Anton Chekov short story, describes the unexpected effects of a surprise wedding.

Glancing one Sunday morning into the kitchen, Grisha was struck dumb with amazement. The kitchen was crammed full of people. The cook, Pelageya, was
Line standing in the middle of the kitchen in a new cotton
(5) dress, with a flower on her head. Beside her stood the cabman. The happy pair were red in the face and perspiring and blinking with embarrassment.

Pelageya's face worked all over and she began blubbering. At last the outer door was opened, there was
(10) a whiff of white mist, and the whole party flocked noisily out of the kitchen into the yard.

"Poor thing, poor thing," thought Grisha, hearing the sobs of the cook. "Where have they taken her?"

Next morning the cook was in the kitchen again. The
(15) cabman came in for a minute. He thanked Mamma, and said: "Will you look after her, madam? And also, madam, if you would kindly advance me five rubles of her wages. I have got to buy a new horse-collar."

Again a problem for Grisha: Pelageya was living in
(20) freedom, doing as she liked, and not having to account to anyone for her actions, and all at once, for no sort of reason, a stranger turns up, who has somehow acquired rights over her conduct and her property! Grisha was distressed. He longed passionately, almost to tears, to
(25) comfort this victim, as he supposed, of man's injustice.

17. One can infer from information in the passage that Grisha

(A) had hoped to marry Pelageya himself.
(B) has little previous experience with weddings.
(C) often makes chauvinistic observations.
(D) is a distant, unfeeling boy.
(E) thinks that all marriages should be based on monetary concerns.

18. The primary purpose of the passage is most likely to

(A) describe a joyous scene.
(B) illustrate the poor living conditions that rural Russian servants experienced in the 19th century.
(C) demonstrate the unfairness that sometimes accompanies a common ritual.
(D) present a comical view of an otherwise tragic event.
(E) chronicle the ways in which marriage has changed for women in the last 200 years.

Homework Passage 2 (Short)

The electromagnetic radiation known as X-rays is generally considered to be invisible to the human eye. In fact, some early observers referred to X-rays as "the
Line invisible light." William Röntgen, the man who did the
(5) first extensive studies of X-rays, concluded in 1895 that "The retina of the eye is insensitive to our rays; the eye brought close to the discharge apparatus registers nothing." Little did Röntgen know that he had already seen X-rays; he just did not recognize them at the time.
(10) In 1896, another scientist observed that, after his eyes had adjusted to near-total darkness, very energetic X-rays produced a faint bluish-gray glow. Strangely, this glow seemed to originate from *within* the eye. After hearing about this phenomenon, Röntgen realized that he
(15) had made note of a similar glow during his experiments, but had dismissed his observation as subjective because he only saw the glow once. As it turned out, the glow could be replicated in other experiments, proving that Röntgen had indeed seen the "invisible light" of X-rays.
(20) You are not likely to see any X-rays the next time you go to the doctor or the dentist, though; those X-ray scans are not nearly powerful enough to produce a visible glow.

19. Based on information in the passage, Röntgen's statement in lines 6-8 ("The retina … registers nothing") can best be described as

(A) metaphorical.
(B) paradoxical.
(C) ironic.
(D) understatement.
(E) allusive.

20. In the context of the passage, the primary function of the final paragraph (lines 20-23) is to

(A) summarize the main ideas of the passage.
(B) connect a technical topic to an everyday experience.
(C) present the internal conflicts of a person described in the passage.
(D) refute an observation made in the previous paragraph.
(E) provide specific, well-documented support for a controversial idea.

education
be smarter.

Unauthorized copying or reuse of any part of this page is illegal.

Version 1.3

Homework Passage 3 (Long Paired)

These passages describe some of the earliest attempts at human flight, particularly in relation to its uses in combat.

Passage 1:

The beginning of humanity's infatuation with flight is shrouded in legend. Ancient tales tell of beasts or half-birds flying through the air. Greek mythology tells the
(Line) story of Pegasus, a flying horse, and the messenger god
(5) Hermes in his winged sandals flying throughout the world. The Valkyries of the Norse myths traveled through the air on winged horses. The ancient Greek myth of Daedalus and Icarus tells the tale of how Daedalus made wings of wax and feathers so that he and
(10) his son Icarus could escape from captivity. But Icarus flew too close to the sun and his wings melted, while Daedelus flew too low and crashed into the rocks. Both died in their attempts to fly.

Other legends about flight abound. Another early
(15) one tells of King Bladud, who ruled in Britain in the ninth century B.C.E. Bladud supposedly constructed a pair of wings with which he proposed to fly. But, according to the monk Geoffrey of Monmouth in a history of the British kings, Bladud was dashed to pieces
(20) as he landed on top of the Temple of Apollo in the town of Trinovantum. Another tale recounts the invention of a Greek named Archytas of Tarentum who was said to have made a wooden bird about B.C.E. This bird was powered by steam and supposedly flew about 50 feet (15
(25) meters).

The wars of Alexander the Great in the second century B.C.E. were illustrated in medieval prints showing chariots being pulled through the air by griffins or other creatures with eagle's heads and wings and
(30) bodies of lions. In Roman times, numerous reports told of men flying like birds and some who attempted to fly and died in the attempt. One story tells of Simon the Magician who attempted a flight in front of the emperor Nero only to fall to his death.

(35) The Chinese were the first to fly kites sometime during the first millennium B.C.E. These have been called the world's first aerial vehicles. The philosopher Mo Tzu in the fifth century B.C.E. reportedly constructed a wooden kite that could fly but was wrecked after one
(40) day's tests. A general in 206 B.C.E. described using a kite for reconnaissance. The kite was also used for carrying bombs in war as well as for more benign purposes.

The Europeans also flew kites, pennons, and other
(45) devices based on European tradition from an early era. They learned to make plane surface kites from people in the Middle East. In recounting his adventures in the Far East in the thirteenth century, for example, the explorer Marco Polo described the binding of a man to a wooden
(50) structure—a primitive kite—and exposing him to the wind so that he was carried aloft.

Passage 2:

The French were the first to use balloons for aerial reconnaissance in 1794, during their conflict with
(Line) Austria. This reconnaissance contributed to the French
(55) victory by providing a way for the French to observe the makeup and activities of their enemies. The world's first military observation balloon, "L'Entrepremant," was constructed in 1793 under the guidance of the scientist Charles Coutelle and assisted by N.J. Conti.

(60) The hydrogen balloon was designed to remain tethered and thus had to be especially strong to withstand buffeting by the wind. Two people would be aloft in the balloon's basket—one to handle the balloon and signal to the ground crew who controlled it, and the second to
(65) observe the area. The observer would communicate with the ground by flag signals or by placing written messages in sandbags fitted with rings that could be slid down the cables. The balloon would have two cables tethering it to increase the degree of control and to reduce the
(70) likelihood of the enemy freeing a balloon by severing a cable.

The balloon corps, or Aérostiers, transported L'Entrepremant to Mauberge where Coutelle inflated it, and the air corps was ready to face the
(75) enemy—or at least to see the enemy. The air corps went into action against the Austrians in June 1794. During the battle, Coutelle and Conti successfully spied on Dutch and Austrian troops from high above Mauberge, They provided detailed reports of the location and composition
(80) of the Austrian and Dutch troops and directed ground fire against the forces. The Austrians protested that the use of a balloon was against the rules of war and attempted to shoot it down, but Coutelle had his ground crew let out more cable, and L'Entrepremant easily rose out of range.

(85) The French triumphed at the ensuing Battle of Fleurus, which took place on June 26, 1794. Ground operations were entirely directed from the air. In addition to providing a tactical advantage, the balloon also demoralized the enemy troops. The Austrians feared the
(90) balloon and looked upon it as an agent of the devil that was allied to the French Republic. The Battle of Fleurus was the first battle in history in which aerial reconnaissance contributed significantly to the victory.

The aerial reconnaissance of the Aérostiers led to
(95) further victories by the French troops and also to the building of three more balloons, the Celeste, the Hercule, and the Intrepide, each with its own corps and equipment. Subsequent balloon observations contributed to French victories, and Coutelle persuaded Napoleon to
(100) allow the Aérostiers to accompany the troops to Egypt in 1797. However, the skills of the Aérostiers were not efficiently used, and at the Battle of Aboukir in 1798, the British destroyed the equipment. Upon returning to France in 1799, Napoleon disbanded the Aérostiers and
(105) the balloon school. With that, the use of balloons by the French military was suspended for 40 years.

21. The main idea behind the "myth of Daedalus and Icarus" (lines 7-8) is most likely that

   (A) people should not build wings out of wax.
   (B) the ancient Greeks had no desire to gain the ability of flight.
   (C) modern aircraft such as airplanes and balloons are unsafe.
   (D) attempting to acquire god-like powers such as flight is very dangerous for humans.
   (E) prisoners should not try to escape from their captors.

22. In the context of the first passage, what is the function of the second paragraph (lines 14-25)?

   (A) to contradict a statement made in the previous paragraph
   (B) to introduce the main idea of the passage
   (C) to proclaim that many legends have no historical basis
   (D) to transition from mythical tales of flight to legends with a more historical basis
   (E) to compare the flying technologies of the ancients to more modern devices

23. The examples of "King Bladud" (line 15) and "Simon the Magician" (lines 32-33) primarily show that

   (A) only educated men dreamed of achieving flight.
   (B) Europeans were the first to attempt to fly.
   (C) ancient flight pioneers were surprisingly skilled.
   (D) historical records of ancient human flight are very incomplete.
   (E) early attempts at flight often met with spectacular failure.

24. Based on information in the first passage, one can infer that the first person to achieve flight likely did so

   (A) in a balloon
   (B) in an airplane
   (C) with wings made of wax and feathers
   (D) on a kite
   (E) on a steam-powered, wooden bird

25. The first paragraph of the second passage primarily serves to

   (A) refute an argument presented in the first passage.
   (B) describe the background of an important figure.
   (C) state the main ideas of the passage.
   (D) provide an interpretation of a historical event that will be contradicted by the rest of the passage.
   (E) compare two kinds of hot-air balloon.

26. Based on the description of "the hydrogen balloon" (line 60), one can infer that the balloon

   (A) required only two men to operate it.
   (B) was used to carry armed soldiers behind enemy lines.
   (C) was meant to fly toward the enemy troops and back during a battle.
   (D) flew so high that those on the ground could not hear the balloonists.
   (E) was not susceptible to enemy fire.

27. According to the second passage, the reaction of the Austrians to the French balloon corps was one of

   (A) fear and anger.
   (B) pride and respect.
   (C) awe and surrender.
   (D) scorn and laughter.
   (E) sadness and resignation.

28. The history of the Aérostiers under Napoleon can best be classified as

   (A) an unmitigated failure.
   (B) a brief period of success.
   (C) a long series of failed attempts culminating in a spectacular victory.
   (D) the beginning of a program that would last for centuries.
   (E) the most important military development of the era.

C2 education
be smarter.

Unauthorized copying or reuse of any part of this page is illegal.

Version 1.3

29. Both passages specifically discuss which of the following military uses for aircraft?

    (A) to aid with reconnaissance in battle
    (B) to help soldiers escape from oncoming forces
    (C) to frighten enemy troops
    (D) to carry bombs
    (E) to provide a better position to fire at the enemy

30. Which of the following best describes the relationship between the structures of the two passages?

    (A) Whereas Passage 1 discusses only wing-powered flight, Passage 2 details several types of flying machine.
    (B) Both passages use humorous stories to counteract tales of failed flights.
    (C) While Passage 1 is structured chronologically, Passage 2 is not.
    (D) Both passages begin by discussing myths relating to flight before moving on to their primary subjects.
    (E) Whereas Passage 1 describes a series of events throughout history, Passage 2 primarily focuses on one development.

31. The tone of both passages can best be described as

    (A) objective.
    (B) poignant.
    (C) contemptuous.
    (D) humorous.
    (E) laudatory.

Homework Passage 4 (Long)

This excerpt examines some of the problems with the American secondary education system.

Internationally, U.S. youngsters hold their own at the elementary level but falter in the middle years and drop far behind in high school. We seem to be the only
Line country in the world whose children fall farther behind
(5) the longer they stay in school. That is true of our advanced students and our so-called good schools, as well as those in the middle. Remediation is rampant in college, with some 30% of entering freshmen in need of remedial courses in reading, writing and mathematics.
(10) Employers report difficulty in finding employees who have the skills, knowledge, habits, and attitudes they require for technologically sophisticated positions. Though the pay they offer is excellent, the supply of competent U.S.-educated workers is too meager to fill the
(15) available jobs.

In the midst of our flourishing economy, we are re-creating a dual school system, separate and unequal, almost half a century after it was declared unconstitutional. We face a widening and unacceptable
(20) chasm between good schools and bad, between those youngsters who get an adequate education and those who emerge from school barely able to read and write. Poor and minority children usually go to worse schools, have less expected of them, are taught by less knowledgeable
(25) teachers, and have the least power to alter bad situations.

If we continue to sustain this chasm between the educational haves and have-nots, our nation will face cultural, moral, and civic peril. During the past 30 years, we have witnessed a cheapening and coarsening of many
(30) facets of our lives. We see it, among other places, in the squalid fare on television and in the movies. Obviously the school is not primarily responsible for this degradation of culture. But we should be able to rely on our schools to counter the worst aspects of popular
(35) culture, to fortify students with standards, judgment and character.

Regrettably, some educators and commentators have responded to the persistence of mediocre performance by engaging in denial, self-delusion, and blame-shifting.
(40) Instead of acknowledging that there are real and urgent problems, they deny that there are any problems at all. Broad hints are dropped that, if there is a problem, it's confined to other people's children in other communities. Then, of course, there is the fantasy that America's
(45) education crisis is a fraud, something invented by enemies of public schools. And there is the worrisome conviction of millions of parents that, whatever may be ailing U.S. education in general, "my kid's school is OK."
Now is no time for complacency. Such illusions and
(50) denials endanger the nation's future and the future of today's children. Good education has become absolutely indispensable for economic success, both for individuals and for American society. Good education is the great equalizer of American society. Horace Mann termed it
(55) the "balance wheel of the social machinery," and that is

Version 1.3

Unauthorized copying or reuse of any part of this page is illegal.

even more valid now. As we become more of a meritocracy, the quality of one's education matters more. That creates both unprecedented opportunities for those who once would have found the door barred and huge
(60) new hurdles for those burdened by inferior education. America today faces a profound test of its commitment to equal educational opportunity. This is a test of whether we truly intend to educate all our children or merely keep everyone in school for a certain number of years; of
(65) whether we will settle for low levels of performance by most youngsters and excellence from only an elite few.

32. "Employers" (line 10) face which of the following problems, according to the passage?

(A) insufficient funds to hire new employees
(B) an economy in a recession
(C) a lack of well-educated workers
(D) too much denial and self-delusion
(E) an excessive number of qualified applicants for each available position

33. Which of the following is NOT a problem faced by "Poor and minority children" (lines 22-23)?

(A) They are unable to escape their unfortunate circumstances.
(B) Separate and unequal schools have been ruled to be constitutional.
(C) Their teachers are not skilled enough.
(D) They are not expected to achieve excellent academic results.
(E) They attend schools that are poorly equipped.

34. According to the author, how can education be used to combat "cultural, moral, and civic peril" (line 28)?

(A) by acknowledging that America's education crisis is a fraud
(B) by imbuing students with greater moral character
(C) by teaching children to be subservient
(D) by keeping children in school until they turn 18
(E) by providing a greater knowledge of mathematics

35. The fourth paragraph (lines 37-48) is primarily at attack on which problem, as seen by the author?

(A) the over-reliance on remedial college courses
(B) the refusal to admit the extent of the educational system's problems
(C) the contempt that other countries have for the United States' secondary education.
(D) the desire to re-segregate schools along economic lines
(E) the degradation of popular culture

36. What is the meaning of the quote from Horace Mann in line 55?

(A) Good education ensures that everyone has an equal chance at success in life.
(B) The importance of education is often overstated.
(C) Education helps turn rich people into poor people, and vice-versa.
(D) A separate, unequal school system is the best way to ensure that elite students get the best education.
(E) Without better technical education, there will not be enough engineers and mechanics.

37. The author's intent in writing the final paragraph was likely to

(A) convince readers of the dangers of not reforming the education system.
(B) summarize the main points of the passage.
(C) provide experimental data to support the main argument of the passage.
(D) refute an argument presented in an earlier paragraph.
(E) show that the dangers facing our nation's future are mostly just "illusions."

38. Which of the following words, as it is used in the passage, does NOT impart negative connotations?

(A) "chasm" (line 20)
(B) "cheapening" (line 29)
(C) "squalid" (line 31)
(D) "fantasy" (line 44)
(E) "equalizer" (line 54)

39. The tone of the passage can best be described as

(A) impartial.
(B) carefree.
(C) admiring.
(D) insistent.
(E) ironic.

Unauthorized copying or reuse of any part of this page is illegal.

Version 1.3

B16HW: Homework and Extra Practice

| **SC TOPIC:** Eliminating Answers (Lesson B14a) | **RC TOPIC:** Analysis Questions (Lesson B15b) |

Homework Set 1

1. Marylou had been expecting her boss to resist her demands for a raise and an increase in benefits, so she became somewhat ------ when he was completely ------ instead.

   (A) rabid . . unrelenting
   (B) bewildered . . digressive
   (C) jaded . . submissive
   (D) cognizant . . dissenting
   (E) astounded . . acquiescent

2. Animals' actions are often described in emotional terms, such as "my cat is so happy," but animals are not actually ------, at least not in the same way that humans are.

   (A) infallible
   (B) crass
   (C) sentient
   (D) aloof
   (E) indiscriminate

3. The twin siblings were so similar in appearance that no one but their parents was able to ------ the identity of one without the other being present as a comparison.

   (A) encumber
   (B) scorn
   (C) depreciate
   (D) discern
   (E) omit

4. Although there were once ------ apple varieties available throughout the United States, today only six types make up ninety percent of the apples sold.

   (A) singular
   (B) manifold
   (C) reclusive
   (D) compulsory
   (E) scanty

5. Although the guest speaker was quite ------ and his arguments were convincing, his attitude of total ------ toward the students left them feeling offended and alienated.

   (A) obtuse . . contempt
   (B) tedious . . aversion
   (C) poignant . . commendation
   (D) lucid . . exaltation
   (E) eloquent . . disdain

6. Despite the chaos of the earthquake, Ivan remained completely ------ and continued to eat his lunch as he did every other day.

   (A) flagrant
   (B) placid
   (C) perplexed
   (D) aroused
   (E) profuse

7. Washing your hands twenty times a day is usually ------; when working in a hospital, however, frequent hand-washing is ------ to prevent the spread of disease.

   (A) gratuitous . . imperative
   (B) requisite . . superfluous
   (C) redundant . . frivolous
   (D) dogmatic . . crucial
   (E) feasible . . contingent

8. Not only was the man ------ the officer's warning to be quiet, he in fact seemed to be ------ by it, as he turned up the volume on his stereo to its highest setting.

   (A) fastidious about . . roused
   (B) deferent to . . incited
   (C) heedless to . . afflicted
   (D) undaunted by . . goaded on
   (E) intimidated by . . invigorated

Homework Set 2

9. Knowing that the project would be a lengthy and ------ one, Penny sought to ------ it by eliminating some of the most difficult and time-consuming tasks.

    (A) onerous . . hinder
    (B) trifling . . ameliorate
    (C) grueling . . exacerbate
    (D) manifest . . thwart
    (E) arduous . . expedite

10. As he read the book, Bob was so ------ that he did not notice that his phone was ringing.

    (A) rapt
    (B) spurious
    (C) naïve
    (D) detrimental
    (E) fickle

11. Claire has been ------ her family for the last five years; she has still not forgiven them for disapproving of her marriage.

    (A) estranged from
    (B) enlisted in
    (C) aggregated by
    (D) immersed in
    (E) coalesced by

12. Rather than take his demotion with grace and good humor, Marcellus reacted with ------, screaming about the unfairness of the situation.

    (A) indignation
    (B) terseness
    (C) penance
    (D) magnanimity
    (E) seclusion

13. The rainy weather did not ------ Wendy's ------ for the concert; she would have sat through a tornado to see her favorite singer perform.

    (A) wane . . ambivalence
    (B) diminish . . zeal
    (C) instigate . . fervor
    (D) subside . . apathy
    (E) exonerate . . keenness

14. Though he never made a lot of money in one year, Jose ------ wealth slowly and was able to retire as a millionaire.

    (A) placated
    (B) detracted
    (C) accrued
    (D) allured
    (E) ceded

15. The ------ furnished apartment did not have enough chairs to seat everyone at the party, so several people had to remain standing.

    (A) astutely
    (B) profusely
    (C) austerely
    (D) ornately
    (E) morosely

16. Tim was ------ to go to work today, but he went anyway because he needed the money.

    (A) portentous
    (B) disinclined
    (C) immaculate
    (D) callous
    (E) deplorable

Homework Passage 1 (Short Paired)

Passage 1:

Consider the sentence "You have a green light." What does this sentence mean? Depending on the context, it could mean several different things. For
Line instance, it could mean that you are holding a green light
(5) bulb; alternatively, it could mean that you are driving and the traffic light in front of you is green. Or, it could be metaphorical: "you now have approval to do something." In a less likely scenario, it could even mean that your body is glowing green.
(10) This example describes a phenomenon known as "structural ambiguity." In linguistics (the study of how languages work), structural ambiguity is used to argue that most language does not have inherent meaning. Rather, it depends on the context of the speaker and the
(15) listener. This remarkable flexibility of language is a testament to the linguistic powers of the human brain.

Passage 2:

At first glance, the languages of the world seem to be quite diverse. And indeed, no two languages share the
Line same structures or conventions. Focusing on the
(20) differences between languages, however, is not as enlightening as focusing on the similarities. According to the followers of *generative linguistics*, certain aspects of language are innate—that is, they are genetically encoded into all humans at birth. Generative linguists examine the
(25) structures of different languages to determine which aspects are universal to all human languages.
One example of this universal grammar is that all known languages distinguish between nouns and verbs. Another is that all languages distinguish between lexical
(30) words (which carry the meaning of a sentence, i.e. nouns, main verbs, adjectives, and most adverbs) and function words (which identify the relationships between lexical words, i.e. prepositions, articles, and helper verbs). All human languages share these and other features.
(35) Presumably this is because the human brain is naturally inclined to make such distinctions.

17. The author of Passage 1 likely considers the concept of "structural ambiguity" (line 11) to be

(A) obvious but trivial.
(B) reasonable and practical.
(C) ultimately meaningless.
(D) dangerously flawed.
(E) plausible but unproven.

18. The two parenthesized passages in lines 30-33 of Passage 2 primarily serve to

(A) refute an argument made by generative linguists.
(B) provide examples of structural ambiguity.
(C) connect linguistics to an aspect of brain chemistry.
(D) show one way in which languages can differ.
(E) define terms that illustrate a contrast.

19. Both passages use which of the following techniques?

(A) unqualified and unjustified assertions
(B) examples that illustrate a technical concept
(C) satirical or ironic language
(D) quotations from authoritative sources
(E) extended metaphors

20. The authors of both passages would most likely agree that

(A) The meaning of all language depends on its context.
(B) Adjectives and adverbs are the source of most structural ambiguity.
(C) Linguists agree that genetics accounts for most characteristics of language.
(D) The human brain has impressive innate language abilities.
(E) Every known language uses metaphors.

Homework Passage 2 (Long)

This article defines the field of linguistics and describes some of the main areas of study within that field

Linguistics is the study of human language. Knowledge of linguistics, however, is different from knowledge of a language. Similar to how a person is able
Line to drive a car without understanding the inner workings
(5) of the engine, so, too, can a speaker use a language without any conscious knowledge of its internal structure. And conversely, a linguist can know and understand the internal structure of a language without being able to speak it.

(10) Formal linguistics is the study of grammar, or the development of theories as to how language works and is organized. Formal linguists compare grammars of different languages, and by identifying and studying the elements common among them, seek to discover the
(15) most efficient way to describe language in general. The ultimate goal of this process is a "universal grammar"— the development of a theory to explain how the human brain processes language. Within formal linguistics, there are three main schools of thought:

(20) The **traditional** approach to grammar is the one that is typically taught to schoolchildren. A typical definition in a traditional grammar is "A noun is a person, place, or thing." "Adjective clause," "noun clause," "complement," and "part of speech" are other familiar terms from
(25) traditional grammars.

Structural linguistics, a principally American phenomenon of the 1940's, was heavily influenced by the work of B.F. Skinner. Structuralists exclude meaning from the study of language, focusing instead on linguistic
(30) forms and their arrangement.

The **generative** approach to the description of language was introduced in 1957 with the publication of Noam Chomsky's *Syntactic Structures*. Generative approaches include meaning in the study of language,
(35) and look for patterned relationships between "deep" structures of meaning and "surface" structures of linguistic forms actually used by the speaker.

The following are the five principal areas of study within formal linguistics:

(40) **Phonetics** is the study of the sounds of language and their physical properties. Phonetics describes how speech sounds are produced by the vocal apparatus (the lungs, vocal cords, tongue, teeth, etc.) and provides a framework for their classification. Two practical
(45) applications of phonetics are speech synthesis, the reproduction by mechanical means of the sounds produced in human language; and speech recognition, the developing capacity of computers to comprehend spoken input.

(50) **Phonology** is concerned with the analysis and description of the meaningful sounds uttered in the production of human language, and how those sounds function in different languages. The letter "p," for example, can be pronounced in several different ways: an
(55) English speaker interprets these different pronunciations

as one sound, whereas a speaker of some other language might interpret the pronunciations as two or more sounds. It is phonological analysis such as this that allows the foreign language teacher to pinpoint and
(60) correct students' pronunciation difficulties in the foreign language classroom.

Morphology is the study of the structure of words. Morphologists study minimal meaning units, or morphemes, and investigate the possible combinations of
(65) these units in a language to form words. For example, the word "imperfections" is composed of four morphemes: *im | perfect | ion | s*. The root, "*perfect*," is transformed from an adjective into a noun by the addition of "*ion*," made negative with "*im*" and pluralized by "*s*."

(70) **Syntax** is the study of the structure of sentences. Syntacticians describe how words combine into phrases and clauses and how these combine to form sentences. For example, "I found a coin yesterday" is embedded as a relative clause in "The coin, which I found yesterday, is
(75) quite valuable." Syntacticians describe the rules for converting the first sentence into the second.

Semantics is the study of meaning in language. The goal of semantic study is to explain how sequences of language are matched with their proper meanings and
(80) placed in certain environments by speakers of the language. A demonstration of the importance of meaning to the grammar of a language is the following well-known example from Chomsky: "Colorless green ideas sleep furiously." This is a grammatical sentence; but
(85) because semantic components have been ignored, it is meaningless in ordinary usage.

21. Which of the following best describes the structure of the passage?

   (A) a chronological history of an area of study
   (B) a comparison between two prominent approaches to a subject
   (C) a persuasive essay with an introduction, evidence, and conclusion
   (D) a broad description of a subject followed by specific information about many aspects of the subject
   (E) a refutation of incorrect principles followed by a statement of more valid ones

22. The description of the "person" driving a "car" in the first paragraph is an example of

   (A) metaphor.
   (B) alliteration.
   (C) paradox.
   (D) personification.
   (E) allusion.

Unauthorized copying or reuse of any part of this page is illegal.

Version 1.3

23. According to the passage, what is the goal of formal linguistics?

    (A) to analyze the sounds made in various languages
    (B) to compose sentences that are grammatical but meaningless
    (C) to understand the universal characteristics of language
    (D) to break down words into the meanings of their individual parts
    (E) to teach schoolchildren the structure of language

24. What is the primary distinction between structural linguistics and generative linguistics?

    (A) Structural linguistics is taught to schoolchildren.
    (B) Structural linguistics is far more concerned with phonology than phonetics.
    (C) Generative linguistics is an older approach.
    (D) Structural linguists must be able to speak the languages that they study.
    (E) Generative linguistics considers the meaning as well as the structure of language.

25. The attitude of the author toward the three main approaches to linguistics can best be described as

    (A) biased toward structural linguistics.
    (B) biased toward generative linguistics.
    (C) critical of all three approaches.
    (D) favoring a new, fourth approach.
    (E) completely impartial.

26. Which of the following statements is most likely related to the study of phonetics?

    (A) The letter "c" can be pronounced in several ways depending on its language and context.
    (B) The sentence "My friend, who turned 30 yesterday, had a party." contains a relative clause.
    (C) There are three units of meaning in the word "undesirable": *un*, *desire*, and *able*.
    (D) To make the "m" sound, speakers must press their lips together and use their throat to make a humming sound.
    (E) The sentence "Endless minutes sprint slowly to their end." has correct grammar but no meaning.

27. The passage implies that the study of phonology differs in what way from the study of phonetics?

    (A) Phonology is more concerned with how sounds are interpreted than how they are vocalized.
    (B) Phonology describes the functions of the anatomy in producing speech.
    (C) Phonology discusses the grammatical effects of various words.
    (D) Phonology has more practical uses than phonetics does.
    (E) Phonetics relies on a traditional approach, whereas phonology prefers a structural approach.

28. How does a morphologist analyze words, according to the passage?

    (A) by breaking them up into sound-based parts, such as syllables
    (B) by breaking them up into parts based on the meaning of those parts
    (C) by considering how they combine to form sentences
    (D) by considering the different pronunciations a word can have in different dialects
    (E) by analyzing the grammatical functions of words

29. A semantician might criticize a syntactician for ignoring what aspect of grammar?

    (A) the ways that the lips and tongue are used to form words
    (B) the ways phrases and clauses are combined to form grammatical sentences
    (C) the ways in which words are combined to create meaning
    (D) the meanings of the individual parts of words
    (E) the different pronunciations of certain letters in different languages

30. Which of the following would make the best title for the passage?

    (A) The Case for the Generative Approach
    (B) How Morphemes Form Words
    (C) An Overview of Linguistics
    (D) Colorless Green Ideas
    (E) The Life and Theories of Noam Chomsky

Version 1.3

Unauthorized copying or reuse of any part of this page is illegal.

Homework Passage 4 (Long)

In the following excerpt from a short story written in 1903, a young man and his father debate the talents and accomplishments of the father's dead friend, "old Pontifex."

My father's face would always brighten when old Pontifex's name was mentioned. "I tell you, Edward," he would say to me, "old Pontifex was not only an able man,
Line but he was one of the very ablest men that ever I knew."
(5)   This was more than I as a young man was prepared to stand. "My dear father," I answered, "what did he do? He could draw a little, but could he to save his life have gotten a picture into the Royal Academy exhibition? He built two organs and could play the minuet in *Samson* on
(10) one and the march in *Scipio* on the other; he was a good carpenter and a jokester; he was a good old fellow, but why make him out so much abler than he was?"

"My boy," returned my father, "you must not judge by the work, but by the work in connection with the
(15) surroundings. Could Giotto or Filippo Lippi*, think you, have gotten a picture into the Exhibition? Would a single one of those frescoes we went to see when we were at Padua have the remotest chance of being hung, if it were sent in for exhibition now? Why, the Academy people
(20) would be so outraged that they would not even write to poor Giotto to tell him to come and take his fresco away. Phew!" continued he, waxing warm, "if old Pontifex had had Cromwell's** chances he would have done all that Cromwell did, and have done it better; if he had had
(25) Giotto's chances he would have done all that Giotto did, and done it no worse; as it was, he was a village carpenter, and I will undertake to say he never did a lazy job in the whole course of his life."

"But," said I, "we cannot judge people with so many
(30) 'ifs.' If old Pontifex had lived in Giotto's time he might have been another Giotto, but he did not."

"I tell you, Edward," said my father with some severity, "we must not judge men not so much by what they do, as by what they make us feel that they have it in them
(35) to do. If a man has done enough either in painting, music or the affairs of life, to make me feel that I might trust him in an emergency, he has done enough. It is not by what a man has actually put upon his canvas, nor yet by the acts which he has set down, so to speak, upon the
(40) canvas of his life that I will judge him, but by what he makes me feel that he felt and aimed at. If he has made me feel that he felt those things to be loveable that I hold loveable myself, I ask no more; his grammar may have been imperfect, but still I have understood him; and I say
(45) again, Edward, that old Pontifex was not only an able man, but one of the very ablest men I ever knew."

Against this there was no more to be said, and my sisters eyed me to silence. Somehow or other my sisters always did eye me to silence when I differed from my
(50) father.

* Giotto, Filippo Lippi: famous Italian painters
** Cromwell: Oliver Cromwell, former ruler of England and leader of the English Civil War

31. The passage implies that, because the narrator is "a young man" (line 5), he is not very likely to be

(A) skilled at carpentry.
(B) skeptical of his father's stories.
(C) a member of the Royal Academy.
(D) tolerant of differing opinions.
(E) silenced by his sisters.

32. The narrator's father most likely mentions "Giotto" and "Filippo Lippi" (line 15) in order to

(A) claim that Giotto was a fair greater painter than was Lippi.
(B) identify the only two painters who are superior to Pontifex.
(C) point out two of Pontifex's artistic influences.
(D) provide evidence that further supports the narrator's position.
(E) demonstrate that the standards of the Royal Academy are not a fair measure of an artist's talent.

33. In the context of the passage, the word "waxing" (line 22) most nearly means

(A) gaining in emotion
(B) polishing
(C) increasing in size
(D) becoming illuminated
(E) removing hair

34. The passage implies that the narrator's sisters perform what role in the narrator's family?

(A) to instigate arguments for the sake of entertainment
(B) to end arguments before they become too heated
(C) to keep conversations flowing by asking interesting questions
(D) to side with the narrator against their father
(E) to verbally taunt the narrator into doing their bidding

education
be smarter.

Unauthorized copying or reuse of any part of this page is illegal.

Version 1.3

35. Which of the following words from the passage is used as a metaphor?

    (A) "surroundings" (line 15)
    (B) "fresco" (line 21)
    (C) "job" (line 28)
    (D) "canvas" (line 40)
    (E) "silence" (line 48)

36. Based on the descriptions in the passage, which of the following best describes old Pontifex?

    (A) unskilled and frivolous
    (B) wealthy and renowned
    (C) witty and hard-working
    (D) severe and uneducated
    (E) argumentative and unpleasant

37. In the passage, the main point of conflict between the narrator and his father is most nearly whether

    (A) old Pontifex was a good person or not.
    (B) sons should always show obedience to their fathers.
    (C) people should be judged based their accomplishments or on the goals that they have aimed for.
    (D) Giotto could have gotten a painting into the Royal Academy exhibition.
    (E) Oliver Cromwell was the greatest leader in England's history.

38. Which of the following best describes the attitude that the narrator's father holds toward old Pontifex?

    (A) skeptical.
    (B) indifferent.
    (C) laudatory.
    (D) stern.
    (E) contrary.

B17HW: Homework and Extra Practice

SC Topic: Vocab Strategies (Lesson B17a)	RC Topic: Analysis Questions (Lesson B14b)

Homework Set 1

1. The teacher noticed that Bruce's schoolwork was ------ and asked him why some of his essays were ------ and others were riddled with spelling and grammatical mistakes.

   (A) erratic . . inept
   (B) recurrent . . elaborate
   (C) monotonous . . pristine
   (D) vacillating . . immaculate
   (E) capricious . . latent

2. Despite his mother's soothing reassurances, the small child remained ------ about going to the dentist.

   (A) acquiescent
   (B) apprehensive
   (C) indubitable
   (D) estranged
   (E) provincial

3. Angie's friends trusted her unconditionally because they knew that she would always be ------ with their secrets.

   (A) cursory
   (B) brash
   (C) imprudent
   (D) remiss
   (E) discreet

4. Though traveling back in time is an intriguing possibility, it is not a plausible one because time is ------, always flowing in the same direction—into the future.

   (A) retrospective
   (B) outmoded
   (C) fickle
   (D) pedestrian
   (E) irreversible

5. After breaking his neighbor's window with a baseball, Hugh seemed genuinely ------ and offered to pay them $200 to help ------ the damage that he caused.

   (A) contrite . . mitigate
   (B) obstinate . . pervade
   (C) remorseful . . proffer
   (D) repentant . . exacerbate
   (E) sullen . . evade

6. The medication was intended to cure Soon-yi's headaches, but its ------ effects, such as nausea and rashes, outweighed its few benefits.

   (A) marginal
   (B) advantageous
   (C) adept
   (D) fortuitous
   (E) deleterious

7. The education expert ------ that all parents try to ------ a love of reading in their children, saying that children who read often become more successful adults than those who do not.

   (A) censured . . extricate
   (B) advocated . . foster
   (C) reproached . . deter
   (D) retracted . . cultivate
   (E) asserted . . avert

8. The reviewer denounced the book as ------, saying that the author had only appropriated well-worn ideas without adding any new or interesting ones.

   (A) obsequious
   (B) innovative
   (C) effusive
   (D) embellished
   (E) prosaic

Homework Set 2

9. Lana was one of the few people in the audience who possessed sufficient expertise to comprehend the ------ presentation.

   (A) esoteric
   (B) decorous
   (C) coherent
   (D) loquacious
   (E) vindictive

10. In an attempt to satisfy its ------ appetite, the blue whale ingests tremendous amounts of water, as well as the ------ marine organisms contained in that water.

   (A) voluminous . . monotonous
   (B) voracious . . manifold
   (C) dubious . . copious
   (D) ravenous . . scanty
   (E) miniscule . . obsolete

11. As a child, Giorgio considered cauliflower to be ------ food, but now that he is an adult, he actually has begun to enjoy it.

   (A) a singular
   (B) an unassailable
   (C) a repugnant
   (D) a laudatory
   (E) an auspicious

12. Samuel recognized that if he ------ his newfound wealth, he would risk offending those who had not been so fortunate, so he did not purchase any ostentatious cars or jewelry.

   (A) despised
   (B) flaunted
   (C) obliterated
   (D) alleviated
   (E) transpired

13. Brett's ------ personality prevented him from ever becoming too ------; no matter what adversities he faced, he was always smiling again before long.

   (A) malevolent . . fervent
   (B) morose . . dejected
   (C) jovial . . amiable
   (D) buoyant . . despondent
   (E) complacent . . aloof

14. Ms. Hurford was both wise and ------; she could enlighten a student more with a sentence than most teachers could with an essay.

   (A) wary
   (B) verbose
   (C) subservient
   (D) omnipresent
   (E) succinct

15. Though the forecast had called for thunderstorms, the weather remained ------ all day, with hardly any clouds and only a gentle breeze.

   (A) serene
   (B) audacious
   (C) turbulent
   (D) precarious
   (E) rapt

16. The proofreader was normally quite ------, but he did not correct two ------ errors in the last article he was assigned, and also missed numerous smaller mistakes.

   (A) diligent . . tenuous
   (B) negligent . . blatant
   (C) exacting . . indistinct
   (D) conscientious . . flagrant
   (E) intermittent . . inconspicuous

Homework Passage 1 (Short Paired)

Passage 1:

For nearly the entire history of art, all paintings, sculptures, and other art forms were representational; that is, they were meant to represent some object from the
Line real world. It was not until the 1920s that abstract art,
(5) which relies on shapes and colors rather than trying to depict a realistic figure, began to be seen as a legitimate pursuit in the art community. Prior to that, the cubist works of artists like Vincent van Gogh and Georges Braque began the transition by depicting real figures that
(10) were nonetheless wildly distorted from their actual appearance.

Probably the first major abstract painter was the Russian Wassily Kandinsky. Kandinsky, who was also a musician, saw each shape and color as representing
(15) sounds and deeper themes. For instance, a circle represented life and completeness, whereas bright yellow was analogous to a brash trumpet blast. His vibrant, complex paintings feature geometric figures that combine to create a unique feeling in the viewer, much as
(20) individual notes combine to create a chord in music.

Passage 2:

One of the most important painters in Mexican history, Frida Kahlo, utilized Mexican and Native American traditions to express her personal suffering and
Line loneliness. Her unique paintings, many of which are self-
(25) portraits, are often surrealist—that is, they depict real figures, but with certain aspects exaggerated or amplified. She used vivid colors to amplify the reality of the images. In her self-portraits, she is always dour and unsmiling, and is often surrounded by exotic or symbolic
(30) figures such as monkeys and birds.

The lack of joy shown in Kahlo's self-portraits was real; her life was turbulent and often filled with pain. As a child, she had polio, which left one of her legs shorter than the other. When she was 18, a bus that she was
(35) riding in collided with a trolley, causing severe injuries and breaking her spinal column as well as her ribs, pelvis, right leg, and collarbone. These injuries required 35 surgeries and continued to cause pain for the rest of her life. They also likely contributed to two miscarriages.
(40) Kahlo's marriage to the great muralist Diego Rivera was also a source of stress for her, as they feuded constantly.

17. The author of Passage 1 would most likely agree that Kandinsky's artwork

(A) was primarily completed before 1900.
(B) expresses his deep dissatisfaction with life.
(C) was heavily influenced by his interest in music.
(D) is less powerful because it does not depict real objects.
(E) is wrongfully classified as "abstract."

18. The second paragraph of Passage 2 (lines 31-41) primarily serves to

(A) criticize Diego Rivera for treating his wife poorly.
(B) use abstract themes to interpret an artist's work.
(C) use events from an artist's life to illuminate an aspect of her work.
(D) provide a brief history of art.
(E) explain a few of the symbolic elements of an artist's work.

19. The two passages indicate that "cubist" (line 7 of Passage 1) and "surrealist" (line 25 of Passage 2) artwork shares

(A) an exaggerated or distorted vision of reality.
(B) a disdain for representational art.
(C) an expression of profound pain.
(D) a belief that colors can represent sounds.
(E) a traditional perspective.

20. Both "Wassily Kandinsky" (line 13 of Passage 1) and "Frida Kahlo" (line 22 of Passage 2) emphasized which of the following in their paintings?

(A) symbolic animals
(B) complex geometric shapes
(C) personal suffering
(D) vivid colors
(E) surrealist figures

Unauthorized copying or reuse of any part of this page is illegal.

Version 1.3

Homework Passage 2 (Long)

The following article, written during the frigid winter of 2009-2010, explains how global warming and cold weather are not contradictory.

That feeling of numbness in your toes, even inside your thickest boots, is not lying to you. It's been very cold so far this winter in most of the U.S. and many
Line places at middle latitudes in the Northern Hemisphere.
(5) Washington, D.C., London and Seoul have already shoveled themselves out from major snowfalls. And over the course of 2009, average temperatures across some parts of the U.S. were cooler than the average temperature for a baseline period of 1951-1980.

(10) To many people's confusion, these weather events happened against a backdrop of increasing man-made greenhouse gas levels in the atmosphere that are gradually warming the planet. But scientists stress this weather does not mean that those gases are no longer
(15) exerting a warming influence. Nor does it go against the grain of basic global warming theory. Cold snaps and bouts of natural cooling that could last years are expected naturally even as the climate continues on a long-term warming trend, forced by man-made emissions.

(20) So, what has been going on out there these past few months? As for the Arctic winter weather, it is exactly that—Arctic. A pattern of high sea-level pressure over the Arctic has led to weaker westerly winds that typically pin cold air closer to the North pole. According to John
(25) M. Wallace, an atmospheric sciences professor at the University of Washington, the weakened jet stream has allowed cold Arctic air to creep into more southern latitudes over the U.S., Canada, Europe and Asia.

This pattern of pressure is called the "Arctic
(30) Oscillation." The oscillation comes in two phases: a "negative phase" where there is relatively high pressure over the North pole and low pressure at the mid-latitudes (at about 45 degrees North); and a "positive phase" in which this pressure system is reversed. This winter, the
(35) Arctic Oscillation has been in an extremely negative state. This has caused unseasonably cold air masses to sweep over what are normally temperate latitudes, and unusually mild air masses to be brought in over much of the Arctic itself, Wallace explained.

(40) "The unseasonable temperatures have been accompanied by well-above-normal sea-level pressure in the Arctic, especially over the Atlantic sector. That's how scientists characterize the Arctic Oscillation," Wallace said. "Winter isn't over yet, we're barely to the halfway
(45) mark. But this will be a winter to remember because of the Arctic Oscillation."

The bottom line is, I don't find it extraordinary," Wallace said. "With or without anthropogenic (man-made) warming, you're going to have big variations in
(50) these patterns."

The 2009 global temperature analysis released by NASA's Goddard Institute for Space Studies (GISS) shows that, globally, 2009 was tied for the second hottest year on record. This comes as news reports and blogs

(55) question whether global warming is even occurring, given local weather conditions and the fact that warming did not occur at the same rate in the past 10 years as it did during the '80s and '90s. But here is the key: While the rate of warming slowed, the decade ending Dec. 31,
(60) 2009 was also the warmest since accurate records began in 1880, according to GISS. And neither the basic chemistry and physics of global warming nor the continuing increase in man-made greenhouse gas emissions has changed.

(65) "Frequently heard fallacies are that 'global warming stopped in 1998,' or that 'the world has been getting cooler over the past decade,'" GISS director James Hansen wrote in a recent essay called "The Temperature of Science." "These statements appear to be wishful
(70) thinking—it would be nice if true, but that is not what the data show."

Hansen explains that the 5-year and 11-year temperature averages (the planet's annual average temperature, averaged over 5 or 11 years) are valuable
(75) because they place less emphasis on single-year variability. These running averages show a consistent rise in the Earth's temperature over the past 30 years. Further, if the El Niño effect (when unusually warm ocean temperatures occur in the tropical Pacific Ocean) is as
(80) strong in 2010 as expected, Hansen said there is a greater than 50 percent chance that it could be the warmest year in the period of instrumental data.

"The bottom line is this: there is no global cooling trend," Hansen wrote in his 2009 temperature analysis.
(85) "For the time being, until humanity brings its greenhouse gas emissions under control, we can expect each decade to be warmer than the preceding one."

21. What is the most likely function of the first sentence of the passage (lines 1-2, "That feeling… to you.")?

(A) It attracts the reader's attention by addressing his or her actual experiences.
(B) It distracts the reader from the actual topic of the passage.
(C) It provides experimental data that supports the essay's thesis statement.
(D) It directly states the main idea of the article.
(E) It provides important background information on a key debate.

Version 1.3

Unauthorized copying or reuse of any part of this page is illegal.

22. What is the meaning of the word "stress" (line 13) as it is used in the passage?

    (A) feel anxious
    (B) emphasize
    (C) test vigorously
    (D) read out loud
    (E) frustrate

23. According to evidence in the passage, what is the primary cause of the unseasonably cold weather of 2009?

    (A) Arctic air moving to lower-than-usual latitudes
    (B) man-made carbon emissions
    (C) a global cooling trend
    (D) below-normal sea-level pressure in the Arctic
    (E) the El Niño effect

24. What is the importance of the "Arctic Oscillation" (lines 29-30) in the global warming debate?

    (A) It casts doubt on the existence of man-made global warming.
    (B) It proves that 2010 will be colder than 2009.
    (C) It helps explain how localized cold weather can coexist with global temperature increases.
    (D) It has been proven to be a fallacy, like most other arguments against global warming.
    (E) It has caused a rift among scientists who argue if it will increase or decrease temperatures.

25. The passage implies that James Hansen has which of the following views regarding "fallacies" (line 65)?

    (A) They are deliberate lies spread by his rivals.
    (B) They are false, though the truth is less optimistic.
    (C) They overstate the dangers of global warming.
    (D) They are true, but they are based on the wrong data.
    (E) Despite common misconceptions, they are actually true.

26. According to Hansen, why are "5-year and 11-year temperature averages" (lines 72-73) the best measure of global warming?

    (A) The planet's temperature vacillates regularly over 5- and 11-year periods.
    (B) These temperature averages utilize fewer measurements.
    (C) Such averages are taken only during the warmest (summer) months.
    (D) Longer-term averages show no variation in temperature.
    (E) A longer time frame reduces the effects of random variation in yearly temperatures.

27. In the passage, the phrase "the bottom line" (line 47, line 83) is always used to indicate which of the following?

    (A) a remark that concludes the article
    (B) a contradictory statement
    (C) an example of data supporting an argument
    (D) an attack on a rival theory
    (E) a summary of an expert's opinions about an issue

28. Which of the following phrases, as used in the passage, is an example of figurative language?

    (A) "major snowfalls" (line 6)
    (B) "against the grain" (lines 15-16)
    (C) "weakened jet stream" (line 26)
    (D) "basic chemistry and physics" (lines 61-62)
    (E) "over the past 30 years" (line 77)

29. Based on the passage as a whole, what would the author's attitude likely be concerning a statement such as the one made in lines 66-67 ("the world … decade")?

    (A) admiring
    (B) apathetic
    (C) skeptical
    (D) nostalgic
    (E) contemptuous

30. Overall, the primary purpose of the passage is to

    (A) reconcile two seemingly contradictory facts.
    (B) explain how the Arctic Oscillation works.
    (C) argue that 2010 will be the warmest year on record.
    (D) convince readers that global warming no longer exists.
    (E) describe the many sources of man-made global warming.

Unauthorized copying or reuse of any part of this page is illegal.

Version 1.3

Homework Passage 4 (Long)

The following is an excerpt from the classic tale of survival in the Alaskan wilderness, White Fang, *by Jack London.*

A vast silence reigned over the land. The land itself was a desolation, lifeless, without movement, so lone and cold that the spirit of it was not even that of sadness.
Line There was a hint in it of laughter, but of a laughter more
(5) terrible than any sadness... It was the masterful and incommunicable wisdom of eternity laughing at the futility of life and the effort of life. It was the Wild, the savage, frozen-hearted Northland Wild.

But there *was* life, abroad in the land and defiant.
(10) Down the frozen waterway toiled a string of wolfish dogs. Their bristly fur was rimed with frost. Their breath froze in the air as it left their mouths, spouting forth in spumes of vapor that settled upon the hair of their bodies and formed into crystals of frost. A leather
(15) harness was on the dogs, and leather traces attached them to a sled, which dragged along behind...

On the sled, securely lashed, was a long and narrow oblong box. There were other things on the sled—blankets, an axe, a coffee-pot and frying-pan; but
(20) prominent, occupying most of the space, was the long and narrow oblong box.

In advance of the dogs, on wide snowshoes, toiled a man. At the rear of the sled toiled a second man. On the sled, in the box, lay a third man whose toil was over—a
(25) man whom the Wild had conquered and beaten down until he would never move nor struggle again. It is not the way of the Wild to like movement. Life is an offense to it, for life is movement; and the Wild aims always to destroy movement. It freezes the water to prevent it
(30) running to the sea; it drives the sap out of the trees till they are frozen to their mighty hearts; and most ferociously and terribly of all does the Wild harry and crush into submission man—man who is the most restless of life, ever in revolt against the dictum that all
(35) movement must in the end come to the cessation of movement.

But at front and rear, unawed and indomitable, toiled the two men who were not yet dead... They traveled on without speech, saving their breath for the work of their
(40) bodies. On every side was the silence, pressing upon them with a tangible presence...

An hour went by, and a second hour. The pale light of the short sunless day was beginning to fade, when a faint far cry arose on the still air. It soared upward with a
(45) swift rush, till it reached its topmost note, where it persisted, palpitating and tense, and then slowly died away. It might have been a lost soul wailing, had it not been invested with a certain sad fierceness and hungry eagerness. The front man turned his head until his eyes
(50) met the eyes of the man behind. And then, across the narrow oblong box, each nodded to the other.

A second cry arose, piercing the silence with needle-like shrillness. Both men located the sound. It was to the rear, somewhere in the snow expanse they had just
(55) traversed. A third and answering cry arose, also to the rear and to the left of the second cry.

"They're after us, Bill," said the man at the front.

His voice sounded hoarse and unreal, and he had spoken with apparent effort.
(60) "Meat is scarce," answered his comrade. "I ain't seen a rabbit sign for days."

Thereafter they spoke no more, though their ears were keen for the hunting-cries that continued to rise behind them.

31. The last sentence of the first paragraph ("It was ... Northland Wild.") is an example of

(A) personification.
(B) simile.
(C) paradox.
(D) irony.
(E) alliteration.

32. Why are the "wolfish dogs" (lines 10-11) in the woods?

(A) They are helping two men on a hunt.
(B) They are searching for some lost men.
(C) They are in a race.
(D) They are pulling a sled.
(E) They are wild dogs looking for food.

33. The passage implies that the "third man" (line 24) is

(A) retired.
(B) handicapped.
(C) resting.
(D) dead.
(E) a statue.

34. Throughout the passage, "the Wild" is portrayed as being

(A) opposed to life and movement.
(B) fearful and gentle.
(C) restless and energetic.
(D) submissive to mankind.
(E) lush and full of life.

35. The passage implies that the men are silent mainly because

(A) they are angry with each other.
(B) they communicate using sign language.
(C) they are conserving energy by not speaking.
(D) they are sad because their friend has died.
(E) they are listening to the sounds of the sled dogs.

36. The passage implies that "the sound" (line 53) is that of

(A) the men's stomachs growling with hunger.
(B) rabbits running through the trees.
(C) the men's sled dogs.
(D) other men, far away in the forest.
(E) animals that are hunting the two men.

37. The author likely includes no dialogue in the first eight paragraphs of the passage in order to

(A) show that the main characters can no longer speak.
(B) put the main focus of the passage on the sled dogs.
(C) imply that the characters can communicate using their minds.
(D) foreshadow that the two men will lose their ability to speak.
(E) heighten the feeling of silence and isolation described in the passage.

38. The tone of the passage is predominantly

(A) jovial.
(B) ironic.
(C) affectionate.
(D) irate.
(E) ominous.

B18HW: Homework and Extra Practice

| **SC Topic**: Vocab Strategies (Lesson B17a) | **RC Topic**: EXCEPT Questions (Lesson B18b) |

Homework Set 1

1. The actress' career got off to ------ start when she had small roles in several hit films, but it did not reach its ------ until twenty years later, when she won a major acting award.

   (A) an auspicious . . apex
   (B) a portentous . . adversity
   (C) a dismal . . summit
   (D) a precarious . . oblivion
   (E) a fortuitous . . delusion

2. The astronomer conceded that the meteor could potentially collide with the Earth, but emphasized that there was little to fear because its chances of doing so were extremely ------.

   (A) remote
   (B) credulous
   (C) equitable
   (D) predisposed
   (E) recurrent

3. Despite the book's ------, meandering prose, it is worth reading, particularly due to the author's ------ use of the fascinating and well-drawn characters.

   (A) coherent . . proficient
   (B) haphazard . . adept
   (C) systematic . . deplorable
   (D) fickle . . fastidious
   (E) wayward . . resolute

4. Aside from price, there was no ------ difference between the two phone plans, so Ines signed up for the cheaper one.

   (A) preposterous
   (B) negligible
   (C) discernible
   (D) infallible
   (E) spurious

5. With a ------ sneer and a dismissive hand gesture, Franz told the maintenance workers to get out of his way.

   (A) contented
   (B) reverent
   (C) ardent
   (D) derisive
   (E) buoyant

6. The judge quickly dismissed the lawsuit, saying that it was ------ to sue someone because he ate a few of your cookies.

   (A) frivolous
   (B) solemn
   (C) astute
   (D) commendable
   (E) serene

7. Recent studies have shown that intelligence is neither fully ------ nor ------; rather, it is affected by one's environment and can change throughout one's life.

   (A) alluring . . pliable
   (B) innate . . immutable
   (C) inherent . . capricious
   (D) marginal . . perpetual
   (E) superficial . . abiding

8. The sportswriter's ------ output included a daily column, a weekly, in-depth interview, and at least one book a year.

   (A) scanty
   (B) remiss
   (C) disinterested
   (D) prolific
   (E) prosaic

Homework Set 2

9. The ------ of Yong's job, which consisted of staring at a featureless landscape for hours on end, was ------ only by the occasional thunderstorm or wild animal sighting.

(A) sentience . . aggregated
(B) revelry . . waned
(C) tedium . . alleviated
(D) monotony . . exacerbated
(E) vitality . . exalted

10. Science-fiction writers of the 1950s predicted that flying cars would be ------ by the early 21st century, but today they are no more common than creatures from Mars.

(A) ascetic
(B) elusive
(C) itinerant
(D) obsequious
(E) ubiquitous

11. No independent study was able to ------ the claims made by the controversial chemist, thus casting doubt on the ------ of the chemist's other observations.

(A) denounce . . resilience
(B) contradict . . zeal
(C) corroborate . . implausibility
(D) refute . . credibility
(E) validate . . veracity

12. The poem ------ feelings of peacefulness and isolation, making one feel as if one is actually experiencing the author's trip to the deserted island.

(A) evokes
(B) evades
(C) perplexes
(D) impedes
(E) averts

13. The failing grade that Glenda received on her first calculus test proved to be ------, for she received nothing but stellar marks the rest of the term.

(A) a premonition
(B) an elaboration
(C) a contrition
(D) an aberration
(E) an acquiescence

14. The conspirators gathered ------ in a secluded cave so as to avoid the notice of the authorities that they were plotting against.

(A) naïvely
(B) callously
(C) clandestinely
(D) brashly
(E) redundantly

15. Brad demanded that all of his employees obey him at all times and ------ any who displayed ------ or otherwise disrespectful behavior.

(A) fostered . . compulsory
(B) reprimanded . . venerable
(C) exonerated . . docile
(D) extolled . . audacious
(E) reproached . . insolent

16. Though she had not yet realized it at that age, the 6-year-old Mary Cassatt possessed ------ abilities that would allow her to become a skillful painter.

(A) overt
(B) indiscreet
(C) omnipresent
(D) superfluous
(E) latent

Unauthorized copying or reuse of any part of this page is illegal.

Version 1.3

Homework Passage 1 (Short)

The university of the twenty-first century is already evolving. Such universities are both local, rooted in their regional communities, and global in the scope of their
Line networks of intellectual contact. The twenty-first-century
(5) university is much more an intellectual space, underpinned by instructional technologies, values, ideas, revenue flows, and sociopolitical legitimacy than a physical space with a specific set of buildings. In any case, institutional and individual branding in which
(10) desirable features are promoted, generated, evaluated, and enhanced over time will become essential. Most universities will identify competitive niches and continually reinvent themselves to meet the changing needs of their constituents.

17. The passages indicates that modern universities are "already evolving" (lines 1-2) in all of the following ways EXCEPT

   (A) broadening the scope of their intellectual connections.
   (B) placing a greater emphasis on a physical location.
   (C) highlighting ideals and knowledge.
   (D) creating a public image that represents each school's distinctive attributes.
   (E) changing to meet demands from their students.

18. Which of the following statements best summarizes the main idea of the passage?

   (A) Universities are becoming obsolete in the modern world.
   (B) A university should ultimately be measured by its revenue flow, not its education.
   (C) The university of the future will have no buildings, and all its classes will be conducted online.
   (D) Universities are beginning to change the ways in which they identify themselves.
   (E) Students should demand that their universities be more responsive to their desires.

Homework Passage 2 (Short)

The art of the Renaissance reached its greatest excellence during the last three decades of the fifteenth and the first half of the sixteenth century. This was a
Line glorious period in the history of art. The barbarism of the
(5) Middle Ages was essentially a thing of the past, but much barbaric splendor in the celebration of ceremonies and festivals still remained to satisfy the artistic sense, while every-day costumes and customs lent a charming quality to ordinary life. As much of the pagan spirit as
(10) yet endured was modified by the spirit of the Renaissance. The result was a new order of things especially favorable to painting.

An artist now felt himself as free to illustrate the pagan myths as to represent the events in the lives of
(15) Jesus, the Virgin and the saints, and the actors in the sacred subjects were represented with the same beauty and grace of form as were given the heroes and heroines of Hellenic legend. St. Sebastian was as beautiful as Apollo, and the imagination and senses were moved alike
(20) by pictures of Danae (a Greek goddess) and Mary Magdalene—the two subjects being often the work of the same artist.

19. According to the passage, the Renaissance was a "glorious period" (line 4) in large part because

   (A) it combined the best elements of pagan and religious traditions.
   (B) scientists were revolutionizing the way that people thought about the world.
   (C) most art venerated Jesus and other Christian figures.
   (D) advances in medicine improved people's quality of life markedly.
   (E) the pagan spirit of the Middle Ages was completely eliminated.

20. The author of the passage would most likely agree with all of the following statements EXCEPT

   (A) The culture of the late fifteenth century enhanced the paintings made in that period.
   (B) Even the everyday lives of ordinary people benefited from Renaissance customs.
   (C) Renaissance artists often painted both pagan and Christian figures.
   (D) Some trappings of pagan religions remained even after the religions themselves faded from popularity.
   (E) In the Middle Ages, religious figures were represented similarly to ancient Greek figures.

Homework Passage 3 (Long)

This passage describes how children acquire language from birth to the time they enter school.

The process of language acquisition for young children is built upon a variety of experiences.

Crying is the earliest form of infant vocalization. But
Line after only a few weeks of experience with language,
(5) infants begin to vocalize in addition to crying: they coo. Cooing is repeating vowel-like sounds such as "oooooh" or "aaaaah." Infants coo when their parents or caregiver interact with them. At around 3 or 4 months, infants start to add consonant sounds to their cooing, and they begin
(10) to babble at between 4 and 6 months of age. Babbling consists of consonant and vowel sounds. Infants are able to combine these consonant and vowel sounds into syllable-like sequences, such as "mamama," "kaka," and "dadadada." Through interacting with parents or
(15) caregivers by such cooing and babbling, infants develop a sense of the role of language in communication by the end of the first year.

In the beginning of the second year, children's first words emerge. The first words are also called
(20) "holophrases" because children's productive vocabulary usually contains only one or two very simple words at a time, and they seem to utter single words to represent the whole meaning of an entire sentence. Children's first words are usually very different from adults' speech in
(25) terms of the pronunciation, and these first words are most frequently nominals—labels for objects, people, or events. In addition, children's first words are quite contextual. They may use a single word to identify something or somebody under different conditions (such
(30) as saying "ma" when seeing mother entering the room), to label objects linked to someone (saying "ma" when seeing mother's lipstick), or to express needs (saying "ma" and extending arms for wanting a hug from the mother). In the initial stage of the first-word utterance,
(35) children produce words slowly. However, once they have achieved a productive vocabulary of ten words, children begin to add new words at a faster rate, called "vocabulary spurt."

By their second birthday, children begin to combine
(40) words and to generate simple sentences. Initially, the first sentences are often two-word sentences, gradually evolving into longer ones. Children's first sentences have been called "telegraphic speech" because these sentences resemble the abbreviated language of a telegram. Like
(45) the telegram, children's first sentences contain mainly the essential content words, such as verbs and nouns, but omit the function words, such as articles, prepositions, and pronouns, auxiliary verbs.

Although children's first sentences seem to be
(50) ungrammatical in terms of adult standards, they are far more than strings of random words combined. Instead, they have a structure of their own. A characteristic of the structure is that some words, called "pivot words," are used in a mostly fixed position, and are combined with
(55) other less frequently used words referred to as "open

words," which can be easily replaced by other words. For example, a child may use "more" as a pivot word, and create sentences such as, "more cookie, "more car," and "more doggie."
(60) Creativity also plays an important role in this first sentence stage. Research has revealed that many of children's early sentences, such as "allgone cookie," and "more read" are creative statements that do not appear in adult speech. Like the first-word creation, context plays
(65) an important role in understanding children's first sentences because both require context in order that understanding can occur. As children's use of simple sentences increases, the amount of single-word use declines, and their sentences become increasingly
(70) elaborate and sophisticated.

By the time children are 3 1/2 to 4 years of age, they have already acquired many important skills in language learning. They have a fairly large working vocabulary and an understanding of the function of words in
(75) referring to things and actions. They also have a command of basic conversational skills, such as talking about a variety of topics with different audiences. Nevertheless, language development, especially vocabulary growth and conversational skills, continues. It
(80) is generally agreed that vocabulary learning is not accomplished through formal instruction. Instead, the meaning of new words is usually acquired when children interact with other more skilled language users during such natural situations as riding, eating, and playing.
(85) From these activities, children are able to construct hypotheses when hearing unfamiliar verbal strings. They then test these hypotheses by further observation or by making up new sentences themselves. Finally, through feedback and further exposure, children revise and
(90) confirm their hypotheses.

By the time children enter elementary school, their oral language is very similar to that of adults. They have acquired the basic syntactic, semantic, and pragmatic elements of their native language. Language
(95) development will continue, however, from early childhood through adolescence and into adulthood.

21. According to the information in the passage, which of the following is most likely to be an infant's first vocalization (other than crying)?

(A) "papa"
(B) "doggie"
(C) "aaaaaaah"
(D) "more read"
(E) "mmmmmmm"

Unauthorized copying or reuse of any part of this page is illegal.

Version 1.3

22. According to the passage, what is the difference between a cooing and babbling?

   (A) Cooing involves more than one word, while babbling consists of single words only.
   (B) Cooing is just a form of crying, but babbling is more complex.
   (C) Cooing uses only nominals, but babbling includes verbs as well.
   (D) Babbling involves vocalizations of multiple syllables, while cooing is usually just one syllable.
   (E) Babbling uses only consonant sounds; cooing uses only vowel sounds.

23. Which of the following statements does NOT apply to the speech of a one-year-old?

   (A) One-year-olds pronounce words very differently than adults do.
   (B) One-year-olds often use a word to mean different things in different contexts.
   (C) One-year-olds' first words are usually names for people and things.
   (D) One-year-olds rarely use more than one or two words at a time.
   (E) One-year-olds use verbs more than nouns.

24. All of the following are age-appropriate vocal expressions for a two-year-old EXCEPT

   (A) "go play."
   (B) "that there."
   (C) "give me."
   (D) "more kitty."
   (E) "no sleep."

25. A child's first sentences are likely to be all of the following EXCEPT

   (A) fairly short and simple.
   (B) ungrammatical.
   (C) dependent on context.
   (D) structured.
   (E) lacking in creativity.

26. As it is used in line 86, "strings" most nearly means

   (A) thin threads
   (B) fundamental parts of matter
   (C) musical instruments
   (D) sequences of words or sounds.
   (E) groups of people

27. In the seventh paragraph (lines 71-90), the author uses language reminiscent of which occupation to describe a child's process of acquiring new vocabulary?

   (A) scientist
   (B) teacher
   (C) musician
   (D) writer
   (E) athlete

28. The primary purpose of the passage is to

   (A) compare four-year-olds' language skills to those of adults.
   (B) explain the difference between "pivot words" and "open words."
   (C) tell parents how to increase their children's vocabularies.
   (D) outline the ways in which children acquire language at several different ages.
   (E) criticize a theory of language development that the author considers to be flawed.

29. The structure of the passage can best be described as a

   (A) list of important terms and their definitions.
   (B) comparison between two disparate concepts.
   (C) chronology of a child's language development.
   (D) statement of a theory's concepts followed by a critique of the theory.
   (E) lighthearted introductory anecdote followed by a serious explanation of a related issue.

30. The passage implies that a child's fastest period of vocabulary expansion occurs between the ages of

   (A) birth and 6 months.
   (B) 6 months and 1 year.
   (C) 1 year and 4 years.
   (D) 4 years and 7 years.
   (E) 7 years and 12 years

31. Which of the following factors does the passage identify as being critically important throughout a child's language development?

   (A) formal study of vocabulary
   (B) the use of "telegraphic speech"
   (C) vocal interaction with parents and peers
   (D) the formation of simple sentences
   (E) using a single word to identify many different things

Homework Passage 4 (Long)

The following excerpt explains how scientists estimate the age of the Earth and determine what it was like in past eras.

The Earth is very old—4.5 billion years or more—according to recent estimates. This vast span of time, called geologic time by earth scientists, is difficult to
Line comprehend in the familiar time units of months and
(5) years, or even centuries. How then do scientists reckon geologic time, and why do they believe the Earth is so old? A great part of the secret of the Earth's age is locked up in its rocks, and our centuries-old search for the key led to the beginning and nourished the growth of
(10) geologic science.

Mankind's speculations about the nature of the Earth inspired much of the lore and legend of early civilizations, but at times there were flashes of insight. The ancient historian Herodotus, in the 5th century B.C.,
(15) made one of the earliest recorded geological observations. After finding fossil shells far inland in what are now parts of Egypt and Libya, he correctly inferred that the Mediterranean Sea had once extended much farther to the south. Few believed him, however, nor did
(20) the idea catch on. In the 3rd century B.C., Eratosthenes depicted a spherical Earth and even calculated its diameter and circumference, but the concept of a spherical Earth was beyond the imagination of most men. Only 500 years ago, sailors aboard the *Santa*
(25) *Maria* begged Columbus to turn back lest they sail off the Earth's "edge." Similar opinions and prejudices about the nature and age of the Earth have waxed and waned through the centuries. Most people, however, appear to have traditionally believed the Earth to be quite young—
(30) that its age might be measured in terms of thousands of years, but certainly not in millions.

The evidence for an ancient Earth is concealed in the rocks that form the Earth's crust and surface. The rocks are not all the same age—or even nearly so—but, like the
(35) pages in a long and complicated history, they record the Earth-shaping events and life of the past. The record, however, is incomplete. Many pages, especially in the early parts, are missing and many others are tattered, torn, and difficult to decipher. But enough of the pages
(40) are preserved to reward the reader with accounts of astounding episodes that certify that the Earth is billions of years old.

Two scales are used to date these episodes and to measure the age of the Earth: a relative time scale, based
(45) on the sequence of layering of the rocks and the evolution of life, and the radiometric time scale, based on the natural radioactivity of chemical elements in some of the rocks. The relative scale highlights events in the growth of geologic science itself; the radiometric scale is
(50) a more recent development borrowed from the physical sciences and applied to geologic problems.

32. According to the author, why is geologic time "difficult to comprehend" (lines 3-4)?

(A) The units of time are far larger than the ones we typically use.
(B) Most people do not believe the Earth to be more than a few thousand years old.
(C) The process of measuring time radiometrically is very confusing.
(D) Even scientists cannot estimate the age of the Earth.
(E) Different measurements of the Earth's age often conflict strongly with each other.

33. In the context of the passage as a whole, what is the function of the second paragraph (lines 11-31)?

(A) to show how current evidence differs from predominant historical perceptions
(B) to provide supporting evidence for a claim made in the previous paragraph
(C) to criticize those who believed the Earth was not round
(D) to explain the author's preference for ancient scholarship over modern science
(E) to distract the reader from the main point of the essay

34. The author would likely agree with some of the geological conceptions of all of the following people EXCEPT

(A) "earth scientists" (line 3).
(B) "Herodotus" (line 14).
(C) "Eratosthenes" (line 20).
(D) "most men" (line 23).
(E) "Columbus" (line 25).

35. The author uses which of the following literary devices when describing the "evidence for an ancient Earth" (line 32)?

(A) metaphor
(B) allusion
(C) hyperbole
(D) sarcasm
(E) paradox

36. As it is used in the passage, "episodes" (line 41) most nearly means

(A) bouts of illness.
(B) television shows.
(C) parts of a narrative.
(D) digressions.
(E) important events.

Unauthorized copying or reuse of any part of this page is illegal.

Version 1.3

37. All of the following are factors that could be used in the "relative time scale" (line 44) EXCEPT

    (A) the thickness and composition of a rock layer.
    (B) the depth of a rock relative to other layers.
    (C) the amount in which a radioactive chemical in a rock has decayed over time.
    (D) the geographic area in which a fossil is found.
    (E) the evolutionary complexity of a fossil in relation to other similar fossils.

38. The author would likely classify the evidence in support of the Earth being billions of years old as

    (A) complete.
    (B) misleading.
    (C) convincing.
    (D) illusory.
    (E) mixed.

| SC Topic: Guessing and Review (Lesson B19a) | RC Topic: EXCEPT Questions (Lesson B18b) |

Homework Set 1

1. Many people sweat ------ when nervous or exposed to ------ heat, but an unlucky few experience excessive sweating even in normal conditions.

   (A) prolifically . . benign
   (B) profusely . . sweltering
   (C) scantily . . balmy
   (D) meagerly . . scorching
   (E) succinctly . . tepid

2. After suffering from a mysterious ------ for five years, Janie's condition was finally diagnosed and she was given medication to alleviate her symptoms.

   (A) benevolence
   (B) decorum
   (C) embellishment
   (D) apex
   (E) malady

3. Lenny would rather be thought of as interesting but inconsistent than be labeled as a constant but ------ sort.

   (A) wary
   (B) esoteric
   (C) eccentric
   (D) insipid
   (E) rapt

4. Mona's ------ efforts to complete her project ahead of schedule paid off when she received a bonus for her hard work.

   (A) assiduous
   (B) intermittent
   (C) detestable
   (D) lethargic
   (E) frivolous

5. After spending decades in prison for trying to end racial segregation in South Africa, Nelson Mandela was finally granted ------ in 1990 and released.

   (A) indignation
   (B) amnesty
   (C) implication
   (D) delegation
   (E) naïveté

6. Unused to such fervent ------, Holly blushed and thanked her newfound fans for their ------ support.

   (A) commendation . . dormant
   (B) adulation . . zealous
   (C) disdain . . obstinate
   (D) malice . . keen
   (E) reconciliation . . subdued

7. The landscape that surrounded the desert town was ------ a ------ one, though a small band of trees did relieve the barrenness somewhat.

   (A) tentatively . . lush
   (B) tacitly . . verdant
   (C) immutably . . pristine
   (D) predominantly . . stark
   (E) clandestinely . . desolate

8. Samir could not believe that he had been so ------ as to have missed the easiest question on the test.

   (A) adept
   (B) conscientious
   (C) cordial
   (D) obtuse
   (E) astute

Unauthorized copying or reuse of any part of this page is illegal.

Version 1.3

Homework Set 2

9. The counselor cautioned the parents not to reward ------ behavior and instead to try to ------ tantrums by modeling a calm and reasonable attitude for the child.

(A) sullen . . advocate
(B) insolent . . foster
(C) submissive . . circumvent
(D) petulant . . avert
(E) serene . . deter

10. The normally reserved singer was surprisingly ------ in her latest interview, admitting that even after ten years of performing she still sometimes got stage fright.

(A) covert
(B) bewildered
(C) candid
(D) digressive
(E) clandestine

11. Alfred was unable to ------ himself from the quicksand, but he remained calm until rescuers arrived to pull him out.

(A) obliterate
(B) extol
(C) extricate
(D) insinuate
(E) exonerate

12. In an effort to reduce teen driving fatalities, the state ------ that all teenagers must complete ----- defensive-driving course before receiving their drivers' licenses.

(A) mandated . . a compulsory
(B) reveled . . a requisite
(C) endorsed . . an outmoded
(D) protracted . . a gratuitous
(E) dictated . . a superfluous

13. After growing up destitute and living in a tiny, dirty ------, Orrin considered his modest but tidy apartment to be just as good as a mansion.

(A) citadel
(B) abyss
(C) felicity
(D) havoc
(E) hovel

14. The piano ------ gave his first concert at age 7 and composed his first symphony at age 13.

(A) sycophant
(B) benefactor
(C) prodigy
(D) oaf
(E) laggard

15. The peace talks quickly turned ------ when one of the diplomats angrily ------ the other side's dishonesty.

(A) vengeful . . lauded
(B) contentious . . acquiesced to
(C) ubiquitous . . reviled
(D) rancorous . . denounced
(E) amiable . . entrenched

16. Those who did not know Fred well often considered him to be stingy or uncaring, but his closest friends knew him to be both kind and ------.

(A) belligerent
(B) munificent
(C) reticent
(D) indifferent
(E) prominent

Homework Passage 1 (Short)

This passage, excerpted from Jane Austen's Sense and Sensibility, *describes the opinions of two older ladies regarding a young man named Edward Ferrars.*

Edward Ferrars was not recommended to their good opinion by any peculiar graces of person or address. He was not handsome, and his manners required intimacy to
Line make them pleasing. He was too diffident to do justice to
(5) himself; but when his natural shyness was overcome, his behaviour gave every indication of an open, affectionate heart. His understanding was good, and his education had given it solid improvement. But he was neither fitted by abilities nor disposition to answer the wishes of his
(10) mother and sister, who longed for him to make a fine figure in the world in some manner or other. His mother wished to interest him in political concerns, to get him into Parliament, or to see him connected with some of the great men of the day. Mrs. John Dashwood wished it
(15) likewise; but in the mean while, till one of these superior blessings could be attained, it would have quieted her ambition to see him driving a carriage for a gentleman. But Edward had no turn for great men or carriages. All his wishes centered in domestic comfort and the quiet of
(20) private life. Fortunately, he had a younger brother who was more promising.

17. In the context of line 18, "turn" most nearly means

    (A) rotation.
    (B) sudden shock.
    (C) inclination.
    (D) change of direction.
    (E) sickness.

18. All of the following are perceived flaws in Edward Ferrars' character EXCEPT

    (A) inadequate education.
    (B) moderate shyness.
    (C) lack of ambition.
    (D) mediocre social skills.
    (E) ordinary looks.

Homework Passage 2 (Short)

Most schoolchildren learn about the building blocks of the atom—the proton, the neutron, and the electron— at a relatively young age. These particles are not equally
Line fundamental, however. Physicists have discovered that
(5) two of these three particles, protons and neutrons, are each composed of smaller particles known as quarks. There are six different types—what physicists call "flavors"—of quarks that can combine to form dozens of varieties of particles, but only two quark flavors make up
(10) protons and neutrons. A proton is made up of two "up" quarks and one "down" quark, while a neutron is made up of two "down" quarks and one "up" quark. Up and down are the two most stable quark flavors, which explains why protons and neutrons are so common. The
(15) particles made up of other quark flavors are highly unstable and can only be created in labs. Consequently, scientists are just beginning to understand the possibilities and theoretical ramifications of various quark combinations.

19. The author most likely places quotes around the word "flavors" (line 7) in order to

    (A) dismiss the term as unsuitable.
    (B) emphasize that quarks can affect the sense of taste.
    (C) show that the word is part of a regional dialect.
    (D) signify that it is a technical term.
    (E) designate a direct quotation from a famous source.

20. The author of the passage would most likely characterize scientists' current knowledge of subatomic particles as

    (A) little better than it was 200 years ago.
    (B) largely worthless.
    (C) extraordinarily comprehensive.
    (D) based on faulty assumptions.
    (E) advanced but far from complete.

Homework Passage 3 (Long Paired)

These two passages describe different aspects of the day-to-day life of Americans living in small villages in the mountains of Nepal.

Passage 1:

I wake to chattering voices, a bus horn, bells ringing, an old man with a hacking cough, the squeak of a rusty latch opening across the hallway. A year ago, any of
Line these noises would have been a disturbance, but now the
(5) morning ensemble is simply a part of my day. I push open the flaps in the mosquito net and step out into my bedroom. I stretch my arms upward to the ceiling and exhale a bearish yawn. It's six in the morning.

Meanwhile, the village has been up for several
(10) hours. At the tea shop two floors below my bedroom window, rush hour has arrived. When I walk downstairs to the ground floor, the shop's four tables are packed with village men dipping *sell roti*, a doughnut-like pastry, into their milk tea. Some of the men draw long breaths of
(15) cigarette smoke as their conversation hammers away above the shop's buzzing commotion. A rice-filled pressure-cooker whistles, spouting white steam like a miniature locomotive while the adjacent pot sizzles to life with the aroma of onions and garlic.

(20) In front of the shop, I sit down on a wooden bench between Janak, a short, amiable teacher at the school where I taught English last year, and Hajurbaa, my 104-year-old host grandfather. From the inside of the shop behind me, I hear someone calling my Nepali name,
(25) "Hare Krishna!" Gita, the shopkeeper, smiles and stretches her hand beyond the counter to hand me a cup of tea. "Namaste!" she says, and then "Good morning!" With this English phrase she lets out an excited giggle in anticipation of my approval. Over the course of my year
(30) in the village, Gita has been learning bits of English and practicing with me, although we rarely get past "Hello…How are you…I'm fine" without her erupting into laughter. Gita is typical of many Nepali women in that she married young—in her case, when she was 14—
(35) and never attended school. Now 30, she gave birth to her son when she was 16 and her daughter at 18. For the past eight years, she's worked alongside her husband at the tea shop, which opens before dawn and closes after dark. Since I arrived last year, I've never seen her take a day
(40) off, nor have I ever heard her complain about it.

Next to me, Hajurbaa asks a question I strain to comprehend, although with Hajurbaa I'm typically able to guess what he's asking. Our conversations tend to be an exercise in stating the obvious. When he sees me
(45) drinking tea, he'll ask, "Are you drinking tea?" "Yes! I'm drinking tea," I'll respond. It's a tacit agreement that helps to bridge our extremely wide lingual, cultural, and generational gap. Today he's wearing a light-blue *dowra surwal*, the traditional dress for Nepali men,
(50) a knee-length lightweight robe and pants with a matching cap. While I might be laughed at if I were to wear a *dowra surwal*, Hajurbaa wears the clothing naturally and gracefully. "Where are you going today, Hajurbaa?"

I ask. I ask him this question every morning and always
(55) get the same response. "Going? I'm 104 years old! I'm not going anywhere. I'll stay here."

Around 8 in the morning, the business of village life slows as people retreat to their homes for their morning meal. The rituals and routine of village life—the work,
(60) the meals, even the conversation—are as unchanging as the seasons. The only thing that seems to be different here is me. But, after a year of living and working here, even I'm starting to fit in.

Passage 2:

Line One day last fall, my Nepalese friend Kumar invited
(65) me to have lunch at his family's home. I was sitting outside talking with Kumar when Kumar's wife rushed out of the kitchen onto the porch, a plume of black smoke following close behind her. She was coughing violently and her eyes were watering, stinging red from the smoke.
(70) I thought maybe the house was on fire.

"Is she all right?" I asked Kumar.

"She's just cooking lunch," he said.

Just cooking lunch? I ventured inside to see what was up. I expected to find an ox, or maybe a buffalo,
(75) roasting on a spit above wild flames, but all I found was a small pot of simmering vegetables, balanced on two adjacent chunks of clay above the kitchen floor. Below the pot, an assortment of small branches and sticks sizzled and cracked, emitting an acrid, black cloud of
(80) smoke that was quickly filling the cramped kitchen area. It was essentially an open fire in the middle of the house, without any real means of ventilation. The first floor of the house, which served as the kitchen and living room, and the living quarters for the family's three goats, had a
(85) total of one small window—about two feet by two feet— and the door to the porch outside, but these two portals didn't provide enough breathing room, given the suffocating cloud of smoke coming from the stove.

In the library a week later, I found research and
(90) information about projects detailing the harmful effects of traditional cooking methods in Nepal and ideas for building improved stoves within our villages. I learned, for example, about the laundry list of health hazards related to traditional stoves: bronchitis, emphysema, and
(95) conjunctivitis—a painful eye infection. Additionally, I discovered how the villagers' dependence on firewood is leading to the deforestation of Nepal's lush green hillsides.

One report detailed an "Improved Cook-Stove"
(100) project, which had taught more than 50 women in one community how to build an improved stove—one that would ventilate the smoke through a chimney—using only mud, bricks, cow dung, and iron rods. It was extremely important both that the materials were cheap
(105) and available locally, and that the women learned how to build the stoves themselves. After reading this report, I decided that the Improved Cook-Stove (ICS) program

was certainly something my village would benefit from.

(110) I enlisted the help of Shiva Raj, who had previously participated in ICS training and had built a stove in his home. When I met with Shiva Raj, I had the opportunity to see an operating improved cook-stove and was impressed with the drastic improvement over the traditional stove: much less smoke, less firewood

(115) required, and a much happier, healthier family at mealtimes. I was also impressed with Shiva Raj—his charisma and his knowledge about the stove. I asked him that day if he'd like to help me give ICS training in my village…

(120) Two months after the training, I went back to three of the homes to check up on the women. With great pride, each woman showed off her new stove and insisted I stay for a demonstration and a cup of tea. One of the women, Sita, had dropped out of school after 10th grade,

(125) but had emerged from our group as a very skilled, capable leader. Her mother seemed pleased with her daughter's new skill. "Our Sita is very smart," she told me. "She built this stove herself, and now there is no smoke in our house. No smoke!"

21. Which of the following would make the best title for Passage 1?

(A) How I Lived to Be 104
(B) Eight Years Without a Day Off
(C) Learning to Fit In
(D) The Noise of My Village
(E) Cooking Without Smoke

22. The statement in lines 3-5 of Passage 1 ("A year ago… my day.") is likely intended to show that

(A) the author has begun to feel at home in the village.
(B) a year ago, the author lived in an even noisier place.
(C) the village has become less noisy recently.
(D) the author now wears earplugs to bed.
(E) the author has become hearing impaired due to the excessive noise.

23. The "tea shop" (line 10) can best be described as

(A) orderly.
(B) expansive.
(C) inhospitable.
(D) chaotic.
(E) quiet.

24. "Gita, the shopkeeper" (line 25) can accurately be described as all of the following EXCEPT

(A) petulant.
(B) diligent.
(C) jovial.
(D) sociable.
(E) uneducated.

25. The conversations between the narrator of Passage 1 and Hajurbaa can be described as all of the following EXCEPT

(A) tentative.
(B) profound.
(C) repetitive.
(D) cross-cultural.
(E) friendly.

26. The narrator of Passage 2 asks the question, "Just cooking lunch?" (line 73) in order to

(A) make the reader think about food.
(B) express his confusion about a seemingly insufficient explanation.
(C) declare that it is too late in the day to be eating lunch.
(D) introduce a question that he will spend the rest of the passage discussing.
(E) let the reader know that he believes his friend is lying.

27. Which of the following is NOT a problem with the "traditional cooking methods in Nepal" (line 91)?

(A) the smoke from the cooking fire causes eye irritation and infections.
(B) the small cooking fire is not large enough to cook meals for a whole family.
(C) there is often insufficient ventilation, causing smoke to fill the home.
(D) breathing the cooking fire's smoke can lead to respiratory illnesses.
(E) the cooking fires use too much firewood, leading to deforestation.

28. All of the following were goals of the "'Improved Cook Stove' project" (lines 99-100) EXCEPT

(A) to teach women to build their own stoves.
(B) to build larger and more powerful stoves.
(C) to reduce the amount of wood used for cooking.
(D) to build stoves from cheap, local materials.
(E) to reduce the amount of smoke that villagers inhale.

Unauthorized copying or reuse of any part of this page is illegal.

Version 1.3

29. The primary purpose of Passage 2 is to

    (A) describe a few of the ways in which an outsider is becoming accustomed to his new home.
    (B) advocate for the implementation of the Improved Cook Stove program in the United States.
    (C) list the advantages of the traditional Nepali cooking method.
    (D) contrast life in America with life in Nepal.
    (E) detail the development of a beneficial program.

30. Compared to Passage 1, Passage 2 is more concerned with

    (A) the ways in which the narrator tries to help the villagers.
    (B) the daily routines of the village.
    (C) the food and drink that the villagers consume.
    (D) describing the personalities of the villagers.
    (E) highlighting the cultural differences between the narrator and the villagers.

31. Based on information from the two passages, how does Gita (Passage 1) differ from Sita (Passage 2)?

    (A) Gita is more of a natural leader than Sita is.
    (B) Sita is more friendly than Gita.
    (C) Sita has had more education than Gita.
    (D) Gita takes more pride in her accomplishments than Sita does.
    (E) Sita works longer hours each day than Gita does.

32. The authors of both passages make use of which of the following literary devices?

    (A) simile
    (B) personification
    (C) foreshadowing
    (D) hyperbole
    (E) onomatopoeia

33. The authors of both passages share what attitude toward the people of Nepal?

    (A) aloofness
    (B) disdain
    (C) disillusionment
    (D) admiration
    (E) bewilderment

Homework Passage 4 (Long)

This passage describes the history of legal cases related to the Fourth Amendment to the U.S. Constitution, which protects against unreasonable searches and seizures.

What is a search? What is a seizure?

What constitutes a search was clearly outlined in one of the earliest Fourth Amendment cases. Decided in
Line 1886, Boyd v. United States involved a federal customs
(5) statute that required businessmen (involved in importing goods) to choose between producing invoices and record books during a government inspection or having the imported goods confiscated by custom officials. Justice Joseph P. Bradley, delivering the opinion of the Court,
(10) struck down the customs statute and in doing so, widened the scope of the Fourth Amendment. He argued, "It is not the breaking of a man's doors and the rummaging of his drawers that constitutes the essence of the offense; but it is the invasion of his indefeasible right of personal
(15) security, personal liberty and private property, where that right has never been forfeited by his conviction of some public offense."

Justice Bradley's interpretation of the Fourth Amendment was reshaped by three technological
(20) developments that occurred during the later part of the 19th century. The telephone, the microphone, and instantaneous photography all created new ways to conduct searches and seizures. In light of these new inventions, the questions for the Court became whether
(25) or not the use of these devices constituted a search and, if they did, were the searches reasonable.

In the 1928 landmark case of Olmstead v. United States, the Court was given the opportunity to decide the constitutionality of wiretapping by the FBI. In a split
(30) decision, the Court ruled that a wiretap was not a search and seizure within the meaning of the Fourth Amendment, therefore, the FBI's actions were constitutional.

The Olmstead decision helped define the meaning
(35) and scope of the Fourth Amendment for the next forty years. However, in 1967 the Court decided Katz v. United States, in which it reversed the Olmstead decision. Katz had been convicted of illegal gambling based on evidence gathered using a wiretap placed in a
(40) public telephone booth. Conversations between Katz and his gambling associates were overheard and recorded by the FBI. Justice Stewart, writing for the majority, stated, "The Government's activities in electronically listening to and recording the petitioner's words violated the privacy
(45) upon which he justifiably relied while using the telephone booth and thus constituted a 'search and seizure' within the meaning of the Fourth Amendment." In Katz, the Court defined a "search" as any governmental intrusion into something in which a person
(50) has a reasonable expectation of privacy and "seizure" as taking into possession, custody, or control.

34. The two questions that start the passage primarily serve to

(A) force the reader to consider his or her opinions on a controversial subject.
(B) introduce the reader to an important historical figure.
(C) define the questions that the rest of the passage will discuss.
(D) convince the reader that the Fourth Amendment is important.
(E) cast doubt on the legitimacy of the Boyd v. United States decision.

35. How does the Olmstead v. United States decision differ from the other two cases discussed in the passage?

(A) It is the only case in which the limits of Fourth Amendment protection is expanded.
(B) Justice Bradley wrote the opinion for that case but not for the other cases.
(C) That case deals with wiretapping; the other two deal with customs searches.
(D) It is the only one of the three cases in which the Supreme Court ruled in favor of the government.
(E) The other cases were historic, but the Olmstead case is considered to be of only minor importance.

36. The passage implies that "Justice Joseph P. Bradley" (lines 8-9) would have reacted to the case of "Katz v. United States" (lines 36-37) by

(A) claiming that wiretapping is not a violation of the Fourth Amendment.
(B) taking offense that the Supreme Court does not use his definition of "search" and "seizure."
(C) preferring to retain the Olmstead v. United States decision rather than expand the Fourth Amendment.
(D) agreeing with the Supreme Court's decision.
(E) declaring that telephone booths can be legally wiretapped because they are in public.

37. All of the following actions, if performed by law enforcement without a warrant, would now likely be seen as a violation of the Fourth Amendment EXCEPT

(A) breaking into a person's house.
(B) tapping a person's telephone.
(C) placing microphones in a person's car.
(D) photographing a person through the window of his apartment.
(E) watching a person as she walks down a public street.

38. Based on information in the passage, it would be reasonable to conclude that, in the future,

(A) the Supreme Court will continue to refine the meaning of "search" and "seizure" in light of new technologies.
(B) the Fourth Amendment will be changed to only protect against seizures, but not searches.
(C) the Supreme Court will overrule the Katz v. United States decision.
(D) the FBI will never again violate a person's Fourth Amendment rights.
(E) the Fourth Amendment's protections will remain exactly as they currently are.

39. The author's tone when discussing the Supreme Court is one of

(A) unrestrained glee.
(B) ironic indifference.
(C) utter despair.
(D) respectful objectivity.
(E) justifiable anger.

Unauthorized copying or reuse of any part of this page is illegal.

Version 1.3

B20HW: Homework and Extra Practice

SC TOPIC: Guessing and Review (Lesson B18a)	RC TOPIC: EXCEPT Questions (Lesson B18b)

Homework Set 1

1. The speech, which praised the governor's policies, wisdom, personality, and good looks, was so ------ as to make the speaker seem like a mere ------.

   (A) adulatory . . sycophant
   (B) malevolent . . charlatan
   (C) rancorous . . toady
   (D) effusive . . cynic
   (E) spurious . . exemplar

2. Oliver's teachers loved how ------ he was in class, but his parents worried that he was too quiet, or even subservient.

   (A) docile
   (B) fervent
   (C) munificent
   (D) contrite
   (E) fickle

3. The ------ scholar was considered to be the foremost expert on Native American art forms.

   (A) eminent
   (B) defunct
   (C) frivolous
   (D) pedestrian
   (E) clandestine

4. Though some considered her way of thinking to be ------, Evita was actually quite willing to accept innovation; she was just well aware of the ------ facing new technology.

   (A) outmoded . . veracity
   (B) cursory . . hindrances
   (C) provincial . . impediments
   (D) scrupulous . . expediency
   (E) portentous . . efficaciousness

5. Once his sister threatened to have their parents ------ the dispute, Rico agreed to ------ one of the cookies in exchange for getting to keep the other one.

   (A) mediate . . adhere to
   (B) disdain . . salvage
   (C) omit . . cede
   (D) intervene in . . relinquish
   (E) meddle in . . elucidate

6. Ulysses turned down several ------ job offers because he valued other factors—especially the quality of the company—far more than he valued money.

   (A) lucrative
   (B) diminutive
   (C) dubious
   (D) arduous
   (E) stingy

7. When his parents caught him sneaking out of the house after his curfew, Yan braced himself for their ------; they were not angry, however, only worried.

   (A) commendation
   (B) amnesty
   (C) allure
   (D) apex
   (E) rebuke

8. When they realized that Katie was the originator of the malicious rumors, her friends ------ her from the group and refused to even look at her for a week.

   (A) accommodated
   (B) ameliorated
   (C) proffered
   (D) proliferated
   (E) ostracized

Homework Set 2

9. The kindergarten teacher greeted each day with ------, for she loved nothing more than teaching and interacting with young children.

    (A) despondence
    (B) apprehension
    (C) joviality
    (D) insolence
    (E) petulance

10. Though the judge ruled that the defendant's actions were technically not illegal, she did not ------ them, and even reprimanded the defendant for his unethical behavior.

    (A) censure
    (B) condone
    (C) corroborate
    (D) condemn
    (E) circumvent

11. Helga was a ------ but ------ movie reviewer; her articles were invariably only a few sentences long but packed with her acerbic wit.

    (A) belligerent . . verbose
    (B) monotonous . . esoteric
    (C) amiable . . loquacious
    (D) caustic . . terse
    (E) deferent . . succinct

12. ------ bargain-hunter, Liam would buy anything if it was on sale, even if he had absolutely no use for it.

    (A) A finicky
    (B) An indiscriminate
    (C) A decorous
    (D) A remiss
    (E) An insipid

13. The author uses such ------ language that even descriptions of ------ events, such as brushing one's teeth, grip the reader's attention.

    (A) scintillating . . mundane
    (B) obtuse . . prosaic
    (C) alluring . . extraordinary
    (D) provocative . . prominent
    (E) tedious . . plausible

14. The journalist was touched by Yusef's gift of $10,000 to the children's hospital and decided to write an editorial in which he ------ Yusef's ------ gesture.

    (A) reviled . . deleterious
    (B) exalted . . miserly
    (C) extolled . . magnanimous
    (D) lauded . . ravenous
    (E) chastised . . munificent

15. Knowing that even the slightest error could result in disaster, the surgeon ------ removed the cancerous tissue.

    (A) flagrantly
    (B) vindictively
    (C) painstakingly
    (D) sullenly
    (E) capriciously

16. Seemingly lacking the capacity for modesty, the millionaire athlete ------ his wealth by wearing gaudy jewelry, including a gold necklace that spelled out his name in diamonds.

    (A) reproached
    (B) obliterated
    (C) flaunted
    (D) deprecated
    (E) scorned

Homework Passage 1 (Short)

How far back in time do you have to go to find a person who is an ancestor of every person currently living on Earth? Perhaps not as far as you think.
Line Anthropologists have used genetics and other knowledge
(5) to estimate that the "Most Recent Common Ancestor" (MRCA) of all humans may have lived as recently as a few thousand years ago. This is true even though certain populations (such as Native Americans and Aboriginal Australians) were almost completely isolated from the
(10) rest of the world for more than ten thousand years, until European explorers "discovered" their lands. The theory is that the descendants of these isolated groups have all interbred with the descendants of groups from the rest of the world in the past few centuries.
(15) If you go back even further in time, you will reach the so-called "identical ancestors point." This is the point at which each living human was either the ancestor of *every* modern human or the ancestor of *no* modern humans. In other words, everyone alive today has the
(20) exact same group of living ancestors at the identical ancestors point. In this sense, we are all family—very distant cousins, perhaps, but family nonetheless.

17. The author uses all of the following techniques in the passage EXCEPT

(A) italics used for emphasis.
(B) a rhetorical question.
(C) quotation marks indicating sarcasm.
(D) an extended metaphor.
(E) definitions of technical terms.

18. Which of the following statements, if true, would most WEAKEN an argument made in the passage?

(A) Anthropologists have yet to identify the location of the Most Recent Common Ancestor.
(B) There were people alive at the identical ancestors point who are the ancestors of no modern humans.
(C) Without isolated populations, the MRCA would have lived only a few hundred years ago.
(D) Many Aboriginal Australian tribes did not contact a European group until 150 to 200 years ago.
(E) An isolated island tribe has not interbred with any other group in at least 600 years—probably much longer.

Homework Passage 2 (Short)

Yes, Art is the great and universal refreshment. For Art is never dogmatic; it holds no brief for itself. You may take it or you may leave it. It does not force itself
Line rudely where it is not wanted. It is reverent to all
(5) tempers, to all points of view. But it is willful: the very wind in the comings and goings of its influence, an uncapturable fugitive, visiting our hearts at vagrant, sweet moments. We often stand even before the greatest works of Art without being able quite to lose ourselves!
(10) That restful oblivion comes, we never quite know when—and it is gone! But when it comes, it is a spirit hovering with cool wings, blessing us from least to greatest, according to our powers; a spirit deathless and varied as human life itself.

19. The author of the passage most likely capitalizes the word "Art" throughout the passage in order to indicate

(A) a distinction between professional and amateur artists.
(B) a personification of a venerated topic.
(C) a deity that represents creative pursuits.
(D) a person's name.
(E) an ironic dismissal of the term.

20. The author of the passage would likely NOT agree with which of the following statements about art?

(A) Art is rigid and demanding to those who hope to enjoy it.
(B) People of any personality type or perspective can appreciate art.
(C) Those who view art cannot control it.
(D) The effects of a work of art are often unpredictable.
(E) A person can lose himself or herself in a work of art.

Homework Passage 3 (Long)

This passage examines some evidence about the origin of Earth's moon, as uncovered by NASA's Solar TErrestrial RElations Observatory (STEREO).

NASA's twin STEREO probes are entering a mysterious region of space to look for remains of an ancient planet that once orbited the Sun not far from
Line Earth. If they find anything, it could solve a major
(5) puzzle—the origin of the Moon.

"The name of the planet is Theia," says Mike Kaiser, STEREO project scientist at the Goddard Space Flight Center. "It's a hypothetical world. We've never actually seen it, but some researchers believe it existed 4.5 billion
(10) years ago and that it collided with Earth to form the Moon."

The "Theia hypothesis" is a brainchild of Princeton theorists Edward Belbruno and Richard Gott. It starts with the popular Great Impact theory of the Moon's
(15) origin. Many astronomers hold that in the formative years of the solar system, a Mars-sized protoplanet crashed into Earth. Debris from the collision, a mixture of material from both bodies, spun out into Earth orbit and coalesced into the Moon. This scenario explains
(20) many aspects of lunar geology, including the size of the Moon's core and the density and isotopic composition of moon rocks.

It's a good theory, but it leaves one awkward question unanswered: Where did the enormous
(25) protoplanet come from? Belbruno and Gott believe it came from a Sun-Earth Lagrange point.

Sun-Earth Lagrange points are regions of space where the pull of the Sun and Earth combine to form a "gravitational well." The flotsam of space tends to gather
(30) there much as water gathers at the bottom of a well on Earth. 18th-century mathematician Josef Lagrange proved that there are five such wells in the Sun-Earth system: L1, L2, L3, L4 and L5.

When the solar system was young, Lagrange points
(35) were populated mainly by the asteroid-sized building blocks of planets. Belbruno and Gott suggest that in one of the Lagrange points, L4 or L5, the miniature planets assembled themselves into Theia, nicknamed after the mythological Greek Titan who gave birth to the Moon
(40) goddess Selene.

"Their computer models show that Theia could have grown large enough to produce the Moon if it formed in the L4 or L5 regions, where the balance of forces allowed enough material to accumulate," says Kaiser.
(45) "Later, Theia would have been nudged out of L4 or L5 by the increasing gravity of other developing planets like Venus and sent on a collision course with Earth.

If this idea is correct, Theia itself is long gone, but some of the ancient mini-planets that failed to join Theia
(50) may still be lingering at L4 or L5.

"The STEREO probes are entering these regions of space now," says Kaiser. "This puts us in a good position to search for Theia's asteroid-sized leftovers."

Just call them "Theiasteroids."

(55) Astronomers have looked for Theiasteroids before using telescopes on Earth, and found nothing, but their results only rule out kilometer-sized objects. By actually entering L4 and L5, STEREO will be able to hunt for much smaller bodies at relatively close range.

(60) The search actually began last month when both spacecraft rolled 180 degrees so that they could take a series of 2-hour exposures of the general L4/L5 areas. In the first sets of images, amateur astronomers found some known asteroids, and new comet Itagaki was imaged just
(65) a couple of days after the announcement of its discovery. No Theiasteroids, however.

Hunting for Theiasteroids is not STEREO's primary mission, Kaiser points out. "STEREO is a solar observatory. The two probes are flanking the sun on
(70) opposite sides to gain a 3D view of solar activity. We just happen to be passing through the L4 and L5 Lagrange points en route. This is purely bonus science."

"We might not see anything," he continues, "but if we discover lots of asteroids around L4 or L5, it could
(75) lead to a mission to analyze the composition of these asteroids in detail. If that mission discovers the asteroids have the same composition as the Earth and Moon, it will support Belbruno and Gott's version of the giant impact theory."

(80) The search will continue for many months to come. Lagrange points are not infinitesimal points in space; they are broad regions 50 million kilometers wide. The STEREO probes are only in the outskirts now. Closest approach to the bottoms of the gravitational wells comes
(85) next year. "We have a lot of observing ahead of us," notes Kaiser.

21. If the Theia hypothesis is true, which of the following statements about the Moon is most likely to be correct?

(A) The Moon is made up of material from two separate astronomical bodies.
(B) The Moon formerly was located in a Lagrange point.
(C) The Earth captured the Moon in its gravitational field without a collision.
(D) The Moon was formed at the same time as the Earth.
(E) Theia collided with the Moon about 4.5 billion years ago.

22. The name "Theia" is an example of which literary device?

(A) metaphor
(B) alliteration
(C) onomatopoeia
(D) paradox
(E) allusion

Unauthorized copying or reuse of any part of this page is illegal.

Version 1.3

23. When determining aspects of the Theia hypothesis, scientists have made use of all of the following EXCEPT

    (A) direct observation of the protoplanet itself.
    (B) computer simulations.
    (C) mathematics.
    (D) geological measurements.
    (E) reasonable suppositions.

24. The use of the STEREO probes to search for Theiasteroids can best be described as

    (A) the result of a carefully planned scientific experiment.
    (B) a process that was completed many years ago.
    (C) an unexpected and fortuitous opportunity.
    (D) a long-delayed and troubled process.
    (E) an unfortunate coincidence.

25. If scientists discover no new asteroids in the L4 and L5 Lagrange points, the Theia hypothesis would likely be

    (A) completely disproved.
    (B) highly praised.
    (C) mostly unaffected.
    (D) weakened but not refuted.
    (E) partially confirmed.

26. Based on evidence from the passage, why does the author describe the Lagrange points as "mysterious" (line 2)?

    (A) The STEREO probes cannot see into the depths of the Lagrange points.
    (B) Scientists are not sure where the Lagrange points are located.
    (C) No one is quite sure how the gravity wells of the Lagrange points operate.
    (D) Theories differ about whether the Lagrange points ever existed.
    (E) The Lagrange points are vast and largely unmapped.

27. Which of the following statements about Theia is NOT accurate, based on evidence from the passage?

    (A) Theorists speculate that Theia was roughly the size of Mars.
    (B) Scientists have confirmed that Theia existed 4.5 billion years ago.
    (C) The existence of Theia would help explain some confusing attributes of the Moon.
    (D) The Lagrange points are the most likely location of the remnants of Theia.
    (E) Any remnants of Theia that still exist would be small asteroids.

28. The quotes throughout the passage from Mike Kaiser reveal a tone that can best be described as

    (A) profoundly skeptical.
    (B) largely disinterested.
    (C) cautiously optimistic.
    (D) hopelessly bleak.
    (E) unreservedly enthusiastic.

29. The author of the passage would most likely describe the evidence in favor of the Theia hypothesis as

    (A) nonexistent.
    (B) inconclusive.
    (C) misleading.
    (D) spurious.
    (E) persuasive.

30. The primary purpose of the passage is to

    (A) analyze several competing theories and select the most convincing one.
    (B) depict the efforts being made to find proof for an interesting theory.
    (C) describe the geology of the Moon.
    (D) argue for a particular explanation of the Moon's formation.
    (E) refute a controversial hypothesis.

Version 1.3

Unauthorized copying or reuse of any part of this page is illegal.

Homework Passage 4 (Long)

The following passage provides an overview of the career of renowned Renaissance artist Michelangelo as well as the critical interpretations of his work.

Michelangelo's place in the world of art is altogether unique. His supremacy is acknowledged by all, but is understood by a few only. In the presence of his works
Line none can stand unimpressed, yet few dare to claim any
(5) intimate knowledge of his art. He is one to awe rather than to attract, to overwhelm rather than to delight. Yet while Michelangelo can never be a popular artist in the ordinary sense of the word, the powerful influence that he exercises seems constantly increasing. Year by year
(10) there are more who, drawn by the strange fascination of his genius, seek to read the meaning of his art.

His subjects are all profoundly serious in intention. Life was no holiday to this strenuous spirit; it was a stern conflict with the powers of darkness in which such
(15) heroes as David and Moses were needed. Like the old Hebrew prophets, the artist poured out his soul in a vehement protest against evil, and a stirring call to righteousness.

Considered both as a sculptor and a painter,
(20) Michelangelo's one vehicle of expression was the human body. His works are "form-poems," through which he uttered his message to mankind. As he writes in one of his own sonnets, "Nor hath God deigned to show himself elsewhere / More clearly than in human forms sublime."
(25) Learning his first lessons in art of the Greeks, he soon possessed himself of the great principles of classic sculpture. Then he boldly struck out his own path; his was a spirit to lead, not to follow. With the subtle Greek sense of line and form, he united an entirely new motif.
(30) In contrast to the ideal of repose that was the leading canon of the Greeks, his chosen ideal was one of action. Moreover, he invariably fixed upon some decisive moment in the action he had to represent, a moment that suggests both the one preceding and the one following,
(35) and which gives us the whole story in epitome. Thus in the David we see preparation, aim, and action. It was a far cry from the elegant calm of the Greek god to the restless energy of this rugged youth.

It was characteristic of Michelangelo's impetuous
(40) nature to spend his enthusiasm upon the early stages of his work, and leave it unfinished. This unfinished effect of many of his statues seems to bring us in closer touch with his methods as a sculptor. Nor is a rough surface here and there inharmonious with the rugged character of
(45) his conceptions. Moreover, as a critic has pointed out, the polished and rough portions enhance each other, giving a variety in the light and shadow that is pictorial in effect.

Michelangelo has been compared to two great masters of dissimilar arts, Milton and Beethoven. There
(50) are striking points of similarity in the men themselves, in stern uprightness of character, in scorn of the low and trivial, in lofty idealism. The art of all three is too far above the common level to be popular; it requires too much thinking to attract the superficial. In poetry, in
(55) music, and in sculpture, all three utter the profoundest truths of human experience, expressed in grand and solemn harmonies.

31. According to the first paragraph (lines 1-11), the attitude of most of those who view Michelangelo's art can best be described as

(A) knowledgeable.
(B) disdainful.
(C) delighted.
(D) indifferent.
(E) awestruck.

32. According to the author, Michelangelo's main emphasis as an artist was on

(A) relaxing, peaceful imagery.
(B) religious messages.
(C) background scenery.
(D) vehicles such as carriages and wagons.
(E) the human body.

33. What does the author mean when he says that Michelangelo "gives us the whole story in epitome" (line 34)?

(A) He paints many different scenes on the same subject.
(B) His works are so peaceful and relaxed that the viewer can imagine the whole story easily.
(C) He writes brief summaries that accompany each of his works.
(D) He focuses on a key moment so that the viewer can infer what happened both before and after.
(E) He sculpts a figure at the beginning of an action and again at the end of the action.

34. The passage implies that the "unfinished effect" (line 41) in Michelangelo's work

(A) is a sign of poor character.
(B) is fitting for his style.
(C) has no significance.
(D) greatly detracts from the viewer's enjoyment.
(E) is the result of deliberate planning and hard work.

35. What is the function of the final paragraph (lines 48-57)?

   (A) to proclaim the Michelangelo is a more influential figure than either Milton or Beethoven
   (B) to compare Michelangelo's key traits with those of other creative masters
   (C) to refute an argument presented in the previous paragraph.
   (D) to prove that Michelangelo was less popular than his contemporaries
   (E) to summarize the main points of the essay

36. Based on information from the passage, Michelangelo can be said to be all of the following EXCEPT

   (A) righteous.
   (B) impulsive.
   (C) daring.
   (D) severe.
   (E) light-hearted.

37. The author's tone toward Michelangelo can best be described as

   (A) stern.
   (B) condescending.
   (C) praising.
   (D) ambivalent.
   (E) unimpressed.

38. The passage as a whole can best be described as

   (A) an examination of Michelangelo's upbringing and family life.
   (B) a thorough description of the history and appearance of a famous sculpture.
   (C) an overview of the most important aspects of Michelangelo's art.
   (D) an argument that Michelangelo wasted his talent by being impetuous.
   (E) a comparison between Michelangelo and other famous artists.

Literature
as
Exploration

THIRD EDITION

LOUISE M. ROSENBLATT

NOBLE AND NOBLE, PUBLISHERS, INC.
NEW YORK · DALLAS
CANADA: EDU-MEDIA LIMITED, KITCHENER, ONTARIO N2G 4H1

Foreword

THE NEARLY FORTY YEARS since the first publication of *Literature as Exploration* have seen a number of shifts in literary theory and the practice of teaching literature in schools and colleges in the United States. Through these permutations, Louise Rosenblatt's magnificent discussion of the relationship between reader and literary work has remained the major document on that subject. Critical and pedagogical theory being two fields noticeably subject to vicissitude, one might be surprised that a book that bridges the two would have so long a life. When one reads the book, however, one can understand why.

First of all, the book is far from narrowly conceived; there is not the polemical bias that mars so many books dealing with literature and its teaching. In treating the literary work, Louise Rosenblatt does not argue for an emphasis on form or content, but recognizes the organic nature of a story, novel, or poem. In discussing teaching, she again asserts the dominance of neither teacher nor student, but envisions a classroom in which teacher and student share honestly. Most importantly, she sets forth one of the clearest descriptions of the literary experience that has been portrayed.

Many have dealt with the literary experience since the time of Aristotle's discussion of catharsis; most of Louise Rosenblatt's predecessors dealt with it as a social experience, as a psychological experience, or as an esthetic experience. *Literature as Exploration* treats each of these aspects of the reader—the individual psyche, the individual as a member of society, and the individual as seeker of form and order—and sees them all as aspects of the essential humanity of the reader, as part of the conceptual baggage that the reader brings to the text and that is modified during and long after the reading of the text. The literary experience —what others have since called response to literature—is, as the "Coda" to this volume indicates, a performance, a transaction between reader and text in which both are modified in many of their aspects.

Literature as Exploration first abetted changes in the teaching of literature in the schools; later it provided the theoretical basis for research in the teaching and study of literature, much of which either explicitly followed from the theory or tended to support it from an empirical standpoint. The research has shown that readers project their world into what they read; that readers tend to ask critical questions directed in part by the text and in part by their culture; that readers gain diverse insights and satisfactions from their reading; and that readers change as they grow. Each act of reading becomes a unique encounter between an individual and a text. Obviously there are some constraints set by the text and some set by the common bonds of humanity, but *Gulliver's Travels* read by a ten-year-old child is not the same experience as *Gulliver's Travels* read by that same person twenty years later.

Most recently, the ideas of Louise Rosenblatt have become an accepted part of literary theory. When *Literature as Exploration* was written, many critics advanced theories based on a "correct" reading of a text, even though that correct reading might never be achieved by any one critic. In the past decade, a number of critics have come to realize that critical truth is illusory and that even the most synoptic of critics cannot give a complete reading of a poem; there is always another performer.

Literature as Exploration deserves republication now for several reasons: it is a classic; it is a superbly reasoned exploration of the reader; and it is a timely warning. The danger that the teaching of literature will slip back into a phase where the individuality and creativity of the reader will be stifled, where the emotions will be neglected, where detachment will replace commitment, always lurks and threatens to produce a generation of people who will spurn literature because the schools have deadened it for them. *Literature as Exploration* speaks against this possibility, and its importance is like that of Milton's *Areopagitica* and Shelley's *Defense of Poetry*: for this time and for a long time to come, it is the major defense of the reader.

ALAN C. PURVES

University of Illinois
July 1976

Preface to the Third Edition

THE MAXIM that a book once published leads a life of its own was confirmed for me when the initiative for this edition came from others. I have therefore been diffident about making substantial changes in its general pattern, despite considerable revision in presentation. . . ."* The preceding opening words from the Preface to the second edition apply also to the present one; again the initiative has come from others,** and the changes consist mainly in the prefatory materials, and the bibliography. I am gratified that teachers of literature in both schools and colleges, as well as those concerned with the education of teachers of literature, have again affirmed the continuing usefulness of this book.

"Since the varied powers of literature cannot be confined within a single phrase, the title of this book should be understood as a metaphor, not as a limiting definition. The word *exploration* is designed to suggest primarily that the experience of literature, far from being for the reader a passive process of absorption, is a form of intense personal activity. The reader counts for at least as much as the book or poem itself; he responds to some of its aspects and not others; he finds it refreshing and stimulating, or barren and unrewarding. Literature is thus for him a medium of exploration. Through books, the reader may explore his own nature, become aware of potentialities for thought and feeling within himself, acquire clearer perspective, develop aims and a sense of direction. He may explore the outer world, other personalities, other ways of life. Liberated from the insularity of time and space, he may range through the wide gamut of social and temperamental alternatives that men have created or imagined. Part of my task will be to outline some of the realms into which the reader may thus penetrate, and to sketch some of the personal and social benefits that may flow from such literary discovery."[1]

As I think back over the years since this book first appeared, I find confirmation of one of my basic points: i.e., what readers make of a work will vary with different situations and at different times, as they bring diverse preoccupations and interests to the text. In their reception to this book, readers have stressed varying implications at different times. I cannot here attempt to give an historical explanation—after all, in these decades we have lived through wars, cold and hot, affluence and recession, times of optimism and times of anxiety. But it has occurred to me that some of these different emphases might be of interest to those coming to this book for the first time, or who knew it in earlier editions. As one advocating change and reforms, I was often a minority voice, yet I am grateful that I was so often listened to, and that I was involved in so many of the important educational developments, even at times when in the colleges and universities very alien theories predominated.

The first edition was given a surprisingly warm reception. (For instance, soon after it appeared I found myself addressing the general session of the National Council of Teachers of English meeting in the Manhattan Opera House in New York. And leaders of the Modern Language Association asked me to join with them in writing a statement on literature.) The book struck a chord most con-

---

* In this discussion, I shall from time to time draw on the first and second prefaces, indicating the source of a "1" or a "2" following the quotation.
** For reasons of space, the acknowledgments listed in the prefaces to the preceding editions have regretfully been omitted. Of the various people involved in launching the present edition, two *must* be mentioned: Richard Adler, of the University of Montana, and especially Paul O'Dea, Director of Publications of the National Council of Teachers of English.

genial to those who were actively seeking to loosen the
bonds of the traditional cut-and-dried English curriculum
—the standard book lists of so-called classics, the emphasis
on generalized interpretations and paraphrases, the organization by historical periods and genres, the barrage
of questions to be answered about each work.

My emphasis on the relationship between the individual
reader and the text was cited by those concerned with
introducing the study of literary works closer to student
interests. (I recall a meeting at Harvard in those early days,
in which I was invited to defend my call for the introduction of contemporary literature into school curricula.) As
the years passed, book lists and anthologies provided an
increasingly diversified fare, and the advent of the paperback enabled enterprising teachers to institute individualized reading programs supplementing the group work.

Some especially welcomed the reminder that readers,
and especially young readers, respond most readily to
literature as an embodiment of human personalities, human situations, human conflicts and achievements. The
life situations and interests of students were more often
seen as the bridge between them and books. Anthologies
and courses organized around human-relations themes became increasingly widespread. (I recall, for example, jour-
neying from Washington to New York, during World War
II, to help plan the first edition of *Reading Ladders for
Human Relations,* which was based on the idea that no
matter what their reading level, young people want to
read literary works that help them understand themselves
and their world. The fifth edition of this work was published by the N.C.T.E. in 1972.)

Such themes and such provision for student differences
continued to concern teachers and educators even during
the period after World War II when Sputnik generated

an emphasis on the intellectualistic and the scientific, and the New Criticism came to dominate many college and university English Departments. In Chapter 4, I cite I. A. Richards' pioneering study of readers' interpretations, *Practical Criticism* (1929). The formalist New Critics drew on Richards also, but, true to my point about readers taking what they want, they took over mainly his close reading and concentrated on the technique of the work. By 1938 I had already absorbed from Dewey, Coleridge and the German philosophers a sense of the subjectivity of all perception, so that Richards mainly reinforced my interest in the reader's response. Like the New Critics, "I was reacting against the predominance of literary history. Like others, too, I rejected the oversimplified social approach of the thirties. But having written a critique of the art-for-art's-sake theorists, I was also disillusioned with the engrossment in technique and so-called purely literary matters. Focusing on the nature of literary experience enabled me to see the mutual interdependence of all facets. Today's readers will recognize that although the discussion opens with the social aspect, emphasis throughout is on the literary experience in its totality. If there is much talk about the social sciences, the purpose is to relegate them to their place as less powerful propagators of social attitudes than the arts, especially literature."[2] Even at the height of the intellectualism and formalism of the early sixties, many in the elementary and secondary schools maintained a lively interest in the personal nature of reading. This approach was supported by work in adolescent and developmental psychology and by the growing preoccupation with the quest for individual identity.

In this retrospective glance at responses to this book, I must not forget the many elementary schoolteachers and librarians who throughout were quick to see the implications for their work with younger children. Perhaps they were less hampered by the baggage of literary history and critical terminology. If it had been possible, I would have liked to deal with the literary experience from the very beginning, before the child learns to read. Although my illustrations tend to be drawn from high school and college years, everything I say about the nature of literary experience and the teaching process applies as well to the youngest readers.

In the late sixties, a strong reaction against the over-intellectualized, pseudo-scientific and analytic educational emphases in the colleges, including the New Criticism, led young people and many of their teachers to be especially receptive to the sensuous and emotional aspects of literary experience. This found special reverberations in the demand for literary works "relevant" to students' interest in the contemporary world, and adapted to their psychological needs. In many ways it seemed to me that the college and university faculties were discovering what the schools had known all along—a responsibility to the students as well as to the discipline. Thus by the time of the second edition, attention was focused particularly on my making the students' response the starting point for all growth in understanding and critical powers. Moreover, I had been saying all along that sound teaching requires a sound underlying theory of the nature of literary experience—and now the dynamics of literary response, rather than the author's technique or the theme or "content" of the work, came into the limelight. The interest in inductive methods of teaching at that time also led me to differentiate between the old method, whereby leading questions were aimed at preordained conclusions, and my view, that "the most fruitful inductive learning arises out of the involvement of the student—in this instance involvement in a literary experience—which leads him to raise personally meaningful questions . . . [and] to seek in the text the basis for valid answers and the impetus to further inquiry."[2]

At the present moment, contradictory forces seem to be at work in the educational arena. On the one hand—a legacy from the social and moral upheavals of the last decade—some are calling for the nurturing of greater spiritual and artistic strengths and personal creativity. The efforts to take over such British methods as the open classroom and creative dramatics reflect this trend. On the other hand, the economic recession has fostered in some quarters narrowly utilitarian demands for eliminating "frills" such as the arts, and concentrating on "basic skills." Only if we possess a philosophy of literature teaching can we justify the importance of literary experience, and make clear the criteria on which we base our classroom methods or curricular patterns. When literature is rescued from its diminished status as a body of subject matter and is offered as a mode of personal life-experience, all other kinds of relevant knowledge and skills can be added to it. Then we can explain that the "basic skills"—whether of beginning reading or sophisticated interpretation—will be learned within a meaningful context: the only reliable mode of learning.

Our courts, in prescribing the education of all the children in our democracy to their fullest capacity, are forcing us to face reality. The need for programs that start with what the student brings to the printed page is surely an idea "whose time has come." This must be the rationale for "efforts to make literature accessible to all in our schools and colleges—including those born outside the mainstream of American culture, those whose tempo of growth is fast or slow, those emerging from the narrow life of the urban ghetto or the affluent suburb, and those who are alienated or seeking new goals."[2] Literature can be an important medium, as various chapters show, for enhancing a pride in ethnic roots while at the same time fostering a sense of community with other Americans of different ethnic heritages—an orchestration of diversities in our pluralistic society.

Research in reading, no matter what else it has demonstrated, has found the teacher to be a most important—perhaps *the* most important—factor in the educational process. Theoretical movements come and go, but change comes slowly. In the classroom, teachers often fall back on the ways of their own teachers, because of lack of practical implementation of new theories or because of fear of failure in trying new methods. Or administrators fail to understand that imposition of change by fiat, without the active understanding of the participating teachers, is doomed. In this book, accounts of classroom discussions and teaching processes are interspersed as illustrations of theoretical points. For those prospective or practicing teachers who might find it hard to make the transition from more traditional methods, I have added to the bibliography, "For Further Reading," a section on teaching methods. This and the "Coda," supplemented by use of the Index, will serve, I hope, as a springboard for returning to those parts of the book that deal directly with teaching methods.

At present, the reaction from the aridity and sterility of much of the formalist analysis of literature has in some quarters become so extreme that I find myself, after years of attacking the New Critics, seeking to redress the balance. The New Critics did make a contribution in rescuing the literary work from being studied mainly as an historical or biographical document. While rejecting the New Critical view of the work as a closed system apart from author and reader, we can broaden the concept of close reading to encompass the reader's close attention to his responses to the text. Some critics and teachers today, in rejecting formalist impersonality, have swung to the opposite pole, insisting on the reader's response as a kind of absolute, a position even more extreme than the old impressionism. Others—especially those who espouse psychoanalysis—use the reader's responses as a basis for analysis of the reader's personality and obsessions. Still others, rejecting the estheticism of the New Critics, nevertheless retain their neglect of the student-reader and use literature simply to indoctrinate political and social ideologies. I believe that mine is a voice warning against all such extremist pendulum swings.

My book has much to say about the impact of the reader's personality and experience on what he makes of the text. But I do not reject responsibility to the text. Similarly, I have much to say about the reader's growth in self-critical insight into his own identity through his intercourse with literature. But I warn also against teachers' assuming the role of psychologists or psychoanalysts. I stress the social as well as personal nature of literature. But I am concerned with the social and cultural role of literature above all in a democracy. Chapters are devoted to the processes through which teachers can foster the growth of more self-aware and self-critical readers, able independently to do greater justice to the text, and able to relate their experience more perceptibly to other literary works and to their own lives.

In our present-day world of rapid social transitions, of changes in the roles of men and women and in family life, in this world beset by the evils of poverty, pollution, and war, no ready-made answers or decisions seem possible. It is imperative that we reflect on the values implicit in the potential long-term human consequences of one or another alternative solution. We need to understand our own priorities so that we may be guided to humane choices. Wrongdoing in high places and the spread of violence and crime have intensified the sense of crisis. This situation has led teachers, parents, and administrators to propose the introduction of a concern for values into school programs. An educational movement has emerged, mainly sponsored by social scientists, setting forth strategies to achieve what they call "values clarification." Studies are also in progress to ascertain stages in moral development that parallel Piaget's findings in cognitive development. Like Molière's M. Jourdain, who discovered that he had been talking prose all his life, teachers of literature find here a new name for something that is inherent, it has been my thesis, in any sound teaching of literature.

A large part of the present book involves students' clarification of the choices they participate in through literary works, the values affirmed and denied, and the light that reflection on the work and their response to it throws upon their own value systems. Without disparaging the approaches used in other disciplines, I try to show how the literature classroom offers something unique—the opportunity to participate directly and imaginatively in value choices, and to reflect on them within an emotionally colored context. In short, we can be helped to think clearly about issues that engage our emotions. Also, I suggest the context within which values are acquired and the processes by which they may be tested and revised.

It happens that these words are being written on the day that our democracy moves into the beginning of its third century. Joy in its survival and achievements is mingled with sadness at failures to achieve fuller economic and social democracy—yet also with hopeful aspirations for the future. Our democratic institutions have resiliently weathered recent threats from within and challenges from without, and there is being rekindled among us that vigilance which from the beginning we were told would be the eternal price of liberty. More than ever, we need to foster the growth of people who will have the inner strength and the humane values needed to face constructively these times of crucial decisions and awesome yet wonderful possibilities. This book is testimony to my belief that teachers of literature can contribute in vital ways to those goals.

L.M.R.

Princeton, New Jersey
July 4, 1976

Contents

PART I

The Province of Literature

CHAPTER 1

The Challenge of Literature

IN A TURBULENT AGE, our schools and colleges must prepare the student to meet unprecedented and unpredictable problems. He needs to understand himself; he needs to work out harmonious relationships with other people. He must achieve a philosophy, an inner center from which to view in perspective the shifting society about him; he will influence for good or ill its future development. Any knowledge about man and society that schools can give him should be assimilated into the stream of his actual life.

Nor is it only for some future way of life that he needs to be prepared. During his school years, he is already part of the larger world, meeting the impact of its domestic and international tensions, adjusting to adults who bear the marks of its successes and failures, discovering the possibilities it holds open to him. As he plays his youthful role, he is creating the personality and ideals that will shape his role as an adult. Young people everywhere are asking, "What do the things that we are offered in school and college mean for the life that we are now living or are going to live?"

Teachers of literature have been too modest about their possible contribution to these demands. Their task, they have felt, is to make their students more sensitive to the art of words, to induct them into our literary heritage. Leaving to others more mundane preoccupations, they had enough to do, it seemed, in busying themselves with purely literary matters.

The demand that the teaching of literature have some relation to the pupil's immediate human concerns has usually been countered by pointing to the horrors of the didactic, moralistic approach to literature. Wise teachers have opposed any tendency to make of literature a mere handmaiden of the social studies or a body of documents illustrating moral points. The Victorians, the argument runs, demonstrated the sterility of seeking in literature only social or moral lessons; those who see literature in such terms reveal their blindness to the special nature and primary value of literature.

Yet when the literary experience is fully understood, it becomes apparent that teachers of literature have indeed been somewhat shortsighted. They have not always realized that, willy-nilly, they affect the student's sense of human personality and human society. More directly than most teachers they foster general ideas or theories about human nature and conduct, definite moral attitudes, and habitual responses to people and situations. Preoccupied with the special aims of their field, they are often not conscious of dealing, in the liveliest terms, with subjects and problems usually thought of as the province of the sociologist, psychologist, philosopher, or historian. Moreover, these attitudes and theories are proffered in their most easily assimilable form, as they emerge from personal and intimate experience of specific human situations, presented with all the sharpness and intensity of art.

The teacher of literature will be the first to admit that he inevitably deals with the experiences of human beings in their diverse personal and social relations. The very nature of literature, he will point out, enforces this. Is not the substance of literature everything that man has thought or felt or created? The lyric poet utters all that the human heart can feel, from joy in "the cherry hung with snow" to the poignant sense of this world "where youth grows pale, and spectre-thin, and dies." The novelist displays the intricate web of human relationships with their hidden patterns of motive and emotion. He may paint the vast panorama of a society in a *War and Peace* or a *Human Comedy*. He may follow the fate of an entire family in a *Buddenbrooks*. He may show us a young man coming to understand himself and life, grappling with his own nature and the society about him, as in *A Portrait of the Artist as a Young Man* and *The Way of All Flesh*, or he may lead us to share in the subtle moods and insights of men and women, as in *The Ambassadors* and *Remembrance of Things Past*. The writer of stories catches some significant moment, some mood, some clarifying clash of wills in the life of an individual or a group. He may give us the humorous tale of *Rip Van Winkle* or the revelation of character in Chekov's *The Darling* or the harsh image of frustration in *Ethan Frome*. The dramatist builds a dynamic structure out of the tensions and conflicts of intermingled human lives. He may use the comic incongruities of social conventions and human affectation, as in *The Rivals*, or he may create a somber symphony out of man's inhumanity to man and the inscrutable whims of fate, as in *King Lear*. The joys of adventure, the delight in the beauty of the world, the intensities of triumph and defeat, the self-questionings and self-realizations, the pangs of love and hate—indeed, as Henry James has said, "all life, all feeling, all observation, all vision"—these are the province of literature.

Whatever the form—poem, novel, drama, biography, essay—literature makes comprehensible the myriad ways in which human beings meet the infinite possibilities that life offers. And always we seek some close contact with a mind uttering its sense of life. Always too, in greater or lesser degree, the author has written out of a scheme of values, a sense of a social framework or even, perhaps, of a cosmic pattern.

No matter how much else art may offer, no matter how much the writer may be absorbed in solving the technical problems of his craft, in creating with words new forms of esthetic experience, the human element cannot be banished. Thus, a writer such as Gertrude Stein, who was preoccupied with technical innovation, will have lasting value only as her work suggests to other writers new means of conveying emotions and a sense of the flow of life. The most sophisticated reader, extremely sensitive to the subtly articulated qualities of the poem or play or novel, cannot judge its technical worth except as he also assimilates the substance which embodies these qualities. Even the literary work that seems most remote, an imagist poem or a fantasy, reveals new notes in the gamut of human experience or derives its quality of escape from its implicit contrast to real life.

Santayana has summed up this basic appeal of literature:[1]

> The wonder of an artist's performance grows with the range of his penetration, with the instinctive sympathy that makes him, in his mortal isolation, considerate of other men's fate and a great diviner of their secret, so that his work speaks to them kindly, with a deeper assurance than they could have spoken with to themselves. And the joy of his great sanity, the power of his adequate vision, is not the less intense because he can lend it to others and has borrowed it from a faithful study of the world.

Certainly to the great majority of readers, the human experience that literature presents is primary. For them the formal elements of the work—style and structure, rhythmic flow—function only as a part of the total literary experience. The reader seeks to participate in another's vision—to reap knowledge of the world, to fathom the resources of the human spirit, to gain insights that will make his own life more comprehensible. Teachers of adolescents, in high school or in college, know to what a heightened degree they share this personal approach to literature.

In contrast to the analytic approach of the social sciences, the literary experience has immediacy and emotional persuasiveness. Will President Madison or Rip Van

[1] George Santayana, *Reason in Art* (New York, Charles Scribner's Sons, 1924), pp. 228-229.

Winkle live more vividly for the student? Will the history of the Depression impress him as much as will Steinbeck's *The Grapes of Wrath*? Will the theoretical definitions of the psychology textbook be as illuminating as *Oedipus* or *Sons and Lovers*? Obviously, the analytic approach needs no defense. But may not literary materials contribute powerfully to the student's images of the world, himself, and the human condition?

The English teacher will urge that his aim is to help students understand what they read, to acquaint them with the history of literature, to give them some insight into literary forms, and to lead them toward a measure of critical discrimination; this seems to have nothing to do with teaching them psychological or sociological theories. The answer is that when he most sincerely seeks to fulfill these aims, he inevitably finds himself dealing with materials that at least imply specific psychological theories and social attitudes. Since literature involves the whole range of human concerns, it is impossible to avoid assuming some attitude toward them. Moreover, because the implied moral attitudes and unvoiced systems of social values are reinforced by the persuasiveness of art, the teacher should bring them out into the open for careful scrutiny.

English teachers are trained to be scrupulous concerning the scholarly accuracy of their statements about literary history. But how often do they stop to scrutinize the scientific bases of the views concerning human personality and society that insinuate themselves into their work? How often have they critically considered the ethical criteria implicit in their judgments on literature, and incidentally, on life? How often is there even an awareness of the ever-present implied generalizations concerning man and society? While attention has been lavished on the historical and technical aspects of literature, these assumptions have been accepted as a by-product requiring no preparation.

WHAT, THEN, ARE SOME OF THE WAYS in which the teaching of literature does impinge on problems usually associated with the concerns of, for example, the psychologist or sociologist? A review of the accepted practice in literature classes—indeed, of much literary criticism as well—would reveal an amazing amount of attention given to topics which could be classified under the heading of psychological theorizing. The creation of vivid characters constitutes a large part of the novelist's, the dramatist's, the biographer's art. How can we read *Hamlet* or *Crime and Punishment* or *The Great Gatsby* without preoccupation with the psychology of the characters?

The student, therefore, is often asked to define the nature of the particular characters in the work he has been reading. He is also encouraged to see some relationship between motive and action: To what influences did Macbeth respond? What can explain Lady Macbeth's early determination and later breakdown? What was the influence of the characters upon one another in *A Separate Peace*? We do not need the abundant evidence of textbook and teacher's manual to know that such questions will arise. After reading *Hamlet*, the high school student, like the Shakespearean authority, often turns to theorizing about the rational and irrational elements in human be-

havior. Conrad's *Lord Jim* imposes reflection on the effect
of a sense of guilt and failure upon personality. Moreover,
the teacher is usually careful to develop the student's
sensitivity to the evidence of changes in character set
forth in such works as *Ethan Frome, Great Expectations,
Huckleberry Finn,* or the plays of Shakespeare.[2]

Once we embark on anything approaching a discussion
of characters, it is impossible for us to avoid committing
ourselves to some definite assumptions. Many different
views of human motivation may lend themselves to the
attempt to understand Othello's rapidly aroused jealousy,
to square that with his nature as it is displayed at the
opening of the drama, and to see why his jealousy should
have led so unswervingly to murder. Of course, these
problems may be evaded by maintaining that the psychological consistency of Othello's character is merely a
theatrical illusion. Professor E. E. Stoll contended that any
psychological interpretation is merely superimposed upon
a series of incidents, actions, and speeches that were
dictated by dramatic conventions and theatrical needs for
the sole purpose of creating a convincing and exciting
play, without concern for subtle psychological consistency.
However, it would still be necessary to explain why
Othello seems a living, integrated personality and not a
mere series of theatrical effects. In thinking back over our
experience of the tragedy, we find that we have fitted
what the dramatist offers us into some preconceived notions about human behavior, about the extent of human

[2] Since the discussion applies to the whole literature program, illustrations will be drawn from both high school and college levels. Chapters
4 and 7 consider the adequacy of the usual reading lists.

credulousness or the effects of jealousy. We judge whether Othello is a credible character in the light of our own assumptions about human nature.

For instance, when high school students make the relationship between Hamlet and his mother the core of their interpretation of his actions, whether or not they even know the name Freud, they have absorbed, somehow, somewhere, certain of the psychoanalytic concepts. Similarly, in interpreting *Othello* students may reveal an extraordinary diversity of theoretical frameworks. One student may emphasize the details offered by the dramatist concerning Desdemona's and Othello's sense of racial difference and may base on that his explanation of Othello's readiness to believe in his wife's infidelity. Another student may see Othello as a man fundamentally insecure, unsure of his ability to hold Desdemona, and thus ready to believe himself betrayed. Still another student may phrase Othello's problem in moral terms as the struggle between the nobler and the baser elements in his nature. There will also be the student who accepts the characters' statements about their acts, assumes that everything they do is consciously willed, and passes judgment accordingly. Each has found the play intelligible in terms of his own understanding of human motivation.

Students (and teachers) often assume that they are merely making explicit the author's particular view of human psychology. The process of interpretation is more complex than that, however. The reader must remain faithful to the text. He must be alert to the clues concerning character and motive present in the text. But he does more than that: he seeks to organize or interpret such clues. His own assumptions will provide the tentative framework for such an interpretation. He may discover that this causes him to ignore elements in the work, or he may realize that he is imputing to the author views unjustified by the text. He will then be led to revise or broaden his initial tentative assumptions.

Such a process surely would have been generated by an interchange among students holding the opinions about Othello sketched above. The challenge would be twofold: to determine whether their interpretations were supported by the text, and at the same time to test the adequacy of the psychological assumptions guiding their responses to the text. The body of critical writings on *Othello* demonstrates that the text permits a wide range of interpretations which bring to bear a variety of psychological hypotheses. The student reader will be less likely to impose irrelevant or unjustified interpretations if he has been led to scrutinize his psychological assumptions and to become aware of alternative possibilities.

When the text provides an unambiguous view of characters and reflects a particular psychological theory, as in the plays of Ben Jonson or in many recent works based on Freudianism, the task of the classroom might seem to be restricted to simple explication. If it were possible not to intrude any direct or indirect comment, the effect would still be implicit approval of each author's view of human motivation. This could result only in the student's being subjected to a series of discrete, inconsistent notions. But such complete neutrality would be impossible. Something of approval or disapproval would be conveyed through tone of voice, kinds of questions raised, length of time devoted to the work, or emphasis on one or another aspect. Hence the necessity remains for the teacher to recognize his responsibility toward the handling of psychological concepts. The students need to be helped both to understand the author's presentation of his characters and to acquire some means of critically relating it to other views of human nature and conduct.

Works of the past—the *Odyssey*, the Arthurian legends, *Beowulf*, Elizabethan drama, Victorian novels—engender a major psychological question: What are the basic human traits that persist despite social and cultural changes? To what extent are the resemblances of one age to another, as well as the differences, due to environmental influences? Indeed, this question of persisting or "universal" human traits is one that arises constantly in discussions of literature. The phrase *human nature* recurs again and again in the discussion of books, and the manner of its use conveys a great many unformulated implications.

Questions such as the following about *David Copperfield* are often encountered:

> One passage in this chapter shows David beginning to read human nature correctly. Where is it?
> What baseness of human nature is revealed by different persons in this chapter? What goodness of human nature?

Or consider a very recent instance, a third grade unit on the fable which suggests to the teacher such psychologically oriented questions as these:

> Why did each of the animals leave home?
> Was the story the bandit told his friends really what he thought he saw?

Did he make it up to shield his cowardice?
How would each of these animals act if they were people?

Or in a sixth grade unit on Chaucer's *Chantecleer and the Fox*:

How do these animals form particularly appropriate pictures
of the human follies, evils, or incongruities which they exhibit?

The term *human nature* is itself a controversial one.
Nevertheless, some set of notions dominates our sense of
human behavior, and discussion of particular characters
or works builds up in the student's mind a predisposition
toward such a set of ideas. "These are the significant
elements in human personality; these are the kinds of
forces that dominate men's lives and lead them to act in
certain ways," are the generalizations constantly implied
in discussion of specific characters. Even if the teacher
desired to, he could not evade transmitting certain generalized concepts concerning character and the ways in
which it is molded and motivated.

IN RECENT YEARS, great strides have been made in the
fields of psychology, sociology, and anthropology toward
a clarification of the fundamental problems of human behavior. The layman's tendency to speak of human nature
as though it were constant and unchanging has been
searchingly questioned; the plasticity of the human creature has been discovered to be almost endless. Anthropologists have revealed to us societies in which human
beings have suppressed or rigidly regulated some of the
drives, such as sex or the desire for self-preservation, that
we tend to consider most fundamental and ineradicable.

Our primary impulse is to equate human nature with the particular motivations, modes of behavior, and types of choice that we have from childhood observed in the society about us. The inescapable molding influence of the culture into which we are born is an extremely important concept. The teacher should have this clearly in mind before discussing questions concerning character and motivation or even before introducing the student to the images of human behavior presented in our own and other literatures.

The danger is in the unquestioning adoption of the general attitudes toward human nature and conduct that permeate the very atmosphere we live in. Unfortunately, the ideas that are taken most for granted are often the ones that merit the most skeptical scrutiny. For instance, the notion that the conscious motives of the individual determine action is implied in most casual discussions of behavior: If man transgresses, it is because he has willed it. The problem of praise and blame is thus a simple one. Yet present-day psychology stresses the importance of unconscious factors that motivate behavior. A classroom discussion of essays, letters, journals, autobiographies, or any of the other literary forms that deal with individual conduct automatically creates the necessity for advancing one or another view. Whether he wishes to or not, the teacher will either reinforce or counteract these assumptions. He will increase the hold of the voluntaristic view of human motivation or replace it with a keener sense of the complexities in the many environmental, physiological, and involuntary psychological factors that influence behavior. Even writers, like Shakespeare, who may not have consciously held this broader view have nevertheless often indicated significant environmental and physiological factors that may explain their characters' personalities and actions. The teacher may or may not make the student aware of the possible relationships between such things. In either case he is helping to determine the student's sense of these questions.

Despite the desire to leave these issues to the specialists in psychology, teachers of literature must resign themselves to the fact that they cannot avoid encroaching upon these extremely important and interesting questions concerning human behavior. The problem is that the average teacher or college instructor in literature is not necessarily equipped to handle these topics in a scientific spirit. Hence the discussion of characters and motivation tends to follow the superficial lines of ordinary everyday conversations about people. The students may thus very easily conclude that merely on the basis of one's own meager experience and casually acquired assumptions, one may make valid judgments on human motives and conduct. To provide a critical framework, the instructor needs some knowledge of the dominant conceptions in psychology.

THE TEACHING OF LITERATURE inevitably involves the conscious or unconscious reinforcement of ethical attitudes. It is practically impossible to treat any novel or drama, or indeed any literary work of art, in a vital manner without confronting some problem of ethics and without speaking out of the context of some social philosophy. A framework of values is essential to any discussion of human life. In most cases the concern with specific episodes or characters may veil the fact that these generalized attitudes are being conveyed. Yet any specific discussion implies the existence of these underlying attitudes.

When the student has been moved by a work of literature, he will be led to ponder on questions of right or wrong, of admirable or antisocial qualities, of justifiable or unjustifiable actions. The average student spontaneously tends to pass judgment on the actions of characters encountered in fiction. Sometimes this tendency is furthered by the type of analysis and discussion of literature carried on in the classroom. Although the practice of many teachers is superior to the level represented by the suggested questions in textbooks and prepared unit materials, and although there has been a reaction—too extreme in some quarters—against "moral" interpretations, questions that ask the student to pass judgment still tend to be common teaching practice. For example, in the third grade unit on the animal fable mentioned earlier, the children are asked to build a "repertory of words and phrases" suggested by the antithesis of the "wise" beast and the "foolish" beast. This would elicit and perhaps crystallize attitudes toward different types of behavior. Or consider the implications of questions such as these concerning *The Scarlet Letter:*

> Which in your opinion is the guiltiest of the three: Hester Prynne, Arthur Dimmesdale, or Roger Chillingworth? Which suffered most?
> What characters do you consider admirable? Why?

There is little in the first question to suggest to the student that perhaps he should seek not to pass judgment but to understand how the whole tragic complication grew out of the way of life in that Puritan community. The question also rules out an interpretation of this novel as a study in the effect of a sense of sin on character.

The teacher would do neither literature nor students a service if he tried to evade ethical issues. He will be exerting some kind of influence, positive or negative, through his success or failure in helping the student to develop habits of thoughtful ethical judgment. The teacher should scrutinize his own ethical criteria, which must color anything that he says or does in the classroom. He should not foist his own bias on students, but objectivity should not create the impression that value judgments are unimportant. The literature classroom can stimulate the students themselves to develop a thoughtful approach to human behavior.

Thus far, only those ethical and psychological assumptions have been mentioned that seem to deal with the more personal elements in the field of human relations. The nature of literature also embraces matters that are special to the historian, the economist, and the sociologist. Such concerns are implied even by the traditional phrasing of the aims and content of the literature program. For example, the object might be to acquaint the student with tales of adventure in exotic settings. Suggested readings might be *The Count of Monte Cristo, Kon Tiki, The Time Machine, Mutiny on the Bounty,* or the *Odyssey.* In these books, the student's attention will be focused on the vigorous action and the foreign scenes. Yet various considerations that might be classified as historical or sociological will creep in. Some novels, for instance, will involve an understanding of the historical periods treated. Such works as the *Iliad* or Elizabethan dramas invite reflection on the idea that in different ages and in different parts of the world man has created extraordinarily dissimilar social, economic, and political structures which pattern the life of the individual in ways very different from our own. Perhaps in some genres, such as science fiction, this is even a too glibly presented cliché.

Social and historical considerations enter even more obviously into the study of any period of literature or the chronological treatment of any form such as poetry or the drama. In presenting these materials, the teacher consciously, and probably even to a greater extent unconsciously, will be stressing various notions concerning historical problems; he will be transmitting various positive or negative assumptions concerning the influence of social and political circumstances upon other phases of man's life. The process of social change (of which literary change is but one aspect), the influence of technological conditions upon the social and intellectual life of a society, the factors that lead men in one age to be obsessed by aspirations very different from those of another age—such problems are necessarily implied by any survey of the history of literature. Even by ignoring them the teacher is affecting, though in a negative way, the student's ability to understand these problems.

And what about attitudes toward personal relationships? Here the role of the teacher of literature is most clear. Think, for instance, of such works as *Ah Wilderness!*, *Romeo and Juliet*, *All My Sons*, or *The Scarlet Letter*: they evoke attitudes toward the relationship between husband and wife, patterns of family life, and the concept of romantic love. Or consider the attitudes toward the child and questions of relationships between parents and children implied in the reading of *Tom Sawyer, David Copperfield, The Ordeal of Richard Feverel, Sons and Lovers,* and many of Wordsworth's poems.

The young people who encounter such works of literature are building up their sense of the socially favored types of adjustment in our culture. In books they are meeting extremely compelling images of life that will undoubtedly influence the crystallization of their ultimate attitudes, either of acceptance or of rejection. Here again the teacher will exert an influence through the whole framework of ideas and attitudes that he builds up around the experience of the particular sense of social relationships presented by any particular work.

Literature treats the whole range of choices and aspirations and values out of which the individual must weave his own personal philosophy. The literary works that students are urged to read offer not only "literary" values, to use a currently favored abstraction, but also some approach to life, some image of people working out a common fate, or some assertion that certain kinds of experiences, certain modes of feeling, are valuable. The teacher who is aware of the potential absorption or rejection of social attitudes will be led to investigate his own role in this process.

How QUICK TEACHERS OF LITERATURE would be to condemn the teacher of history or zoology who interlarded his discussions with dogmatic statements about literature. How unscholarly they would think the biology instructor who felt that what he had absorbed about literature from newspapers, magazines, and perhaps a random course at college justified his passing on the merits of Milton's poetry, insinuating that free verse was a ridiculous innovation, or making casual judgments as to the authorship of the disputed passages in *Sir Thomas More*. Yet too often literature teachers feel that the social concepts and attitudes absorbed from everyday life, plus a scattered reading on a subject here and there or a rapid survey of the field in a college course, are ample preparation for using literature as the springboard for discussions of human nature and society. They are forced to the rejoinder that the very nature of literature necessitates such discussions; these matters cannot be evaded by judicious selection. But this should bring recognition of their responsibility to equip themselves to handle a vital and inevitable phase of their teaching.

Probably the comparative youth and lack of unanimity of the social sciences partly explain this casual encroachment upon their territory. A more respectful attitude developed long ago toward the natural sciences. The English teacher would be considered grievously lacking who propagated in his classroom the idea that the sun moves around the earth (cf. *Paradise Lost*, Book Eighth) or that incantation was the approved method of curing the sick. From a "purely esthetic" point of view, which ignores the fact that the person experiencing the work of literature comes to it out of a particular world and will return to it, this may not matter. One could appreciate many literary works just as well esthetically though holding these exploded beliefs. The fact is, nevertheless, that the student will return to the world of today. His literary experience will have been confusing rather than helpful if he brings from it ideas that are relics of an outgrown past.

A parallel scrupulousness is needed concerning psychological, social, and ethical concepts that the student may absorb from his reading. Just as the student will be able to enjoy Milton's *Paradise Lost* without necessarily accepting Milton's cosmology, so he must be able to absorb from the literature of the past and of the present what is sound and relevant to his own needs in this age. A zestful reading of, let us say, Walter Scott is compatible with a sense of the anachronism, particularly for an American, of an acceptance of Scott's feudalistic philosophy. The literature teacher may not be primarily concerned with giving scientific information; yet it is his responsibility to further the assimilation of habits of thought conducive to social understanding. He shares with all other teachers the task of providing the student with the proper equipment for making sound social and ethical judgments. Indeed, the English teacher can play an important part in this process, since the student's social adjustments may be more deeply influenced by what he absorbs through literature than by what he learns through the theoretical materials of the usual social science course.[3]

The already overburdened literary scholar, aware of the great mass of materials and information that he must absorb, will probably protest that he is now being called

[3] This argument cuts both ways, of course, and leads to the conclusion that literary materials have their place also in the social science curriculum. See Chapter 7.

upon to assimilate the great body of knowledge accumulated by the social sciences, too. This obviously is impossible. The prospective teacher of English cannot be given the training demanded of the social scientist. It is imperative, however, that undergraduate and graduate programs provide time for building up a sound acquaintance with at least the general aspects of current scientific thought on psychological and social problems. Many undergraduate programs now include some introductory work of this kind, but rather haphazardly. The practicing teacher must feel the necessity for constantly increasing such knowledge. Teachers of literature cannot neglect to establish a rational basis for this inevitable and highly important phase of their work.

THIS CHAPTER HAS SOUGHT to suggest how intimately the concepts of the social sciences enter into the study of literature. Many problems remain to be clarified concerning the relation between this much neglected aspect and the more widely recognized concerns of English teaching. The emphasis thus far may seem to resemble "the social approach" to literature. Unfortunately, the champions of this view, in a pendulum-swing reaction against extreme estheticism, have sometimes been led to neglect the fact that literature is a form of art. The defenders of "esthetic" or "literary" values, on the contrary, have often felt it necessary to reject all social concerns. The thesis of this book is that no contradiction should exist between these two phases of art—that, in fact, they are inextricably interrelated. Those who see in literature only social documents and those who admit only so-called pure esthetic values offer equally limited insights. The increase of literary sensitivity, no less than the fostering of social awareness, requires a concern for the issues raised in this chapter. A philosophy of teaching based on a balanced recognition of the many complex elements that make up the literary experience can foster the development of more fruitful understanding and appreciation of literature.

To view literature in its living context is to reject any limiting approach, social or esthetic. Although the social and esthetic elements in literature may be theoretically *distinguishable*, they are actually *inseparable*. Much of the confused thinking about the esthetic and the social aspects of art would be eliminated if the debaters realized that an object can have more than one value: It can yield the kind of fulfillment which we call *esthetic*—it can be enjoyed in itself—and at the same time have a social origin and social effects. The task of the coming chapters will be to make this point clear and to elaborate its implications for the reader and the teacher.

CHAPTER 2

The Literary Experience

TERMS SUCH as *the reader, the student, the literary work,* have appeared in the preceding pages. Actually, these terms are somewhat misleading, though convenient, fictions. There is no such thing as a generic reader or a generic literary work; there are only the potential millions of individual readers of the potential millions of individual literary works. A novel or poem or play remains merely inkspots on paper until a reader transforms them into a set of meaningful symbols. The literary work exists in the live circuit set up between reader and text: the reader infuses intellectual and emotional meanings into the pattern of verbal symbols, and those symbols channel his thoughts and feelings. Out of this complex process emerges a more or less organized imaginative experience. When the reader refers to a poem, say, *Byzantium,* he is designating such an experience in relation to a text.

Teachers at all levels should have the opportunity to

observe the child's entrance into the world of the printed page. The child must have attained the physical and intellectual capacity to perform this highly complex operation, the act of reading. He should be emotionally ready to meet this challenge. Essential, too, is a sufficiently rich experience, so that words are signs for things and ideas. A set of marks on a page—CAT—becomes linked to a certain crisp sound in the ear, but is read as a word only when that sound points to a certain class of furry, four-footed creatures.

It is easy to observe how the beginning reader draws on past experience of life and language to elicit meaning from the printed words, and it is possible to see how through these words he reorganizes past experience to attain new understanding. Those who work with older students in school and college do not always recognize that they are faced with a similar situation. Like the beginning reader, the adolescent needs to encounter literature for which he possesses the intellectual, emotional, and experiential equipment. He, too, must draw on his past experience with life and language as the raw materials out of which to shape the new experience symbolized on the page.

The teacher of literature, then, seeks to help specific human beings discover the satisfactions of literature. Teaching becomes a matter of improving the individual's capacity to evoke meaning from the text by leading him to reflect self-critically on this process. The starting point for growth must be each individual's efforts to marshal his resources and organize a response relevant to the stimulus of the printed page. The teacher's task is to foster fruitful interactions—or, more precisely, transactions—between individual readers and individual literary works.[1]

Literature lends little comfort to the teacher who seeks the security of a clearly defined body of information. He does have "knowledge," of course. There are even those reassuring things called facts—facts about the social, economic, and intellectual history of the age in which literary works were written; facts about the responses of contemporary readers; facts about the author and his life; facts about the literary traditions he inherited; facts, even, about the form, structure, and method of the work. Yet all such facts are expendable unless they demonstrably help to clarify or enrich individual experiences of specific novels, poems, or plays. The notion of "background information" often masks much that is irrelevant and distracting.

The uniqueness of the transaction between reader and text is not inconsistent with the fact that both elements in this relationship have social origins and social effects. If each author were completely different from every other human being, and if each reader were totally unique,

---

[1] The usual terminology—e.g., "the reaction of the reader to the literary work," "the interaction between the reader and the work," or references to "the poem itself"—tends to obscure the view of the literary experience presented here. Hence at times the need to differentiate between *the text*, the sequence of printed or voiced symbols, and *the literary work* (*the poem, the novel*, etc.), which results from the conjunction of a reader and a text.

In various disciplines *transaction* is replacing *interaction*, which suggests the impact of distinct and fixed entities. *Transaction* is used above in the way that one might refer to the interrelationship between the *knower* and what is *known. The poem* is the transaction that goes on between reader and text. Cf. John Dewey and Arthur F. Bentley, *Knowing and the Known* (Boston, Beacon Press, 1949).

there could, of course, be no communication. There are many experiences that we all have in common—birth, growth, love, death. We can communicate because of a common core of experience, even though there may be infinite personal variations. Human beings participate in particular social systems and fall into groups such as age, sex, occupation, nation. These, too, offer general patterns upon which individual variations can be played. The forces of social conditioning are also pervasive in the formation of specific emotional drives and intellectual concepts.

Just as the personality and concerns of the reader are largely socially patterned, so the literary work, like language itself, is a social product. The genesis of literary techniques occurs in a social matrix. Both the creation and reception of literary works are influenced by literary tradition. Yet ultimately, any literary work gains its significance from the way in which the minds and emotions of particular readers respond to the verbal stimuli offered by the text.

In the past the danger has been that one aspect or the other of the literary experience has been emphasized. On the one hand, literature deals with and ministers to human life and human needs. On the other hand, this is accomplished by means of artistic form, through the exercise of literary craftsmanship creating works of high esthetic appeal. To treat literature merely as a collection of moralistic pamphlets, a series of disquisitions on man and society, is to ignore that the artist is concerned not with indirect commentary on life but with the addition of a new experience in life, namely, the work of art.

When concern with the human elements in literature has become confused with the purely practical approach to those elements in life itself, distortion and critical confusion have followed. Literary works have then been judged solely in terms of their conformity to conventional aims and standards. Such an approach made possible the elevation of the novels of the now unread Miss Yonge over those of George Eliot or Charlotte Brontë. This approach is possible only when the nature of literature as an art is forgotten.

When, usually in reaction against the practical point of view, only the formal and technical elements of the work have been considered important, an equally disastrous distortion has resulted. An excessive preoccupation with the externals of form and technical brilliance, such as Oscar Wilde exemplifies, has led to a breakdown of sound critical standards. The very remoteness of a work from the living core of human preoccupations comes to be considered a merit. The literary craftsman is elevated above the true artist.

In recent decades the influence of the "New Criticism" and other critical approaches has also tended to diminish the concern with the human meaningfulness of the literary work. The stress on "close reading" was unfortunately associated with the notion of the "impersonality" of the poet and the parallel impersonality of the critic. "The work itself" was said to be the critic's prime concern, as though it existed apart from any reader.[2] Analysis of the technique of the work, concern with tone, metaphor, sym-

[2] See Louise M. Rosenblatt, "The Poem as Event," *College English*, Vol. 26, No. 2 (November 1964), pp. 123–128.

bol, and myth, has therefore tended to crowd out the ultimate questions concerning relevance or value to the
reader in his ongoing life.[3]

Since to lead the student to ignore either the esthetic
or the social elements of his experience is to cripple him
for a fruitful understanding of what literature offers, the
teacher of literature needs much insight into the complex
nature of the literary experience.

WHAT, THEN, HAPPENS IN the reading of a literary work?
Through the medium of words, the text brings into the
reader's consciousness certain concepts, certain sensuous
experiences, certain images of things, people, actions,
scenes. The special meanings and, more particularly, the
submerged associations that these words and images have
for the individual reader will largely determine what the
work communicates to *him*. The reader brings to the
work personality traits, memories of past events, present
needs and preoccupations, a particular mood of the
moment, and a particular physical condition. These and
many other elements in a never-to-be-duplicated combina-

---

[3] "The pernicious practice of converting every literary work into a moral
homily is perhaps the abuse most frequently committed. But the Commission believes that no discussion, no study, no reading of any work is
complete without some consideration of possible extrinsic meaning,
meaning that brings that work directly against the reader's own philosophical convictions and experience. It may be ironic that, after so
many years of complaint about teachers who taught the moral instead of
the work, warning should now be given against the incompleteness of
any study of literature that avoids this consideration. But the Commission believes that 'close reading' may as readily sterilize the study of
literature as moralizing once stultified it." *Freedom and Discipline in
English*, Report of the Commission on English, College Entrance Examination Board (Princeton, New Jersey, 1965), pp. 72–73.

tion determine his response to the peculiar contribution of the text. For the adolescent reader, the experience of the work is further specialized by the fact that he has probably not yet arrived at a consistent view of life or achieved a fully integrated personality.

Another factor which adds to the variability of the teaching situation is the great diversity in the nature of the literary works themselves. There is a decided difference between the emotional satisfactions to be derived from a lyric by Sir Philip Sidney and a lyric by Browning; an even greater diversity of appeal is made by works of different literary types and moods, such as *The Brothers Karamazov* and *As You Like It*. Obviously, very different kinds of sensitivity and knowledge are required for the fullest appreciation of each of these works. The infinite diversity of literature plus the complexity of human personality and background justify insistence on the special nature of the literary experience and on the need to prepare the student to engage in the highly personal process of evoking the literary work from the text.

Those who associate psychological or social interests with a narrow didacticism or instrumentalism tend to misinterpret the thesis of Chapter 1—hence the need to reiterate that we are concerned with social and psychological insights as they flower from the actual esthetic experience. Grammar and syntax are involved in any literary work, yet no one would mistake a novel for a treatise on grammar. One should be just as careful to avoid the confusion of seeming to discuss literary works as though they were treatises on sociology or psychology. The crux of the matter is that the text embodies verbal stimuli toward a special kind of intense and ordered experience—sensuous, intellectual, emotional—out of which social insights may arise. The following discussion will seek to dispel the confusion that so often results from a fixation *either* on something called pure art *or* on the social implications of literature, cut off from their roots in personal esthetic experience.

Philosophers, to be sure, have defined the esthetic experience in a great many ways. Often they have been concerned with fitting art into previously developed metaphysical systems, or they have emphasized one out of the many springs of esthetic enjoyment. The play impulse, the instinct for imitation, the urge for self-expression, the desire to communicate, the religious or the mythic impulse, are some of the many suggested sources of man's drive to create and enjoy art. This is merely further documentation that art satisfies a great many different human needs and impinges upon the broad range of man's personal and social concerns.

In our everyday lives, preoccupied as we are with accomplishing some task or attaining some goal, we must often ignore the quality of the moment as it passes. Life presents a confused mass of details from which we select for attention only those related to our practical concerns. Even then our attention is focused not on the details themselves but on their practical bearing. We usually cannot stop to savor their quality. In our approach to a work of art, interest is centered precisely on the nature and quality of what is offered us.

This illuminates the difference between reading a literary work of art and ordinary reading. When we read for some practical purpose, our attention is focused on the information or ideas or directions for action that will remain when the reading is over. Hence a paraphrase or a summary of a biology text or a rephrasing of the technical language of a law may be quite as useful as the original. Someone else can read the newspaper or a scientific work for us and summarize it acceptably. But no one can read a poem for us. The reader of the poem must have the experience himself. It may later have repercussions in actual life, but as he sees the play or reads the novel or poem, he is intent on the pattern of sensations, emotions, and concepts it evokes. Because the text is organized and self-contained, it concentrates the reader's attention and regulates what will enter into his consciousness. His business for the moment is to apprehend as fully as possible these images and concepts in relation to one another. Out of this arises a sense of an organized structure of perceptions and feelings which constitutes for him the esthetic experience.

Definitions of the esthetic experience often postulate that art provides a more complete fulfillment of human impulses and needs than does ordinary life with its frustrations and irrelevancies. Undoubtedly, such a sense of fulfillment and emotional equilibrium is largely due to the intense, structured, and coherent nature of what is apprehended under the guidance of the text. Yet those engaged in the task of developing sensitivity to a particular art form will not need to be reminded that any such complete experience depends not only on the work itself, but also on the reader's capacities and readiness. Sound literary insight and esthetic judgment will never be taught by imposing from above notions of what works should ideally mean. Awareness of some of the things that actually affect the student's reactions will allow the teacher to help the student in handling his responses and achieving increasingly balanced literary experiences.

WHEN IN THE COURSE OF OUR DAILY AFFAIRS we exclaim "How funny!" or "How tragic!" we have engaged in an embryonic artistic process. We have seen a pattern in human life; we have juxtaposed certain events in our minds, have perceived their relationships, and have thus disengaged their humor or tragedy. The author does this in a more completely creative form, since he enables us to share his vision. No one would question that in the creation of the literary work the writer does more than passively reflect experiences as through a photographic lens. There has been a selective force at work. From the welter of impressions with which life bombards us, the writer chooses those particular elements that have significant relevance to his insight. He leads us to perceive selected images, personalities, and events in special relation to one another. Thus, out of the matrix of elements with common meaning for him and his readers, he builds up a new sequence, a new structure, that enables him to evoke in the reader's mind a special emotion, a new or deeper understanding—that enables him, in short, to communicate with his reader.

The reader, too, is creative. The text may produce that moment of balanced perception, a complete esthetic experience. But it will not be the result of passivity on the reader's part; the literary experience must be phrased as a *transaction* between the reader and the text. Moreover, as in the creative activity of the artist, there will be selective factors molding the reader's response. He comes to the book from life. He turns for a moment from his direct concern with the various problems and satisfactions of his own life. He will resume his concern with them when the book is closed. Even while he is reading, these things are present as probably the most important guiding factors in his experience.

The same text will have a very different meaning and value to us at different times or under different circumstances. Some state of mind, a worry, a temperamental bias, or a contemporary social crisis may make us either especially receptive or especially impervious to what the work offers. Without an understanding of the reader, one cannot predict what particular text may be significant to him, or what may be the special quality of his experience. Hence it is important to consider some of the selective factors that may mold the reader's response to literature.

The reader seeks in literature a great variety of satisfactions. These sometimes quite conscious demands are in themselves important factors affecting the interrelation between book and reader. A freshman class at a New England women's college was unexpectedly asked, "Why do you read novels, anyway?" Here are some of the spontaneous answers:

> I like to read a novel for relaxation after I have been studying hard all day.
> I like to read anything that is well written, in which the author gives you interesting descriptions and exciting adventures.

I like to find out about the things that happen to people, and how they solve their problems.

I had an interesting experience with a novel a few weeks ago. I discovered that one of the characters was in the same fix that I was in. I got a great deal from seeing how the character in the book managed.

I like to read about as many different kinds of situations as possible—just in case I, myself, might be in such a situation some day.

These students summarized, in simplified form perhaps, a number of the personal satisfactions that adolescent and adult alike seek from literature. Their remarks are akin to de Maupassant's comment:

The public as a whole is composed of various groups, whose cry to us writers is:
"Comfort me."
"Amuse me."
"Touch me."
"Make me dream."
"Make me laugh."
"Make me shudder."
"Make me weep."
"Make me think."
And only a few chosen spirits say to the artist:
"Give me something fine in any form which may suit you best, according to your own temperament."

In its simplest terms, literature may offer us an emotional outlet. It may enable us to exercise our senses more intensely and more fully than we otherwise have time or opportunity to. Through literature we may enjoy the beauty or the grandeur of nature and the exotic splendor of scenes in far distant lands. Furthermore, it may provide experiences that it would not be either possible or wise to introduce into our own lives. The love of action and adventure, the interest in kinds of people and ways of life alien to our own, the delight in scenes of strong emotion, in pictures of physical violence, even in images of hatred and evil, may be due to the release they provide for drives repressed by our culture. Nor does literature afford an outlet only for antisocial emotions. A great work of art may provide us the opportunity to feel more profoundly and more generously, to perceive more fully the implications of experience, than the constricted and fragmentary conditions of life permit.

The college students, bearing out the contention of the preceding chapter, placed greatest emphasis on literature as a means of broadening one's knowledge of people and society. This reflected their curiosity about life, a curiosity shared with younger adolescent and preadolescent students. For the average adult reader as well, literature contributes to the enlargement of experience. We participate in imaginary situations, we look on at characters living through crises, we explore ourselves and the world about us, through the medium of literature.

The capacity to sympathize or to identify with the experiences of others is a most precious human attribute. Scientific studies of reactions to works of art have revealed how pervasive is our tendency to identify with something outside ourselves. This has been found to be true even of nonhuman subjects. We tend to "feel ourselves into," to empathize with, the painting of the tree that is swaying in the wind, until the successful artist will have somehow made us that very tree itself. Even the delicate poise of an architectural column or the symmetry of a Greek vase will be felt in the pull and balance of our own muscles, though we may not be conscious of the source of our pleasure. How much more directly and completely is this tendency to project ourselves into the object of our contemplation fulfilled when we are concerned with the personalities and joys and sorrows, with the failures and the achievements, of characters in literature!

This tendency toward identification will certainly be guided by our preoccupations at the time we read. Our own problems and needs may lead us to focus on those characters and situations through which we may achieve the satisfactions, the balanced vision, or perhaps merely the unequivocal motives unattained in our own lives.

The students valued literature as a means of enlarging their knowledge of the world, because through literature they acquire not so much additional *information* as additional *experience*. New understanding is conveyed to them dynamically and personally. Literature provides a *living-through*, not simply *knowledge about*: not the fact that lovers have died young and fair, but a living-through of *Romeo and Juliet;* not theories about Rome, but a living-through of the conflicts in *Julius Caesar* or the paradoxes of *Caesar and Cleopatra.* In contrast to the historian's generalized and impersonal account of the hardships of the pioneer's life, they share these hardships with Per Hansa and Beret in Rölvaag's *Giants in the Earth.* The sociologist analyzes for them the problems of the Negro in our society; in Wright's *Native Son,* Baldwin's *The Fire Next Time,* Ellison's *The Invisible Man,* they themselves suffer these problems in their human dimensions. The anthropologist can teach them the ethnology of the Eskimo and the social patterns in the Philippines or India;

in Peter Freuchen's novel *Eskimo*, in Bulosan's *The Laughter of My Father*, and in Markandaya's *Nectar in a Sieve*, they themselves become part of these cultures. They may read encomiums on the devotion and disinterestedness of the scientist; in *Madame Curie* or *Arrowsmith* they share his single-minded zeal, his frustrations, and the intellectual and emotional rewards of his success.

The college girls were equally frank about the escape value of literature. They were especially ready to speak of release from the circumstances and pressures of their everyday lives. This term *escape* has perhaps been used too often in an indiscriminately derogatory sense; there are useful and harmful forms of escape. Anything that offers refreshment and a lessening of tension may have its value in helping us to resume our practical lives with renewed vigor. The unfavorable overtones of the term are due to the failure of much of the so-called literature of escape to accomplish this.[4] The greatest literary works may have for a particular reader the value of an "escape." Our lives may be so monotonous, so limited in scope, so concentrated on practical survival, that the experience of profound and varied emotions, the contact with warm, subtle personalities, the understanding of the wide range of human capacities and human problems, may be denied us except through the medium of literature. Or a great work may give even to the person living a full and happy life a moment of change, of "escape" from the demands of "reality." The capacity of a particular book to offer such values will be directly related to the emotional needs of the reader and his particular situation and preoccupations.

[4] See Chapter 7, pp. 209–214.

Another important potential satisfaction from literature, which the students only implied, is the possibility of compensating for lacks or failures through identification with a character who possesses qualities other than our own or who makes fuller use of capacities similar to our own. The young girl may in this way identify with Juliet or with Elizabeth Bennet; the boy, chafing at his childish status, may identify with an epic hero. This compensatory mechanism may in part explain our vivid identification with characters very different from ourselves. Here again, the force of the reader's emotional reactions will be channeled in ways dictated by his sense of his own lacks. This process is usually considered in terms far too crude, since literature may provide very subtle kinds of compensation. The human being has latent capacities for many modes of life and action that he would not elect, but whose exercise through literature will nevertheless give him satisfaction.

The ability to understand and sympathize with others reflects the multiple nature of the human being, his potentialities for many more selves and kinds of experience than any one being could express. This may be one of the things that enables us to seek through literature an enlargement of our experience. Although we may see some characters as outside ourselves—that is, we may not identify with them as completely as we do with more congenial temperaments—we are nevertheless able to enter into their behavior and their emotions. Thus it is that the youth may identify with the aged, one sex with the other, a reader of a particular limited social background with members of a different class or a different period.

One student made rather surprisingly articulate another personal value of literature: its objective presentation of our own problems. It places them outside ourselves, enables us to see them with a certain detachment and to understand our own situation and motivation more objectively. The young girl irked by the limitations of the small-town environment may derive such objectivity from Anderson's *Winesburg, Ohio*. The boy unconsciously rejecting an overpossessive mother may gain insight from Howard's *The Silver Cord*. This process of objectification may also go on in a disguised form. Without conscious admission of the relevance of the literary experience to our own practical situation, our attitudes may be clarified either by a violent reaction against what we have read or by assimilation of it.

To have impact, a work need not treat circumstances overtly similar to the reader's situation. The power of the work may reside in its underlying emotional structure, its configuration of human drives. Thus, an adolescent boy may resent restraints imposed by accepted authority —family, school, or employer. At this moment of his life, he might find in *Mutiny on the Bounty* satisfying expression of his rebellion; he might react with extraordinary intensity to *The Devil's Disciple* or *The Loneliness of the Long Distance Runner*. College freshmen have been known, very disconcertingly, to sympathize inordinately with Lear's unfilial daughters. Similarly, the youth who has just experienced disillusionment with friends might find the relationship between Othello and Iago the most significant part of the entire play. When *Hamlet* is a moving experience for the adolescent today, may it not be because the play gives form to a prevalent mood of uncertainty and disillusionment, of reluctance to undertake aggressive action in a world gone awry?

An intense response to a work will have its roots in capacities and experiences already present in the personality and mind of the reader. This principle is an important one to remember in the selection of literary materials to be presented to students. It is not enough merely to think of what the student *ought* to read. Choices must reflect a sense of the possible links between these materials and the student's past experience and present level of emotional maturity.

There is an even broader need that literature fulfills, particularly for the adolescent reader. Much that in life itself might seem disorganized and meaningless takes on order and significance when it comes under the organizing and vitalizing influence of the artist. The youth senses in himself new and unsuspected emotional impulsions. He sees the adults about him acting in inexplicable ways. In literature he meets emotions, situations, people, presented in significant patterns. He is shown a causal relationship between actions, he finds approval given to certain kinds of personalities and behavior rather than to others, he finds molds into which to pour his own nebulous emotions. In short, he often finds meaning attached to what otherwise would be for him merely brute facts.

SUBSTANTIATING DE MAUPASSANT's complaint, none of the students made articulate a sense of that emotional equilibrium which is a mark of a complete esthetic experience. This omission is undoubtedly explained in part by the difficulty of describing such moments of mental and emotional poise or illumination. It is probably even more largely explained by the fact that the adolescent's attention is to an extraordinary degree focused on the personal import of what he reads. We have glanced at several of the factors that produce this preoccupation with the human contribution of literature.

Yet for the adolescent, too, these human concerns are embodied in the esthetic experience. The student who has lived through the experience of *Othello* will have been carried along on the wave of feeling and insight to the moment of ultimate resolution. His sense of the gamut of human experience and emotion will have been broadened. He will have entered, for the time, into a world of strange moral values and responsibilities. But this participation in human affairs will have been possible only because *Othello* is above all a work of art. The resonant blank verse, the opulent imagery, the swiftly paced structure of the play, are an integral part of this reliving of Othello's and Desdemona's tragedy. The entire experience has a structure and an inner logic, a completeness that only the great work of art can offer. The student would tend not to speak of this phase of the matter, precisely because these formal and stylistic elements of the drama were an aspect of his apprehension of its human import.

It is possible to do justice to this problem of form and style without being false to the psychological process involved in the relationship between book and reader. Note that we have been discussing those social insights and the human understandings that may arise specifically from the experience of literature. *The enhancement of these human values will therefore depend upon the intensification and enrichment of the individual's esthetic experience.*

Any theory about art that tends to break up the response to literature into distinct segments, whether under the headings "social" versus "esthetic" or "form" versus "content," is misleading. Of course, the teacher must himself have a zestful appreciation of the sensuous and formal aspects of literature if he is to be of any help to his students. Yet if he does not in addition see these aspects of literature in their organic relation to those broader human aspects that we have been discussing, he will merely tend to impoverish his students' sense of both literature and life.

More than merely the intellectual "content" of literature was involved in the discussion in Chapter 1, and in the preceding consideration of factors molding the reader's response. Those factors influence the reader's sensitivities to all aspects of the work of art as an integral whole. Indeed, although one may talk about qualities of form and style or about content, this theoretic division has little to do with the actual psychological situation when we are responding to a given literary work. Each of these aspects of the work exists by virtue of the other aspects.

We may, for example, talk about something called the sonnet form, but such a form can be apprehended only as it is embodied in a particular sonnet made up of particular words. We cannot dissociate from the total effect of the poem the meaning of the words—the images, concepts, and emotions that they denote, the nuances of feeling and the associations that cluster about them. It is equally impossible to distill from the total effect the sound of the words or the beat of the verse. We can tap out the rhythmic pattern of a poem, but will anyone contend that our sense of that tapping is the same as our experience of the rhythmic pattern when it is embodied in a sequence of sonorous and meaningful words? Obviously, the effect of a sonnet on a person who does not know the language can offer few clues to the impression that would be produced by the sound and rhythm upon a person who understood the meaning of the words as well. The complete effect of a particular sonnet results from the fact that different elements act on us simultaneously, reinforce and, one might almost say, create one another. Similarly, in music we may define a particular form such as the fugue, but we can never experience the form abstracted from the complex texture of some specific musical work.

It is equally impossible to experience "content" apart from some kind of form. It is a cliché to say that a paraphrase of a poem does not represent the actual content of the poem. Certain of its concepts and implications have merely been abstracted and rephrased. One might, for example, state the various ideas and name the various emotions encountered in "The Rime of the Ancient Mariner," but this would, in a sense, be offering not only a different form but also a different "content." The various concepts and images take on significance and emotional and intellectual overtones from precisely the form in which they are experienced in the poem. Even a transposition of the different stanzas would have given them a different significance. To encounter an idea after our emotions have been aroused through various images and rhythms gives that idea a very different significance from what it would have if presented in another rhythmic pattern or in another sequence. Hence the term *content of the literary work* is confusing when used to indicate abstract intellectual import.

If we think in terms of the total experience of the reader, we shall not be thus misled. We shall see that the formal relationships in the literary work—the verse form, rhyme scheme, sentence structure, plot structure—or the other sensuous elements, such as the imagery, do not have a separable or even a clearly distinguishable effect. How can we legitimately dissociate anything called the content of a poem from the interplay of sensations and concepts and emotional overtones produced by the particular words in the particular relations to one another in which they are found in the text itself? Only as we become sensitive to the influence of subtle variations in rhythm and in the sound and emotional overtones of words, only as we become more refined instruments upon which the poet can play, will we be able to experience the full import of the poem.

Similarly, it is essential to hold firmly to the totality of the reader's experience of the literary work whenever we are tempted to speak as though the structure of a play or novel were distinct from the specific sensations, emotions, personalities, events, presented in the work. The sense of the form or structure of the play or novel results from the fact that these particular elements and no others are *experienced* in particular relations to one another. Just as in a melody a particular note takes on color and character from its context, so in a play or novel, the significance of any particular scene or personality is the result of the context in which it is encountered.

To return to *Othello*: recall the scene in which Desdemona sings the "Willow Song." This has great poignancy; we have lived through the mounting tension of the intrigue, and now the innocent Desdemona sings as Emilia prepares her for the night. This episode would have little pathos or even interest for anyone who knew only that scene of the play or if that scene were placed at some different point in the play. It would be hard to say whether the transposition would be a change in form or in content. The actual result would be to make the reader or the audience see and feel fewer human implications in the scene. Similarly, although we may speak of the structure of the play and even make diagrams that purport to represent the rising tension and the climax, we must remember that the rising tension results from the reader's identification with certain personalities presented to him and from his vicarious experience of emotions and ideas.

Thus we find ourselves involved in a circular argument. If we start with form or structure, we find that we are merely talking about the particular relationships of certain human sensations, concepts, and emotions. If we talk about so-called content, we find that we are merely dealing with the significance that arises from a particular series of relationships among certain sensations, concepts, and emotions. Teaching practices and assignments should be scrutinized to make sure that students are not given the idea that the formal relationships in a literary work exist apart from, and are merely superimposed upon, something called the *content*. Much truer to the reality of both literary creation and literary experience is the sense of how organically interfused are these two phases of the work of art.

Of course, students need to understand the nature of the diverse literary forms—the lyric, the epic, the novel, the essay, the drama—forms that our literary ancestors and contemporaries have developed through the cyclic process of "convention and revolt." We want to share with our students the pleasure to be derived from a discriminating response to the means that the author has employed and the variations or reversals he has based upon the traditional pattern. Knowledge of the problems of artistry, a recognition of the author's aims and of the technical difficulties involved in achieving these aims, often tend to increase enjoyment. Pleasure arises from discovering the kind of structure that the artist is creating, from seeing things fall into a pattern. Awareness of the function of various characters or episodes or images illuminates what the work as a whole "means." However, that perception of order or pattern is important to the average reader only in relation to the impact of the work as a whole. And these sensitivities to the author's technique are not necessarily best fostered or manifested through a labeling of devices or an analysis of forms.

One of the best ways of helping students to gain this appreciation of literary form and artistry is to encourage them to engage in such imaginative writing. In this way they will themselves be involved in wrestling with the materials offered them by life or by their reaction to it; they will discover that problems of form and artistry are not separable from the problems of clarifying the particular sense of life or the particular human mood that the work of art is destined to embody.

The reader's role, we recall, is an active, not a passive, one. The artist using the medium of words must, like other artists, make his appeal primarily to the senses if his desire is "to reach the secret spring of responsive emotions." Because he cannot tangibly represent what he offers, the writer must select significant images that will stimulate his reader to undertake the process of sensuous and intellectual recreation. The greater the reader's ability to respond to the stimulus of the word, and the greater his capacity to savor all that words can signify of rhythm, sound, and image, the more fully will he be emotionally and intellectually able to participate in the literary work as a whole. In return, literature will help the reader to sharpen further his alertness to the sensuous quality of experience. Such training is extremely necessary in our society, geared as it is toward a neglect of the quality of the means in an obsession with practical ends.

Here again, even a discussion of the writer's artistic medium necessarily leads to emphasis on the kinds of human experience toward which words point. Words themselves, it is true, not only refer to something else but also possess a sensuous quality of their own. The child, long before he understands the meaning of the words, will derive pleasure from the sound, the rhythmic movement, and subtle inflection of a lyric by Blake. But this represents only the thinnest and most fragmentary response to words. Those pleasant sounds can evoke for him extraordinarily rich experiences as his mental and emotional capacities are enlarged and he comes to know what the words symbolize. We must foster the child's delight in the music of words, but we must also help him to link up definite experiences and concepts with those sounds as they occur in different contexts; he must come to understand more and more what a word implies in the external world. These aims apply, of course, throughout the whole process of the individual's acquisition of language. Perhaps adolescent students are often impervious to the appeal of literature because for them words do not represent keen sensuous, emotional, and intellectual perceptions. This indicates that throughout the entire course of their education, the element of personal insight and experience has been neglected for verbal abstractions.

The teacher who himself possesses a lively awareness of the world about him will seek to develop the student's sensuous endowment so that he may gain from life and literature the greatest measure of enjoyment of sound, color, and rhythm. As the student looks more closely at the world of sight and sound, he will also come to distinguish their effect upon his own moods. He will come to notice dominant impressions, to see certain patterns in events, to sense the clues to the states of mind of other people. Sensuous details will acquire significance as they lead him to glimpse the emotional undercurrents that flow so swiftly beneath the surface of everyday life. In the same way, greater receptivity to the sensuous stimuli offered by literature must be paralleled by enriched emotional associations with them.

On the one hand, emphasis on abstract verbalization, on intellectual concepts cut off from their roots in concrete sensuous experience, is destructive of responsiveness to literature. On the other hand, image, form, structure, the whole sensuous appeal of literature, can be fully apprehended only within the framework of a complex sense of life. Sensitivity to literary technique should be linked up with sensitivity to the array of human joys and sorrows, aspirations and defeats, fraternizings and conflicts.

THE TEACHER REALISTICALLY concerned with helping his students to develop a vital sense of literature cannot, then, keep his eyes focused only on the literary materials he is seeking to make available. He must also understand the personalities who are to experience this literature. He must be ready to face the fact that the student's reactions will inevitably be in terms of his own temperament and background. Undoubtedly these may often lead him to do injustice to the text. Nevertheless, the student's primary experience of the work will have had meaning for him in these personal terms and no others. No matter how imperfect or mistaken, this will constitute the present meaning of the work for him, rather than anything he docilely repeats about it. Only on the basis of such direct emotional elements, immature though they may sometimes be, can he be helped to build any sounder understanding of the work. The nature of the student's rudimentary response is, perforce, part of our teaching materials.

The individual reader brings the pressure of his personality and needs to bear on the inextricably interwoven "human" and "formal" elements of the work. If his own experience of life has been limited, if his moral code is rigid and narrow or slack and undiscriminating, the quality of his response to literature will necessarily suffer.

Conversely, any sensitivity to literature, any warm and enjoyable participation in the literary work, will necessarily involve the sensuous and emotional responsiveness, the human sympathies, of the reader. We shall not further the growth of literary discrimination by a training that concentrates on the so-called purely literary aspect. We go through empty motions if our primary concern is to enable the student to recognize various literary forms, to identify various verse patterns, to note the earmarks of the style of a particular author, to detect recurrent symbols, or to discriminate the kinds of irony or satire. Acquaintance with the formal aspects of literature will not in itself insure esthetic sensitivity. One can demonstrate familiarity with a wide range of literary works, be a judge of craftsmanship, and still remain, from the point of view of a rounded understanding of art, esthetically immature. The history of criticism is peopled with writers who possess refined taste but who remain minor critics precisely because they are minor personalities, limited in their understanding of life. Knowledge of literary forms is empty without an accompanying humanity.

When literary training is viewed as primarily the refinement of the student's power to enter into literary experiences and to interpret them, there will be little danger of excessive emphasis on one or another approach. We shall be aware of the need to sharpen the student's responses to the sensuous, technical, and formal aspects of the literary work. But we shall see these as merged with— reinforcing and reinforced by—responses to those elements in the work that meet the reader's need for psychological satisfactions and social insights. Particularly for the adolescent reader, the desire for self-understanding and for knowledge about people provides an important avenue into literature. The young reader's personal involvement in a work will generate greater sensitivity to its imagery, style, and structure; this in turn will enhance his understanding of its human implications. A reciprocal process emerges, in which growth in human understanding and literary sophistication sustain and nourish one another. Both kinds of growth are essential if the student is to develop the insight and the skill needed for participation in increasingly complex and significant literary works.

THIS VIEW OF THE literary experience raises a number of questions. What does it signify for actual teaching aims and methods? How can students develop sensitivity to all the organically related facets of the literary work? What adolescent needs and interests should the teacher be aware of? How can the study of literature enable students to understand themselves better and to see human beings and society in a broader context of emotions and ideas? In short, how can students be helped to achieve literary experiences of higher and higher quality? Parts Two and Three will consider such questions.

PART II

The Human Basis of Literary Sensitivity

CHAPTER 3

The Setting for Spontaneity

During a reorganization of education on the Indian reservations some years ago, it was discovered that in some classes the Indian boys and girls were being required to read Restoration comedies. It seems ridiculous that these children, whose past experience had been only the conditions of the reservation village and the vestiges of their native culture, should be plunged into reading the sophisticated products of a highly complex foreign country remote in space and time. Can it be doubted that the children could "make nothing of it"? Any show of "understanding" a Restoration play would undoubtedly be only a parroting of empty words and phrases to satisfy a teacher's demand.

The plight of these Indian children probably differs only in degree from the average American child's relation to much of the literature he reads in his classroom. The relevance of literary materials has too often been measured in terms of purely verbal operations. To demonstrate "understanding" of a work has been primarily a matter of paraphrasing, defining, applying the proper rubrics. This can be accomplished even when the work presents nothing that awakens an intimate personal response. Too often, the average student might utter Coleridge's lament in "Dejection" when he gazed at the sky and the stars, and could only "see, not feel, how beautiful they are!" The teacher is concerned with making the student "see" what in the work of literature has made *others* deem it significant. Whether the student himself "feels" this is an entirely different question, and one that is rarely considered.

Undoubtedly in many English classes today the student functions on two separate and distinct planes. On one plane, he learns the ideas about literature that his teacher or the literary critic presents to him as traditional and accepted by educated people. On the other plane, he reads the literature and reacts to it personally, perhaps never expressing that reaction or even paying much attention to it. Only occasionally will there be a correlation of these two planes of activity. Teachers frequently approach a book or a poem as though it were a neatly labeled bundle of literary values to be pointed out to the student. If the consensus of critical opinion recognizes certain virtues in a given work, the critics' direct experience of it has led them to perceive those values. The student's repetition of that critical opinion would have validity only when he himself had lived through an experience similar to the critics'. When the images and ideas presented by the work have no relevance to the past experiences or emotional needs of the reader, only a vague, feeble, or negative response will occur.

It is not at all surprising that so few of even our college graduates have formed the habit of turning to literature for pleasure and insight. The novel or play or poem has been made for them too much something to know "about," something to summarize or analyze or define, something to identify as one might identify the different constellations on a star map or define the qualities of a particular chemical element. For is there a great difference, after all, between the process of memorizing the properties of hydrogen or its peculiar reactions to changes in temperature, and the process of memorizing that the romantic movement was a reaction against eighteenth-century classicism, was concerned with the individual, and produced a great deal of "nature poetry"? How many students have reeled this off for an examination and yet never have felt the full impact of a romantic poem! Literary history has its values as have the various approaches developed by literary critics and scholars. But all the student's knowledge about literary history, about authors and periods and literary types, will be so much useless baggage if he has not been led primarily to seek in literature a vital personal experience.

Far from helping the student in this direction, much literature teaching has the effect of turning him away from it. He is to a certain degree insulated from the direct impact of the work. He comes to it with the idea that he should see in it first of all those generalized values or kinds of information that the "literature class" stresses—

summaries of plot and theme, identification of certain characteristics that mark its period or genre, certain traits of style and structure. Much of even the best literature teaching is analogous to typical American "spectator sports." The students sit on the sidelines watching the instructor or professor react to works of art. Though the student may develop a certain discrimination in the appreciation of professorial taste, this often tends to obscure the need for the student himself to develop a personal sense of literature.

The great value of the various scholarly and critical approaches to literature *in their proper place* will be considered later.[1] But they can be very easily transformed from useful aids into preoccupations that claim the center of attention and crowd the student's personal experience with literature into the dim outer fringe of vision. One could, for instance, become quite proficient in the history of Italian literature without knowing the language and without having read any Italian work even in translation. One would be able to sketch the sweeping lines of literary change, to discourse glibly on the special characteristics of the different periods, to name the contributions of its great writers, and to recount their biographies. It would be possible to learn summaries of the so-called content of their works, as for example, the story and the philosophy of *The Divine Comedy*. One might even hold forth on its relations to the dying medieval culture and the dawning Renaissance. Without acquaintance with the works themselves, all this information would lack essential substance. Much of the activity concerning literature with

[1] See Chapters 5, 7, and 8.

which the average student busies himself in school and college has something of this character. The frame is elaborately worked out, but there is a blank where the picture should be. Missing are the personal experience and understanding of the literary works which historical and biographical information should enhance.

The problem that the teacher faces first of all, then, is the creation of a situation favorable to a vital experience of literature. Unfortunately, many of the practices and much of the tone of literature teaching have precisely the opposite effect. They place a screen between the student and the book. The solution of this primary problem is therefore complicated by habitual attitudes and academic practices. The majority of English teachers still need to concentrate on this problem, for in many English classes today the instructor never even glimpses the student's personal sense of the work discussed. The teacher may be interested in, let us say, *Pride and Prejudice* from the point of view of the history of the novel form in England, or he may be eager to discuss the relation of style and theme. The student, however, may be impressed by the revelation that then, even as now, the business of finding a mate was no simple matter, and that then, even as now, personality clashes and the gap between generations were important. In many cases there is an unbridged gulf between anything that the student might actually feel about the book, and what the teacher, from the point of view of accepted critical attitudes and his adult sense of life, thinks the pupil should notice.

This often leads the student to consider literature something academic, remote from his own present concerns and needs. He recognizes a traditional aura about literature, but discards it when his school days are past. (We all know the student who says, "but I have *had* Shakespeare," as though it were something to suffer through and forget, like the measles.) Thus he does not learn to turn spontaneously to the literature of the past or to the comparably good literature of the present; such works, he feels, must be approached only in full dress and with all the decorum of critical method handed down by the teacher. He is cut off from the personal value they might have for him. Instead he turns to the pseudo-literature of the "pulp" magazines, comic books, or lurid drugstore paperbooks.

For many students, the only thing approaching a personal literary experience is provided by such "trashy" writings. This is certainly not because there is no good literature that could arouse their interest and fulfill their needs. Obviously, one reason for this situation must be the frequently defensive attitude toward "good books" built up in the mind of the student in school and in college. He has been given to understand that there are proper ways to react, there are certain things to look for—that he must be ready to discuss the "characterization" or to analyze "plot and subplot" or to talk about the author's "choice of words." To some extent this is a reflection of that blight on our educational system, its emphasis on the attainment of good marks rather than on the value of the work or the knowledge for its own sake. Instead of plunging into the work and permitting its full impact, he is aware that he must prepare for certain questions, that his remarks on the work must satisfy the teacher's already crystallized ideas about it.

The teacher of college freshman literature courses is often perturbed to find this attitude affecting the work of even the most verbally proficient students. They read literary histories and biographies, criticism, introductions to editions, so-called study guides, and then, if there is time, they read the works. Their interest in the author's life is often on a par with the Hollywood gossip column; or they have learned at best to view the work as a document in the author's biography. Their quest is for the sophisticated interpretation and the accepted judgment. If they have learned techniques of close analysis, they tend to look upon the work as a means of displaying their analytic virtuosity. They seem shut off from the personal nourishment that literature can give. Hence they are often insecure and confused when given the opportunity and responsibility to express their own honest responses to the work.

I. A. Richards published the classic documentation of this point in 1929. He asked his class at Cambridge University to write comments on unidentified poems, giving no clues to title, authorship, period, school, or literary value. As he reports in *Practical Criticism*,[2] the students found it extremely difficult to make up their minds about the poems or even to work out possible opinions from which to choose. They set forth an extraordinary variety of views, and the "reckless, desperate" tone of many of their comments revealed their bewilderment. Instead of

[2] New York, Harcourt, Brace and Company, 1929.

being able to apply to the poems neatly ticketed interpretations and judgments appropriate to their authorship and their literary period, the students were forced to base their comments on their own intimate reactions. In most cases, their training in literary history and their fund of critical dicta on good poetry were of very little help in handling their unvarnished primary personal responses. They were thus at the mercy of personal obsessions, chance associations, and irrelevant conventional opinions about poetry. Hence they often failed to understand the poems or to discriminate differences in literary quality.

Evidently, in most cases an unprecedented demand was being made upon these students. Yet during the whole course of their literary training they should have again and again been given the opportunity to handle their primary responses to the text. A secure approach to poetry would have utilized the "background" they possessed; but it would have been a tool, not a crutch.

Surely the majority of American students, subjected to similar experiments, would not yield a different picture even today, after several decades in which "close reading" has been increasingly stressed in colleges and secondary schools. The average American student probably would not reveal as much "literary background," let alone the ability to utilize it. We insist that students should not consult histories of literature or works of criticism in order to find out what to think about an author, but we have usually not sought to discover why they are so lacking in self-reliance.

Few teachers of English today would deny that the individual's ability to read and enjoy literature is the primary aim of literary study. In practice, however, this tends to be overshadowed by preoccupation with whatever can be systematically taught and tested. Or the English program becomes what can be easily justified to parents and administrators, whose own past English training has produced skepticism about the value of the study of literature. The professional preparation of the English teacher, moreover, often has little relation to actual conditions in the classroom.

How THEN CAN STUDENTS be enabled to have such vital experiences with literature that they will indeed come intimately and lastingly into their literary heritage? This has always been the concern of the teacher who is also a lover of literature. He has known that without this all his conscientious lecturings and questionings, all his "techniques" are valueless. To attempt a comprehensive answer to this problem would, of course, be fatuous. The following discussion will naturally tend to emphasize those aspects that seem to have been most generally neglected. The purpose is not to set a pattern or formula for any one teacher or class to follow, but to underline general considerations that should influence practice.

Unless the teacher himself values literary experience, revision of his aims or his methods will be futile. By implication, any definition of the ideal relationship between the student and the literary work applies also to the teacher. As long as an artificial and pedantic notion of literary culture persists, students will continue in their indifference to the great works of the past and present.

The teacher's personal love of literature, however, has

not always been proof against the influence of routine, pedantic notions concerning teaching methods. He is dismayed at the results indicated by the low level of taste about him; he undergoes constant frustration, or he consoles himself by focusing on the rare student who seems to possess the divine spark. To develop many such students the teacher must liberate himself as well as his pupils from self-defeating practices. He should not relinquish his own zestful sense of literature as a living art.

The persistence of many of the routine procedures in literature teaching makes it necessary to phrase some primary duties in negative terms. First is the necessity not to impose a set of preconceived notions about the proper way to react to any work. The student must be free to grapple with his own reaction. This primary negative condition does not mean that the teacher abdicates his duty to attempt to instill sound habits of reading or sound critical attitudes. Nor does this imply that historical and biographical background material will be neglected. The difference is that instead of trying to superimpose routine patterns, the teacher will help the student develop these understandings in the context of his own emotions and his own curiosity about life and literature.

The youth needs to be given the opportunity and the courage to approach literature personally, to let it mean something to him directly. The classroom situation and the relationship with the teacher should create a feeling of security. He should be made to feel that his own response to books, even though it may not resemble the standard critical comments, is worth expressing. Such a liberating atmosphere will make it possible for him to have an un-self-conscious, spontaneous, and honest reaction.

When the student feels the validity of his own experience, he will cease to think of literature as something that only a few gifted spirits can enjoy and understand in an "original" way. How often, when urged to speak out for himself, a student will respond, "But I'm not literary, the way Jane or John is!" Nothing is more conducive to this than the attitude of the instructor that he is one initiated into the esoteric mysteries of art, suffering with amused tolerance the Philistine reactions of the class. His function is to help the student realize that the most important thing is what literature means to him and does for him.

Another negative means of furthering a spontaneous response is to avoid placing undue importance upon the particular form in which the expression of the student's reaction should be couched. He should be able to express himself freely. Nor should there be constant insistence on summaries or rehashes of the work. That may become as artificial and inhibiting as any of the other routine methods. The young reader should feel free to let his comment take the form dictated by what he has lived through in reading the book. To set up some stereotyped form will probably focus the student's attention on what is to be required of him after he has read the book, rather than on the work itself as he evokes it from the text.

The effect of such assignments is illustrated by a father's report of his twelve-year-old daughter's experience with *Great Expectations*, which she had selected for individual reading. Her reaction was intense. She said to him, "This is a very, very deep book. You're thinking about the story, the strange things that happen to Pip—and all of a sudden you see another meaning back of it." She groped toward a phrasing of those "deeper" symbolic meanings and offered an unusually mature interpretation of the book. Later, her father found her at her desk, in despair before a blank sheet of paper with only the title of the book written on it. To his remark that surely she had much to say, she replied that none of those ideas would serve; she had to write a book report—summarize the plot, sketch the setting, describe any two characters, write a brief opinion or blurb. The little formula provided by the teacher as a guide had instead divorced the youngster from her actual experience of the novel. The book report she finally ground out revealed none of this response. Fortunately, her involvement in this powerful work had made her temporarily forget the assignment. The next time, she would be on her guard, less likely to pay attention to much beyond what would be useful for the book report. Conscientious teachers often thus unwittingly defeat their long-term aims by classroom methods, day-to-day assignments, and devices for evaluation.

An experience reported by a teacher documents this point: "As I was leafing through a tenth-grade poetry text, I found myself drawn into rereading the old Scottish ballad 'Edward, Edward' with its step-by-step revelations of a crime and its fearful aftermath. In the dialogue with his mother, you recall, he reveals that the blood on his sword is that of his 'fadir deir.' He utters his desperate decision to do penance wandering over the seas, leaving his halls to fall into ruin, his wife and children to wander the world as beggars. And then there is that final stanza:

> 'And what wul ye leive to your ain mither deir,
>   Edward, Edward?
> And what wul ye leive to your ain mither deir?
>   My deir son, now tell me O.'
> 'The curse of hell frae me sall ye beir,
>   Mither, mither,
> The curse of hell frae me sall ye beir,
>   Sic counseils ye gave to me O.'

"As I finished the poem, it was as though I had been participating in a Greek tragedy in capsule. Associations with Oedipus and Orestes were a measure of my involvement. And then I turned the page—'What is the name of this kind of poem? What characteristics does it share with other poems of this type? What is the effect of the refrain?'

"The shock of these questions drew me away from all that I had undergone in reading the text—the structure of feeling called forth by the pattern of events, my darkening mood as I saw the destruction of the family by the son's desperate crime and desperate penance, the horror of the final interchange. For the moment, I was the student, rudely torn from all this by the textbook editor's questions."

Is this not typical of what often happens in the classroom? Out of misguided zeal, the student is hurried into thinking or writing that removes him abruptly and often definitively from what he himself has lived through in reading the work. It therefore becomes essential to scrutinize all practices to make sure that they provide the opportunity for an initial crystallization of a personal sense of the work.

Although all students should not be required to give the same sort of expression to their reaction, in most cases a personal experience will elicit a definite response; it will lead to some kind of reflection. It may also lead to the desire to communicate this to others whom the boy or girl trusts. An atmosphere of informal, friendly exchange should be created. The student should feel free to reveal emotions and to make judgments. The primary criterion should not be whether his reactions or his judgments measure up to critical traditions, but rather the genuineness of the ideas and reactions he expresses. The variety and unpredictability of life need not be alien to the classroom. Teachers and pupils should be relaxed enough to face what indeed happened as they interpreted the printed page. Frank expression of boredom or even vigorous rejection is a more valid starting point for learning than are docile attempts to feel "what the teacher wants." When the young reader considers why he has responded in a certain way, he is learning both to read more adequately and to seek personal meaning in literature.

There is no formula for giving students the assurance to speak out. One experienced teacher has found that his students are encouraged by mention of comments made by other students in past discussions. Another finds that classes that are accustomed to the traditional recitation pattern may be reluctant to engage in spontaneous discussion but will welcome the chance to write brief anonymous comments on a work at the beginning of a meeting. Some of these comments selected at random will serve to elicit further frank reactions and interchange. This teacher sometimes analyzes the written comments and later reports on trends and contrasts as a way of focusing on problems of importance to the group. Sometimes a general "unstructured" question, to borrow a term from the psychologist, will be enough to open the discussion. The teacher needs to maintain the conviction that it is important to place the discussion of the text in this matrix of personal response. He will also need to develop the security to permit a rather free-flowing discussion to begin with, before the group can be helped to focus on problems and skills of interpretation relevant to them.

A situation conducive to free exchange of ideas by no means represents a passive or negative attitude on the part of the teacher. To create an atmosphere of self-confident interchange he must be ready to draw out the more timid students and to keep the more aggressive from monopolizing the conversation. He must be on the alert to show pleased interest in comments that have possibilities and to help the students clarify or elaborate their ideas. He must keep the discussion moving along consistent lines by eliciting the points of contact between different students' opinions. His own flexible command of the text and understanding of the reading skills it requires will be called into play throughout.

One of the most valuable things the students will acquire from this is the ability to listen with understanding to what others have to say and to respond in relevant terms. If they have thus far been subjected to the typical school routine, the tendency is at first for them to address themselves only to the teacher; the conversational ball is constantly thrown to the teacher, who then throws it to another student, who again returns it to the teacher, and so on. In a more wholesome situation, the ball is passed from student to student, with the teacher participating as one of the group. This interchange among students must be actively promoted.

BUT SHOULD NOT THE TEACHER or instructor enter more positively into the picture? Should his function be only to select a sufficiently wide range of good books, place them upon the shelves of a library, turn the students loose to seek their own mental and emotional nourishment, and then listen to their spontaneous comments? Even the decision as to what should be placed on the shelves of this library would make the teacher's task an influential one. Ideally, general considerations such as have been suggested thus far would guide his choices: an understanding of adolescent needs and conflicts, and a recognition of any circumstances in their personal and social background that would make certain books of the past or present particularly interesting and illuminating.

This need to select from the body of literature those works to which particular students will be most receptive implies a knowledge not only of literature but also of the students. If the language, the setting, the theme, the central situation, all are too alien, even a "great work" will fail. All doors to it are shut. Books must be provided that hold out some link with the young reader's past and present preoccupations, anxieties, ambitions. Hence, a standard literary diet prescribed for all has negated the reality of the school situation. In our heterogeneous society, variations from group to group, and from individual to individual, require a wide range of literary materials that will serve as the bridge from the individual's experience to the broad realms of literature. Such factors as the students' general background, level of maturity, linguistic history, major difficulties and aspirations, would guide the teacher's selection of works to bring to their attention.[3]

There is much to be said for Newman's vision of a university as a place where young people have access to books. Until quite recently, after all, English literature was not a subject for organized study and teaching. Yet it was a vital and absorbing interest to many, perhaps because there was no superstructure of traditional teaching practice connected with it. If the student turned to English literature, it was because he felt its personal value. He read with a free spirit, not because the academic powers decreed a knowledge of it necessary, but perhaps precisely because it was outside the stultifying routines

[3] Much in the following chapters will relate to this matter of selection. Ultimately, of course, students should learn to select their own books. An account of how high school students developed increasing maturity and breadth of choice when permitted to choose the books to be added to the school library is to be found in Professor Lou L. LaBrant's *An Evaluation of the Free Reading in Grades Ten, Eleven, and Twelve* (Columbus, Ohio State University Press, 1936). See also *Were We Guinea Pigs?* (Holt, 1938), and the report on these students as adults, Margaret Willis, *The Guinea Pigs after Twenty Years* (Ohio State University Press, 1961). Under the restricted conditions of most public school systems, however, the pressing need is that teachers should be aware of what books students require and should exert pressure for their introduction into the school library.

of the curriculum. Unfortunately, it sometimes seems that it would be much better if students were turned loose in a library to work out a personal approach to literature for themselves.

Nevertheless, the teacher of literature may have a powerful and beneficial influence. The basic postulate is that such influence will be the elaboration of the vital influence inherent in literature itself. Important as it is, the selection of a humanly significant book list is only the first of the teacher's important functions. To reject the routine treatment of literature as a body of knowledge and to conceive of it rather as a series of possible experiences only clears the ground. Once the unobstructed impact between reader and text has been made possible, extraordinary opportunities for a real educational process are open to the teacher.

A situation in which students did nothing but give free rein to their reactions, their likes and dislikes, would undoubtedly have psychiatric value. The psychologists warn us about the neurotic effects of the driving nature of our whole culture. In the compulsive atmosphere of the average school and college today, there is a tremendous pressure on students to fulfill requirements and to meet standards. A literature class where the student could feel that everything that he thought or said was equally valuable might possibly have a therapeutic effect. But the development of literary understanding is a more positive goal. The study of literature should give the student the form of emotional release which all art offers and, at the same time, without strain or pressure, should help him gain ever more complex satisfactions from literature. A spontaneous response should be the first step toward increasingly mature primary reactions.

CERTAINLY, LIVELY, UNTRAMMELED discussion bespeaks an admirable educational setting. The fact that the student is articulate and eager to express himself is a wholesome sign. The teacher has given the student a feeling of adequacy, a sense that his experiences and ideas are worthy of consideration. Yet all of this, as great an achievement as it represents, only means that the obstacles to real education have been eliminated. The student still needs to acquire mental habits that will lead to literary insight, critical judgment, and ethical and social understanding. There still remains the necessity for positive aids to intellectual development. Though a free, uninhibited emotional reaction to a work of art or literature is an absolutely *necessary* condition of sound literary judgment, it is not, to use the logician's term, a *sufficient* condition. Without a real impact between the book and the mind of the reader, there can be no process of judgment at all, but honest recognition of one's own reaction is not in itself sufficient to insure sound critical opinion. Given this free response, all things shall be added unto us. The implication is that there are other things to be added. Teachers who have been pioneers in freeing themselves from the old routines will be especially aware of the importance of envisaging this constructive phase of the problem.

One occasionally meets a student who has been given unlimited scope and is refreshingly honest in expressing his reactions to literature. Often, nevertheless, although his attitude toward books may be unspoiled by false reverence for what is "correct," his is not an emotionally organized or reasoned approach to literature. He is still at the mercy of his raw reactions, still uncritically ready to proffer every judgment dictated by the chance circumstances of his own personal life. Undoubtedly he is much better off than students who have been deadened to any direct sense of literature, but he is still functioning at the lowest critical level. He needs to retain his spontaneity and yet to develop further, to make each literary experience the source of enhanced capacities for his next experience. For he can begin to achieve a sound approach to literature only when he reflects upon his response to it, when he attempts to understand what in the work and in himself produced that reaction, and when he thoughtfully goes on to modify, reject, or accept it.

THIS CHAPTER HAS UNDERLINED the importance of a relationship between teacher and students that will permit the student to respond intimately and spontaneously to literature. This aim, it was seen, has sweeping implications for classroom procedure and for the choice of works to be read and discussed. Yet enabling the student to approach the text without artificial restrictions and to respond in his own terms is only one aspect of the teacher's role. He has simply established the conditions for carrying out another equally important aspect of his task: to initiate a process through which the student can clarify and enlarge his response to the work. This entails complementary objectives: on the one hand, a critical awareness of his own re-actions, and on the other hand, a keener and more adequate perception of all that the text offers. Both kinds of advance will go on simultaneously, each making the other possible. The complementary character of these two phases of the development of critical powers has hitherto been insufficiently recognized. They will be the concern of the next two chapters.

CHAPTER 4

What the Student Brings to Literature

ONLY CERTAIN ASPECTS of the teaching process have thus far been considered; in any actual class the different phases will not be so sharply separate. The creation of a setting for personal response is basic, as is a situation in which students stimulate one another to organize their diffuse responses and formulate their views. But as the discussion proceeds, the teacher will become involved in the further task of leading the students toward a fuller participation in what the text offers. This requires that the student critically revaluate his own assumptions and pre-occupations. The teacher can help in this process only if he understands some of the possible forces molding the student's response and can anticipate some of the major needs and concerns of adolescents in our society.

In the interchange of ideas the student will be led to compare his reactions with those of other students and of the teacher (later, if necessary, of established critics).

He will see that a particular work may give rise to attitudes and judgments different from his own. Some interpretations, he will discover, are more defensible than others in terms of the text as a whole. Yet he will also become aware of the fact that sometimes more than one reasonable interpretation is possible.[1] From this interplay of ideas questions will arise: Why was his reaction different from the other students'? Why did he choose one particular slant rather than another? Why did certain phases of the book or poem strike him more forcibly than others? Why did he misinterpret or ignore certain elements? The attainment of a sound vision of the work will require the disengagement of the passing or irrelevant from the fundamental and appropriate elements in his response to the text. What was there in his state of mind that led to a distorted or partial view of the work? What in his temperament and past experience helped him to understand it more adequately?

The reading of a particular work at a particular moment by a particular reader will be a highly complex process. Personal factors will inevitably affect the equation represented by book plus reader. His past experience and present preoccupations may actively condition his primary spontaneous response. In some cases, these things will conduce to a full and balanced reaction to the work. In other cases, they will limit or distort.

The experienced teacher will undoubtedly be able to recall many illustrations of responses to literature colored by some personal factor. A personal preoccupation or an automatic association with a minor phrase or an attitude

[1] See Chapter 5.

toward the general theme will lead to a strong reaction
that has very little to do with the work. A word such as
home or *mother* or a phrase such as *my country*, with its
many conventional, sentimental associations, may set off
a reaction that tends to blind the reader to the context of
these words. The same thing happens on perhaps an even
larger scale in connection with fiction and drama. A
young college graduate, for example, expressed herself
most forcibly concerning *Anna Karenina*. She had no
sympathy, she said, for Anna, who was so preoccupied
with her own affairs and who did not appreciate her husband; he was undoubtedly the kind of man who loves
deeply but is unable to communicate his feeling to others.
When asked to point out in the text itself the basis for her
interpretation, she replied, "But there are people like
that, with very warm hearts and intense affections, who
are unable to let others know it. Why, my own father is
like that!"

The personal sources of this reader's response were revealed here more clearly than is usually possible in a
classroom or a school situation. Something accidental to
the book had caused her to identify Karenin with her
father. This is typical, however, of the less obvious ways
in which we tend to project something out of our own
experience which probably has been only vaguely suggested by the text. Some such projection of the student's
own experience or preoccupation may also cause the
reader to have a much more intense emotional experience
than is appropriate. Rosamond Lehmann might have been
astonished at hearing a seventeen-year-old girl pronounce
Invitation to the Waltz "the greatest tragedy I ever read."

It is not difficult to deduce that this girl's own personal history and present preoccupations would explain her reaction to this wistful story of a young girl's first formal dance.[2]

It is easy to detect the influence of the reader's preoccupations and past experiences when, as in the preceding instances, they lead to an interpretation unsupported by the text. Richards labeled this kind of misreading "mnemonic irrelevance." Sometimes emphasis on the negative influence of the reader's personal concerns obscures their positive contribution. The reader's fund of relevant memories makes possible any reading at all. Without linkage with the past experiences and present interests of the reader, the work will not "come alive" for him, or rather, he will not be prepared to bring it to life. Past literary experiences make up an important part of this equipment which the reader brings to literature, but these have usually been emphasized to the exclusion of other elements derived from general life experience. In order to share the author's insight, the reader need not have had identical experiences, but he must have experienced some needs, emotions, concepts, some circumstances and relationships, from which he can construct the new situations, emotions, and understandings set forth in the literary work.

---

[2] A college teacher who read this chapter in manuscript was reminded of an example of such "overweighting" that occurred in one of his classes. "A young man of lax views, and, I fear, lax practice, suddenly discovered to his immense delight that he had Shakespeare's authority for what he was saying and doing. Quoting Sir Toby's 'Dost thou think, because thou art virtuous, there shall be no more cakes and ale?' he solemnly announced, 'That is the greatest sentence ever written!'"

Moreover, that work will have been a vital experience to the extent that these new elements can be assimilated into, and perhaps even modify, the original background of personality. The reader must possess not only the intellectual potentialities but also the emotional readiness to participate in just this vicarious experience. In a motion-picture theater a ten-year-old boy was heard to exclaim, just as the hero and heroine fell into the traditional closing embrace, "This is the part I always hate!" That feeling is evidently not shared by the millions of adults who view such pictures weekly. Another instance: The vocabulary of Hemingway's "The Killers" is probably within the range of fourth-graders, but they would be unable to organize the words into a meaningful story. They would not possess the awareness required to recreate it with all its implications. This quite obvious point concerning emotional readiness is often forgotten. In the molding of any specific literary experience, what the student brings to literature is as important as the literary text itself.

Under usual teaching conditions the opportunities for coming to know the individual student are unfortunately rare. All the more reason, therefore, for the teacher to acquire some general understanding of the possible experiences and preoccupations typical of the particular group of students with which he is dealing. This will aid him in his choice of appropriate literary works and in his handling of the students' spontaneous responses to literature. What, then, does the adolescent bring to literature?

One approach to this question would be to consider in detail the segment of the present adolescent generation self-consciously in revolt against the older generation and "the Establishment." Under the threat of global war, taking an existential stance in the face of the "human condition," rejecting the practical values of the society, distressed at the slow advance of civil and social rights for the Negro, eager to enter into adult sex life, seeking intensity of experience through music and drugs—surely, these young people reveal the seriousness of the problems of their whole generation. Yet basically they are manifesting in extreme form processes that have been inherent in the situation of the adolescent in our society for decades. The following pages will not attempt a detailed picture of the (by no means homogeneous) present adolescent generation, but will instead suggest some persistent underlying factors affecting the adolescent in our culture.

THE ADOLESCENT READER comes to the experience of literature out of a mass of absorbing and conflicting influences. It has become a cliché to describe as a time of storm and stress this period when the child is coming into possession of the physical and temperamental endowments with which he will function as an adult. The marked physical changes that occur at this time have probably been excessively blamed for the difficulties that beset the adolescent years. Anthropologists have pointed out societies such as Samoa where these physical changes occur without emotional upheaval. In other cultures the period of personal turmoil may fall at an entirely different age and without reference to physiological changes. Nevertheless, although not the sole reason for the problems of adolescence in our society, these changes do have certain emotional repercussions. The girl or boy recognizes transformations in his emotional drives and personality traits. A heightened self-consciousness and curiosity about the self usually follow. Obviously this will color his attitude toward the essentially human art of literature.

The self-consciousness of the adolescent often centers about a concern with normality. His size, his height, his weight, his speed in movement, his strength, are constantly measured against what is considered appropriate for his age and social group. Philip Carey's sensitivity about his deformed foot in *Of Human Bondage* or Piggy's self-consciousness in *Lord of the Flies* can symbolize the agonies of embarrassment that many boys and girls suffer because of much slighter and perhaps almost undetectable deviations from what they have come to consider normal. Temperamental traits are subjected to equally searching scrutiny: aggressiveness or shyness, physical courage or timidity, the capacity to make friends, will be measured against some kind of norm.

Even the subtler emotional traits, feelings of anger and envy, of loyalty and affection toward others, may trouble him if he is not sure that others have similar feelings. He seeks some standards against which to measure himself and derives his sense of them from a great many different sources, among which may be literature.[3] This preoccupation is at least a possible factor in students' responses to particular works.

The distress, insecurity, and bewilderment that often accompany these physical and social changes are probably in large part due to the lack of mental preparation for

[3] See Chapter 7, pp. 200–204.

them. Particularly is this true of attitudes toward sex. In some societies, sexual maturation brings with it no insecurity because from early childhood the youth has been prepared for it. The adolescent in our culture often must seek knowledge about sex from surreptitious and unwholesome sources. Even when he has been adequately informed, the nervousness, prudery, and even prurience about sex in the society about him will undoubtedly cause complications. These difficulties have been intensified in recent years by a paradoxically rapid change in legal and social attitudes toward frankness about sexual behavior in, for example, the mass media. Another complicating factor is that youth are seeking to adopt adult behavior at progressively younger levels. Many of the interests and problems formerly characteristic of the high school years are now encountered in the junior high school. In this context of fluctuating attitudes toward sex, the boy and girl must make an adjustment to this newly recognized phase of their nature.

Even teachers who are aware of this preoccupation of youth too often tend to evade or gloss over anything in literature that might have a direct bearing on this vital concern. They thus rule out one of the most unfailingly powerful factors in the student's experience with literature. There is, of course, the opposing danger: the adult excessively zealous to prove his emancipation may initiate a crude pendulum swing that will reinforce a self-conscious sexuality, already sufficiently exploited by advertisements, mass media, and recent fiction. The adult's responsibility is to free himself and the youth from the distortions of both prudery and exaggerated reactions against it. Then understanding of the potential beauty and dignity of this aspect of man's life can be honestly fostered.

The youth, like Maugham's Philip Carey, wishes to find out "man's relation to the world he lives in, man's relation with the men among whom he lives, and, finally, man's relation to himself." The adolescent becomes more conscious of himself as a member of a family and a community. He becomes eager to impress others, to gain their friendship, and to be admitted into special groups, particularly of his peers. This often leads to intense self-consciousness about his own personality and to a great interest in the ways in which people influence one another. Adolescents experiment with various ways of approaching people; they seem to "try on" different social personalities as one might "try on" new clothes. And, indeed, they are making clothing an important aspect of the "adolescent culture" that is emerging.

The initiated adult tends to forget the awakening curiosity of the adolescent eager to see behind the façade of appearances. During childhood he has accepted the bare framework of relationships as they have presented themselves to him, in his family, in his neighborhood, and in the larger world. Now as he nears adult years, he finds these relationships acquiring new and unsuspected meanings. Parents who had been taken for granted, their relation to one another summed up in their common parental role, are suddenly seen to have hitherto-unsuspected intense emotional ties. In many biographical novels the adolescent hero or heroine is shown suddenly discovering the complex, hidden emotional life of the parents.

Thus it is with much of the adult world. The boy and girl question: What are the emotional realities behind the world of appearances? What indeed does it mean to the individual—and potentially to me, the adolescent, about to "live"—to be a leader or a follower, to be a member of a community, to earn one's living, to create a family, a circle of friends, to meet the ups and downs of fate, to know love and birth and death? What does it "feel like," from within, to be this kind of person or that? To be angelic, cruel, dominating, passive? What are the satisfactions, what are the elements, of the many roles that may be played? No longer satisfied with a childlike acceptance of the mere external gestures and trappings, he wishes to experience these things from within. It is often to literature—and principally fiction—that he turns. Here he seeks emotional release for the impulses already strong within him but denied satisfaction in his life as a minor; he seeks also the insight he craves into the possibilities that life offers, the roles perhaps open to him, the situations in which he might find himself.

STILL IN THE DEPENDENT childhood relation to the family yet feeling himself practically an adult, the youth often begins to question its authority. Even in a fairly stable society the period of adolescence brings with it a heightened tension within the family group. The youth strives to assert his existence as an individual apart from it. He sets up the goal of psychological as well as economic independence. These attitudes frequently come into conflict with the desire of the family to continue its dominance, and with the psychic need of the parents to feel themselves still an essential force in the life of their offspring. In the present period of great social transformations such strains and stresses have been tremendously intensified, and emancipation from the family becomes of even greater concern to the adolescent. Moreover, many who are members of minority groups, in effect, subcultures, will have grown up in families structured differently from the dominant pattern. The adolescent needs to understand that different cultures or ethnic groups assign different functions to the family. He will profit also from comprehension of the role of both dependence and independence in the development of the individual.

In recent years increasing attention has been given to study of the individual in relation to the cultural environment. The theories of personality development represented by the various schools of psychology have also become quite generally known. They are often incorporated into the training of teachers and are discussed in books and newspaper columns for parents. Yet in the education given the adolescent in America there is still little to enlighten him along these lines. He will sense needs and curiosities, and here again, it will often be only from the reflection of life offered by literature that he will acquire such insights.

The difficulties of the present-day adolescent are tremendously complicated by the fact that he is living at a moment when our society is singularly lacking in consistency, when economic and social changes are going on with unprecedented speed, and when few of the traditional ideas remain unquestioned. The boy and girl are suddenly catapulted from the relatively stable environment of the family into a world of innumerable alternative patterns; the burden of many choices is placed upon them. They often find the ways of life, the ideas, and the activities valued within the family to be ill adapted to the conditions of a changing world.

More probably than any other generation, the adolescents of today have the opportunity—sometimes felt as an awesome task—to formulate their own ideal life patterns. It is no longer assumed that the families they establish will be organized on one pattern; an extraordinary range of possible relationships with their mates and with their children can be envisaged. Similarly, in their choice of work the settled values need no longer hold. The prestige of the successful businessman has dwindled; the social value of the scientist, the artist, or the technician is increasingly recognized. Similar breadth of choice and challenge to personal creativity meet the adolescent as he seeks to develop a social philosophy and a set of values. Formerly, political questions or possible alternative organizations of society often seemed remote and academic to the adolescent involved in plans for his own personal life. Today, even the least socially conscious individual is forced into some recognition of the influence of the surrounding society. As he turns to literature, he cannot ignore this welter of shifting and uncertain social conditions.

This jolt to habitual attitudes has probably increased awareness of the indirect ways in which these attitudes are usually assimilated. In a stable society, the image of the rights and the responsibilities appropriate to, for example, the various family roles would be absorbed from childhood experience in the family and the community. Although more of these aspects of behavior have been forced into consciousness in our changing age, the processes of social patterning must be recognized. Ready-made standards and attitudes are derived from the family background, from the actions of neighbors, from repeatedly encountered images of accepted behavior. The very emotions with which a situation is spontaneously met have, after all, been learned through the force of cultural suggestion. A woman is indignant at the thought of her husband taking a second mate because from childhood on she has constantly observed that situation coupled with that reaction. For the same reason, a woman in certain African tribes will automatically acquiesce when her husband proposes to take a second wife. Notions of right and wrong, of approved behavior and appropriate responses, are in largest measure the result of such unconscious assimilation.

The present-day youth must often mediate between conventional ideas of life roles and the unprecedented circumstances of contemporary life. Innumerable influences in his environment will have given him a definite image, for instance, of the ways of behavior and feeling, even of the kind of temperament, appropriate or possible for a man or a woman. His parents and his family, through their own example and through explicit statement of the accepted attitudes, will have done much at an early point to set this mold. These will have been reinforced not only by the men and women about him but also by the distinctions between the things proper for men and for women repeated endlessly in the newspapers and popular magazines, by the types presented with monotonous similarity on the screen. Literature, it should be recalled, is another of these image-forming media. The human complications that are recognized as important and valid enough to be given explicit attention in fiction, in the newspapers or other mass media, reflect overwhelmingly the stereotyped notions of masculine and feminine nature and behavior. The man, dominant, masterful, superior; the woman, emotional, dependent, clinging, are the images most often and most forcibly presented even in this supposed age of woman's emancipation. These stereotypes will affect in some way the actions, feelings, and choices of the individual.

The post-World War II generation that seems in such large measure to have broken away from these conceptions still feels the pressure of these older, more deeply rooted images. The redefinition of possible roles for man and woman has gone on constantly in terms of revolt or readjustment to the older attitudes which still permeate our environment. On the one hand, the traditional notions of the behavior of man and woman are being constantly reiterated; on the other hand, the adolescent meets with increasing frequency images of men and women behaving in ways alien to the traditional ideas. Women enter into activities thought appropriate only for men; children are given freedom that would formerly have been considered dangerous; grandmothers behave in ways formerly thought scandalous.

The adolescent's own assumption of adult roles cannot therefore be as automatic as in the case of the youth in a more stable society. Indeed, the adolescent group is increasingly self-conscious in its relation to the older generation, and many are seeking much earlier entrance into adult roles. The adolescent's choices, nevertheless, will probably in large part be made on an emotional basis. Against the weight and pressure of the traditionally accepted image, there will be exerted the dramatic appeal of the new and perhaps more practical image. Many today seem to have retreated into a "teenage culture" as a way of evading the effort to sort out what is sound in the adult world. The assumption of the new type of role will often be made under the compulsion of new economic and social conditions. The old attitudes and habits of response will be constantly intruding themselves, complicating the individual's life, creating insecurity and confusion.

Out of such preoccupations the adolescent comes to his experience of literature today. Anything that his reading may contribute must take its place in the complex web of influences acting upon him. His attention will be diverted to those phases of any work that apply most clearly to his own emotional tensions and perplexities. He may often conceal the reactions dictated by his particular obsessions, yet a teaching situation such as was outlined in the preceding chapter would encourage him to articulate his response.

Still another conditioning factor affects the student's sensitivity to literature. The individualistic emphasis of our society builds up a frequent reluctance to see the implications for others of our own actions or to understand the validity of the needs that motivate other people's actions. The fact that the success of the individual must so often be at the expense of others places a premium on this kind of blindness. Teachers of literature need to take this cultural pressure into account, since it is so directly opposed to the attitude of mind they are attempting to foster. For literature by its very nature invokes participation in the experiences of others and comprehension of their goals and aspirations.

Furthermore, much of what the student reads and sees will tend to coarsen his sensibilities and to make him less able to respond fully to the complex and subtle nature of good literature. It would be fatuous to ignore the crude, oversimplified, and false pictures of human behavior and motivation presented by the mass media and the drugstore paperbacks. Not even the school as a whole, let alone the teacher of literature with his much more limited scope, can hope fully to counterbalance the great weight of the influences met in the surrounding society and in such institutions as the newspaper or television. The mere reading of a play by Shakespeare or a novel by George Eliot or Henry James cannot in itself be expected to wipe out the effect of all the desensitizing influences met outside the school or college.

Yet this does not justify a defeatism that would despair of influencing any but the gifted or those with unusually favorable backgrounds. On the contrary, understanding of the function of the literature teacher must be revised and broadened. He must do more than merely expose the student to great art. Although the reading of a novel will not in itself counteract all the unfavorable pressures, it can be a means for helping the student to develop conscious resistance to those influences. And this requires constant alertness to the nature of the social forces acting upon the student.

WHEN A STUDENT reads a particular work, one of innumerable possible variations upon this general picture of adolescent concerns will come into play. The particular community background of the student will be a factor; whether he comes from the North or the South, from city or country, from a middle-class or underprivileged home, will affect the nature of the understanding and the prejudices that he brings to the book. Lillian Smith's *Strange Fruit* or Paton's *Cry the Beloved Country* will elicit a very different response from students of Northern and Southern (or Westchester and Harlem) background. *Main Street* and *Manhattan Transfer* will not mean the same thing to the city boy and the country boy. The daughters of a mill owner and of a factory worker will probably react differently to Norris' *The Octopus* or Anderson's *Poor White*. And similar differences appear in responses to the literature of the past and of England. The fact that the American people are becoming increasingly urban may explain the growing difficulty of keeping alive the love of English poetry, so permeated by country imagery.

THE STUDENT WILL BRING to his reading the moral and religious code and social philosophy assimilated primarily from his family and community background. His parents may stem from a Main Street setting, or they may have turned from a life such as Marquand pictured to assume the duties of parenthood. Or like James Baldwin, he may have survived a ghetto childhood. The adolescents of the mid-century especially reflect this diversity of social climate. The religious background of the student might also play an important part. In a class studying Milton's *Paradise Lost,* a devout Catholic responded very differently from the student who had been brought up in an agnostic milieu. Similarly, a discussion of *Romeo and Juliet* was given a rather unusual turn by one student's insistence that there was no tragedy since the lovers would be reunited after death. Such diversity of response arises also from varying social and economic views. The child of well-to-do, middle-class parents who, after reading Henry Roth's *Call It Sleep,* insists that "some people like to be dirty and ragged and just won't work" will have rather a special approach to Dickens' *Hard Times* or Hugo's *Les Misérables.* Students will necessarily differ in the sensitivity they bring to many aspects of literary works.

Nor is it only these broader and more easily detected differences of equipment that affect reading. The adolescent preoccupation with family relations may take a wide variety of forms. For example, the degree of adjustment or maladjustment between the student's parents may be reflected in the student's receptivities or rejections. An extreme instance is the woman who confessed that she had hated almost every story or play she had read in high school because they ended on the note "they lived happily ever after," so contradictory to her own parents' unhappy disagreements. Authors, she felt, must be in some vast conspiracy of untruth. Here, certainly, is an instance in which acquaintance with some of the novels dealing with marital maladjustments might have led her to realize that writers attempt to illuminate the whole range of human experience and that, therefore, their images of possible happiness might also be given some credence. As for this woman's daughter, growing up in the present era of explicitness about sexual relations, perhaps her literary fare is equally narrow but her need is to encounter some portrayals of fulfillment in marriage!

Anything, of course, that has entered into and shaped the development of the student's personality may be significant for his literary development. The teacher cannot hope to glimpse many of these factors, of whose import the student most of all will be unaware. Yet such general social attitudes will ultimately condition the whole texture of the student's experience of life as well as of literature. In the interplay between the book and the personality, failures in sensitivity, misinterpretations, and distorted reactions often have their roots in such influences. The effort to help the student arrive at a more balanced and lucid sense of the work thus involves the parallel effort to help him understand and evaluate his personal emphases.

THERE IS VERY LITTLE systematic information available concerning the specific ways in which the individual personality colors the responses to literature. The book by I. A. Richards cited earlier [4] offers some valuable illustra-

---

[4] See p. 63. This is a work that every teacher of literature should read. It has been a seminal book for two generations of critics and teachers. See also James R. Squire, *The Responses of Adolescents While Reading Four Short Stories* (Champaign, Illinois, NCTE Research Report No. 2, 1964), James R. Wilson, *Responses of College Freshmen to Three Novels* (Champaign, Illinois, NCTE Research Report No. 7, 1966), and Walter D. Loban, *Literature and Social Sensitivity* (Champaign, Illinois, National Council of Teachers of English, 1954).

tions of individual reactions to poetry. His elaborate and subtle analyses of his students' comments on poetry reveal some of the typical patterns of response, and his discussion of "Irrelevant Associations and Stock Responses" is especially pertinent here. Illustrations from his book as well as from the experience of other teachers will serve to place these findings in a social and psychological context.

The impact of the literary work is dulled when the reader brings to the text a fund of ready-made, sharply crystallized ideas and habits of response. These responses are so easily touched off that they sometimes interfere with interpretation. Richards gives an illustration of this in several students' comments on Edna Millay's sonnet, "What's this of death, from you who never will die?" The mention of death at once elicited ready-made responses concerning the question of immortality. These prevented the students from understanding either the idea or the effect that the poem was aiming at. The students made a number of irrelevant comments on death or responded to only those phrases in the poem that had some connection with their own preconceived ideas on the subject.

A similar instance occurred in a high school discussion of "The Eve of St. Agnes." One of the students announced that she thought the poem silly and sentimental. She defended this by adding that the poem was all about "romantic love twaddle." In her early adolescent rebellion against the seeming adult obsession with this subject, she had not been willing to respond and had completely misunderstood the tone of the poem.

Subjects such as "home," "mother," "childhood," "birth," "death," "my country," possess whole constellations of fixed attitudes and automatic emotional reflexes. The popularity of such authors as Edgar Guest, Ella Wheeler Wilcox, and James Metcalfe depends in large part on the emotion-arousing efficacy of such subjects, regardless of what the poet may phrase about them. The discussions of D. H. Lawrence's "Piano" by Richards' students offers further examples of how ready-made responses and irrelevant associations may interfere with the reading of any work that deals with a familiar subject (in this case childhood recollections of a mother playing the piano). The Cambridge students were sufficiently sophisticated to be on their guard against the automatic appeal of such elements in Lawrence's poem. For some of them, however, this fear of sentimentality became a barrier to understanding the poem. They recognized the stereotyped nature of the sentiments aroused by elements in the text and blamed the poem for a conventionality inherent in their own feelings. They were so busy resisting the possible automatic response to the idea of home and mother that they failed to perceive how the text itself creates safeguards against sentimentality.

When in wartime mediocre poetry on patriotic themes elicits an intense response, the whole environment is creating the emotions which the text seems to arouse. An antipathy to war may similarly vitiate critical judgment. An intelligent young man of pacifist beliefs picked up *A Shropshire Lad* and glanced at "1887," written on the occasion of Queen Victoria's Jubilee. Shocked and indignant, he did not wish even to finish this poem that, by the very swing of its verse and the use of such traditional phrases as "God has saved the Queen," "saviours," "the land they perished for," seemed designed to arouse patriotic and warlike sentiments. Others have read the poem, especially its last stanza, as an ironic warning against blind patriotism. Whatever may have been the author's intention, the text permits either interpretation. At any rate, the reader's problem is to be aware of how much his own preconceptions enter into his interpretation of its tone, and to dissociate his attitude toward war from his judgment on the effectiveness of the poem.

Students will undoubtedly come to literature with increasingly strong attitudes toward political and social themes. Such subjects are being discussed frequently and heatedly in their homes, in the newspapers, over the radio and television. This suggests a whole complex of definite attitudes and automatic responses which may cause difficulties.

Richards reports such a stock response in the case of students whose antipathy to the glorification of royalty led them to object to a poem on George Meredith's eightieth birthday which referred to him as "king of our hearts today." (It must be recalled that the students did not have the benefit of the clue provided by the title.) At a performance of *King Richard the Second* in New York, one of the spectators revealed a similar blindness owing to antiroyalist sentiments. He was annoyed at the appeal that the play patently had for him. "Why should I care about whether Richard or Bolingbroke wins out? The whole idea of kingship is an anachronism for us today." This antipathy blinded him to the play's more universal interest, its subtly nuanced portrait of a man unable to wield the power thrust upon him, yet histrionically delighting in going through the motions of command, and as histrionically savoring the drama of his own downfall. If the protagonist had been a present-day dictator or the president of a great corporation or university, this irate spectator would have been able to grasp the revelation of human character that his automatic reaction to the idea "king" had obscured. We may sympathize with his political views and yet regret that he was not able to handle his primary response in such a way as to appreciate the basic values of the work before him. The controversial nature of much of the literature being written today often creates such obstacles to sound literary judgment. Students should be helped to handle their responses to the political and social tendencies of a work. These should not block attention to the sensuous, emotional, and intellectual elements actually embodied in the text. An attitude toward the work's social implication is by no means irrelevant, but it should be brought to bear upon the text itself, in its specific terms, and should not be a screen between the reader and his evocation of the work.

This type of predetermined response elicited by the general subject of the work is rather easily detected. The same kind of excessive reaction may be produced by a word or a phrase or an episode in a work whose general theme has nothing to do with this particular prejudice or emotional fixation of the reader. An instance of this is the Cambridge students' misreading of the poem on George Meredith merely because the word "king" set off an irrelevant automatic response. The young girl's reaction to the love element in "The Eve of St. Agnes" is another illustration.

The earlier discussion of some of the conditions affecting the adolescent today suggested various other factors that would encourage narrow or stereotyped preconceptions. For example, a rural or urban background or regional loyalty would tend to build up stock responses. The Southern girl who praised as "good books" all that offered a romanticized picture of the South and condemned such works as *To Kill a Mockingbird* obviously was not functioning on a literary level.

The fixed ideas and emotional associations that cluster about family and sex relations also may lead to irrelevant responses. An example is a Cambridge student's condemnation of D. H. Lawrence's poem "Piano" on the ground that no sensible person would want to give up his adult independence and return to the limitations of childhood. Resentment at restraints placed upon him in childhood may explain this reader's misunderstanding of the poem. His response was to something in his own mind and background, not the text. A group of college girls arguing about *Tom Jones* revealed the extent to which each girl's reactions were affected by her image of the ideal young man, an image, in some instances, sufficiently crystallized to hinder understanding of the various phases of Tom's character that Fielding presents.

IN ADDITION TO PREVENTING an understanding of what is read, rigid attitudes may seriously impair the reader's judgment even of what he has understood. Richards reports instances in which the reader had understood the fresh interpretation that the poem presented but condemned it because he was still dominated by stereotyped ideas and conventional feelings. Here the difficulties arise from the fact that a student will have absorbed from his environment cruder standards than are worthy of the literary experiences made available to him.

This was forcibly brought home to a teacher who in his course in short-story writing was perplexed by the superficial nature of the students' work. In his discussion of the problems presented by the short-story form, he had selected from such writers as Poe, Hawthorne, de Maupassant, Flaubert, and Mansfield those stories that seemed to handle in more subtle ways problems dimly suggested in the students' writings. However, he discovered that the usual literary diet of the students was not the work of writers of this caliber but the stereotyped products of third-rate magazines.

The students' justification of their reading was in psychological terms. These stories were easy to read, offered no difficulties to the understanding. They ended happily and gave one a sense that success was not too difficult of attainment. In some cases the explanation was merely that these cheap stories were more easily available. Obviously, the instructor's expression of disapproval would have accomplished little. He wisely started from the level at which he found his students. By getting them to discuss some of the stories they liked, he helped them to become aware of the stereotyped formulas and trick effects. The class then turned to other kinds of "escape" writing, such as Poe's stories, which require a more complex response and a more subtle perception of the writer's technique. The instructor's aim was gradually to lead the students to approach without resistance those stories he considered most significant.

At once the human element entered, for obviously the students were seeking in the cheap success stories a release from the sense of pressure and defeat that permeated the world in which they lived. They had to be willing to relinquish the easy relaxing drug that made up their reading diet and to welcome the challenge of those stories that attempted to present an honest and searching image of life.

The instructor had to dissipate any feeling that the stories he suggested were to be studied principally from the formal point of view. The concern with technique had to be subordinated to a concern with the state of mind, the attitude toward people and life situations revealed by great writers of the short story. Fundamentally, this also proved to be the sounder approach to the problems of technique. The subtle qualities of mood, the ironic contrasts between personality and situation, the nature of conflicts between characters as well as the solutions of the conflicts—all these things were involved in an understanding of the technical means that the writers had employed. The students had been unable to assimilate the examples of technical success in the short story because they had been unable or reluctant to understand and assimilate the insights that the writers of those stories had sought to give.

The teacher of literature should be on the alert for such possible "stock responses." In large part they represent the dogmatic, platitudinous ideas about people and life that one meets on all sides: in the newspapers and the mass media, or on the lips of the man on the street. Similarly, they show themselves in ways of feeling that have became so conventional as to have lost all individual quality or fine shades. Popular songs are repositories of such sentiments. Such responses are aroused with great ease in the commercialized appeal to stock sentiments represented by Mother's Day and Father's Day and by much of the advertising in the mass media.

Yet the very essence of literature is a rejection of such stereotyped, superficial, and unshaded reactions to the mere outlines of situations or to the appeal of vague and generalized concepts. A poem or a novel should provide fresh insight. The reader, therefore, must be helped to develop flexibility of mind, a freedom from rigid emotional habits, if he is to enter into the esthetic experiences the artist has made possible.

OBVIOUSLY, THE AIM should not be to create in the student such a state of flexibility and such a passivity to new kinds of experience that he will lose all the advantages of an integrated personality or a settled structure of ideas of his own. In one of his letters Keats describes the poet as possessing no character of his own because he could identify himself so completely with other forms of being and could adopt so readily new and untried forms of response. Precious as that capacity may be for a poet, in such an extreme form it is not a practical asset for the conduct of everyday affairs! A stock response, as Richards says, may often be a convenience. Just as it would be disastrous if at every occasion for walking we had to reason out the best way of putting one foot before the other, so in our intellectual and social life crystallized attitudes and ideas are useful. By automatically taking care of the major part of our lives, they leave us energy for meeting the new and unprepared-for situations.

Sufficient flexibility is needed to free oneself from the stock response when it prevents a response more appropriate to the situation. This is as true of the problems encountered in our daily lives as it is of our encounters with literature. Much of the mismanagement of personal relationships results from following a stereotyped and automatic reaction to the general outlines of a situation instead of responding to the special characteristics and changing qualities of that situation. The mother, accustomed to her children's dependence upon her for the management of their lives, continues to expect the same kind of dependence long after the children have grown beyond the need for it. The years of America's economic expansion promote the idea that the man without a job is shiftless and unenterprising; when the Depression makes it impossible for many of even the most enterprising to have jobs, this same attitude toward the unemployed persists in many quarters. The young man who has been accustomed to his mother's housewifely attention to his physical well-being becomes irritated when his wife, employed in business, overlooks these things.

In the experience of literature, free of the demands that practical life makes for speedy, economical response and action, this capacity for flexibility should surely be exercised and enlarged. Fundamentally, the goal is the development of individuals who will function less as automatic bundles of habits and more as flexible, discriminating personalities. Our great heritage of literary experiences can be fully enjoyed and understood only by such personalities.

These remarks concerning "stock responses" can be translated into terms of the breadth or adequacy of the individual life experience. Something in the reader's own background or personality prevents him from understanding fully all that the work offers. His notions about possibilities of human character may be too limited, or his moral code too rigid to encompass the complex human situations and emotions presented in literature. In its simplest terms, as we have seen, this inadequacy of experience may take the form of the city child's inability to respond fully to country imagery; or a more extreme example is the Indian children's difficulties with Restoration comedy. How much of the adolescent's indifference to great literature is the result of inadequate experience? How much of the shallowness or captiousness of his opinions on books is a by-product of a similar approach to situations in life?

Just as in medicine much of the knowledge about normal physiological processes is derived from the study of pathological conditions, so in literature understanding of what goes on when an individual reads a poem or a novel or a play is illuminated by study of the causes for inadequate responses. They document the basic fact that any sound response to literature is dependent on the quality of the reader's personal contribution. He does violence to a poem or a story when some obsession or blindness clouds his vision of what the author has presented. He does justice to it when his own temperament, his own experience, and a flexibly receptive attitude permit him to see clearly what the text itself offers and to perceive its significance. Precisely because it appeals to certain elements in his nature as his past experience has molded it, is the literary effect intense.

IF THE STUDENT'S STRUCTURE of attitudes and ideas is built on too narrow a base of experience, he should be helped to gain broader and deeper insight through literature itself. That is why throughout this discussion the emphasis has been on the interaction between the reader and the text. When the reader becomes aware of the dynamic nature of that interaction, he may gain some critical consciousness of the strength or weaknesses of the emotional and intellectual equipment with which he approaches literature (and life). Since he interprets the book or poem in terms of his fund of past experiences, it is equally possible and necessary that he come to reinterpret his old sense of things in the light of this new literary experience, in the light of the new ways of thinking and feeling offered by the work of art. Only when this happens has there been a full interplay between book and reader, and hence a complete and rewarding literary experience.

The work of art can have this effect because it does more than merely recall to us elements out of our own past insights and emotions. It will present them in new patterns and new contexts. It will give them new resonance and make of them the basis for new awarenesses and enriched understanding. It will tend to supplement and correct our own necessarily limited personal experience.

Through the work of art, our habitual responses, our preoccupations and desires, may be given added significance.
They will be related to the emotional and sensuous structure created by the author, and they will be brought into
organic connection with broader and deeper streams of
thought and feelings. Out of this will arise a wider perspective and a readjustment of the framework of values
with which to meet further experiences in literature and
life.

THESE CONSIDERATIONS reinforce the belief concerning the
teacher's opportunities set forth at the end of Chapter 3.
The fact that the personal contribution of the reader is an
essential element in any vital reading of literature justifies
the demand that the teacher create a setting that makes
it possible for the student to have a spontaneous response
to literature. But the preceding discussion makes more
apparent the basis for the view that this represents only
the first step, absolutely essential though that first step
is. Once the student has responded freely, a process of
growth can be initiated. He needs to learn to handle with
intelligence and discrimination the personal factors that
enter into his reaction to books. Through a critical scrutiny of his response to literary works, he can come to
understand his personal attitudes and gain the perspective
needed for a fuller and sounder response to literature.

This chapter has been concerned with the preoccupations and needs that the adolescent may bring to literature. To help the student critically to understand his own
contribution to the literary experience becomes an aspect
of helping him to do justice to the text. The thesis of

Chapter 1—that the teaching of literature necessarily involves helping the student to handle social, psychological, and ethical concepts—now falls into place. The next chapter will approach the problem of the clarification of the student's response more specifically in terms of the kinds of knowledge that will contribute to his understanding of the literary work.

CHAPTER 5

Broadening
the Framework

A FREE EXCHANGE of ideas will lead each student to scrutinize his own sense of the literary work in the light of others' opinions. The very fact that other students stress aspects that he may have ignored, or report a different impression, will suggest that perhaps he has not done justice to the text. He will turn to it again in order to point out the elements that evoked his response and to see what can justify the other students' responses.

The preceding discussion of adolescent concerns has dealt with some of the factors that lead the individual to be especially receptive to some of the stimuli offered by the text, to ignore others, or even to "read into it" unfounded implications. All of this has assumed that a personal response can be either more or less relevant to the text itself. Therefore, in any teaching situation an awareness of the student's preoccupations and emotional needs should constantly be brought to bear upon the problem of insuring that the student has responded to what is actually offered by the text. The teacher aims to help the student evoke its sensuous, emotional, and intellectual import as fully as possible.

Those least in sympathy with the point of view of the preceding chapters will probably maintain that the only task of the teacher is to help the student understand what he has read, and that therefore the teacher need not be concerned with the personal preoccupations or reactions of the students. The crux of the whole problem lies in the word *understand*. The preceding chapter has shown that understanding is a much more complex personal process than many are willing to admit.

One oversimplified interpretation of understanding was rejected earlier when it was pointed out that the paraphrase is not the poem. A mere intellectualized definition of the meaning of a poem diminishes the work. The student will not be helped to understand if he is restricted to the plane of verbalization, of translation of the literary work into generalizations and abstractions. The ability to express the heart of an idea in clear terms that reveal its possible general application is indeed a rare and valuable one. But understanding does not begin on this level, certainly, nor does it necessarily culminate on this level.

Even if we take the word *understand* in a most limited sense, as it would apply to the definition of particular words, we ultimately become involved in elements of direct human experience that lead into all of the complex considerations concerning the social significance of English teaching. For to understand a word is to see implications in a context significant for human beings. In our everyday lives we often use words as mere empty counters swishing over the surface of the mind with little or no direct sense of what they point to. Thus it is that much of our speech and writing has only the vaguest significance. Certainly this habit will not be counteracted by having students translate one set of words thus vaguely sensed into another set equally devoid of outline and content.

Understanding implies the full impact of the sensuous, emotional, as well as intellectual force of a word. It requires linking the word with what it points to in the world of man or nature. This involves awareness of the sensations it symbolizes, the systems or categories into which it fits, the complex of experiences out of which it springs, the modes of feeling or practical situations with which it is associated, the actions it may imply. Above all, the word cannot be understood in isolation; it must be seen in the variety of its possible contexts. Moreover, we must relate it to our own experience in order that it may become part of our working equipment. Only then, as we place it in its relation to other sensations, ideas, attitudes, and patterns, all equally realized, shall we be in a position to say that we understand it.

The word *love*, for instance, cannot be defined without reference to some context. The varied experiences in life and literature that different individuals associate with the word will also affect the way in which they understand it. The words *virtue, justice,* or *democracy* would represent a similar necessity for encroaching upon the whole framework of ethical and social implications. Thus, even so narrow an aim as the understanding of words leads back to the field of human experiences. And that process becomes involved at once in implied assertions concerning human nature and society. In this vital sense, understanding of even one word demands a framework of ideas about man, nature, and society.

With like inevitability, the task of helping a student to understand a work of literature as a whole involves the context of the student's past experience as well as the historical, social, and ethical context into which he must fit the particular work. This will be true whether the work be "The Solitary Reaper" or *Paradise Lost, Hamlet* or *The Importance of Being Earnest, Anna Karenina* or *A Passage To India.*

Every time a reader experiences a work of art, it is in a sense created anew. *Fundamentally, the process of understanding a work implies a re-creation of it, an attempt to grasp completely the structured sensations and concepts through which the author seeks to convey the quality of his sense of life. Each must make a new synthesis of these elements with his own nature, but it is essential that he evoke those components of experience to which the text actually refers.*

Hence, even when limited to clarification of the student's understanding of the literary work, the teacher finds himself concerned with the student's personality and background, and with the whole range of facts, problems, and theories implied by the text. The student will not experience it (nor understand it) in a vacuum. The heightened sensuous observation, the keener and subtler perception of human emotions and actions, will not etch themselves on a blank page. There must take place an integration between the framework of interests, ideas, and feelings that the student brings, and the structure of ideas and emotions offered by the text. As the student is led to clarify his own sense of it, the teacher will be able to lead him to the various kinds of knowledge that will enable him to achieve the experiences offered by this particular text.

Thus, the clarification of the reader's personal understanding of the novel or poem or play carries with it a responsibility to the text itself. He seeks to recapture the particular approach to nature or society that dominates the work. He evokes the particular kind of awareness it embodies—whether it be the stark terror of "The Pit and the Pendulum" or the sense of time and slow change of *To the Lighthouse*. He becomes self-critical in order to see whether his own emphasis corresponds to what the text actually presents. He returns to the text to make sure that he has done justice to the particular words in their particular order—sound and rhythm, image and metaphor, structure and point of view, indications of tone, clues to character. The discovery of what he overlooked will be as valuable in revealing his own blind spots and emotional fixations as it will be in giving him a sounder participation in the work itself.

The import of any work will remain thoroughly personal, since it is re-created by a specific personality with its own sense of values. Thus there is not necessarily only one "correct" interpretation of the significance of a given work. Not even an author's statement of his aims can be considered definitive. The text exists as a separate entity that may or may not fulfill his intentions and can possess for us more values than he foresaw. The work must carry its own message to each of us. Nevertheless, the student should be led to discover that some interpretations are more defensible than others. A complex work such as *Hamlet* offers the basis for various interpretations; yet their acceptability will depend, first, on whether they take into account as many as possible of the elements present in the text, and second, on whether they do not imply elements that are not present in it.

An interpretation of *Hamlet*, no matter how subtle, that ignored his soliloquies or his conversations with his mother would obviously be inadequate. Similarly, an interpretation that assumed ideas and attitudes for which no basis could be found in the text, or ignored the fact that the language has changed since Elizabethan times, would certainly be capricious. Thus, understanding of the work can be nourished through study of what is sometimes called "background materials."

An undistorted vision of the work of art requires a consciousness of one's own preconceptions and prejudices concerning the situations presented in the work, in contrast to the basic attitudes toward life assumed in the text. Often the reader integrates the work into a context of psychological or moral theories different from those that the author probably possessed. Always, therefore, a full understanding of literature requires both a consciousness of the reader's own "angle of refraction" and any information that can illuminate the assumptions implicit in the text.

STUDENTS WILL BENEFIT from their cooperative attempt to embrace all phases of the work in their formulation of its dominant effect. An example of this is a discussion of Keats' "The Eve of St. Agnes." A number of the students first spoke of the poem as a delightfully gay and ornamental story of romantic love. Others, accepting this characterization of the poem, condemned as irrelevant and jarring the introduction of the old Beadsman, the tombs, the cold chapel, in the opening of the poem, and the death of old Angela and the Beadsman at the end. The group then found it necessary to decide what function these details might serve. They reread the text more carefully and decided that these elements provided an emotional background or undertone for the glowing colors and medieval atmosphere of the lovers' story. The contrast enhanced the warmth and sensuous vividness of the episode, threw over it an atmosphere of remoteness in time and space, and interwove the elegiac theme of death and the passing of all lovely things. The discussion stimulated the students to attend to all the components of the work, the minor chords as well as the major. Out of this came a fuller and more adequate response.

The effort to organize all the elements present in the text may also lead to considerations of human life and literary history. Thus the students' discussion of "The Eve of St. Agnes" helped to make them aware of the presence in much of Keats' poetry of the sense that

> Ay, in the very temple of Delight
> Veiled Melancholy has her sovran shrine.

They sought in Keats' letters and in the story of his brief life and literary enthusiasms, the source of this feeling for the fleetingness of joy and beauty. They placed the work in the context of the life and personality of the author. Note, however, that the movement here was from interpretation of the text to author's life. This is diametrically opposed to the usual procedure in textbooks and many classrooms. To derive an interpretation of a text from the author's life or stated intentions is, of course, critically indefensible.

To see the writer as part of a literary tradition can also clarify personal response, especially for the more sophisticated students. Melodramatic or inconsistent elements in the form and plots of Shakespeare's plays may no longer trouble the reader when placed in the setting of Elizabethan theatrical traditions. Similarly, the attempt to differentiate between the special type of sensibility of different members of the same literary movement, such as Wordsworth and Coleridge, or Conrad and James, will heighten perception of the special quality of the effects each sought to produce.

Thus students may find themselves embarked upon a study of the biographical and literary background of the work. They will come to understand better the particular medium of expression that the author selected. They may see how reactions against the dead weight of literary tradition or the exhaustion of an earlier vein of literary sensibility, as in the case of Wordsworth or T. S. Eliot, will have led him to his particular emphasis. They will thus gain a profounder sense of the communal basis of even the most highly individualized insights and emotions.

The desire to understand a particular work will produce ever widening circles of interest. Yet the focus of these concerns should continue to be the student's own sense of the work and his desire to clarify and refine his perception of it. Knowledge about the author's life and the literary influences acting upon him will create the need for understanding the intellectual and philosophical, the social and economic, conditions surrounding him. If the work is not a contemporary one, the contrasts and similarities between the conditions of that past age and the present will illuminate ways in which present-day reactions to the work may differ from those of the author's contemporaries.

Robinson Crusoe is for us the absorbing tale of man's ingenuity in wresting a livelihood from nature; the account of his religious meditations and conversion is much less stirring. The much pitied Pamela may seem to the young girl of today merely a shrewd and designing hussy. Hamlet's perplexities about whether the Ghost may be a benevolent visitant returned from Purgatory or an evil spirit who has assumed his father's form seem unimportant to those who question the existence of ghosts at all. Similarly, there is much in the work today that has special and perhaps hitherto unexploited overtones. Hamlet's hesitations and melancholy questionings in a world out of joint have a compelling significance for the twentieth-century reader.

Here again, there will be profit in seeing that the reader's own reactions, like the work of art, are the organic expression not only of a particular individual but also of a particular cultural setting. Literary history will not seem like a clear stream flowing between banks which enclose but do not affect it. Rather it will be seen that the literary stream is fed by thousands of rivulets which have their sources in the surrounding intellectual and social environment.

THESE CONCENTRIC CIRCLES of interest focused on the student's sense of a work will involve him in still deeper concern with human relations. He will see in the work a specific reflection of general ideas concerning good and evil. He will work out the scale of values that the writer applies to personalities and to relations between people. The student will apprehend Shakespeare's sense of the individual dominating even an adverse fate by the intensity and resonance of his nature. Or he will adjust to Jane Austen's "human scale," her characters measured against only the society and the world they have created. Or he will share Hardy's sense of individual man as a helpless atom in the cosmic stream.

The young reader will be especially alert to the treatment of character. The writer does more than present human beings in action; he offers clues to the motives and the repercussions of those actions. He shows, too, many of the forces that shape human personality and conduct. Pamela's constant reference to the moral and social code differs greatly from Tom Jones' uncalculating behavior. George Eliot, Thackeray, Aldous Huxley, and D. H. Lawrence each provide a different view of the determining traits of human character. Often, too, the writer reveals the broader influences at work in man's collective life. F. Scott Fitzgerald manifests the influence of social aspirations; Zola and Steinbeck show the force of economic pressures; Emily Brontë and D. H. Lawrence, each in a different way, evoke the power of human impulse and passion. Understanding of the individual sensibility or individual problems presented by the text may thus lead to understanding of the implicit system of values and sense of man's relation to the world.

Such analysis of the work, such acquisition of new insights and information, will have value only as it is linked up with the student's own primary response to the work. His own judgment on it will thus be thrown into sharper relief; for if he is indeed functioning freely and spontaneously, he will undoubtedly reflect not only on the work itself but also on the problems it presents and on the personalities and actions of the characters. The attempt to work out the author's system of values and assumptions about man and society should enable the student to discover the unspoken assumptions behind his own judgment. His conclusions about this particular work imply the unarticulated theories of human conduct and ideas of the good that shape his thinking.

During group discussions the students, in a spirit of friendly challenge, can lead one another to work out the implications of the positions they have taken. They may discover that they are making assertions based on fundamentally contradictory concepts. A student who espoused with equal vigor the causes of Pamela and Tess, and maintained that each of them was "virtuous," found herself involved in arriving at some consistent understanding of that term. Becky Sharp and her humbler daughter, Scarlett O'Hara, led another student into similar difficulties. By bringing their own generalizations into the open, students may be led to feel the need of putting their mental houses in order. They will see how often they have been dominated by ideas only because they have heard them repeated again and again. They will develop a more critical, questioning attitude and will see the need of a more reasoned foundation for their thoughts and judgments, a more consistent system of values.

The teacher's challenge, as well as the challenge of the other students, will stimulate each of them to search for knowledge that will clarify the problems he encounters and will supply the basis for valid judgments. Here the teacher of literature may legitimately see it as his function to point to the existence of helpful bodies of knowledge. He will have made a valuable contribution if the student leaves his experience of the literary work eager to learn what the psychologist, the sociologist, and the historian have to offer him. The core of direct emotional experience at the heart of the critical process outlined here should keep alive the sense of the immediate personal value of the objective knowledge these experts provide. Thus, a teacher of tenth-graders in an affluent and divorce-ridden community was nonplussed by their rejection of *Ethan Frome*. They refused to take it seriously: the whole story was contrived, they said, because to begin with, Ethan's meek acceptance of his lot was unthinkable. As the teacher led them to look more closely at the text, and as they grappled with their own reactions, they discovered how little they knew about recent history and about economic, social, and cultural climates different from their own. They learned something about these matters, but they also learned something about entering into the structure of assumptions of a literary work. They gained both literary and social perspective.

Just such spontaneous recourse to the other disciplines was illustrated by a group of freshmen in a woman's college who had read Ibsen's *A Doll's House*. One of the students attacked the play as profoundly insignificant since "Nora was a fool to have become so dependent on her husband." Others objected that she could do nothing else. You couldn't judge Nora, they pointed out, as you would a woman of today. Her relationship with her father and with Torvald reflected the position of women in the nineteenth century. Yet even those who recognized the historical background of the play could give very little accurate information about the status of women at that time. The students tried to find out what were women's legal and political rights in the nineteenth century as contrasted with the present. They discovered the differences among periods, countries, and even various states within the United States. They emphasized the extent of woman's emancipation since the date of the play, but admitted that some problems still persisted. They were also interested to discover the extent to which the greater emancipation of women had transformed their relationships with husband and children.

These insights deepened the students' sense of the play's significance. They no longer tended to regard Nora as an individual solving an individual problem. They considered her to a large extent the victim of a vast complex of conditions. They saw Torvald's attitude as the expression of a view of his rights sanctioned by the whole force of the society. To see the individual as shaped by a great many factors rooted in the society about him creates a broader perspective. The students also realized the value

of suspending judgment until they had acquired a basis
of information.

At certain points in the discussion the teacher had had
pedantic twinges of conscience about the attention paid
to subjects that could not be strictly defined as literary. He
later realized that he need have had no qualms. Increased
awareness of the complexities of human relationships led
the students toward a fuller appreciation of the play itself. Some of the students became more aware of Ibsen's
dramatic methods. Quite spontaneously, they discussed his
extraordinary economy in conveying significant information about Nora's past relations with her father and her
husband. They pointed out the clear structure of the play
with its swift presentation of complex problems and its
skillful creation of suspense. The final scene, although it
presented no psychological or social solution, was judged
to be theatrically effective because it involved overt action
that clearly defined Nora's dilemma. Because they themselves raised the questions, there was nothing academically remote about these matters of form and technique;
the students saw them as the author's choices, intimately
related to what he was seeking to convey.

BACKGROUND MATERIALS ALREADY receive much attention
in school and college literature programs. The danger,
however, is that such study tends to become an end in
itself. This chapter has proposed a major criterion of the
usefulness of background information: it will have value
only when the student feels the need of it and when it is
assimilated into the student's experience of particular
literary works.

Challenged to establish the validity of his interpretation and judgment of the work, he will be stimulated both to examine the text more closely and to scrutinize the adequacy of his own past experience and basic assumptions. He will test whether what he brings to the text has enabled him to do justice to all that it embodies. This may lead him to probe further into literary techniques and forms. It may also impel him to acquire various types of knowledge—literary and social history, biography, philosophy, psychology, anthropology—that may deepen his understanding of the work. Such a process of clarification and enrichment of successive literary experiences will foster sound critical habits. From this kind of literary study there should flow, too, enhanced understanding of himself and the life about him. The coming chapters will consider in greater detail how literary sensitivity may contribute to such insight.

PART III

Literary Sensitivity as the Source of Insight

CHAPTER 6

Some Basic Social Concepts

TEACHERS OF LITERATURE deal inevitably with its human implications. Must they then become experts in the social sciences? The answer obviously is, No. But they are responsible for scrutinizing their own assumptions about human nature and society in the light of contemporary thought. This chapter will turn away from literature itself to clarify some of the concepts about human relations which underlie the preceding discussion of the relation of social insight to literary sensitivity and judgment. This may elucidate a few of the key ideas with which the teacher should be familiar, and which are more important than any of the specific findings of the various disciplines that study human behavior.

Some of these ideas have in recent years become generally current and are undoubtedly already known to the reader. They are formulated here in order to provide a coherent basis for considering their special relevance to the sphere of the teacher of literature. Chapters 7 and 8 will explore how basic social concepts may illuminate, and be illuminated by, the study of literature.

An axiom of contemporary educational thought is that, under the unprecedented and rapidly changing conditions of present-day life, to give the youth a rigid set of dogmatic ideas and habits is a certain method of producing insecurity and bewilderment. Members of the older generation know that many of the habitual attitudes and ideas they took most for granted have with changed conditions become inappropriate and even antisocial. Habits of thrift were much prized, only to have the economists decree that the socially valuable rule is to spend and invest, not hoard. Women dutifully restricted the scope of their interests to the home, only to find that the functions of the home itself had changed, and that as mothers, wives, and citizens they needed to develop broader interests and understanding. The traditional belief was that every American of any ability could rise unaided above the economic and social stratum into which he was born; now the ideal of equal opportunity is buttressed by a great network of laws. The doctrine that punitive measures prevent crime has been replaced by the view that the criminal is a symptom of weaknesses in our educational and social systems, and should be cured, not punished. In politics, in the relations between men and women, in the adjustments between parents and children, in all phases of our personal and social life, similar discrepancies between habitual attitudes and changed circumstances have developed. Everything points toward a prodigious acceleration of changes demanding such readjustments during the life-time of those who are adolescents and children today.

Obviously, a rigid set of dogmatic ideas and fixed responses to specific conditions is the worst kind of equipment for the contemporary youth. As soon as actual conditions prove that his passively acquired code is useless or even harmful, he has nothing else to cling to. Having been made dependent upon ready-made props, he will be precipitated into painful insecurity. This kind of insecurity, this craving for some easy, reassuring formula, makes the youth of other countries and sometimes of our own a ready prey to those enemies of democracy who hold out the delusive bait of ready-made solutions to all problems. Unprepared to think independently, the young man and woman seek to return to the infantile state in which there is no responsibility to make decisions; they are thus willing to blindly follow some "leader" whose tools and prey they become.

The conditions of human life, the complexities of the interaction of personality upon personality, the shifting images offered by human history, and the rapid flux of the life about us show how evasive of reality a dogmatic approach to human relations would be. Our literary heritage itself, with its reflections of the varied and contrasting forms of human life and personality, with its expression of so many different life goals and values, is eloquent rebuttal of any absolutistic approach to life. However satisfactory may be the system of values the teacher has worked out for himself, he is not justified in "teaching" it to his students, as one might "teach" a method of solving a problem in calculus. There is no proof that the conditions of life this generation of students will face, or the highly diverse personal problems they will have to solve, will be commensurable with any arbitrary measuring rod provided by the teacher.

The teacher, however, must do more than merely avoid explicit dogmatism. He must also avoid the insidious unconscious inculcation of dogma. Only a bundle of miscellaneous and unintegrated responses—in other words, not a functioning individual at all—could avoid conveying some attitudes toward experience. The teacher will inevitably possess some scheme of values, some particular way of approaching and judging people and situations. He should be critically aware of these attitudes instead of imposing them indirectly and unconsciously upon his students.

Nor should the teacher try to pose as a completely objective person. The assumption of a mask of unemotional objectivity or impartial omniscience is one reason why teachers and college professors sometimes seem not quite human to their students. A much more wholesome educational situation is created when the teacher is a really live person who has examined his own attitudes and assumptions and who, when appropriate, states them frankly and honestly. He does not have to seem to possess "all the answers," which the students then need only passively absorb. Admitting his own uncertainties and perplexities will stimulate the students to join him in the common task of seeking the knowledge that may clarify these problems.

But even this awareness of his own point of view and

his frankness are not enough. The teacher needs to see his own philosophy as only one of the possible approaches to life, from which his students should be given the opportunity to select for themselves. Tolerance of other points of view is extremely important for the teacher— an attitude those who are insecure and fearful of challenges to their authority find most difficult to maintain.

To rule out the conscious or unconscious transmission of an explicit set of ready-made answers to personal problems and ready-made judgments on people and society does not, however, mean an end to the teacher's responsibility, nor does it imply a nihilistic approach to life. Reluctance to impose a dogmatic philosophy may lead to an equally dangerous attitude of noncommittal relativism that refuses to admit any standards and tends to produce a paralysis of judgment on the part of the student. Such pseudo-liberalism can lead to the feeling that there is nothing to believe, that there are no values to be sought in this confused world. Wholesale negativism will leave youth completely unprepared. In times of crisis when the inevitable choices must be made, they will tend to fall back on the old, stereotyped attitudes, or to follow chance, irrational appeals.

Although no one code should be taught dogmatically, the need for the individual to work out his own principles and his own hierarchy of values is imperative. The task of education is to supply him with the knowledge, the mental habits, and the emotional impetus that will enable him to independently solve his problems—hence the teacher's need to clarify for himself the basic approaches to experience and the basic concepts concerning human nature and society that will be a useful preparation for the adolescent facing the uncertain future.

In order that the student may be prepared for the unpredictable demands that life will make upon him, our schools and universities must be transformed, as C. S. Peirce said many years ago, from "institutions for teaching" into "institutions for learning." The student should go to school and college, not for the purpose of being taught ready-made formulas and fixed attitudes, but in order that he may develop the will to learn. He must gain command of techniques that make possible a constantly closer approximation to the truth, and he must develop the flexibility of mind and temperament necessary for the translation of that sense of truth into actual behavior. Instead of judgments accepted in whole cloth, he must acquire a curiosity about the causes of human actions and social conditions; he must be ready to revise accepted hypotheses in the light of new information; he must learn where to turn for this information. He needs, in short, to develop a dynamic sense of life, a feeling that an understanding of causes makes for greater control of conditions. Instead of drifting with the stream of circumstance, he will be able to set up more rational personal and social goals and to understand better the conditions under which they can be achieved.

The implication here is that the social sciences have something positive to offer toward a solution of personal problems and toward a framework of ideas that will make possible constructive social action. In order to arouse in the student a desire for social understanding, the teacher of literature needs himself to be aware that such knowledge exists or at any rate that the foundation for it has been laid by the social sciences.

The literature teacher's responsibility toward the kind of information represented by the social sciences can be summed up in general terms: He should be aware of the existence of the various behavioral sciences and should possess a general understanding of what phases of man's life they treat. Even though he may not have a detailed knowledge of these fields, he should at least understand their methods of approach and the basic concepts concerning man and society which they have developed. Without such knowledge he will probably be very effectively undoing in the English classroom whatever the teachers of social studies may have succeeded in accomplishing. Moreover, there is no reason why the English teacher's knowledge should stop at this minimum level. The training of English teachers should include carefully planned work in the behavorial sciences, and the practicing teacher should recognize his responsibility for constantly adding to his knowledge in these fields as well as in the field of literature.

TEACHERS OF LITERATURE and the arts often think of themselves as saving the student from the stultifying effects of our present scientific age. The early romantic opposition to the scientist as one who "murders to dissect" lingers on. Teachers of English tend to consider themselves defenders of a lost cause, keepers of an imaginative or emotional oasis in the midst of our materialistic, science-ridden life.

This attitude toward science is to some extent due to a

prevalent confusion between the effects of science and the effect of the practical, materialistic emphasis of our society. It is not science, but the way in which it has been misused, to which the English teacher should feel himself opposed. More and more evidence is accruing to demonstrate that science, properly exploited, may eventually so reduce time devoted to work that the entire population will have the leisure and the energy for the rich imaginative life that literature and the arts offer.

Even some of those who will admit this continue to assume that there is a fundamental and irreconcilable opposition between science and literature.[1] It is still fashionable in some circles to stress the complexity of human personality and human affairs as an insuperable obstacle to the application of scientific method. The disagreements and conflicts among different schools of thought are pointed to as proof. Only lack of contact with the finest and soundest expressions of the scientific spirit, however, could enable opponents of the social sciences to make these unqualified claims.

An understanding of the spirit of scientific method and its application to human affairs is the most fundamental social concept that the teacher of literature should possess. A lively sense of the essential nature of scientific method will compensate for lack of detailed knowledge of the

[1] Another aspect of the literary person's antagonism to science is his reluctance to recognize that scientific works are often also works of literature. Cf. Huxley's *Man's Place in Nature*, Darwin's *Origin of Species*, Adam Smith's *Wealth of Nations*, Eddington's *Stars and Atoms*, William James' *Principles of Psychology*, Loren Eiseley's *The Immense Journey*.

social sciences. In fact, without this basic understanding of the scientific attitude, any specific facts or theories drawn from the social sciences which he might introduce into discussions of literature would very likely be confusing to his students.

The artist, we are reminded, always conveys the special quality, the peculiar attributes, the unique flavor, of some personality or situation. The scientist, his artistic opponents assert, reduces life to its lowest common denominators and centers attention on whatever in a particular object makes it like every other one of its class. The layman tends to think of the contribution of the scientist as being a body of laws or a system of classifications to be applied to nature and society. This on the surface would seem to negate the artistic approach to life, which seeks to individualize rather than to generalize. But this view of science does it gross injustice.

Wholesale application of broad categories, lumping together many personalities or situations under broad labels, adoption of stereotyped attitudes or sweeping judgments, are alien to the very spirit of science. Contemporary logic and theories of knowledge recognize the spontaneous quality of existence, the novel elements in nature, as much as do the arts. Part of the scientist's duty is to note in a given situation those factors that are unique or that are met here in new combinations which differentiate it from any other situations of the same type. Of course, the scientist recognizes that the human and physical world offers certain recurrent patterns upon which can be built theories concerning the correlation of their various elements. These theories, he hopes, will enable us to understand the consequences that flow from particular combinations of qualities or events.

This desire of the scientist to work out fundamentally recurrent patterns evidently has given rise to the idea that the scientific approach is inimical to the artistic.[2] It is essential to see how the scientist uses his generalizations or broad categories. His tentative generalizations are offered as a framework of ideas and guiding principles to be applied to specific situations. This framework will help to identify in a given situation those elements that possess a particular characteristic pattern. But, equally important, they help him to further discriminate wherein this situation differs from other situations.

This process in no way violates the approach of the artist to life; the artist is not only concerned with the unique. If every author were entirely different from every other human being, and if each of us were totally unique, there could be no art at all.

Fundamentally, comprehension of the author's theme must be based on the general or typical emotions or situations that are present in the work he is creating. At the

[2] Unfortunately, the social scientists themselves are largely responsible for the prevalent misconception. Their tendency has been to formulate their theories in such a way that their meaning for human lives is obscured. Economists, sociologists, political theorists, historians, have too often developed a technical jargon that makes their findings seem remote from ordinary life. They must deal with mass movements, statistical data, the broad sweep of events; yet this should not entail the neglect of the individual human behavior and personal motivations that give rise to these social phenomena. The more creative thinkers in all of these fields, however, are aware of the human import of their work. The view of the social sciences presented here rests on them, in the hope that it will be more and more generally operative. See also pp. 174 seq.

same time, he seeks to render its peculiar and special overtones, its subtle departures from the typical. For example,
there is much that is unusual in the personalities and
situations presented in Hardy's *Jude the Obscure;* yet
without the elements common to many human beings, no
matter how specially combined in the character of Jude
or Sue, we should not be able to understand the work at
all. Intent on the peculiar qualities or the strangeness of
the situation created by the artist, we assume ideas concerning the general or the characteristic. The point of
view of the artist requires a recognition of recurrent patterns, paralleled by the recognition that every personality
and every situation has its own unique qualities.

The artist orders and classifies the data offered by life as
much as does the scientist. The artist aims to make us
experience imaginatively these common patterns and
special qualities; the scientist seeks to discover a framework of ideas concerning what is general and what is
unique that we may apply to such experiences. This
framework of knowledge, these guiding principles, offered
by the scientist are never irrelevant to the experience derived from either life or art.

Science starts with the complexity of human nature
and society, but conquers the variety and intricacy of its
subject matter by working out fruitful principles of explanation for limited phases of it. *Divide et impera,* the
old Roman principle for success in conquering enemies,
is the principle that science has used in overcoming the
complexity of its materials. By approaching human affairs
from different angles, anthropology, economics, psychol-

ogy, and sociology have been able to discover a considerable body of information that furnishes the basis for a provisional understanding of human beings.

Often the generalizations of the social sciences hold only for certain historical epochs, particular culture areas and cultural patterns. The scientist recognizes that his findings within these limited areas must be compared to findings drawn from other areas, such as civilizations other than the Western. The scientist works out a certain hypothesis concerning human personality and society, and then attempts to discover all the facts that will tend to prove or disprove it. He admits that his results are always tentative, that there are many gaps in his knowledge, and that new information may lead to the adoption of new theories.

This very tentativeness of the scientific attitude has been said to make it extremely unsettling to the child or the adolescent. It is feared that great mental insecurity will result from the fact that there is nothing absolutely certain, that all ideas are subject to future revision. Such insecurity evidently arises when the scientific spirit is not thoroughly presented. Though prepared to relinquish belief in any particular findings or conclusions of science, we can still hold firmly to our faith in the scientific method itself.

Scientific knowledge is essentially a cooperative product. Only as a fact or theory is tested and verified by many competent minds, often widely scattered in time and space, does that fact or theory come to be accepted. The important thing is not that one generation rejects a particular theory of psychology worked out by the preceding (paralleling, say, the substitution of an Einsteinian for a

Newtonian physics), but that there are innumerable minds all over the world working at these problems, building on what others have done before them, and contributing, each in his own way, to a greater approximation toward sound understanding. Bringing up young people to base their security upon the idea of absolute certainty has led only to disillusionment and insecurity. They will be much better equipped if they place their faith in the co-operative striving toward greater and greater exactitude and universality that is the essence of the scientific spirit.[3]

The social sciences already offer much that can be assimilated into the fabric of our everyday life. If they do not provide rigid formulas for action, it is precisely because the scientific spirit stresses the need for understanding the special conditions that qualify any particular situation. Our society is seeking more and more to take advantage of what the social sciences can already explain about the various factors involved in its operations. Understanding of the typical as well as the special

[3] "What is science? The dictionary will say that it is systematized knowledge. Dictionary definitions, however, are too apt to repose upon derivations; which is as much as to say that they neglect too much the later steps in the evolution of meanings. Mere knowledge, though it be systematized, may be a dead memory; while by science we all habitually mean a living and growing body of truth. . . . That which constitutes science, then, is not so much correct conclusions, as it is a correct method. But the method of science is itself a scientific result. It did not spring out of the brain of a beginner: it was a historic attainment and a scientific achievement. So that not even this method ought to be regarded as essential to the beginnings of science. That which is essential, however, is the scientific spirit, which is determined not to rest satisfied with existing opinions, but to press on to the real truth of nature. To science once enthroned in this sense, among any people, science in every other sense is heir apparent." Charles Sanders Peirce, *Collected Papers*, Vol. VI (Cambridge, Harvard University Press, 1935), p. 302.

characteristics of any problem is the prelude to more intelligent and more successful solutions. The teacher of literature should cling to this understanding of the flexible, questing nature of the scientific spirit—its readiness to utilize the insights which man's collective endeavors have thus far attained, and its dynamic sense of truth.

THESE OVERARCHING CONSIDERATIONS will protect the literary specialist from the danger of a dogmatic application of scientific theories or a substitution of scientific terminology for scientific insight. A bane of many discussions about human beings (and especially of much educational theory) is the use of a scientific jargon that masks from the speaker and the listener their lack of real understanding.

An illustration of this type of misuse of science is the employment of the jargon of psychological terminology. Recall, for instance, those people who swallow the Freudian or Adlerian theory unquestioningly and who use their various categories loosely and lavishly. Accepting such labels as the *Oedipus fixation* or the *inferiority complex*, they evidently feel that they have clarified their understanding of a personality when they have applied one of these labels to it. Their facile use of such terms merely reveals their lack of understanding of the psychoanalytic approach itself. Any of the accounts of particular analyses recorded by Freud or his disciples reflects their sense of how special each case is. The operation of any such general emotional patterns as the Oedipus fixation or the inferiority complex differs in its particulars in each case. Even the recognition of these broad, typical patterns was arrived at only after prolonged study of the specific cases.[4] Having determined the general pattern, the analyst's concern was to see how it had worked itself out in terms of the particular personality and the particular situation in which the person found himself. Only in this way, not by a mere process of labeling, could the psychiatrist offer any help. Equally valid illustrations of misuse of terminology might be drawn from other schools of psychology and other social sciences, e.g., the nineteenth-century use of *the survival of the fittest* or the indiscriminate application of phrases such as *the law of supply and demand, the class struggle* (economics), *the relativity of morals* (anthropology), *evolution and progress* (sociology), or *the inevitable decay of civilizations* (Spenglerian history).

That the teacher of literature inevitably deals with psychological problems does not argue that he should learn all the systems of classification of human types or all the theories of behavior. Nor should the discussion of literature necessarily be at all concerned with psychological classifications or terminology. Suppose a student docilely learned to classify literary characters according to whether they were extroverts or introverts, or according to whether they showed signs of an inferiority complex, or according to whether their actions could be phrased in Freudian or Jungian terms. Does it seem likely that such

[4] In fact, this recognition of human variability and the need for an ever broader base for generalization explains psychiatrists' current revision of their theories in the light of a study of other cultures. Cf. some early contributions: Karen Horney, *The Neurotic Personality of Our Time* (New York, W. W. Norton, 1937); James S. Plant, *Personality and the Cultural Pattern* (New York, The Commonwealth Fund, 1937); John Dollard, *Criteria for the Life History* (New Haven, Yale University Press, 1935).

a student would be much better off than one who had
passively learned to think in terms of "the good people"
and "the bad people" or to classify them as types, such as
"the gossip," "the bully," "the old maid," or who might
have been led to consider them only as "Aryan" and
"non-Aryan"? Any rigid *a priori* classification used in this
way merely becomes an obstacle to understanding people.
As soon as he has labeled them, the student feels relieved
of any further obligation to get at their inner qualities, to
understand their special motivation, or to observe as many
as possible of the factors that may enter into the external
conditions influencing them.

Hence the teacher of literature should be conversant,
not so much with the details, as with the spirit of psychological inquiry. If the teacher himself espouses any
one school of psychology (and that might lend his teaching a consistency that the remarks about "human nature"
uttered in most literature courses lack), he should be willing to recognize the existence of other schools and the
student's right to know about them. For if the student is
given a sense of the approach to human nature out of
which psychological inquiry springs, he will be ready and
eager to seek from the psychologists themselves the tentative answers they offer to his questions.

The same principle holds for the other behavioral
sciences. The teacher of literature needs to convey the
spirit of scrupulous inquiry and the flexible approach
which is their characteristic. His contribution may be
phrased largely in negative terms: he will not impose a
dogmatic framework upon the concept of "human nature";
he will not allow conventional assumptions to go unchal-

lenged; he will not permit his students to fall back upon pat, stereotyped formulas. In positive terms, he will awaken his students to an awareness of the complexity of human behavior and society and will stimulate them to seek the understanding that the social scientists are endeavoring to establish. He will share the psychologist's belief that knowledge concerning human nature must be the result of careful, controlled observation, that any hypothesis must be tested and retested, and that we must be particularly on our guard against imputing to human beings those traits or those psychological mechanisms that would justify or rationalize our own habitual method of dealing with them.

WHAT, THEN, ARE SOME of the basic concepts that should permeate the discussion when the reading of literature raises questions about human nature and experience? Perhaps an economical way of dealing with these questions within the limits of a chapter will be to start with certain ideas that often appear in the student's thinking and with which the English teacher must therefore deal. With these current conceptions as starting points, it will be possible to see what light the scientific approach can offer. This will have relevance to the problems that teachers constantly face in the classroom, and may indicate how certain concepts can function in ordinary thinking about people and society. The object will be to further illustrate the value of a firm hold on certain fundamental concepts and the importance of bringing such concepts to bear upon current attitudes.

One of the most glaring of the widespread assumptions

encountered in students' reactions to literature is the traditional voluntaristic conception of human nature and conduct mentioned briefly in the first chapter. This view is based on the idea that any behavior can be interpreted as having been willed by the actor. The assumption is that in all situations the individual is free to accept or reject various modes of behavior. If a person is pleasant or unpleasant, social or antisocial, it is largely because he wishes to be so. One needs only to know the "rules," the commandments of the society about one, in order to be provided with a guide to one's own conduct and a code for sitting in judgment on one's fellowmen. Although, stated thus baldly, these assumptions seem almost to condemn themselves, and although this view has lost its hold in many areas of our political and social life, it still often dominates the average man's thinking. We see this reflected in his actual judgments on people or in the attitudes toward whole groups of people.

Scientific investigation and analysis, particularly in the fields of psychology, sociology, and anthropology, have during the past quarter century generally undermined this oversimplified theory of human nature and conduct. The plasticity of the human creature is being recognized. The human personality is thought of by the scientist as a complex of qualities and habits which are the end result of a great many different factors converging upon and interacting with the individual organism. The innate physical and mental endowments of the individual are not ignored, but the individual, as we meet him functioning in society, is seen as the product of the particular ways in which these innate elements have been molded, stimulated, or repressed by external conditions.

The conception of the child as a little savage whose rebellious will must be broken and who must be coerced into civilized ways lost its currency at least a century ago. Equally mythical is the romantic conception of the child as an unspoiled angel who is corrupted into the ways of the world as its "prison walls" close about him. Instead, the human creature is seen to possess potentialities for an infinite variety of behavior. The circumstances into which he is born, the temperaments that act upon him in his earlier years, the kinds of stimulation or repression to which he is subjected, and the satisfactions or frustrations he meets will have a powerful influence in patterning the mental and physical potentialities with which he is born.

Present-day psychology is devoting a great deal of attention to attempting to discover significant forces that contribute to molding the personality. These forces are attributed differing degrees of importance by the various schools of psychology. Some focus their attention upon such seemingly external factors as methods of feeding during babyhood. Others stress more the emotional relationships with the parents and with brothers and sisters as important factors in patterning the child's personality. Still others stress the environment in which the child grows up; the economic conditions that surround him, whether an affluent environment permits unhampered activity or whether, as in the city slums, he is often forced to seek an outlet for his energy in destructive and underhand activities.

No matter which aspect of the forces acting upon the child is stressed, and no matter how much contemporary schools of psychology may differ concerning the methods, behavioristic or introspective, of studying the individual, they share this basic approach to human development. The behavior, the emotional patterns, the ideas and dominant drives that make up a personality, are seen as the result of a process by which the particular mental and emotional habits are, so to speak, learned. Thus, a particular temperament or a particular action cannot be judged in itself. It has to be seen in relation to the whole stream of the individual's life, the various influences to which he has been subjected, the situations and events through which he has passed. This does not eliminate the concept of the will. But it does mean that we have to get back of any particular action to see the context within which "the will" operates.

This view of the plasticity of human nature has been strengthened by the sociologists and the anthropologists, attacking the problem from other angles. From the immediate environment, particularly from the family group, the child acquires not only such things as physical mannerisms, habits of gesture and language, but also emotional habits and major ideas concerning behavior. Similarly, the particular social group of which the child is a part contributes certain elements to his personality patterns and his mental and emotional habits. One illustration of how the ideas and attitudes of the surrounding society are incorporated into the individual personality is the acquisition from the environment of ideas of masculinity and femininity. These mold the individual's own behavior and his expectations concerning the behavior of others. In the same way are built up the patterns of feeling and behavior, the expectations and values that constitute the content of the individual's personality and sense of life.

In our own heterogeneous society this concept of the influence of the family and social environment upon the individual is particularly important. The effort to fully carry out the democratic dream has brought the realization that in our highly complex civilization, people may be the products of practically different subcultures. In our cities, for instance, we find people who superficially seem to be conforming to the ways of life of the average city dweller, and yet who, coming from different parts of the country and from different family, social, and ethnic backgrounds, may be motivated by entirely different conceptions of personal relationships. The young couple who have met and married in the city may represent the conjunction of two different patterns; the young husband coming from a small New England town with its leisurely tempo and thrifty, disciplined, undemonstrative way of life will have very different images of behavior from his wife who may have grown up in the easygoing atmosphere of a Western town where heartiness and vigorous action are valued more than discipline and decorum. Or they may have very different images of what constitutes the family, one perhaps used to a household in which several generations shared their activities and their pleasures and troubles, and the other thinking of the family in terms of the biological unit of parents and children, seeing all others as outsiders toward whom no responsibility need be felt. Other patterns may reflect the high incidence of divorce or perhaps the home built around an unmarried mother.

Beyond such broad patterning factors exists an even more complex and perhaps even more powerful set of influences. The boy who has grown up as the subject of the excessive care and emotional attentions of a doting mother may seek in any other relationships as, for instance, in marriage, similar cherishing protection and emotional dependence. This may be so powerful as to prevent his assuming the emotional responsibilities that are usually associated with marriage and parenthood.

THE ANTHROPOLOGISTS have contributed still another and broader framework within which to place this basic concept of psychological conditioning. By studying a great variety of societies or, to use the anthropological term, *cultures*, they have revealed the diversity of patterns into which man has poured his personal and group life. Around the universal activities of food-getting, propagation, child-rearing, have been developed modes of behavior, types of personal relationships, ideas of good and evil, religious beliefs, social organizations, economic and political mechanisms, that result in cultures with seemingly nothing in common.

Some cultures may organize their economic life on the basis of the individualism of the Eskimo or on the basis of the economic communalism of the Zuni. Kinship may be reckoned according to matrilineal or patrilineal lines. The family may be organized on the basis of the biological unit of parents and children, or on the system whereby a whole community constitutes the family group, or in such a way that the child looks to his mother's brother as his guardian and protector rather than his biological father. One folk may people the universe about them with malevolent spirits, another with benign spirits. Ethical codes may be set up that require the ruthless taking of human life, or that deem it an unpardonable sin, or as in our own society, that make the taking of human life at times sinful murder and at other times (in war) a glorious social deed.

One culture may make the generous bestowal of property upon others the means of social prestige, or as in our own society, prestige may depend upon the ability to accumulate and retain possessions. Some peoples may rear their children from the earliest age as a functioning part of the economic and social group, as among the Samoans; others may let them grow up almost completely outside the adult pattern, as among the Manus; or still others, like the Batciga, may let them create an organized "child society" of their own. For each item of social and personal relationships within any culture, other societies have erected not only contrasting and contradictory but almost incommensurable ideas and arrangements. Everything, from the structure of language or the ways of measuring time and indicating direction, to social and economic organizations or ethical and religious codes, will reveal this extraordinary capacity of the human race to create diverse cultures on the basis of the biological needs of the individual and the group.

In terms of the individual, this implies, of course, that his personality, his needs and aims, will be molded by the particular cultural group in which he has been reared.

Each culture tends to stimulate or nourish certain aspects of personality and to repress others. There would be a great difference in the resulting personality according to whether a particular human organism, whatever its innate tendencies, was born into a cultural pattern that values gentleness, moderation, and cooperativeness, or into a culture that values aggressiveness, violence, and individualism. In one society the pugnacious, acquisitive man will be an admired leader; in another society he will be a misfit or an outcast. Everything from physical traits to the ability to dream dreams and see visions may receive different valuations in different cultures. An illustration of this from within our own cultural stream is the social value placed by medieval society upon the seers of visions as opposed to our present-day interpretation of them as abnormal. In other words, what is considered the approved or "normal" temperament or behavior in one culture, or even at one epoch in a civilization, may be disapproved of as abnormal in another.

The anthropological approach to the concept of normality is particularly useful to teachers of adolescents, since this is a problem that troubles many of them. Within the broad scale of temperaments and actions of which the human creature is potentially capable, different societies have placed the range of normality very differently. We especially need to recognize how powerful a hold the norms of our own group have on us. Whatever the concept of the normal, it is to a certain extent the result of historical causes, since ideas of normality have changed from country to country and from age to age. Therefore our own ideas of the normal have no particular divine sanction, but must be judged rationally by their social effects.

Teachers sometimes fear that such a sense of the cultural "relativity of norms" will be unsettling to the adolescent. Will he not feel that there are no standards—that anything, any kind of behavior, is "as good" as any other? This, of course, is an attitude that could only lead to moral and intellectual chaos, and should be carefully guarded against. Such a conclusion, however, can arise only out of a stress on one part of the anthropological facts. For if anthropology shows us the diversity of norms, it also shows us how closely personality and behavior are related to the whole framework of the culture.

The concept of the relativity of standards must be related to the anthropologists' emphasis on the need for seeing the culture as a whole. They warn against the tendency to think of different phases of society as distinct and unrelated. The ideas about physical beauty or attitudes toward property or the possession of intuitive powers in any one society will often tend to be colored by certain underlying drives, certain basic ways of envisioning human nature, certain values typical of the culture. Although it is unlikely that any culture is completely integrated, the elements of culture influence one another.

> All the miscellaneous behavior directed toward getting a living, mating, warring, and worshipping the gods, is made over into consistent patterns in accordance with unconscious canons of choice that develop within the culture. Some cultures, like some periods of art, fail of such integration, and about many others we know too little to understand the motives that actuate them. But cultures at every level of complexity, even the simplest, have achieved it.[5]

[5] Ruth Benedict, *Patterns of Culture* (Boston, Houghton Mifflin Company, 1934), p. 48.

Hence, we must not view in isolation any detail of behavior in our own or any other society but must study it against the background of the motives and emotions institutionalized in that culture. The individual will be liberated from blind subservience to the norms of his group, not by throwing overboard all standards, but by seeing them in relation to the whole complex of attitudes and values into which they fit.

Thus, it was not enough for women to resent the norms set up by the Victorian image of the submissive, self-effacing female. They had to learn in what ways this image was linked with economic dependence and the habits of mind derived from acceptance of political and intellectual authoritarianism. It is not enough for the artist to chafe at the indifference or scorn of the average American. When the artist sees that indifference as a corollary of the dominant emphasis upon practical action, he is ready to inquire into the historical sources and economic and social causes of these attitudes. The very fact that our society places such emphasis upon being an average "good fellow," the fact that so often our college professors consciously seek to look and talk like solid businessmen, the fact that we are so painfully aware of an unusual individuality in dress or belief, require similar explanation. How often is personality or achievement valued according to its translatability into terms of potential income? To what extent have these dominant attitudes been qualified during the past fifty years by recognition of contributions to general social welfare and by a growing emphasis on the value of every individual human being?

If we consider the norms concerning the relations between husband and wife, or parents and children, for example, we must again see how pervasive are the fundamental drives of our culture. The institution of the family, which concentrates within itself so many economic and social functions, will necessarily be affected by the emphasis on material possessions or the extent to which co-operation or rugged individualism is socially approved. Thus it is futile to discuss recent changes in family rela-. tions or to forecast their future development without considering recent economic and social changes or what possible direction our whole society will take. If we are going in the direction of greater valuation of individual personality, family relations will be very different from what they would be if we moved toward approval of conformity and the suppression of the individual. Labels such as "the organization man" and "the hippie" reflect current extremes.

Far from furthering the rejection of all standards, an understanding of cultural conditioning illuminates the intimate relation between individual lives and the whole social fabric. The adolescent is thus provided with a broader perspective from which to view his own struggle to conform to or to modify the dominant norms. He must live within the framework of our own culture, of course. But he need no longer give unthinking adherence to its images of success. Unthinking total rejection should also be seen as conformity, a conformity in reverse, so to speak.

The youth can be liberated from submission to standards that may be peculiar to the particular environment in which he finds himself. If he is brought up in some limited geographic or social setting, or if he is aware only of the most generally accepted standards, he may be equally in danger of too narrow a view. Our society is strikingly heterogeneous; a number of cultural subpatterns exist side by side. Ethnic, regional, and economic groups have developed very different images of the approved kinds of temperament, behavior, or social success. Often the individual born within one of these groups and measuring himself against its particular norms develops a feeling of inferiority which would disappear if he could become aware of the standards developed by other groups.

As our society demonstrates, the concept of cultural patterns and group norms does not rule out the possibility of individual differences within groups. Every society permits a certain degree of acceptable variation. Early childhood experiences and the particular society within which the individual finds himself set certain general patterns, but after all, the experience of no two people, not even of two children within the same family, is identical. That in itself, even without the factor of congenital differences, would lead us to expect a diversity of personalities.

The study of the influences acting on the individual is therefore also concerned with the attempt to see at what points or in what ways emotional and mental habits are set up and the personality becomes crystallized. Despite the original plasticity of the human creature, once the personality pattern is formed, there is a certain resistance to change. Present-day psychology considers early childhood the most important period in the formation of basic tendencies and mechanisms. The psychoanalytic school especially emphasizes this phase of the individual's development and considers that if any remolding of the personality is attempted, it is necessary to penetrate the deep strata of feeling and habit shaped by early experiences in the family. Other schools of psychology postulate that under favorable conditions the structure of personality can be decisively affected in adolescence and adulthood, although such conditions are more likely to occur in childhood. This theoretical position leads to methods of inducing change in personality different from the prolonged analyses carried on by the depth psychologists.

The study of personality should prevent us from falling into the view directly opposed to the voluntaristic one, but equally erroneous: namely, that the individual is merely a kind of automaton entirely at the mercy of external pressures. Too often the youth is given only one side of the picture. He is encouraged to think of man either as an entirely free agent or as the helpless pawn in a completely deterministic system.

The concept of cultural conditioning in no way implies a fatalistic notion that man is a puppet in the hands of some mythical, external power called the "environment" or the "culture." Rather, the anthropologists view the human organism as interacting with the cultural environment. Every child is born into some kind of social environment, and this immediately exerts a patterning influence. But the individual in turn reacts upon the physical and cultural environment and hence influences it in some manner. The process of conscious cultural change can be conceived in such terms. The more conscious the individual is of the nature of the cultural forces with which he is interacting, the more intelligently can he accept or resist them, and the more intelligently can he modify their power and their direction.[6]

The influence of the cultural environment can be envisioned as setting the broad limits within which the individual can develop and within which he has freedom of choice. This may apply to choices permitted by his physical and temperamental development. It may apply to such choices as whether or not he will read a new book and whether or not he will attempt to change the surrounding society through the advocacy of new laws. In other words, in terms of his own temperamental bent, he can accept or resist environmental pressures and can choose one line of behavior rather than another.

The more unthinkingly and mechanically the human being follows the patterns set for him by his environment, the nearer he approaches the state of the automaton. If the individual understands the important molding influences in his own past and in the history of mankind, if he becomes aware of alternative social patterns or of alternative types of happiness, he will be better able to make choices, to dominate, and if necessary, to remold his environment. Thus he will be in a position to exercise his

[6] The psychoanalysts utilize the same principle in their technique of helping the individual to gain insight into the nature and influence of his past experiences. When these are brought into his consciousness and their relation to his present anxieties and obsessions is understood, he becomes capable of dealing with them rationally, and is thus enabled to remold or readjust his personality. (This analogy was pointed out by Lawrence K. Frank in a letter to the writer.)

Other schools of psychology have applied this principle in the development of different techniques, e.g., David C. McClelland's work in achievement motivation.

"will" and to consciously influence his own future and the future of the society about him.

The anthropologist and the psychologist offer a critical approach to another widespread tendency: to accept the familiar or the traditional as possessing a fundamental rightness and, conversely, to consider the strange and the unfamiliar as necessarily inferior or reprehensible. Since the individual unconsciously absorbs the particular modes of behavior, views of human nature, and ideas about socio-economic arrangements, of the culture into which he is born, he takes them for granted and often cannot even imagine any possible alternatives or variations. Hence, when he does encounter another cultural pattern, as when the white man comes into contact with the African or the Samoan, he tends to look upon it as inferior. An extreme illustration of this is the fact that many primitive peoples have as the name for their cultural group only the word in their language that signifies "human being." Any who do not belong to their cultural group automatically fall outside that category.

The anthropologist helps us to realize that merely because we have grown up in a particular cultural pattern, we have no legitimate basis for considering it, *ipso facto*, the only possible, or even best possible, pattern. Much is to be gained from the knowledge that other cultures have developed working alternatives to the customs and institutions with which we are familiar. Similarly, we can compare the ethical and social ideals of our culture with those created by other cultures or other possible cultures.

Different societies, then, set up different images of the

most highly desirable human satisfactions—as in the
contrast cited above between those valuing violent com
petitive behavior and those valuing peaceful cooperation
Societies also differ in the degree to which their variou
institutions and customs make the valued satisfaction
either more or less easily attainable. Sometimes there i
a decided discrepancy between those two aspects of a cul
ture. An example is the gradual elimination of such a dis
crepancy from our own society during the past few gen
erations: sexual experience was valued, yet a frustrating
atmosphere of guilt or shame was cast about it. The satis
faction of this strong culturally reinforced need is more
and more being freed from culturally imposed feelings o
guilt or shame. Another example from our own society
individual self-determination, freedom of thought and
speech, and self-respect are values that have received
cultural sanction and have therefore become needs fo
which the individual craves satisfaction. Our politica
institutions were designed to fulfill them, but in the live
of many people conditions tended to frustrate these de
mands. Government has played an increasing role in fos
tering economic and social changes designed to narrow
this gap between ideal and reality. The civil rights move
ment comes as the culmination of a whole series of step
in this direction. That this struggle has not been immedi
ately successful, and that unremitting effort will be
needed to bring lasting results, does not contradict the
fact of a great shift in institutionalized attitudes and ex
pectations.

We can judge the society about us, then, in terms o
the kinds of basic satisfactions it values and the degree to

which it permits or stifles the attainment of those satisfactions. Self-consciousness about our cultural pattern means that we no longer need accept it as unthinkingly as the air we breathe. Probably more than any other cultural group before, we have the knowledge to consciously influence the future development of our customs and institutions.

The concept of the cultural pattern can also counteract the tendency to look upon different phases of the society or different groups as distinct and unrelated. In so complex a civilization as ours, anything affecting one element in it—whether that be a geographic or economic section, an ethnic minority, or a particular category such as women or coal miners—will tend to have repercussions upon the rest of society.[7]

This view of the interaction between different aspects of the culture has been given a special interpretation by those who believe that man's economic life—his particular methods of food-getting, manufacture, distribution of goods, and property regulation—tends to determine the nature of all the other aspects of his life, such as social

---

[7] The concept of the cultural pattern is particularly rich in implications for the study of literature. Through literature we are constantly coming into contact with cultural patterns of the past or of other societies. Often, literature gives clear expression to the characteristic ways of feeling, the types of temperament and behavior valued by the society as a whole. It would be unfortunate if, in the study of literature, the student were permitted to forget that man's life is lived in a web of crosscurrents that tend to take on a basic pattern. Literature itself cannot be viewed in isolation from other aspects of man's activity in society. Moreover, the particular images of life presented in literature should be approached with a sense of the complexity of man's life and an awareness of its tendency to reflect some dominant pattern. These questions will be discussed more fully in Chapter 8.

organization, religion, and art. Although this theory of economic determinism has often been applied in a crudely oversimplified way by the "economic determinists," the economic factor is generally recognized by social scientists. The distribution of wealth among various classes in a society, for example, affects a great many different phases of life. Thus, even in the history of literature, it surely was not an accident that the type of fiction represented by the novels of Richardson, Fielding, and their literary descendants began to flourish at the time when the middle class in England was attaining increasing economic power. Moreover, the particular economic group from which a writer springs surely plays some part in his view of life, his sense of values, and his particular choice of subjects. The teacher of literature, like any other student of the products of man's social life, cannot ignore economic influences.

THE PRECEDING PAGES have sketched only a few of the topics that enter into the problem of the patterning of human personality and human society. A great many subjects and considerations that are live concerns of present-day social scientists have not even been broached. In psychology, for instance, a center of much illumination and controversy, psychoanalytic theories concerning the role of unconscious processes and the ways in which they find expression have only been touched upon. Numerous other omissions can be listed: in anthropology, the studies that undermine belief in racial superiority or inferiority, or the problems involved in understanding cultural contact and change; in sociology, studies of the results of increasing industrialization and urbanization; in economics, the development of a "welfare capitalism" and the elimination of the cyclic nature of unregulated competitive enterprise.

The discussion may suffice at least to suggest the general way in which an acquaintance with certain basic concepts in psychology, sociology, and anthropology have a direct bearing upon the subject of human personality and conduct—a subject that is an integral part of any consideration of literature. Such a structure of ideas should make it possible to turn to the literature of other ages and other societies with an open mind, and to look upon the expressions of our own world with critical freedom.

It is not surprising that the older approaches to human nature and society tend to persist. Even those who have come into contact with the newer theories often fail to assimilate them into their attitudes in actual life, and in their personal relationships are still dominated by automatically absorbed prejudices and expectations. Marriage consultants, for instance, reveal that often relationships are shattered by the inability of each of the partners to recognize the causes of the behavior they dislike. The reaction is entirely one of rejection and blame. There is no sense that behavior grows out of a complex network of factors, some of them environmental, some physical, and some the result of emotional attitudes and habits whose source is in the early psychic frustrations of the individual. Each spouse also fails to understand his own motivations and to see that perhaps his own resentments and irritations may be due to certain factors in his environment or past history which have no validity in themselves. An attempt to understand the possible origins of the disapproved behavior may lead to modification of these causes;

a changed external situation and temperamental read-justments may be brought about.

Contemporary behavioral scientists have substituted for the older, voluntaristic approach the effort to understand the factors that generate behavior. Given such habits of mind, the possibility of the adjustment of personalities to one another is greatly enhanced. Such an approach might also tend to prevent people from entering into relationships in which there were fundamental elements that would probably lead to misunderstanding and maladjustment.

During the past quarter-century, many of the concepts presented in these pages have received wide currency in college courses, in newspaper columns on child-rearing, and in legal judgments and actions. On all sides, nevertheless, the student is still being bombarded with expressions of the old approach to people and affairs. In the mass media, in our governmental practices, in our law courts, and above all, in the average home itself, this view often prevails. Hence, it is particularly important that any phase of the student's educational experience concerned with human relations should responsibly present attitudes growing out of the newer approaches to personality. The potential influence of the teacher of English is therefore considerable. Only if the teacher is himself imbued with a more reasoned approach to human personality and society, will he be able to help the student build the attitudes toward people that the psychologists and others concerned with mental health have demonstrated to be most constructive. Instead of the old defeatist notion that "human nature is what it is and will never be changed," there should arise the vision of human beings as responding to many forces that can be modified and directed.

The view that insights offered by the social sciences may lead to more successful living or to a redirection of life or a remolding of society, immediately raises the problem of values. For as both the moralists and the opponents of science are eager to remind us, science may give us the facts, but it cannot give us the standards of what is desirable or undesirable, good or evil. Indeed, long before the invention of nuclear bombs, it was clear that the use of scientific knowledge could raise crucial moral questions. A lesser illustration is the application of psychological knowledge to advertising that creates a demand for useless or harmful things.

The social sciences, then, are slowly building up a body of knowledge concerning important factors in the development of human personality and in the patterning of human society. But where shall we turn for some scale of values that will help us to judge what kinds of personality and what kind of society are desirable?

This problem does not consciously present itself to great masses of people (and they include many of the "educated"). They have unthinkingly acquired from the cultural atmosphere their ideas concerning desirable and undesirable ends, moral or immoral acts, acceptable or unacceptable social arrangements. In other words, they are completely guided by the dominant system of values assimilated from their environment. Almost automatically they have at their disposal a yardstick by which to measure their own and others' conduct and a basis for rejecting personal or general social arrangements that deviate from the customary.

Such unthinking acceptance of any system of values is undesirable. The anthropologist, the historian, and the sociologist (as well as the philosopher) point out that many alternative systems of values are possible. This constitutes a challenge to inquire objectively into the varying effects of these different social and moral codes upon the human beings whose lives they regulate.

Those who find the task of working out their own philosophy too difficult, or are not sufficiently mature to assume the responsibility for their own choice of goals and moral code, turn to authority—to some institution such as a church or to an individual such as a dictator. Comfortable as throwing off the burden of decision might seem to be, the social sciences reveal that institutions often tend merely to reinforce and crystallize the particular customs and traditional values built up by the past. They are not necessarily safe guides in a changing world. In fact, historically they often seem to stand in the way of any adjustment of old values to new conditions. Hence, a blind following of their postulates may lead to painful maladjustment and conflict, and perhaps defeat the very ends of human happiness or social peace for which they first were formulated. Within such institutions today, as, for instance, in the churches and the educational enterprise, there are individuals with sufficient perspective to question whether the traditionally perpetuated codes and practices are relevant to changed conditions.

A sound system of values must guide the search for a

more adequate moral code and social philosophy. The students of other societies will give us information about the personality types, the social institutions, that other cultural groups may have developed. The historians of philosophy will explain to us the various value systems that men have applied in the past or in the present age. And today's social philosophers will be suggesting new guidelines. Our ultimate choice will be influenced by all these, particularly by the philosophies that have directly contributed to our own cultural stream. Certainly, present-day attempts to solve this problem of values would be very different if the Greek and the Judeo-Christian philosophies and the ethical theories developed under feudal and capitalistic social organizations were not part of our cultural heritage. The individual will thus have available alternative schemes of value which his own culture has produced, and he may sometimes seek to import a hierarchy of values derived from another culture. The very fact that he reacts forcibly against some of the points of view in his own society may lead him to emphasize those values and ideals that they neglect. The current interest in Oriental thought—in, for instance, Zen Buddhism—suggests such a quest for alternative possibilities.

One basic value judgment has been implied throughout this discussion: Any system of values can be scrutinized in terms of its consequences for human life. Any form of conduct, any social mechanism, any custom or institution, should be measured in terms of its actual effect on the individual personalities that make up the society. To use the culturally sanctioned terminology, every human being is entitled to "life, liberty, and the pursuit of happiness."

This means that the human being is recognized as having value in himself and that anything which reduces him to the status of a thing, instrument, or automaton is condemned. It sets up as an ideal the social situation in which each member of society is given the opportunity for the greatest fulfillment of those culturally valued satisfactions of which he is potentially capable. The corollary of this is that if a conflict of interest should arise, no individual and no group would be justified in gaining their own satisfactions through exploitation of any other individuals or groups.

This rests upon belief in the fundamental dignity and worth of the human being. It sets up the well-being and fulfillment of the individual in opposition to any abstractions for which might be claimed a superior reality or value such as the Elect, the Supermen, the Proletariat, the Nation, the Race, or the State. This basic postulate of value is obviously one that receives support from many elements present in our cultural heritage. Implicit in various religious philosophies and in the democratic philosophy, it applies not only to our political but also to our social and economic life.

This fundamental principle provides a measure for individual lives, as well as the customs and institutions, the ideas and assumptions that make up our culture. It provides a standard, too, for utilizing and applying the knowledge that the scientists are so laboriously cooperating to acquire. Often, only the scientist can tell us what is best for man's physical and mental health. The sciences that propose to study man as a biological organism and as a social creature are slowly becoming aware of their common function, their responsibility to contribute to this core of knowledge about the factors that enter into the creation of freely and fully functioning human beings. Thus the physician finds that he cannot think of man as a biological organism in a vacuum but must concern himself with the particular social and economic setting within which that biological organism functions. The sociologist, studying man's behavior under the varying conditions created by our social and economic system, can provide information to be judged in terms of successful or unsuccessful human lives. The psychologists are increasingly aware of the fact that psychology of the individual is part of what is known as social psychology. Various specialists in the field of mental hygiene have already reached the point of being dissatisfied to merely readjust scattered individuals among the increasing numbers who are known to be suffering from nervous maladjustment and disorder. On the basis of psychiatric study of these individuals, experts will be better and better able to tell us at what points our particular cultural pattern sets up deep psychic disturbances or stifles and condemns fundamental human drives. In the field of psychology, too, preventative therapy will develop a body of information by which we can apply the basic value judgment indicated above. We shall probably be increasingly able to judge the degree to which any particular cultural pattern satisfies the requirement that it permit the greatest possible fulfillment and enrichment of human lives. Then, too, economists are studying the functioning of methods of production and distribution and of regulations concerning property in various societies, so that these practices may be judged by the standard of the maximum social welfare.

Those who are principally students or practitioners of an art, such as literature, can also place their knowledge and interests within the context of this broader system of values. Surely it is hardly necessary to speak of the joy of artistic activity and the satisfactions of the experience of art. Moreover, the artist can tell us much about man himself. Many of the subtler potentialities of human feelings and behavior that could have been given common utterance in no other way are revealed and embodied in artistic form.

The fundamental values of democracy, the criteria of the dignity and the worth of the human being, require the corollary of freedom for the artist. For not only does the artist give expression to innumerable facets of the life about him. He also has served an important function by recalling his fellowmen to a sense of basic human needs when they forgot them under the sway of destructive symbols and slogans or the compulsion of materialistic ambitions. The opportunity for this kind of activity, at once creative and critical, is essential. Equally essential is freedom for youth—and indeed all citizens—to experience those works of art that reveal weaknesses in the contemporary world or that create a vision of greater fulfillment of human values.

YET IT MAY BE ASKED, why should the school or college be concerned with the development of emotional attitudes or with preparing the student for his personal as well as his broader social relationships? Are there not many other social agencies concerned with precisely these problems? Indeed, has not the importance of the family and community environment just been pointed out? Why then place this additional burden upon the school, which in our society already has so large a task in giving information and developing skills? Why, above all, involve literature, which offers experiences that would be precious in themselves even if they had no further practical justification?

The answer is that the generations of young people now in school and college will have to meet conditions and problems very different from those their parents and grandparents faced. During periods of relative stability or extremely slow social change, the home and the community could be relied upon to furnish the emotional conditioning and attitudes that would automatically fit the kind of society the child was eventually to enter. At no time, of course, has the school been entirely free from the responsibility of influencing character and mental habits. In a stable society, however, that influence would principally be a reinforcement of attitudes acquired by the child outside the school.

Present-day conditions no longer automatically provide the youth with the habits of mind and images of behavior that will be appropriate to future social conditions. The development of an urban industrial society, with all its changes in technology, and the emergence of the "one world" of the "space age" have produced a welter of new relationships and new images of the values to be sought for. The multiplicity of alternative choices in personal relations and social philosophy is particularly characteristic of American society. The old habitual responses, the old images of what is to be taken for granted in relations between people, can no longer be followed unquestioningly. Many of the old attitudes continue, of course, to be valid. No matter how drastic and revolutionary social change may seem, the anthropologist and the historian will remind us that the new elements are infinitesimal in comparison with the mass of cultural attitudes that persist. Nevertheless, failure to cope emotionally and intellectually with the changing political, economic, and social situation can produce much unhappiness and frustration. In a world of such vast technological change, of such a desperate sense of international tensions, the individual needs to build for himself a mental and emotional base from which to meet the fluctuating currents about him.

Since the old attitudes, the old habits of response, the old goals and images of success can no longer be automatically relied upon, youth are increasingly plunged into an unprecedented self-consciousness in the choice of their patterns of life. They must be prepared to test and perhaps to modify the emotional responses their childhood environment transmits to them from the past. The home and the community, whose educational influence operates principally in undirected and unconscious ways, are being called upon to contribute to such flexibility but cannot be expected to do this alone. The school, also, must step in to deliberately provide preparation for the unpredictable future.

Because in so many areas old patterns have crumbled and no clearly defined new patterns have crystallized, young people more than ever before must be sufficiently nature to assume responsibility for making their own judgments and working out their own solutions. The concept of "maturity" is stressed in the disciplines concerned with mental health. They see in our failure to develop a population of mature, self-reliant individuals the explanation of much of the unhappiness, the frustrations, the cruelties, often characteristic of personal relationships in our society. The same lack of emotional maturity explains many of the weaknesses in the functioning of our democratic system of government. The individual who is still in the infantile state of needing an outside authority to make his decisions for him cannot be expected to participate constructively in the creation of a rational society.

The concept of emotional security is closely related to this problem of maturity. Because the surrounding intellectual and social atmosphere is in such a state of flux, the youth needs help in attaining his own intellectual and emotional base. The aim of providing employment and economic security for all, and hence eliminating one great source of insecurity, no longer seems visionary.

But there is another source of security that each individual in our culture should be able to draw upon. This, the behavioral scientists tell us, depends very much on childhood experiences. If the child has been given a feeling of being wanted and loved, if he has been able to feel that he is an accepted member of the family and social group, he will tend to develop the kind of inner security that will enable him to meet constructively much of the external insecurity and struggle of later life. The less he is given assurance of affection and concern, the less strength of character and sense of self-esteem he is likely to develop. These insecurities will color his approach to the people and the world about him. The feeling of being worthless or inadequate or unloved may express itself in hostility to others and in the resort to physical force as a way of meeting the threat of life. So far as present studies indicate, the most important factor seems to be the degree of warmth experienced by the child, rather than any particular techniques of child training.

During the past quarter-century, many parents and teachers have been made intensely aware of the far-reaching influence they can have on the child's personality development. They recognize that he should not be made to feel guilty because he is a child and therefore cannot always live up to adult demands. Life should not be for him a formidable series of rules and prohibitions against which he is naturally a sinner. Throughout the whole course of his home and school life, he should be given the feeling that he is a person worthy of consideration. As in so many instances, the reaction against earlier authoritarianism and rigidity has sometimes led to what is now considered an excessive permissiveness. Evidence seems to suggest that the absence of rigid controls is not in itself enough. For example, inconsistency in the demands made on the child by different parents, or by the home and the school, may be a more important factor than the degree of authority or permissiveness.

Problems of maturity and mental security—much too complex to be adequately treated here—ultimately involve our whole economic and social setup, as well as the methods of child-rearing in the home and the fundamental characteristics of our educational system. A recognition of the importance of these problems strengthens one of the main ideas upon which the foregoing chapters have been based: that although the school should not force upon the student subject matter and materials beyond his intellectual and emotional level of comprehension, it should permit him to function at his fullest emotional and intellectual capacity.

Particularly in the adolescent years, students are often confined to too childish a plane of thought and feeling. They too frequently are encouraged to passively accept what the teacher wishes them to think and feel, without becoming aware of themselves as personalities with definite patterns of their own. The emphasis in earlier chapters on the importance of the personal relationship between the student and the literary work, which grew out of an attempt to understand the literary experience realistically, can be related to this broader concern with the need for fostering the individual's attainment of greater maturity.

American society today—often with too-unquestioning cooperation of school and university—is increasing its demands on youth, "accelerating" the educational pace, and extending the number of years of preparation for adulthood and career. Much effort, often successful, is being expended on tapping the latent intellectual potentialities of children and youth. But there is a glaring lack of general concern, to say nothing of concerted efforts, to provide the basis for an equally successful emotional life. Both in the preadolescent and adolescent years, an em-

phasis on emotional development should parallel the cur
rent emphasis on the intellectual. Here literature and th
other arts can make an important contribution.

Such pressures and overintellectualized demands on th
post-Sputnik generation have had repercussions in th
extreme reactions of some and in the sense of disorienta
tion of many. It is sheer abdication of responsibility o
the part of the older generation, for example, either t
ignore or to condemn adolescent efforts to discover fo
themselves the meaning of sex and love—efforts necessaril
confused and often self-defeating in a world that offers n
clearly defined satisfactory patterns and assumes that a
emotional life can be postponed as easily as a professio
or a career. The social scientists—the historian, the socic
logist, the economist, the psychologist—deal with subject
about which cling strongly emotional, culturally trans
mitted attitudes. Political and economic questions, topic
involving racial or national prejudices, or such matters a
the relations between parents and children, or husban
and wife, almost automatically arouse strong feeling. Th
social scientist must therefore clear the ground for ration
discussion by first eliminating or reducing any prejudice
or fixed emotional attitudes that may obscure a clear viev
of the facts. He has striven for unemotional treatmen
of these explosive subjects. The general effect has been t
"de-emotionalize" not only the scholarly investigations i
the social sciences but also the teaching in those fields.

To bring the student under the dominance of the scien
tific spirit is a most valid aim. The means by which this i
to be accomplished is another matter. One may questio
whether plunging the student at once into abstract con

siderations of generalized social conditions and problems is the best way to lead him to adopt a scientific approach to individual life and to society. May this not strengthen the tendency to deal with words as empty counters, to brush lightly over their surface meanings without any vivid perception of the actual material and emotional elements to which they point? This abstracting, generalizing, and devivifying tendency will not be counteracted by the type of materials usual in social science courses. In reading his psychology textbooks, for instance, the student may tend to dissociate theories or phenomena from the thought of actual human beings. In his history classes, mass movements and national changes may be thought of without ever translating them into terms of the individual human lives that made up these vast historical sums. The information drawn from sociology and economics courses may also be kept on the plane of the general and the impersonal.[8]

If the purpose of the social science courses in high school and in college were solely to give information, complete objectivity might be an end in itself. The teaching of such courses, however, seems to imply a more practical aim than information for its own sake. The assumption seems

[8] This tendency to deal with abstractions called "social forces" apart from any sense of the human beings who embody these forces may explain why so many adolescents seem to have derived only a pessimistic view of the individual and society from their social studies. They have developed the feeling that the individual is merely an impotent puppet at the mercy of inexorable "forces." This result might largely be averted through a more human presentation of social theory. This is an illustration of the extent to which the so-called form in which ideas are presented actually determines the meaning that they will have for the student.

to be that such understanding will enable students to handle better their own observations and experiences. Should it not be assumed that a comprehension of the forces at work in society may help them to play a more socially useful role? Therefore, without abandoning the emphasis on objective scientific knowledge, the educator still has to inquire whether such understanding is being conveyed in a form that will affect social attitudes and influence social behavior.

The aim, surely, is to enable the student to make intelligent judgments. In the choices open to him, he needs to be guided not by the blind reflex of unconsciously absorbed prejudices but by ideas based on scientifically valid facts. Can the unemotional, impersonal recital of facts and the objective scientific analysis of problems be counted on in themselves to give the youth the power of rational choice? Will the information thus acquired outweigh the force of irrational attitudes absorbed from the lagging social atmosphere? In its simplest terms, the question is: Will this objective knowledge affect his actions, inside and outside the school today, and will it influence his actions in later adult life as a member of a family and as a member of a national and world community?

Investigations of changes in attitude resulting, for example, from courses in the social sciences have usually proved nothing more than that the students changed their articulate opinions. They no longer echoed jingoistic sentiments but approved international cooperation; they advocated racial tolerance; they rejected the "devil take the hindmost" theory in favor of the idea of community responsibility. Whether these opinions had struck deep enough to affect emotional response and actual conduct under the pressure of practical circumstances is a highly debatable matter and a question seldom investigated.

Impersonally presented information, thoroughly understood, may influence behavior. For one thing, there are individuals who respond most readily to abstract ideas. Yet, even in this case, those abstract ideas are practically worthless unless the student is led to recognize their application to specific, concrete situations. The fact remains that the influence of this type of impersonal, theoretical instruction is not as obviously visible or as profound as one might hope. How often even high school and college graduates seem unable to resist the pull of disingenuous slogans, specious appeals to emotion, or the contagion of mob hysteria!

It must not be forgotten that the student—no matter whether he is a young child or a college boy soon to enter adult life—is already functioning in society. He has to make choices; he must set up goals for himself in his daily life; he must develop a sense of values. And these demands he will continue to meet throughout his life. The pressure of actual living does not permit prolonged meditation and analysis in precisely those person-to-person and general social situations where such reflection is most needed. Hence, in moments of indecision the emotionally rooted attitudes come to the surface to guide behavior.

The young man in school or at college may have become thoroughly acquainted in his courses in history or sociology with, for instance, the more modern ideas concerning woman's potential equality with man. He may even have become convinced of the desirability of the new ideal of marriage as a partnership and a mutual give-and-take, in which sometimes one and sometimes the other will be dependent or dominant. The success with which he carries out his program for a modern marriage, however, will largely depend on the degree to which these intellectual convictions have been translated into emotional attitudes and have displaced the old automatic sets. Probably, from his family background and many other sources in the society about him, he would earlier have absorbed the image of woman as weaker, more dependent, more emotional than man. He is still being indoctrinated with this image daily in the society about him. If these older, deeply ingrained images still persist, he will unconsciously demand those qualities from the women with whom he comes in contact. He may often find himself irritated at the absence of the conventional feminine qualities in his mate. Particularly in moments of tension, the older, culturally weighted attitudes will tend to assert themselves. He may find himself seeking the sense of dominance and superiority associated with the early acquired image of the husband.

When such moments of conflict and irritation arise, they can be handled successfully only if he and his wife are able to recognize his reaction as the irrational following of deeply grooved patterns which may no longer be justifiable. In order to overcome this, he must possess some strong emotional impulsion toward achieving the kind of marriage that his reason approves.

The gap between the individual's intellectual perceptions on the one hand and his emotional attitudes on the other must be bridged. If such a linkage of opinion with the emotional springs of action does not occur, there are two dangers. First, in moments of crisis the individual may be dominated, not by his rationally worked out opinions, but by the no longer appropriate attitudes absorbed from his childhood environment. Or, if the critical point of view has succeeded in breaking down the old attitude, he may be capable of only a negative approach to the situation. To revert to the illustration, the family: Have we not all encountered the "emancipated" man or woman, whose only attitude toward marriage was a sense of all the things it must *not* be?

The objective study of man in society should do more than illustrate the absence of a valid basis for many of the attitudes and images surviving from former social conditions. There should also be provided a valid emotional basis upon which to build more appropriate and more successful patterns of thought and behavior. Only then can we hope that the present knowledge concerning man and society will bear fruit in more rational social development and in happier, more complete human beings.

This phase of the problem, the transmutation of scientific knowledge and critical opinion into emotional attitudes guiding behavior, has usually been either neglected or evaded by the social science teacher as well as by the others. Obviously it offers difficulties and even some possibilities of abuse. Yet to go on blithely with objective "de-emotionalized" procedures is a betrayal of the practical value of social understanding. The young boy or girl still under the sway of anachronistic compulsions will be a ready victim of the emotional appeals made by less scrupulous, less disinterested social agencies, such as the biased press or partisan groups. The cause of youth's confusion and sense of futility today is often that they recognize the inadequacy of the old images and yet lack any clearly felt emotional drive toward new choices and new patterns of behavior. The quest for new images and social goals must be given sufficient emotional sanction to carry the younger generations through to a more successful solution of their problems.

EDUCATION IN THIS ERA of social transformation must serve both critical and constructive ends. On the one hand, youth need the knowledge and the intellectual tools required for objective appraisal of ideals and social mechanisms—new and old. On the other hand, youth need to develop positive emotional drives that will quicken intellectual insight. Thus they will be enabled to free themselves from antisocial attitudes and will be impelled to achieve a world that will safeguard human values.

Teachers of literature share these responsibilities with all others in the educational enterprise. The theory of literary experience presented earlier explains why the literature classroom can serve these broader aims while fulfilling its esthetic purposes. The following chapters will consider some of the ways in which this can be accomplished.

CHAPTER 7

Personality

LITERARY MATERIALS—the poem, the short story, the novel, the drama, and by extension, the motion picture and television—can contribute powerfully to both phases of the twofold educational process that we have outlined. Contemporary psychology encourages the belief that "the really important things in the education of youth cannot be taught in the formal didactic manner; they are things which are experienced, absorbed, accepted, incorporated into the personality through emotional and esthetic experiences."[1]

Of all the elements that enter into the educational process—except, of course, the actual personal relationships and activities which make up the community life of the school—literature possesses the greatest potential for that kind of assimilation of ideas and attitudes. For literature

[1] Lawrence K. Frank, "Some Aspects of Education for Home and Family Life," *Journal of Home Economics*, Vol. 23, No. 3 (March 1931), p. 214.

enables the youth to "live through"—and to reflect on—
much that in abstract terms would be meaningless to him.
He comes to know intimately, more intimately perhaps
than would be possible in actual life, many personalities.
He vicariously shares their struggles and perplexities and
achievements. He becomes a part of strange environments,
or he sees with new emotions the conditions and the lives
about him. And these vicarious experiences have at least
something of the warmth and color and immediacy of life.

Any insight or clarification the youth derives from the
literary work will grow out of its relevance to certain
facets of his emotional or intellectual nature. The whole
personality tends to become involved in the literary experience. That a literary work may bring into play and
be related to profoundly personal needs and preoccupations makes it a powerful potential educational force. For
it is out of these basic needs and attitudes that behavior
springs. Hence, literature can foster the linkage between
intellectual perception and emotional drive that is
essential to any vital learning process.

The criterion for judging the success of any educational
process must be its effect on the actual life of the student;
its ultimate value depends on its assimilation into the very
marrow of personality. What, then, are the results in terms
of personality and behavior to be expected from the kind
of literary experience and training that has been defined
as desirable?

This question will be answered first in the light of the
individual student's relation to books. The present chapter
will thus deal with the potential influence on personality
inherent in literary experiences themselves. Chapter 8 will

then apply this question to the type of literature study outlined in the first half of this book. Both of these chapters will reflect the view of personality development sketched in the preceding chapter and will indicate how an awareness of the suggested approach to human relations may grow out of the experience and study of literature.

We are now venturing on ground that is thorny with unexplored difficulties. Much emotion has been expended upon this problem of the influence of literature, but little careful or controlled study has been made of it. The following discussion is offered principally for the purpose of focusing attention on this extremely important problem. The aim is to arouse an increased awareness of some of the elements that enter into this question, rather than to suggest a set of neat formulas. As teachers themselves become aware of the dynamic and complex nature of the literary experience, and as students of literature give it added attention, a body of more accurate information on this phase of the problem will slowly be built up.

If we keep this view of the interaction between the individual mind and the literary work in the center of our attention, we shall not be misled into thinking that only books read in the most solemn and pedantic manner will have an influence. The power of literature to offer entertainment and recreation is, despite the pedants and moralists, still its prime reason for survival. Books read solely for entertainment satisfy, after all, definite needs and answer definite preoccupations. Such works have therefore a potential capacity to influence the reader's personality and behavior, perhaps even more than those he may read in the course of the school routine. The discussion that follows envisages any writings that elicit a vivid personal response from the young reader.

PROLONGED CONTACT WITH LITERATURE may result in increased social sensitivity. Through poems and stories and plays, the child becomes aware of the personalities of different kinds of people. He learns to imaginatively "put himself into the place of the other fellow." He becomes better able to foresee the possible repercussions of his own actions in the life of others. In his daily relations with other people, such sensitivity is precious. Through literature the individual may develop the habit of sensing the subtle interactions of temperament upon temperament; he may come to understand the needs and aspirations of others; and he may thus make more successful adjustments in his daily relations with them.

This increased ability to imagine the human implications of any situation is just as important for the individual in his broader political and social relationships. Many political blunders or social injustices seem to be the result not so much of maliciousness or conscious cruelty as of the inability of citizens to translate into human terms the laws or political platforms they support. Political slogans tend to take on an emotional coerciveness regardless of their human implications. Whole nations have been, and indeed are today, so dominated by such dogma in their political and social life that they follow its dictates no matter how disastrous the consequences to themselves or others. A democratic society, whose institutions and political and economic procedures are constantly being developed and remolded, needs citizens with the imagination to see what political doctrines mean for human beings.

It has been said that if our imaginations functioned actively, nowhere in the world would there be a child who was starving. Our vicarious suffering would force us to do something to alleviate it. The reading of the morning newspaper with its accounts, say, of war, famine, the suppression of human freedoms, the death of scores of people here and there in automobile accidents, may take place with hardly an emotional quiver on the reader's part. He registers only the abstract sense of the words and may never even glimpse what they mean in actual human experience. This habit of mind has its immediate value, of course, as a form of self-protection. Yet this callous shell is there to be dealt with in any attempt to inculcate new understanding and new attitudes. Because of the reluctance of the average mind to make this translation into human terms, the teacher must at times feel the responsibility for stimulating it.

Many young people today seem to have withdrawn into some such defensive attitude of callousness. Not to feel anything very deeply, not to care about anything too much, is one way of dulling the effect of quite possible defeat or disillusionment. In a highly competitive world, it also seems necessary not to think too much about the feelings and needs of others. The way the youth in many countries has lent itself to a philosophy of force and brutal sadism is proof of the great social dangers inherent in that kind of disillusioned cynicism and flight from altruistic feeling. The totalitarian ideologies capitalize on this when they callously preach that their ends justify any means, no matter how brutal.

Lack of such imaginative sympathy is probably back of many of our present-day difficulties. No matter whether the problem is just distribution of taxation or universal civil rights or federal-state relations, the basis of any ultimate decision should be its meaning for actual human lives. It is easy enough to understand the possible effect of a point of view upon ourselves and upon the human beings with whom we feel the kinship of family, class, nation, or race. We must also develop the capacity to feel intensely the needs and sufferings and aspirations of people whose personal interests are distinct from our own, people with whom we may have no bond other than our common humanity.

If there has been any "progress" during the past few centuries, it has fundamentally resulted from a certain extension of this kind of imagination. For is not "humanitarianism" ultimately the result of this sense of the prime importance of the human being, based on the ability to transcend selfish interests and to feel the needs of others? Despite the horrible persistence of war, the record shows an extension of increasingly humane social practices.

It would be absurd to suggest that literature was the cause of this (*Oliver Twist* and *Uncle Tom's Cabin* notwithstanding!), for the writing of such works was in itself the result of social conditions conducive to increased humanitarianism. Yet it can be maintained that literature undoubtedly contributes to the diffusion of more humane sentiment. And this applies not only to works like *Oliver*

Twist that preach such sensitivity but also to works written without propagandistic social or moral aims. The ability to enter vicariously into the experience of others can be fostered by a great many different kinds of literary experience.

Constant reading of a wide range of literature may in itself, without any contribution from the teacher, tend to develop social sensitivity. The teacher, however, can have an influence: he can help the student retain his living sense of the experiences through which he has just passed or, by pedantic "literature study," lead him to dismiss them as unimportant. By helping to focus the student's attention upon the actual emotions through which he has entered into the lives of others, the teacher can reinforce the power of literature to develop social imagination. Hence, in attempting to foster a vital personal relationship between the student and the literary work, the teacher will also be making an important social contribution.

LITERATURE CAN PLAY an important part in the process through which the individual becomes assimilated into the cultural pattern. Just as the young child and the adolescent acquire images of behavior and ways of thinking and feeling from the actions and lives of the people about them, so they may assimilate such images from the experience offered by books—from sharing the emotions and ideas of the poet, from participating in the lives of the people created by the novelist, the dramatist, or the biographer. The child and the adolescent often learn from books the culturally appropriate emotional response to types of situations or people (cf. p. 90). Similarly, they may absorb from their reading ideas concerning the kinds of behavior or types of achievement to be valued, and they may acquire the moral standards to be followed under various circumstances.

Undoubtedly, the human influences encountered in the family, the school, and the community tend to be the most powerful and lasting. In recent years, however, it has been increasingly recognized that television, the radio, the motion picture, the newspaper, and the literary work often take their place beside other social agencies in the important task of molding the individual. Probably not enough attention has been given to the fact that literature is one of the important media through which our cultural pattern is transmitted.

Any individual born into a society must somehow learn not only its language, its gestures, its mechanics, but also the various superstructures of ideas, emotions, modes of behavior, and moral values that this society has built on the basic human relationships. It has been maintained, for instance, that if it were not for literature most people would never even have suspected the possibility of romantic love. The whole superstructure of affection, admiration, idealization of the loved one, desire to sacrifice oneself for his or her welfare, and all the other attributes of the romantic relationship, does not inevitably and automatically grow out of the basic fact of sexual attraction. These are ways of feeling and behaving that in some parts of our culture have become associated with this basic physical factor. After all, even within Western culture there are groups who dispense with much of this idealizing aura cast about the sex relationship. They see it associated with the need for a mate who can bear healthy children, or cooperate in the business of life on a farm, or bring the necessary wealth or social prestige. In any case, the feelings and attitudes associated with the basic fact of sexual attraction will have been learned.

Even in the case of romantic love, it would be ridiculous to suppose literature the sole agency through which it was propagated. It would never have found expression in literature if there had not been present in the society the social and economic conditions out of which such a complex of attitudes could have flowered. And there are many other agencies through which this view of love can be inculcated. Yet undoubtedly literature, oral and written, has played an important part in its perpetuation.

This theory does, at any rate, emphasize one of the social effects of literature—its inculcation of images of behavior and accompanying emotional attitudes. This applies potentially to all the phases of man's life and aspirations that have found expression in literature. With the increase of literacy and the wider dissemination of books, it can be expected that literature may play an increasingly important role in helping the individual to assimilate the superstructure of attitudes that he must erect on the basis of his fundamental human impulses.

In contrast to abstractly phrased statements concerning mankind or abstract formulations of moral codes that may be encountered in books, the peculiar power of the literary work of art resides in its influence on an emotional level, analogous to the kind of influence exerted by people and situations in life. Much more important than the explicit general ideas are the kinds of personalities and the emo-

tional overtones ascribed to particular situations or conduct.

The very things most taken for granted in a work may
have the most powerful influence on the adolescent reader. He is avidly curious about what it means in intimate
personal terms to fulfill various adult roles. In literature
the adolescent finds, for instance, certain traits of temperament, certain kinds of emotions, certain ways of
achieving prestige, associated with women characters
that are very different from the traits or satisfactions
associated with the concept of the male character. Again,
certain kinds of physical expressions of emotions such as
fear, anger, or love are encountered, or certain emotional
reactions are presented as appropriate to specific situations. Because of the personal quality of literary experience, it can be an important force in the transmission of
the culturally shaped images and options of behavior.

The power of literature to transmit those elements of
our culture that are most taken for granted may be more
easily seen operating in a past age. The image of the
delicate Pamela with her tiny waist and her hands too
tender to scour a pewter dish had many even more exaggerated counterparts in eighteenth-century literature.
Innumerable maidens of fragile physique, too ladylike to
engage in even the slightest practical activity, sighed and
wept and fainted their way through the pages of intermin-
able eighteenth-century novels. Letters and biographies of
women of the time, particularly of those women who
came to revolt against this image, demonstrate how inextricably these attributes came to be associated with the
idea of being a lady.

Veblen, in his *Theory of the Leisure Class*, treats some of the social and economic factors that probably produced this ideal of the lady; the novelist did not create her out of whole cloth, for obviously he was reflecting standards in process of crystallization. The novelists, however, clearly did much to perpetuate and disseminate this image. It has tended to persist in slightly modified form long after the conditions that produced it had changed. It began as a picture of the aristocratic or upper middle-class woman, but with changing social conditions and with the extention of literacy, women of the lower classes sought also to approximate this picture in their appearance and behavior. That this was not necessarily the aim of the novelists who created such heroines does not minimize the incidental influence of this image.

Thus, notions of complex patterns of behavior, such as courtship, or moral and social attitudes can be assimilated from books. Goethe's *Werther* and Byron's poems influenced whole generations. Scott's novels undoubtedly played a part in the hold of feudalistic ideas on the South. This kind of influence may reinforce acceptance of rigid class differences or suggest the possibility of overcoming them. Books may propagate stereotypes; consider the influence, for instance, of the fact that for so many generations the child usually encountered the Negro presented as an object for laughter or at best a prized servant, as in so many of the novels of the South purporting to show the kindness of masters. The repeated impact of such images in poems, novels, plays, and biographies surely added to the complex pressures acting on the individual and leading him to crystallize his sense of the world about him and of the appropriate attitudes to assume toward it.

THUS FAR, parallels have been drawn between the nature of the influence exerted by literature and the nature of the influence of the family or community environment. Literature, however, possesses special characteristics of its own. In so-called primitive societies, only those elements of the culture present in the minds of specific human beings at that time can possibly be transmitted to the child born into the culture. The only chance for him to suspect the existence of any other way of life is through particular individuals in the society who may have had contact with other cultural groups. The basic factor that distinguishes our own society from primitive societies is that we possess a written literature. Books are a means of getting outside the limited cultural group into which the individual is born. They are, in a sense, elements of societies distant in time and space made personally available to the reader.

Books are one important means of transmitting a much more complex cultural pattern than could be derived from any particular family or community environment. Without the additional contribution offered by the written or printed word, it would be impossible for the personal or community agencies of cultural transmission to give to youth an adequate sense of the complex fabric of our society. (Any kind of systematic education through the electronic image still remains a hypothetical thing of the future, and even this would undoubtedly incorporate the printed word.) Hence, the illiterate or unread person usually participates only in a very narrow and limited sub-culture in our society.

Literature offers a release from the provincialism of time and space. In this way it may exert a powerful influence upon the youth's future behavior. In a heterogeneous, democratic society more and more explicitly seeking to create new social and economic patterns, literature can perform an increasingly important function. Any new synthesis, any integrated American culture, must be more than a mere aggregate of its many, often conflicting, social and economic groups. More than ever before it is essential that the individual be liberated from the provincialism of his own particular family, community, or even national background. Democracy requires a body of citizens capable of making their own personal and social choices. The corollary of this is that they should be emotionally and intellectually aware of the possible alternatives from which to choose.

A third generalization concerning the potential influence of literature is, then, that literature offers an important source of awareness of possible alternatives. This constitutes the social value of that "enlargement of experience" which the college girls quoted in Chapter 2 attributed to literature.

Books can be a liberating influence in many ways. They may reveal to the boy and girl that there can be modes of life different from the ones into which they have happened to be born. They can learn about the extraordinary diversity of subcultures to be found within the framework of our society, with its sectional, economic, and social differences. Their reading can early make them aware that there are families organized very differently from their own. They will discover in our complex society culturally accepted patterns of behavior and socially approved formulations of personal and social goals completely alien to their own background.

Particularly important is this discovery that various groups within our society hold up diverse images of success, and that there are kinds of work despised or ignored by his own group that others consider socially valuable. This diversity of patterns is undoubtedly one of the most valuable aspects of American society. The craftsmen, the technologists, the artists, the scientists, the scholars, offer personal goals and systems of value often strongly in contrast to those represented by the dominant image of the successful businessman. Literature may often provide the first emotionally vivid realization of these facts. Young readers glimpse types of temperament, kinds of work, intellectual and moral atmospheres, very different from anything they have known. They come to realize that there are wide possibilities for choice open to them within the framework of American society.

Vicarious participation in different ways of life may have an even more broadly liberating influence. The image of past civilizations or of past periods within our Western civilization, as well as images of life in other countries today, can help the youth to realize that ours is only one of a great variety of possible social structures. The individual is thus able to look at the society about him more rationally. He can evaluate it, judge what elements should be perpetuated and what elements should be modified or rejected.

Literature not only makes possible the experience of diverse patterns of the past and present; it also offers the opportunity to envisage new and more desirable patterns. Wilde's dictum that "nature imitates art" is after all only a paradoxical expression of the fact that the artist often makes his fellowman aware of new aspects of life and new angles from which to view it. Perhaps Wilde was quite accurate in calling a sunset a poor Turner painting. Without Turner his contemporaries might never have learned to look for and perceive certain effects of light and color in that sunset. Surely the same thing applies to what the artist and particularly the writer can reveal about new emotional overtones in relations between human beings, new aspirations toward greater fulfillment of human personality, or new points of view, moral and esthetic, from which to judge experience.

Thus the writer often becomes the medium through which the future is forecast. Often especially sensitive to the new tendencies at work in the society about him, he disseminates images of new goals. These may kindle in his readers emotional drives toward setting up new patterns of conduct and new social structures. As the history of literature reminds us, writers have set forth scathing revelations of the life about them or have created attractive images of alternative ways of life. Of course, their writings have had influence because many other factors in the society at that time were conducive to it. Conversely, writers have many times created images of life that their own age and succeeding ones were not yet ready to understand or to assimilate.

THIS LATTER CONSIDERATION should allay the typical fear that literary works may incite the youth to rush into all sorts of untried modes of behavior. This view is based on the unrealistic idea of the social effects of literature that is usually associated with Victorian moralism. The Victorian critic often seemed to believe that the mere reading about particular actions in a book would in itself lead to the performance of the same actions in life.

Fortunately or unfortunately, the human being is not plastic enough to be easily moved to any new action simply by reading representations of it. The Victorians mistakenly thought of the reader as a blank photographic plate upon which was projected the series of images offered by a literary work. Some of the factors that make the individual reader anything but such a blank photographic plate have been noted in earlier chapters. Various influences in his environment have already left their imprint on him. For the youth especially, literature can be only one of the many elements that help to channel the intensely dramatic process which is so casually called "growing up." Books contribute an additional influence that must take its place beside the others.

In the interplay of forces acting upon the individual, the literary work, unaided, will probably have little weight if its emphasis is opposed to images that many of the agencies in the society about him are reiterating. If the work does not fit in with dominant conceptions, the reader may indignantly reject what the book offers. In fact, the great body of literature probably exerts its most powerful influence in reinforcing and perpetuating the cultural pattern. Therefore the images or ideas presented by literature function in the context of other environmental influences.

The reading of a book, it is true, has sometimes changed a person's entire life. When that occurs, the book has undoubtedly come as a culminating experience that crystallizes a long, subconscious development. In such cases the book usually opens up a new view of life or a new sense of the potentialities of human nature and thus resolves some profound need or struggle. The probability of any particular work having so profound and transfiguring an effect cannot, however, be predicted or planned for. It would result from the convergence of a great many intangible factors. The possibility that literature may offer such inspiration should, nevertheless, make us eager to stimulate our students to roam freely through a great many types of literary experience.

Literature characteristically operates in less direct and sudden ways. The "influence of literature" will usually be the result of the cumulative effect of a long series of literary experiences, interacting with, or parallel to, the many other forces acting upon the young person.

Only in rare cases would the literary image of a new and aberrant interpretation of a personal role outweigh the influence of frequently encountered conventional images of that role. When the power of the old patterns sanctioned by society is surmounted, it is probably because conditions have so changed that there is a pressing need for a new adjustment. Moreover, even then the new image probably must be reinforced by constant repetition over a long period of time. The emancipated woman, for instance, appears in literature at least from the time of Shelley and Mary Wollstonecraft, very infrequently at first and only with any significant frequency after about 1880. Yet it was not until early in the twentieth century that that image caught the imaginations and was translated into the practical lives of an appreciable number of women.

This may seem a decidedly pessimistic estimate of the possible contribution of literature to constructive social change. That is not the case. Yet it is evident that no oversimplified theories about its influence can be accepted. Since any one literary work is only a strand in a complex fabric of influences, the social situation out of which the reader turns to a particular book will, in large part, determine its possible impact on him.

The rather negative implications of the preceding paragraph are counterbalanced by the overarching fact about our age: we are living in a time of extraordinary social flux. Because there is such a lack of unanimity in our society, because even the agencies committed to transmitting the conventional images are often self-contradictory or at cross purposes, the individual is freer than in other periods to accept or to reject the images offered by literature. Hence the insight of the adolescents who claimed that "enlargement of experience" is an important function of literature. Because conditions are ripe for it, people today are eager for the new vision and new sensitivities that books may stimulate.

Someone has said, "The fool learns only through experience. The wise man anticipates experience." This suggests two essential traits of literature: its power to give vicarious experience and its delineation of a great diversity of personalities and conduct. Is not the capacity for imagination—the ability to picture oneself in a variety of situations and to envisage alternative modes of behavior and their consequences—the thing that gives the "wise man" his advantage? C. S. Peirce, in stressing the value of "ideal experimentation," was referring to the same thing. In imagination we rehearse various possibilities of action in a given situation. We go through a process of imaginative trial and error, trying out different modes of behavior and working out their probable effects. When the situation arises in actual life, we are better prepared to act successfully.

Literature permits something resembling "ideal experimentation" because it offers such a wide range of vicarious experiences. We can live different kinds of lives; we can anticipate future periods in our own life; we can participate in different social settings; we can try out solutions to personal problems. We are able to apprehend the practical and emotional results, the reactions of others, the social praise or blame, that may flow from such conduct; we find some of these temperamentally more satisfactory than others. Literature may thus offer us a means of carrying on some of the trial-and-error experimentation that might be disastrous in real life. *Hence the emphasis in*

*earlier chapters on the necessity for equipping the student
to evaluate the diverse images of life that he encounters
in books.*[2]

THE VICARIOUS EXPERIENCES OFFERED BY LITERATURE can
have a particularly significant effect when they are related
to problems and conflicts intimately involving the reader.
The students mentioned in Chapter 2 remarked that often
in books one comes across people like oneself or people
with problems similar to one's own: Other adolescents
carry on the struggle to achieve a new working relationship with their families; other husbands and wives live
through irritations and misunderstandings; other men and
women seek recognition and the opportunity to exercise
their talents in an indifferent world. The very fact that
the reader's situation is not unique, that it at least parallels what others evidently understand and have lived
through, gives him some perspective. Through seeing his
problems apart from himself, he is helped to think and
feel more clearly about them. This constitutes another
phase of the potential influence of literature.

Lawrence K. Frank has suggested [3] that ideally a series
of literary experiences could perform something approaching a psychoanalysis if the reader were encouraged to
react fully and freely. In large part, the psychiatrist serves
his patient by helping him to bring into consciousness
various experiences, attitudes, or impulses that have been
repressed or "censored." The patient is then encouraged to

---

[2] See also page 262 for comment on the fact that literature does not
simply mirror life.
[3] In a letter to the writer.

look upon them as rationally explicable and hence manageable. Thus he is led to free himself from his fears and obsessions. In order that he may readjust his environment as well as himself, he is also helped to see at what points his environment imposes unnecessary frustrations. The experience of literature may effect a similar liberation. Vicariously experiencing the life of a character in fiction or participating in another's emotion expressed in a poem may enable the reader to bring into consciousness similar elements in his own nature and emotional life. This may provide the basis for a release from unconscious fears and guilt.

The adolescent particularly may be helped to interpret his own acutely self-conscious emotions and motivations. As a child he has built up a sense of himself in relation to other people. Now he finds that "self" undergoing various modifications and expansions. Often he feels that he must be abnormal because of unsuspected tendencies within him. Often, too, he develops a sense of guilt, a feeling that he is highly sinful because his fantasies lead him into forbidden fields or because he resents restrictions on his behavior. If he has been brought up to have religious belief, the growth of agnosticism may lead to intense inner turmoil and disillusionment. The young boy or girl frequently hesitates to confide these conflicts or fears to adults because they might view them as rejections of their standards. Sometimes such anxieties create nervous tension and neurotic distortions of the personality. Literary experiences may at least militate against the growth of neurotic tendencies.

Books may help the adolescent perceive the validity of

his own temperamental bent, even when that may not be valued by his own environment. Thus, the young boy and girl may find encouragement to set up for themselves goals undreamed of in their own families. For example, a contemplative youth in a family of extroverted business-men or a mechanically minded boy in a family with intel-lectual traditions might be particularly in need of reas-surance that he is not eccentric or a failure. This sense of aloneness or estrangement creates much adolescent in-security. Through books each of these boys might learn that other milieus valued his kind of temperament and ability. For the first boy, works such as Willa Cather's or Thomas Mann's stories or Joyce's *Portrait*, for the second boy, works such as Michael Pupin's autobiography or the books about George Washington Carver, might offer the sense of sharing common values and goals. In the litera-ture of both the past and the present they might have found strong contrasts to the norms of their environments.

The range of human temperaments that have been ad-mired and held up as a standard are perhaps best revealed through literature. The autobiography of a Franklin with its disciplined, prudent narrator may be contrasted with the reckless, swashbuckling heroes of romance or with the sensitive, introspective characters in a Henry James novel. The passionate, impulsive folk of Elizabethan drama may be compared with the intellectualized, cynical creatures of Restoration plays, their most vigorous act some sharp thrust of phrase, or with the characters in contemporary dramas such as Shaw's, O'Neill's, or Arthur Miller's, where dramatic conflicts often take place within the mind and are revealed through a technical device. Portrayals of the successful man of power may be placed beside characters whose success lay in self-abnegation or in spiritual and intellectual achievement. The poets, too, offer a wide gamut of temperaments that we can come to know intimately.

The young girl may need to be liberated from the narrow view of the feminine role imposed by her milieu. It hardly seems necessary to point out that through literature an extraordinarily broad range of feminine temperaments and a great variety of views of woman's place in society may be encountered: Pamela's determination not to offend the social code, the common sense conformity of Elizabeth Bennet, the passionate struggles of Meredith's Diana, the striving for independence of Hardy's Sue, or the merging of feminist aspirations with the broader struggle for human rights that characterizes lesser-known heroines of recent fiction. The adolescent worry over the need to conform to the culturally dominant pictures of the temperamental traits, types of work, and modes of behavior appropriate to each of the sexes can be lessened through a wide circle of literary acquaintances.

For the younger adolescent, we have seen, the concern with normality extends even to the problem of conformity to a particular physical type. Here, again, literature may show what a great diversity of physical traits have been admired, and that physical characteristics, even those considered handicaps, need not prevent successful and happy lives. If one approaches fiction from this rather special angle, one is amazed to find how many novels and stories do reflect this concern with conformity to physical standards. Cyrano de Bergerac and Falstaff by no means stand alone. In our own day, Thomas Wolfe recounts the experiences of an extremely tall man, or Vardis Fisher, in *April*, tells the story of a girl who thinks herself hopelessly unattractive.

Frequently literature is the means by which the youth discovers that his own inner life reflects a common experience of others in his society. He finds that the impulses and reactions he feared are "normal," that they are shared by many others in our society, and that there may merely be a convention (or a conspiracy) of silence about them. In this way, a particular poem or an autobiographical novel may provide liberation from blind fears or guilt. Having learned that others have lived through and dominated these supposedly strange impulses, the adolescent can achieve sufficient objectivity to proceed to work out an integrated sense of his own emotional nature. This kind of influence is especially difficult to document. All that psychologists and psychiatrists have been telling us recently about adolescent conflicts, however, tends to suggest that it may be very important.

A point introduced earlier in another connection is especially relevant. Often the reader, without necessarily being aware of it, projects his own present emotional preoccupations on fictional situations and personalities that seem on the surface very remote. The reader responds not so much to the situation presented in the work as to the structure of emotional relationships it implies. Thus, *Mutiny on the Bounty* or *Catcher in the Rye* might strike a responsive chord because a boy was passing through the process of psychological weaning from the authority of his parents. Or the relationship between Othello and Iago may have significance because of the boy's own preoccupation with the need for loyal friends. Similarly, the biography of a great statesman may symbolize the reader's own struggle to make others sympathize with his aims and enthusiasms.

This basic emotional parallelism is most obvious when an author selects a legend like the Prometheus myth or a story set in the past, such as the tale of Tristan and Iseult, and infuses into it values and emotional overtones significant in terms of contemporary life. (Perhaps emphasis on the underlying emotional structure would counteract recent tendencies to be satisfied with the classification of works according to their archetypal or mythic categories. The labeling should be incidental.) Each age finds new significance in the structure of emotional relationships in works like *Hamlet* or *Faust*. It is not usually recognized that in responding to a work of literature, even one that deals with contemporary people and situations, the reader may also be transposing its emotional patterns into his own special situation.

Talking about these matters in terms of the situation in the book merely makes it easier for the reader to bring his own inner problems into the open, and to face them or seek the help of others without the embarrassment of explicit self-revelation. Thus he often reveals what he cannot or will not say about himself. The teacher cannot afford to ignore this tendency to respond to the implicit emotional pattern of poems or novels or plays. Even books that seem to have little to do with the externals of a student's life may provide vicarious experience and occasion discussion that will lead to increased self-understanding for the student.

This is a perfectly valid way of responding to literature —in some ways the most valid, since it means that the work has profound importance to the reader. However, the aims of the literature classroom dictate a prime qualification: If in projecting his own situation into the work he has actually created something alien to its intention, the reader should be helped to discover this. The major task of the teacher (cf. Part One) will consist in such clarifications through group discussion of alternative responses and interpretation. Actually, in thus learning to read the text more closely, the reader often becomes aware, not only of unnoticed verbal clues, but also of his own biases or blind spots.

In recent years there has been much discussion of literature as a means of "sublimation" of socially disapproved impulses. The desire for violence and cruelty; the wish to dominate others; the need for sexual expression when, as in the case of the adolescent, society prevents it; the impulse to strike back at those who place restrictions on us—these are tendencies for which literature is said to provide an outlet. Certain aspects of this theory are related to the function of literature set forth in Aristotle's much-debated remarks about the catharsis, or purgation, of the emotions of fear and pity that results from the experience of tragedy.

Literature may perform an even more constructive service for the individual. It can suggest to him socially approved channels for expression of his impulses. A young boy whose fantasies had taken a consistently antisocial form might be directed through fiction and biographies toward goals that society would consider highly valuable. Domination of others might be sought not through physical violence, but rather through the possession of superior knowledge and even the ability to help others, as through the knowledge of medicine.

IN SOME RARE CASES the teacher might consciously attempt to use literature in this way. One extremely perceptive teacher who has had training in psychology reports that she has done this. She has been able to create an unself-conscious relationship with the students and has led them to express themselves very freely in their writing for her classes. Thus she is often able to glimpse some of their conflicts and obsessions. In one instance it became apparent that the boy's sympathy for his mother and antagonism toward his father were the source of strong feelings of guilt and were creating much friction. The teacher casually suggested that the boy read such books as Bennett's *Clayhanger* and (admitting its meretricious elements) Deeping's *Sorrell and Son.* These helped to bring directly into consciousness the problem of his own relations with his father. He was sufficiently freed from his sense of guilt to be able to discuss the matter and to work out a more adequate handling of it.

Unless the teacher is in an almost psychiatric relationship with the student, however, any attempt to use literature in this way would probably create more conflicts and tensions than it solved. Many teachers would probably be led into officious meddling with the emotional life of their students. (Unfortunately, like members of any other group, many teachers are themselves laboring under emotional tensions and frustrations. Given the right to meddle in this way, they would be tempted to find solutions for their own problems by vicariously sharing the student's life. They might also project upon the student their own particular preoccupations and lead him to think that he was suffering difficulties and frustrations that in reality were the teacher's.) Assuredly, even worse than the old indifference to what is happening psychologically to the student is the tampering with personality carried on by well-intentioned but ill-informed adults. The wise teacher does not attempt to be a psychiatrist. The essential thing, he knows, is to be a complete human being in his relations with his students—bringing to bear in his work with them all of the sensitivities that he would bring to bear in his relations with people outside the classroom.

On the whole, then, the teacher should avoid any too literal application of what might loosely be called the psychiatric possibilities of literature. It is highly important, however, to recognize that books may often perform such functions for young people. The teacher's responsibility is to provide a wide selection and to help the student develop sufficient independence to seek out those works for himself. Thus there may be at least the chance of his coming upon those that will be psychologically helpful. Moreover, if the teacher is aware of the conflicts and anxieties that recur most frequently among adolescents in our society, he will be able to make available works that have some relevance to these tensions. If a segment of our youth today take an almost completely negative stance toward the adult world, this may be because they have encountered in literature classrooms, as elsewhere, materials consistently irrelevant to their own concerns and needs. Above all, the adolescent should have a wide range of alternative experiences in works that speak to him as he now is. In an earlier day, the need was mainly for a certain iconoclasm; today, the need is not only for challenge but also for the frank treatment of themes that may lead beyond rejection toward affirmation of new and more satisfactory attitudes.

These considerations were an additional reason for the discussion of adolescent needs and conflicts in Chapter 5. Since any vital literary experience is possible only when the work strikes some responsive chord, the teacher should present to the student literary works that have this personal import. Such literary experiences will make it possible for him to grow in critical ability. At the same time, they may have valuable psychological repercussions. Probably in most cases the wisest thing for the teacher is to keep his attention focused on the relationship between the text and the student. If he does this part of his job well, in the spirit outlined in the earlier chapters of this book, he can probably feel assured that he has created the basis for a great deal more than purely "literary" insight.

THE CONSIDERATION OF psychological values that may be derived from literary works suggests a related problem that causes many teachers difficulty. They are aware that, both during school days and afterward, the great mass of the American people feed on shoddy reading matter.

The stilted academic approach to good literature in the schools may contribute to the student's feeling that he can get little personal enjoyment from it, so that he turns to a type of writing about which there hangs no academic aura. The more generally assumed reason for American reading habits is, however, that they reflect the desire for "escape." Undoubtedly, the causes for this wish to escape from reality are deeply rooted in our society.

It is sometimes argued that the teacher's condemnation of cheap escape fiction is merely an expression of professional snobbery. If this "trash" gives pleasure and momentary release from pressures or permits the compensation, at least in fantasy, for personal lacks and frustrations, why should the reader be denied this? An earlier comment is relevant here: The criterion for discriminating between helpful and harmful kinds of escape is that escape through literature should not leave the reader less able than before to cope with reality.

Someone dealing with extremely maladjusted individuals would probably use various means, including this type of literature, for even a temporary effect. In such cases, however, the literature performs only the function of a drug that momentarily releases tension. The work of returning the patient to mental health, of giving him greater capacity for meeting situations in life, still remains to be done. Repeated indulgence in the drug of escape fiction can lead only to an increased craving for such escape.

To be sure, it is not always trashy fiction that provides escape. The reader who immerses himself in medieval romance, or reads and rereads the works of Scott as a steady literary diet, or turns constantly to such works as Trollope's stories of quiet cathedral towns, may be indulging in the same flight from reality as the girl who avidly reads the stories about "the international set" on the Riviera. In either case, there has undoubtedly been a period of pleasant escape from the difficulties and disappointments of the present-day world. Surely, only the most ascetic of Puritans would wish to cut us off completely from this relaxation and enjoyment.

In most cases, however, the escape function is served by writings that present a false image of life. The obstacles placed in the way of the characters are oversimplified. The ease with which problems are solved, or the absence of any real problems, probably constitutes one appeal of this type of writing. Even more subtly enervating are the emotions undiluted with thought and lacking in individual quality. Purportedly successful personal relationships in marriage or business are usually presented in naively simple terms. And the crudest elements in our society, the ruthless competition, the emphasis on wealth, the respect for the winner no matter what his methods, often provide the framework of the story. The reader will return to life from this kind of fare probably less capable than before of understanding and coping with the complex situations, the mixture of frustrations and satisfactions, that life offers. Such fiction fosters the notion that the level of vitality required for a full life is lower than is actually the case.

A striking phenomenon in recent years has been the widespread sale of writings purveying crude images of violence, sadism, and sexuality. Such materials jostle the classics on the paperback shelves and fill magazine racks in stores throughout the country. The other mass media also manifest this trend, which has been interpreted as a reflection of the tensions and violence characteristic of twentieth-century life. Psychiatrists have disagreed about the effect of such materials on young readers. Some have suggested that these provide an outlet for aggression, while others have found that they contribute to delinquent behavior. Under different circumstances and with different individuals, both of these effects seem possible. Much more systematic study of the problem is needed, with both literary critics and psychologists contributing.

Some have justified such writings by pointing to the presence of violence and eroticism in serious contemporary works, such as those of existentialist and "absurd" writers. The necessary rejoinder is that the presence or absence of such elements is not in itself a basis for judgment. Such writings may serve a function as expression for the author; whether they serve the needs of a particular reader remains a legitimate question. The educator, who knows that freedom is essential to the health of any literature, will oppose censorship. His responsibility is all the more clear—to develop discriminating readers able to evaluate the human import of the literary fare offered to them.

The fundamental social causes for this national craving for the drug of "escape" literature are beyond the scope of the classroom. At least the literature class can counteract the tendency to follow the path of least resistance. One way is to discuss examples of poor fiction. It is wise, after all, to start with the student at whatever level of understanding and appreciation we may find him. There is no point in just condemning the reading he most enjoys. He will only develop a feeling of shame about it without being able to resist indulging in it. Reading forbidden books "in the attic" or "behind the barn," or whatever the modern equivalent may be, seems one of the persistent traits of our culture. Condemnation or prohibition alone can have only pernicious effects.

For adolescent students, a calm analysis of the appeal of this kind of reading might lessen its attraction. A critical attitude toward its silly, dishonest, and sensational pictures of life can have a wholesome influence. The contrast between cheap and honest treatments of similar themes can help to accomplish this. This will help them to judge by other criteria of happiness the picture, for example, of wealth as equivalent to success. In contrast to "love" as limited to the physical, they will be made aware of the many values that can be integrated into the love relationship.

Without assuming a "holier than thou" attitude, the teacher should keep in mind the adolescent psychology that leads students to this low-grade fiction, and should try to provide more wholesome and invigorating satisfactions for these needs. Educators and parents have come to recognize the importance of this in the field of sex education. They realize that the attempt to prohibit any knowledge about sex causes the adolescent to seek it from undesirable sources, often sensational fiction. They admit, therefore, that it is better to provide this information in more wholesome ways and to permit the adolescent to read literature that deals frankly and honestly with sex as a fundamental and enriching element in man's life. This principle should not be restricted to the field of sex knowledge, however. There is certainly something wrong with a literature curriculum if the students turn from it to magazines and books purveying violence and the crudest sexuality under a veneer of cynicism. Adventure and vigorous action, on the one hand, and honest treatment of the sex relationship, on the other, are to be found in abundance in good literature. Probably in many cases the school is still too much dominated by nineteenth-century ideas about the literature that the cultivated person should read, when it would be very easy to find equally good literature that has the swift pace and vigorous action the student craves. Of course, even when such books are read in a classroom, there still remains the danger that they may be drained of all their tang and zest by routine study. When the teacher and the school seriously carry out such professional responsibilities, they have earned the right to exercise them without external censorship.

Victorian notions about the influence of literature led to a rigid censorship of books by publishers and critics as well as by parents and teachers. Particular books were valued because they offered approved models of conduct which young people were expected to imitate. The view of literature presented here has led to a rather different emphasis: in a democracy, the more varied the literary fare provided for students, the greater its potential as an educationally liberating force. In this way, through literature, the necessarily limited influence of their environment will be supplemented and corrected by contact with expressions of other phases of society and other types of personality.

This means that the student will not be limited to one kind of literary diet. He will not read exclusively the works of the past or the present. He will not be nourished entirely on the literature of England and America. Instead, he will be permitted an insight into ways of life and social and moral codes very different even from the one that the school is committed to perpetuate.

These generalizations about the choice of books apply to several specific problems that can be mentioned only briefly. Very often in school, children are required to read works that demand a constant effort at comprehension because the vocabulary and sentence structure represent "the next stage" toward which they are being led. Or they may be required to read works written in an archaic language, very different from the language that they hear about them or that is used by accepted contemporary writers. Few adults—even college professors!—impose upon themselves the task of constantly reading works with a vocabulary that is strange to them or with a complicated style that demands unusual efforts of attention. Only rarely do they undertake such tasks. Most of the time their reading is at the level of their present vocabulary and powers of attention. In our zeal to give our students the proper literary training, we constantly set them tasks a step beyond their powers, or plunge them into reading that practically requires the learning of a new language. Belated efforts to help the disadvantaged child have revealed that standard English is indeed often a strange dialect, to be learned almost as a second language. No wonder that many students, middle-class and disadvantaged, do not learn to read, or read only the simplest of crude escape literature!

The question of command of language leads to another controverted subject: the literature of the past versus contemporary literature. When one objects to intensive study of words and syntax as withering any possible love of the "classics," the answer is usually that the students will not otherwise understand what they are reading. If a work presents such linguistic difficulties, one may question whether a direct attack on the linguistic problems offers a solution. By the time the student has acquired enough understanding of the unusual language, the work as a whole has probably lost its power to affect him. If the work presents experiences and ideas highly relevant to the student's own preoccupations, his interest will often carry him over the hurdle of the language difficulty and give him sufficient motivation to study the language. Many of the great classics have elements of vivid action, strong emotion, and suspense that may provide an incentive for the more mature or the more intelligent student to clear away the obscurities due to unfamiliar language or literary forms. Too often, however, the classics are introduced to children at an age when it is impossible for them to feel in any personal way the problems or conflicts treated.

Difficulties in understanding, as indicated in Chapter 5, are usually not merely a matter of words and syntax, for words must be apprehended in some context of experience. The teacher who feels that if he can only get the students to understand the individual words he will have eliminated all obstacles, is often mistaking the symptom, the language difficulty, for the real seat of the trouble, which is the student's lack of readiness for what the work offers.[4] For the great majority it would probably be much wiser to postpone such reading and to gradually build linguistic flexibility through the use of more familiar materials. When the students are more mature, more experienced, they will then be able to apprehend enough of what the great classics offer to be willing and eager to clarify any linguistic obscurities.

When one thinks of all that great literary works can yield, one is horrified to see them so often reduced to the level of language exercise books for the young. The antipathy of many students to Latin and Greek arose from this use of masterpieces beyond their powers of appreciation as texts for acquiring the language. Those who cram the classics down students' throats long before they are ready are careless of the fate of the great works of the past.

[4] Obviously, this does not imply a neglect of any of the means by which the student can acquire a clearer understanding of words themselves. The dictionary can become a very interesting book for the student, if what he gets from it is not left on the purely verbal level. He should develop the habit of using it, just as the motorist uses a road map, as a tool to get him to the right place.

See pages 111–119 for other references to this problem of understanding. There has been increasing interest in this basic problem of meaning, owing to the influence, e.g., of the writings of C. S. Peirce, Bertrand Russell, P. W. Bridgeman, I. A. Richards, and Gilbert Ryle. Two highly influential works have been *The Meaning of Meaning* by C. K. Ogden and I. A. Richards and *Philosophical Investigations* by Ludwig Wittgenstein.

Even though the majority were to graduate from school and high school without having encountered many of the great authors, we should not need to be alarmed if they had the ability to read with understanding and had acquired zest for the experience that literature can give. Those who try to crowd into the school years everything that "ought to be read" evidently assume that the youth will never read again after school years are over. People who read for themselves will come to the classics at the point when particular works will have particular significance for them. To force such works upon the young prematurely defeats the long-term goal of educating people to a personal love of literature sufficiently deep to cause them to seek it out for themselves at the appropriate time.

The difficulty presented by works of the past is that not only the language but also the externals of life and the manners and morals represented may seem so peculiar that the student's attention is focused almost completely on these aspects rather than upon the major experiences the authors sought to convey. Even those works that deal with personal emotional problems still vital today are often clothed in an atmosphere and deal with ways of life that make the whole thing seem artificial and remote. Many teachers are aware that before the student can enjoy a work, he must feel that it has some relevance to his own experience. They therefore often devote much time and energy to indicating the equivalents in our own society of the different aspects of life represented in the work. Like all background information, however, this should not obscure their purpose, to reveal the basic emotional patterns of the work itself.

There are many works of the past in which the strange mores do not block comprehension of the basic emotional relations; the older work may offer just as intense a personal experience as would a more contemporary work. The friendship of Achilles and Patroclus might seem as personally important to a boy as would a treatment of friendship such as in Steinbeck's *Of Mice and Men*. The story of Lear and his daughters might seem as near to a girl as the family relations in E. M. Forster's *Howard's End*. *Dombey and Son,* just because it was written at a time when problems of parent-child and husband-wife relations were still drawn in their broadest terms, might, at a certain stage, be more comprehensible than the treatment of similar problems in a book by Virginia Woolf. The fact that some writers of this century, like James Joyce or T. S. Eliot, are themselves so much the product of a long literary heritage might make them less comprehensible to the young reader than a nineteenth-century writer would be. The student himself needs to go through the experience of relevant literature of the past before he can understand some contemporary writers.

Nevertheless, most contemporary authors offer no such difficulty but write about a life that the student can understand. For instance, Benet's *John Brown's Body* would be more easily understood than *The Idylls of the King;* Carl Sandburg and Langston Hughes would have more personal impact than Matthew Arnold; Orwell and Salinger than Thackeray and Hawthorne. The question of literary comparisons must wait until the students can handle the historical obstacles to participation in the older works.

Certain other considerations relate to the use of classical or contemporary literature. It is usual to think that classics survive a winnowing process that guarantees them to be repositories of the accumulated wisdom of the race. There is much in this view. Even so, it is hard to find any great work that has been consistently recognized as such. Shakespeare has had his ups and downs, as have lesser writers. And when different ages agree in their exaltation of a work, it may be for widely differing reasons. Moreover, in any work, the elements of "lasting truth" are intermingled with much that was special to the particular age in which it was written. This is as true of the work of Shakespeare, Milton, and Goethe as it is of Jane Austen.

Surely, many "works that every person should have read" lend powerful reinforcement to emotional attitudes and assumptions about human nature that our contemporary life and our contemporary thinkers have discarded as outmoded and false. What is the possible influence of a steady diet of literature produced out of social systems and ethical philosophies very different from our own? Ideas about the relations between men and women, employer and employee, between citizen and state, and indeed between man and the universe, as they are reflected in much of the older literature, would seem to exalt much that the person of average enlightenment today considers reactionary or limited. To what extent is such literary training in the schools contributing to the persistent hold of images and ideals no longer appropriate to our present-day life and knowledge? Are the students offered literary

fare that provides opportunity only for imaginative identification with images of behavior irrelevant to actual life
or whose relevance they are not equipped to see? [5]

Obviously, these questions are presented in oversimplified form. Books, it has been seen, do not function in a
vacuum, and their influence is always part of a complex
network of social factors. For instance, the boy who has
come into contact with the present-day skeptical scientific
attitude will naturally be less likely to absorb the authori-
tarian point of view that permeates much of the writing
of the past. Yet in a conflict between the two attitudes,
a steady fare of such literary experiences might tend to
strengthen subservience to intellectual authority. It is
realistic to think of particular literary works as tending
either to reinforce or to weaken attitudes and images the
young person may encounter through other social influences.

It is generally recognized that students should read
works of both the past and the present. The fact that a
work is written by a contemporary is certainly no automatic proof of its value. Still, in the mass of literature
produced today there is much that represents those areas
of thought and experience that are the points of growth
and change in our own age. If the youth is to develop a
critical understanding of his world, he must be exposed

[5] To what extent, for example, can the influence of literature be held
responsible for the fact that many women today find within themselves
emotional obstacles to their sincere ambition to be independent emotionally and intellectually? Throughout their entire experience with
literature, they have been led to identify themselves most often with the
older image of woman as temperamentally, as well as economically,
subordinate and dependent. See Chapter 8, p. 265, for further discussion
of this problem.

to contemporary expressions of personal and social attitudes. The novel, the poem, the play—whether encountered in the printed page or other media—provide a sense of the adult world he must enter. Through the processes of "ideal experimentation," they help him to forge some of the necessary intellectual and emotional tools.

This leads back to the principle so often reiterated in these pages, that the test of what books the child or adolescent should read is his intellectual and emotional readiness for what they offer. The classics will be more appropriate than some esoteric contemporary author, but in many cases comparatively recent works will speak more profoundly and constructively to the boy and girl than will much "greater" works of the past.

We should not, then, set up arbitrary ideas in this matter of classic and contemporary works. The teacher should be eager to find those books of the past and present that will have a live meaning for his students. In most schools and colleges even today, this principle would lead to a greater liberality in introducing contemporary literature into the curriculum. For the teacher's desire will be to give the youth as wide a range of relevant experiences as possible at his level of development.

To SUM UP: Because the literary work of art is a form of personal experience, literature has many potentialities that dynamic and informed teaching may sustain.

Literature fosters the kind of imagination needed in a democracy—the ability to participate in the needs and aspirations of other personalities and to envision the effect of our actions on their lives.

Literature acts as one of the agencies in our culture that transmit images of behavior, emotional attitudes clustering about different social relationships, and social and personal standards.

Literature can reveal to the adolescent the diversity of possible ways of life, patterns of relationship, and philosophies from which he is free to choose in a heterogeneous, rapidly changing democratic society.

Literature may help him to make sound choices through imaginative trial and error or experimentation—through experiencing in the literary work the consequences of alternative actions.

Literary experiences may enable the reader to view his own personality and problems objectively and so to handle them better.

Literature, through which the adolescent reader encounters a diversity of temperaments and systems of value, may free him from fears, guilt, and insecurity engendered by too narrow a view of normality.

Literature may suggest socially beneficial channels for drives that might otherwise find expression in antisocial behavior.

CHAPTER 8

Emotion and Reason

IN THE PRECEDING REFLECTIONS on literature as a source of insight and emotional liberation, the emphasis was primarily on the relationship between the individual student and the book. The teacher entered the picture mainly through his power to limit or broaden the range of books with which the student might come into contact. But the teacher's function does not end there. The role and the teaching process sketched for him in earlier chapters can also be viewed in terms of its potential influence on personality and behavior. This will involve, too, a consideration of how the study of literature may create an understanding of the various basic social concepts discussed in Chapter 6.

In sum, the teaching process outlined consists in helping the student to develop the habit of reflecting upon his primary response to books. Having given him the essential opportunity to react freely, the teacher then seeks to create a situation in which the student becomes aware of possible alternative responses and is led to examine further both his own reaction and the text itself. In this way he is helped to understand his own preoccupations and assumptions better. He considers whether he has taken into account everything that the text offered. He thus becomes more aware of the various verbal "clues"— the diction, the rhythmic pattern, structure, and symbol— and develops or deepens his understanding of concepts such as voice, *persona*, point of view, genre. This process of reflection leads the student to seek additional information concerning the work, the author, and their social setting, as a basis for understanding of himself and of literature. These new technical, personal, and social insights may ultimately lead to a revision of his original interpretation and judgment and may improve his equipment for future response to literature.

Now if we were to substitute the words *situation* or *personality in life* for *text* or *work* in the preceding paragraph, the description would apply equally well to the kind of thinking that is most fruitful whenever an individual meets a new situation in life or must adjust to a new kind of personality. His first need is to understand his own emotional response to the person or situation. He realizes that preoccupations and prejudices may have led him to exaggerate some things and ignore others. He has to bring his basic moral or psychological assumptions out into the open in order to test the validity of their application to this new situation. He may find that his own past experience and information must be supplemented before he can make an adequate judgment or plan appropriate action. The result of these considerations may be a rejection or revision of his original reaction. Through this process of self-scrutiny, he may have come to understand himself, as well as the outside world, better. A certain inner readjustment may have started which will modify his response to the next person or situation encountered.

In the case of either the literary experience or the life experience, a process such as the one outlined constitutes reflective thinking. If the individual is stimulated often enough to engage in this kind of reflection, it may tend to become habitual. There will have been set up a readiness to reflect upon his own attitudes toward people and situations as a prelude to passing judgment or deciding on action.

It seems reasonable to suggest, therefore, that in building up the habits of mind essential to the attainment of sound literary judgment, the student will also be acquiring mental habits valuable for the development of sound insight into ordinary human experience.

There is more than a verbal parallel between the process of reflective thinking arising from response to literature and the process of reflection as a prelude to action in life itself. John Dewey reminded us that in actual life constructive thinking usually starts as a result of some conflict or discomfort, or when habitual behavior is impeded and a choice of new paths of behavior must be made. Such thinking, therefore, grows out of some sort of tension and is colored by it. The tension contributes the impetus to seek a solution, but intelligent behavior results from thought brought to bear upon the problem. Moreover, the validity of the thought will usually depend on whether emotion has been controlled and has not obscured the actual situation. "Impulse is needed to arouse thought, incite reflection and enliven belief. But only thought notes obstructions, invents tools, conceives aims, directs technique, and thus converts impulse into an art which lives in objects." [1]

Educators are more and more recognizing this view of constructive thinking. It is comparatively easy for the student to think rationally about difficult human problems when impersonal academic treatments make them abstract subjects of thought. Unfortunately, that kind of thinking is probably not very useful; it lacks the conflicting impulses or emotional perplexities out of which thinking usually grows in real life. Reason should arise in a matrix of feeling:

> The conclusion is not that the emotional, passionate phase of action can be or should be eliminated in behalf of a bloodless reason. More "passions," not fewer, is the answer. To check the influence of hate there must be sympathy, while to rationalize sympathy there are needed emotions of curiosity, caution, respect for the freedom of others—dispositions which evoke objects which balance those called up by sympathy, and prevent its degeneration into maudlin sentiment and meddling interference. Rationality, once more, is not a force to evoke against impulse and habit. It is the attainment of a working harmony among diverse desires.[2]

That kind of rationality may be fostered by literature. It may provide the emotional tension and conflicting attitudes out of which spring the kind of thinking that can later be assimilated into actual behavior. The emotional

[1] John Dewey, *Human Nature and Conduct* (New York, Henry Holt and Co., 1922), pp. 170–171.
[2] *Ibid.*, p. 195.

character of the student's response to literature offers an opportunity to develop the ability *to think rationally within an emotionally colored context*. Furthermore, the teaching situation in which a group of students and a teacher exchange views and stimulate one another toward clearer understanding can contribute greatly to the growth of such habits of reflection.

Several specific classroom discussions may serve to illustrate this. The students who discussed Ibsen's *A Doll's House* (see p. 122) provide an example of processes that might also be evoked by many more recent works. After they had clarified their historical approach to the play, they still found themselves involved in a lively difference of opinion. "Nora should never have left her children, no matter how unhappy she was," declared one. "Her main duty was toward them and toward maintaining a home for them." This was vigorously opposed by others who claimed that Nora's duty was first of all toward herself. She needed to develop her own mind so that she might consider herself truly an individual. Without this she could be of little service to her children.

The young women had obviously identified very strongly with Nora; the discussion seemed to have personal immediacy for them. The rights of a woman to self-expression and personal dignity were thoroughly canvassed. Nevertheless, all of the students, even the most decided individualists, hesitated to say that Nora had no responsibilities toward her children. A number of the students found it difficult to take one position or the other. Their sympathies were involved in Nora's gesture of independence; they shared her desire to stand completely alone; yet they were equally ready to see the value of marriage and children. At this point an "emotional tension" had developed.

Although the discussion seemed to be moving in circles, the teacher did not rush the class over this hurdle. Finally, one of the students pointed out that Ibsen's ending had not provided a solution to Nora's problem, but had only underlined her dilemma. Certainly an individualism that entailed the sacrifice of important relationships could not be very desirable. A valuable kind of independence for Nora would have permitted her to be a complete human being, yet to remain in the home and to function as a wife and mother. Another student added that it is often necessary to sacrifice certain satisfactions—such as the right to complete, untrammeled independence—in order to satisfy other needs in our nature. On the other hand, it was agreed that the role of wife and mother should not have required submergence of Nora's personality. Furthermore, one student pointed out that even if Torvald had been an ideal man, there still would have remained the need for adjustment between the personalities of the husband and wife as equals.

The students here were groping toward ideas that authorities on family problems and mental hygiene consider extremely important. They remind us that in order to achieve an integrated personality the individual must reconcile or adjust conflicting impulses and aspirations within himself. Moreover, much friction would be avoided by recognition that any personal relationship necessarily entails compromises between different temperaments. The family group, for example, should provide scope for each of the personalities within it; yet if it is to be a smoothly functioning group, each individual must to a certain extent be willing to adapt himself to the others. The adolescent, in his present family or in future relationships, will be better prepared to make the necessary adjustments if he has thoroughly assimilated this approach.

In this discussion, there was not only a clash of opinion among various students; certain students discovered conflicting emotional attitudes within themselves. Thus these students lived through something analogous to the inner conflict that must often attend choices in life.

Furthermore, in this phase of their discussion the students were not considering the demands and responsibilities only of the marriage relationship. They also achieved some understanding of the complex adjustments required in any relationship. And each individual, they concluded, should seek to reconcile his different needs; he must attempt to satisfy the most important with as little sacrifice as possible of other valued tendencies in his nature. Such insights were much more valuable than any conclusion that the students might have reached concerning the "rightness" of Nora's final act.

More significant than any statements made by the students was the fact that these ideas grew out of emotional tension and lively personal feeling. There is no proof that the insights achieved were retained. But it can safely be said that they were more likely to be retained than if the same ideas had been encountered in an impersonal way in a traditional psychology or sociology course.

The fact that Ibsen's *A Doll's House* is a "problem

play" may possibly obscure the point. A similar process might have grown out of the experience of a play that was in no way designed to focus attention on a controversial problem. Works that are read solely because of their literary significance may arouse interest in such issues.

For example, in a discussion of *Antony and Cleopatra* carried on by a freshmen literature class in a women's college, the play was rejected by the majority of the group. Their dislike for the tragedy, it became apparent, grew out of their antipathy to Cleopatra. "I hate that kind of woman. She is selfish, conceited, grasping for power. I am not interested in what happens to her." Like most students, they had responded to the character as they would in real life. The instructor's job was to help them maintain that personal sense of the work and yet react to it in rational terms.

The students were challenged to consider the basis for their antipathy. It finally became obvious that theirs was the point of view of the average woman to whose marital peace a person like Cleopatra would be a decided menace. (When this episode was related to an authority on adolescent psychology in charge of guidance in a large California high school, she commented that the students' reaction to Cleopatra was as much in terms of their present adolescent relationships as of any future adult situations. We tend to forget, she pointed out, that adolescents in their boy and girl relationships are already engaged in an intense emotional life parallel to adult experiences. They are already, for instance, experiencing the disillusionments and triumphs of sex rivalry.)

The students felt that their judgment of Cleopatra's ruthlessness and egotism was justified by the text. This led them to inquire what her function was in the play. Obviously, the reader was being led to feel that the fate of Cleopatra and Antony was important. Much as the class might disapprove of Cleopatra in real life, they came to perceive that her very vices and weaknesses, like those of Antony, are intermingled with traits that make their struggle and their downfall significant. Although morally some of Cleopatra's actions merit condemnation, she possesses great vitality, the ability to feel and act on a grand scale. Approaching the character in this way, they were able to comprehend the intermingled childish and queen-like actions that characterize her. They responded more perceptively to the verse. Shakespeare, the students concluded, helped them to grasp the complexity of such a character; there is understanding to be gained from living through the fugue of emotions that the play presents, to their resolution in those noble last scenes.

From this discussion of Cleopatra there emerged, first of all, a clearer understanding of the esthetic attitude. Cleopatra's significance for them was obviously not what it might have been if she were part of their own lives. They could set aside their practical reaction toward her and participate in the complex and heightened form of experience that the play offered. One student phrased in her own terms the value of esthetic distance, which made this possible.

These literary perceptions tended to modify the students' initial reaction. They came to see that their practical judgments on people, in either a play or real life, need not be the limit of their insight. They might attempt to comprehend the human drives that lead people to act in ways potentially injurious or repugnant to them. In some cases, they realized, their own aims and satisfactions might seem equally alien or objectionable from the point of view of other people.

Implied in this discussion, therefore, was the germ of a new moral attitude, as well as the development of critical objectivity. Instead of simply approving or condemning, one might seek to understand. Instead of fixed rules of conduct unconditionally applied to all under all circumstances, judgment should be passed only after the motives of the behavior and the particular circumstances had been understood. One might condemn the act and yet wish to understand what produced it. Moral judgment itself would thus become more humane.

Much less complex works than Shakespeare's plays may lead to similar insights. A class in a coeducational Southern school was reading plays and short stories. The group was at first content to condemn the possessive mother in Sidney Howard's *The Silver Cord* or to talk about how much they disliked the vain posturing of Mr. Reginald Peacock in Katherine Mansfield's story. Because of the way the anthology for the course was arranged, they tended to speak in terms of "types" of people, such as the boor, the sadist, the gossip. One or two of the students tried to suggest some excuse for these characters' behavior; the discussion ultimately veered toward the idea that, after all, the important thing was not to condemn but rather to find out what produced such personalities and behavior. The students felt that their reading had led them to observe themselves and other people much more carefully. That in itself was useful because one might then learn "how to live with them." It might also be better not to think that one necessarily has the right to try to change other people, or that mature personalities are easily modified. However, one might at least attempt to see what explained behavior in order to help create conditions that would in the future produce more socially valuable people.

The class had started with a decidedly moralistic attitude, sitting in judgment upon the characters encountered in their reading. Their point of view changed appreciably in the direction of greater human sympathy and objectivity. Instead of thinking only of individual human beings, they saw them in relation to the social forces that had molded them or that gave them scope for expressing their special temperaments.

Another instance: the demand in some quarters that the *Merchant of Venice* be barred from the schools. In a class in which a number of students were Jewish, it is argued, Shylock would create self-consciousness and resentment in that group and reinforce the prejudices of the rest of the class. This argument assumes a number of things that the preceding discussion has rejected. The first assumption is that the class would read the play and react to the character of Shylock without any interchange among themselves or with the teacher. The second assumption is that even if they did express themselves, their original ideas would remain unchanged.

The desirable kind of classroom situation outlined in

the preceding chapters would negate both these assumptions. If the literary experience offered by this play did give rise to decided reactions to Shylock, that should then serve as the beginning of a process of clarification such as was described earlier. Obviously, the kind of classroom atmosphere predicated, reflecting a relationship of confidence, would be extremely important. The students would not be encouraged merely to express their attitude toward Shylock. The discussion would become a means of leading them back to the text, to understand Shylock's situation, to see the adverse conditions against which he struggled, and to recognize the connection between that and his behavior. In other words, that part of the play would have enabled them to live through the experiences of a member of a minority group and to understand his behavior even when it was distasteful or ridiculous to them.

It might be contended that Shakespeare shared the prejudices of his age and that therefore this excursion into the development of racial understanding would be irrelevant to the play. Even if one grants the view concerning Shakespeare's attitude (his text provides its own antidote to that attitude), the English teacher could not justifiably ignore the fact that the students are reacting to the play in terms of their own present-day lives. He could not shirk the opportunity to contribute to a more rational, unprejudiced approach to human beings. Young people in school function as whole personalities; they are not creatures that can be neatly divided into literary or sociological segments, each segment to be ministered to by a different teacher. Hence the English teacher must feel some responsibility for dealing with whatever repercussions, no matter how controversial or "nonliterary," the experience of such a play may have. The fact that the play is "great literature" may have determined its selection in the first place, but that means nothing unless it has human significance today.

SOME WILL CONCEDE that the school and the teacher have the responsibility of developing constructive attitudes toward human relations but will ask: Why suggest this roundabout way of transmitting such insight? Why not have given the first group lectures on the need for adjustment of the different temperaments within the family? Why not have presented to the other groups a clearly worked-out exposition of the factors conditioning personality and behavior? Why take the time of a literature class for discussions suggested by the haphazard accidents of student reactions? Topics may not be brought into the discussion in any logical order, and there may be important subjects that the students may not introduce in their discussions at all. Would it not be preferable to eliminate any such topics from the literature classroom and to depend on a more orderly method of presenting this information to the students?

The considerations set forth in the first five chapters of this book offer an answer to one aspect of these questions. The student's personal response to literary works will be primarily colored by his attitudes toward the characters and situations they present. To attempt to ignore these student reactions would destroy the very basis upon which any greater *literary* sensitivity could be built. Even when the English teacher's responsibilities are interpreted in the narrowest terms, the discussion of such topics remains relevant to the literature classrooms.

If, on the other hand, one were not at all concerned with whether students developed sounder literary appreciation, one should nevertheless recognize literature as a potential means of developing social understanding. A formal course in psychology or social problems could not perform quite the function illustrated by the discussions in literature classes reported earlier in this chapter. Their special characteristic was the element of personal emotion that permeated the students' treatment of these topics. In the argument about *A Doll's House*, some sort of identification with Nora had occurred. Yet the students felt free to show their feeling because ostensibly they were talking about Nora, not themselves. The discussion of any general topic concerning human nature or social relations arose from the students' own vicarious experience and their feelings about it. Their concluding insights grew out of a process accompanied by definite emotional pulls toward various points of view. The whole discussion was *felt* as well as thought.

If the literary works had had little emotional impact, any discussion would have been empty verbiage. The discussions reported above were fundamentally attempts by the students to work out some rational understanding of their own reactions. They were involved in the task of managing their emotions—something very different from ignoring or repressing them. In this way, they were encouraged to bring thought to bear upon emotional responses—the starting point for intelligent behavior.

Thus, discussion of literary experiences makes possible rehearsals of the struggle to clarify emotion and make it the basis of intelligent and informed thinking. This possesses a certain parallelism to those situations in life which engender conflicting inner attitudes. The insights and ideas that result from such an experience tend to be assimilated into the individual's active equipment because they are embedded in a matrix of emotional and personal concern. Hence, literature provides an educational medium through which the student's habits of thought may be influenced. When this is more widely recognized, we may expect that literary materials will be introduced into many different phases of the curriculum.

The emotional quality of literature has sometimes caused the social scientist to look askance at it as something that strengthens the student's natural tendency toward undisciplined emotion. Dewey offers the rejoinder that rationality does not exist in opposition to emotion, but rather represents the attainment of a working harmony among diverse desires. The social scientist should recognize that literature may provide a means of helping the student to achieve a functioning rationality.

The power of literature to develop capacity for feeling, for responding imaginatively to the thoughts and behavior of others, was treated in earlier chapters. This chapter has considered how, through discussion and reflection on his response to literature, the student may learn to order his emotions and to rationally face people and situations he is emotionally involved in. Power to transmit understanding of society in terms that will be personally assimilable is lacking in traditional social science teaching methods. When literary experiences are made the material for reflective thinking, they may be one means of providing this sorely needed linkage between feeling, thought, and behavior.

Teachers of the social sciences usually demonstrate a rather limited view of the value of literary treatments of their subjects. History textbooks append references to historical novels, or students are assigned short stories and novels about foreign countries or about different types of social background. If the French Revolution is being studied, for example, *A Tale of Two Cities* is read. The idea seems to be that the literary work adds sharpness to the information that the teacher wishes to convey. The student is helped "to understand" the information better through the more vivid and detailed descriptions; a novel, for instance, helps him to visualize the people and scenes mentioned in his history book. That, certainly, may be one of the contributions of literature. But the matter is usually left on this level, with literature considered merely a tool for vividly conveying facts.

The repercussions of such understanding gained through vicarious experience do not end there. From enhanced perceptions may flow a sense of the human and practical implications of the information that has been acquired. This information is no longer words to be rattled off; the words now point toward actual human situations and feelings. Thus, the reading of *Hiroshima* or Kelley's *A Different Drummer* will bestow emotional reality in terms of human beings, their suffering, their needs and struggles. The meaning attributed earlier to the term *understanding* transcends the view of literature as a pedagogic device for giving sugar-coated information.

The teacher of social sciences as well as the teacher of English should hold firmly to this fact that literature is something "lived through," something to which the student reacts on a variety of interrelated emotional and intellectual planes. Therein lie its many educational potentialities.

This stress on the value of the literary experience in no way rules out the organized study of psychological and sociological subjects. On the contrary, students should be given even greater opportunities for that kind of knowledge. The social sciences, however, could be made more practically fruitful than they are at present. The question as stated at the end of Chapter 6 is: How can the student come to assimilate the scientific approach to man and society so thoroughly that it will translate itself into the very attitudes, decisions, and actions that constitute his own life? Unfortunately, this has too seldom happened. Many even of the college graduates among present adult generations tend to think only of the conditions that affect them most directly. They do not reconsider their own opinions in the light of social, economic, or psychological theory, nor do they attempt to imagine the human effects of the social measures they espouse as immediately beneficial to themselves.

The will to learn, it has been said, rests on a state of

dissatisfaction with present knowledge. The interchange of ideas in class discussions can lead the student to dissatisfaction with his present knowledge about human relations, since lack of information limits his ability either to participate in the experience offered by the book or to fit the experience into some rational structure of ideas. The reading of literature, therefore, might be made a means of arousing the will to learn. Furthermore, sociological or psychological information sought in this way is more likely to be integrated into the stream of the student's thought and behavior.

The social science teacher must, of course, determine the extent and manner of his use of literary materials, questions beyond the scope of this book. There are similarities between literary experience and direct observation through field trips, another source of personal response to social facts.[3] His special concern will be to bring about a perception of the general implications of what is experienced vicariously through literature. The purposes of the social science classroom require the transition from concern with particular instances to concern

[3] Literature, for instance, might be used as a substitute when such direct observation is not possible. Literary materials might even be an excellent means of introducing the student to the subject or problems to be studied, as a preliminary to direct observation of actual conditions. The analysis in the preceding chapter of the development of social sensitivity through literature is also relevant here.

The case history is another approximation toward personal experience. Its value will depend, probably more than is recognized, on the literary effectiveness with which the case history is presented. In addition to the more scientifically controlled and studied case history, the social science teacher should probably utilize the surer emotional and intellectual effects of literary treatments of the general social conditions with which his particular science concerns itself.

with the general social conditions or basic factors involved.[4]

The teaching processes described in Part Two of this book and in the present chapter can further that transition to general concerns. Conversely, social science discussions of general ideas should more frequently be translated back into terms of individual human beings. Such a shuttling back and forth between the abstract and the concrete, the general and the specific, which the use of literary materials might foster, would give social science study immediacy and lasting value. The student would develop the habit of recognizing that behind any particular situation there exists a general social situation whose causes and effects should be understood. Equally important, he would be aware that any generalizations or statistical data about society, politics, economics, refer to the behavior of living, feeling people.

The preceding remarks reflect the belief that the social science teacher shares with the literature teacher, and indeed with all other teachers, the responsibility toward the student as a complete person. The emphasis and methods of the social science teacher may be different; he

---

[4] The teacher whose main responsibility is the development of literary sensitivity will be less impatient for this transition to occur and will depend on repeated literary experiences and discussions to accomplish it. The social science teacher will probably consider this too time-consuming, given his desire to impart a body of relevant information. To read a book like Claude Brown's *Manchild in the Promised Land* and then to study Harlem might contribute to such generalization.

Students will need to question whether the picture is an accurate one and whether there may not be contrasting or contradictory considerations that he did not offer. This will illuminate the value of the impersonal scientific investigation based on the study of as many cases as possible.

is interested in initiating his students into an understanding of the methods of research in his particular field and in giving his students some knowledge of the nature of its materials. Ultimately, however, these techniques and this information must become a part of the equipment with which the student encounters actual life situations. In the functioning personality, there should not be any conflict between the attitudes toward man and society engendered by literature and by the social sciences.

Teachers of different subjects will be helped by an understanding of how their various contributions toward a common goal are related to one another. The view that the literature teacher should have some knowledge of the fundamental methods and concepts of the social sciences implies with equal force that the social studies teacher should have some understanding of the special nature of the experience provided by the literary work of art. The social science teacher should be aware of the emotional and intellectual factors entering into the students' literary experience.

The necessity for such mutual understanding among members of the different disciplines has been demonstrated where teachers have worked together in an integrated course. They need to share a common approach to literature and human relations. The great weakness in such courses has been that a lack of insight into the special nature of the literary experience has caused both social science and literature teachers to reduce the literary work of art to the status of social document.

THE CLASSROOM DISCUSSIONS of *A Doll's House, Antony*

and Cleopatra, and other works are isolated instances representing a wide variety of possible illustrations. The intention has been to avoid any suggestion of a routine procedure through which students are docilely led to predigested slogans about social understanding. One of the banes of educational systems today is the pressure on the teacher to work out neat outlines of the ideas about literature that his students are to acquire. Once such a plan is made, there is a great temptation to impose it arbitrarily. The teacher becomes impatient of the trial-and-error groping of the students. It seems so much easier all around if the teacher cuts the Gordian knot and gives the students the tidy set of conclusions and labels he has worked out. Yet this does not necessarily give them new insights. Hence the emphasis throughout this book on the teacher's role in initiating and guiding a process of inductive learning.

A teacher of English in a high school, unusually aware of the adolescent's need to understand human development, decided to give his class a period of several weeks in which they could read novels that presented a life history, ranging from *David Copperfield* to *Sons and Lovers.* He began by lecturing on the main points in developmental psychology. He provided an outline of some of the major problems and influences that enter into the development of any personality. The students were then required to write essays on each novel read, discussing the hero's development in the terms provided by the teacher's outline. The essays indicated that the pupils had read the novels with the aim of finding details to illustrate just those points mentioned by the teacher. The papers gave little indication of what the novels had meant to the youngsters themselves. The whole thing took on the nature of an exercise in which they attempted to apply the teacher's labels to each novel as it passed in review.

Despite his admirable initiative in breaking away from the usual routine of literature teaching, this teacher's aims were defeated by his unfortunate tendency to be satisfied when students had learned a vocabulary. He did not let the desire for organized understanding grow out of the reading of the novels. The pupils should have first been permitted to read these books in ways significant to themselves and thus to have participated emotionally in the growth and aspirations of the heroes and heroines. The class should have become involved in an interchange of ideas and feelings produced by their experience of the novels. Discovering certain similar problems in the lives of these characters, the students would then have been ready for the analysis of life patterns which the psychologist can offer. The perception that the development of a personality is not a haphazard process would have grown out of the reading, not have been imposed upon it. The teacher would have played an extremely important role in fostering this. The students themselves would have played an equally important role, however, and they would have achieved insights related to their own tensions and their own world.

Given the spontaneous and largely unpredictable character of specific literary experiences and the great diversity of temperaments and backgrounds in most student groups, any discussion will tend to develop a special character and focus. To take advantage of this, the teacher will not impose a routine but will let the discussion grow out of the ideas and the perplexities formulated by the students themselves. However, this does not imply sheer improvisation. In order to see the possibilities present in the students' responses, the teacher needs to have a firm grasp on the work and the major concepts relevant to it. He will then be able to carry on an inductive process, in which the students are stimulated to raise questions and to arrive at understandings that have personal significance.

The necessity for presenting isolated classroom illustrations may do injustice to another very important point. Certainly a few scattered discussions of literature could have little or no influence on students' attitudes toward people. Any such influence would be the cumulative effect of many experiences with literature, many free interchanges of opinion among students and teachers, many such emotionally motivated insights. Moreover, the intellectual tone of the school and the habits of thinking fostered by the entire school experience will modify the nature of the discussion in any single class. And within the class, the basis for such spontaneous discussions must be slowly and steadily built up. The give-and-take of ideas and the interplay between different personalities will in itself have a liberalizing influence. If under the repeated stimulus of literature the students have again and again been able to start from their emotional uncertainties and work through to some rational understanding, it is probable that a gradual revision of their habits of feeling and thinking will occur. They will at least have been set upon the path that leads to the development of a rational approach to experience.

THE PERSONAL NATURE OF THE LEARNING PROCESS places a decided responsibility upon the teacher. In seeking to create a vital relationship between his students and literature, he will become imbued with a feeling for the complex process by which social insights can grow out of response to literature. The areas of intellectual and emotional ferment are the points at which growth is possible in the student's mind and personality. The teacher who learns not to become insecure when lively discussion arises will also learn to sense the right moment to introduce new concepts relevant to these growth points. The thesis of Chapters 1 and 6 can now be seen more clearly in its educational context: The teacher can perform his function successfully only when aware of the attitudes toward human nature and society that he is helping his students to assimilate.

This view of literature study is completely alien to the old notion of "character building through literature," which consisted in giving the student, without any regard for his own needs and state of mind, a series of models of behavior to imitate. Equally unacceptable are attempts to treat literature as a body of documents that may be brought forth to illustrate various subtopics under the heading of human relations. Lists of books dealing with topics such as family, war, labor relations—let alone such moralistic topics as noble characters or great deeds of the past—will not in themselves do the job that has been formulated in this book.

The teacher's responsibility would be much reduced if he could think entirely in terms of the "subject matter" of literature. His task then would be principally the assembling of such lists of books. That is not the situation. Literature offers not merely information, but experiences. After all, the important thing is not whether a particular book presents a picture of contemporary marriage relations or describes the activities of the Eskimo, but the way these subjects are treated by the author, and the context into which they are integrated in the reader's mind. Does the image of marriage relationships present an attitude of resentment toward one or the other sex? Or does it offer the possibility of sensing the subtlety of temperamental adjustments involved in the achievement of happily shared lives? The significant thing is not that a book tells how the Eskimo fishes, builds his house, and wins his mate, but whether the book presents the Eskimo as a remote being of a different species or as another human being who happens to have worked out different patterns of behavior.

To catalogue the great body of literary materials according to the basic attitudes they might convey would be a colossal task. It would be almost impossible to find general standards of judgment, principally because the effect of any book will vary with the attitudes and assumptions that each reader brings to it. Although in the following pages terms drawn from the social sciences will be used, the focus is on the subtler, least easily catalogued modes of social understanding that literature makes possible.

There is a tendency to feel that one can create social understanding by simply assigning to students a group of novels or plays dealing with a social science topic. The value of book lists depends on how they are used and whether the teacher selects from them in the light of his students' or his classes' needs.

Moreover, it is necessary to reiterate that the teacher must play an active part in the development of social understanding. He himself needs to possess an enlightened sense of human relations in order to help his students derive new sensitivities from literary experience and evaluate it in personal and social terms. In the long run, therefore, this kind of illumination cannot be prescribed for by means of book lists, outlines, and routine procedures. It will depend in each case on the particular personalities and backgrounds of each group of teacher and students as well as upon the nature of the particular school setting.

The preceding qualifications should prevent the misinterpretation that sometimes arises when ideas illuminated by literary materials are emphasized. Moreover, given the point of view and the teaching process set forth in Part Two, literary history, biographical information, and critical analysis of technique will not degenerate into routine studies considered as ends in themselves. They will have value because they throw light upon the total literary experience, with all that it implies of personal emotion and social awareness.

The study of literary history, for instance, is often insufficiently motivated. The student learns about the sequence of literary movements, he memorizes the chronology of authors and works, but only because this seems to be information arbitrarily demanded. He learns it for examinations, but forgets it very quickly. Despite the study of periods and chronology, Chaucer, Swift, and Thackeray come to inhabit the same vague region.

The history of literature recounts the social activities of man in one special realm, just as does the history of politics or of industry. The various approaches to the study of literature parallel the approaches to the study of any of man's activities and institutions. Failure to empha- size this partially explains the usual sterility of the study of literary history in school and college.

The study of literary history constitutes a study of social history in two ways: First, since the writer is always a member of a particular society and a particular group within that society, his work grows out of the various social, economic, and intellectual conditions of his time. Literary scholarship has generally assimilated this approach. Especially in the treatment of American litera- ture, the writer is studied as a member of society, and his work is viewed in relation to the various social and intel- lectual pressures of his time.

Second—and this is the point that is least often recog- nized or exploited—the various *processes* of social history may often be studied more dramatically through literary history than through any other phase of man's activities. Literature is a social institution in the sense that the family or church is a social institution, each with its own history. Because man's literary behavior takes the explicit form mainly of a body of written or printed works, its his- tory is perhaps somewhat more clearly delimited. Yet it seldom is utilized to initiate students into an understand- ing of general social mechanisms. Literary history reveals clearly the nature of the individual's relations to the social group, as well as the nature of the forces molding the group itself. The student should be helped to apply to other phases of man's life the ideas concerning historical processes derived from literary history.

Literature is not a photographic mirroring of life but is the result of a particular socially patterned personality employing particular socially fostered modes of communication. Much of what is considered purely literary, technical, or textual criticism involves definitions of the special temperamental attitudes of the author, the precise emotional tone of his work, and its particular philosophic approach. All of this is essential to appreciate the literary merits of his work. The study of his manipulations of literary technique (to which the term *literary criticism* is often too narrowly limited) is incidental to the desire to apprehend the special qualities of the novel or poem or play. Walter Pater, the apostle of esthetic criticism, limited his duties as critic to a clarification or definition of the impression produced on him by literary works. Yet in a study such as his *Wordsworth,* this aim encompasses social and psychological considerations.

From these literary concerns should arise an added awareness that any individual—writer or bricklayer—with his special traits and techniques is the result of interaction with his environment.[5] This concept is often presented to

[5] "Environment" here necessarily includes physical nature as well as the cultural setting. Various geographical determinists at the end of the last century exaggerated the influence of man's natural environment; nowadays we may tend to underestimate its influence, particularly on literature. See Aldous Huxley's entertaining essay on what Wordsworth's sense of nature might have been if he had lived in the tropics rather than in the gentle atmosphere of the Lake Country.

the student only in the study of such topics as crime, juvenile delinquency, or politics. Yet this view of the individual is illustrated just as dramatically in the creation of the artist as in the acts of criminals or statesmen. By seeing how a concept of this sort applies throughout the whole range of his studies—social, scientific, or artistic—the student will be able to build up an integrated approach to human relations.

One of the usual approaches to the study of literature is the history of different forms—the novel, the drama, poetry, the essay. The student learns that in different periods these forms reflect different literary traditions. He is not made aware that literary traditions represent one type of crystallized social behavior. After all, environmental influences operate as much in an author's treatment of literary form and choice of theme as in any other phase of man's activity. The imagination of the Elizabethan dramatist, for instance, necessarily functioned within the framework of the conventions and dramatic formulas of his day. Knowing them can help us to differentiate between what in Elizabethan plays the contemporary audience accepted as dramatic convention and what reflected the actual life about them. The very themes the dramatist selected were similarly nourished by the intellectual climate of his time. From study of a particular literary form at different periods there can arise the perception that the individual's activities and ideas in any sphere are necessarily directed by attitudes and patterns absorbed from his cultural environment.

Similarly, the study of a literary period as a whole may

illuminate this concept of the shaping pressure of the environment upon the individual. If he lives in a time when prose forms are highly valued and poetry neglected, he will tend most readily to express himself in prose. If he lives in an age when the drama is the dominant form, he will probably express himself through that medium. Or if he uses some minor form, it will probably be selected from those admired in his milieu, as in the case of the Elizabethan sonnet. Indeed, the pressure of literary conventions is even more pervasive than that. Having grown up at a time when the heroic couplet is the common poetic mold, he will tend to express himself in its balanced and measured phrases, and freer patterns will seem rough and unpleasant to his ear. The study of eighteenth-century poetry or of eighteenth-century criticism of Elizabethan literature can serve to illustrate this concept of cultural conditioning.

It is often hard for the student to realize in a vivid or personal way that the ideas and behavior he accepts most unquestioningly derive their hold upon him from the fact that they have been unconsciously absorbed from the society about him. He can be led from a perception of how this happens in literary activity to an understanding of the similar process which crystallizes the individual's ideas concerning ways of behavior and ideas of right and wrong. Having observed so explicit a demonstration of how even the most gifted and intelligent authors are shaped by their environment, the student may come to recognize similar pressures upon all other phases of men's thought and activity. He should see that the existence of literary periods with marked characteristics of style and subject matter is the reflection of a general sociological phenomenon.

The student who becomes acquainted with this concept of cultural conditioning often may tend to exaggerate its implications. He may think of the individual as completely at the mercy of the dominant forces in the environment about him. This is as erroneous, of course, as is the earlier notion that the individual has complete free choice and self-determination. The study of Shakespeare in relation to the other Elizabethan dramatists may illuminate this problem in a way highly interesting to students. They have accepted the idea of Shakespeare as a supreme genius. Their introduction, however, to the tragedies of blood, and particularly to Thomas Kyd's *Spanish Tragedy*, usually brings keen disillusionment. They find that much in Shakespeare's *Hamlet* follows the outlines of earlier plays which also use ghosts calling for revenge, avengers who are mad or feign madness, heroes who hesitate and soliloquize. They discover that Shakespeare often followed very literally the theatrical conventions of his own day. The student's first reaction usually is to remove Shakespeare from his pedestal and to exclaim that he was merely a man of his own time, after all.

Reflection, however, brings revision of this judgment. They begin to see that Shakespeare was thoroughly a product of a particular environment, and yet, working within the patterns set by his time, he modified them and put his own unique stamp upon them. A comparison between his plays and contemporary ones of the same type, such as the romantic comedies or the tragicomedies, reveals the pervasive influence of his literary environment upon the individual, but it reveals also his ability to create something new and superbly individual out of the elements provided by his age. Moreover, these unique creations will influence writers who come after him. Through the study of easily recognized literary details, the student can be led to perceive within a limited sphere something of how in all phases of man's life the average individual, too, not only is molded by but also molds his environment.

EVEN MORE STRIKING is the light that the study of literary history may cast upon the process of social change. This should be understood as a process in time, involving the constant adjustment and readjustment of particular individuals to particular cultural patterns. This human view of social changes can grow out of a study of the modifications over a period of time in authors' selections of subjects and choices of literary forms. The study of English literature from 1750 to 1830, for instance, offers dramatic possibilities for developing a sense of the complex factors involved in any change in man's ways of thinking and behavior.

For example, the concept of "cultural lag" applies as much to literature as to any phase of history. A study of verse forms, poetic diction, and themes shows how attitudes and social patterns tend to persist even when they no longer serve a vital need. The hold of the heroic couplet, the endless minor variations on themes fully exploited earlier in the century, the development of tricks of poetic diction to the point of absurdity, illustrate very forcibly the tendency of the average mind to follow already channeled grooves.

Against this background of persisting habits and conventions, the study of the beginnings of the romantic movement in the eighteenth century and its flowering in the early nineteenth century can illustrate the slow cumulative process of social innovation—the few signs earlier in the century of a slight departure from accepted attitudes toward man and nature in a poem here and there by a Lady Winchelsea or a Parnell; the evidence of an increasing body of sentimental minor poetry, like the "graveyard poems," that hints at new tendencies; the partial break with tradition represented by the Wartons or by Thomson; the harking back to literary precedents of the Middle Ages and the Renaissance to sanction rejection of the contemporary conventions; the curious transitional quality of Gray's poems or of Wordsworth's earliest verse; the full revolt bursting forth in the *Lyrical Ballads;* the resistance that Wordsworth, Keats, Shelley, and the others met from critics and readers still dominated by the Pope tradition in poetry; the slow education of an audience that would understand and appreciate their work.

These literary materials give vivid evidence that social change often comes about slowly and almost imperceptibly. At first a few minds here and there free themselves from the worn-out attitudes and procedures that no longer satisfy new needs. Gradually the number of these nonconformists increases; their influence spreads; and ultimately their ideas may become the dominant ones automatically assimilated by young authors and readers, as in the case of the romantic view of poetry. Thus, in his study of the rise of romanticism, the student can find dramatically portrayed the pull and tug of contending social phenomena. The tendency to hold on to old attitudes, on the one hand, is opposed by the struggle, on the other hand, to find fresher and more completely satisfying patterns. In other words, the relation between the processes of cultural lag and social innovation is revealed as legitimately in literary history as it is in the history of technology or of political institutions.

The anthropologist's idea of the interdependence of the various aspects of any culture can be related to the history of literature. An understanding of what happens in the realm of literary activity requires the study of the accompanying economic, social, and political conditions. It would, for example, be false to explain the romantic movement entirely in literary terms as a revolt against eighteenth-century formalism. (Of course, this popular view of eighteenth-century literature is also oversimplified.) It is necessary to be aware also of the political ideals, the emphasis on a static and stratified society, which paralleled the eighteenth-century concern with balanced form and disciplined emotion. Romantic exaltation of free expression of individual feeling often arose from rejection of social as well as literary limitations.

Similar interdependences can be noted no matter what period is studied. What, for example, were the forces at work in Elizabethan society that helped to make possible the flowering of the drama? What were the economic and social conditions that created so heterogeneous an audience for the theatre? How did the fact that the Court still

played so central an economic and social, as well as
political, role influence the drama? How did the religious
and philosophic developments affect the sense of significant human problems? The history of literature cannot be
viewed as completely separate from other aspects of
society.

The anthropologists point out also that through this
interaction of its different elements, a culture tends to
develop some degree of integration, a recognizable basic
cultural pattern. Out of the interplay between the different forces at work in the society will arise a set of
dominant values or drives. These will determine whether
a society values human life or military glory more,
whether it phrases success in terms of material acquisition
or ceremonial generosity, whether it gives greater prestige
to wealth or craftsmanship or learning. The nature of this
dominant pattern will make a great difference in the
emotional overtones and in the very character of the
various personal relations within that society.

Within the range of even a single literature we may
encounter the reflection of a number of different cultural
emphases—in the literature of England, for example, the
sharp contrast between earthly and otherworldly values
in medieval society, with its intense appreciation of both;
the greater flexibility of Renaissance institutions, with the
attendant zest for free expression of individual personality; the increasing importance of materialistic bourgeois
values in the eighteenth and nineteenth centuries, with
accompanying stress on property and on social prudence;
the paradoxical reflection of bourgeois economic individualism in the romanticists' demands for personal freedom

and their break with the utilitarian bourgeois view of life when the romantic artists translated their individualism into esthetic and spiritual values; the development of the physical and biological sciences creating a crisis in religious thought through their reinforcement of a naturalistic interpretation of man and the universe; and the increasingly frequent expression today of a philosophy that stresses the individual's inescapable bonds with his fellowmen. The societies that express themselves through English literature seem to have developed varying degrees of integration. In some ages, one perceives a number of clear-cut subpatterns, or even a number of contradictory patterns in a state of unstable equilibrium; in other ages, many aspects of the society seem to reflect similar or parallel emphases.

Even such a sketchy listing indicates that a literary work reflects or refracts the characteristic emphases of its own age. The literature program has always included works produced in a great many different periods and social settings. Students read (or should read) books that treat both contemporary and past American life; British, French, German, Russian novels; modern versions of the Scandinavian epics; or Greek drama. An increasingly large body of Oriental literature is becoming available in translation. In addition to this, the growing body of fiction, such as Freuchen's *Eskimo*, dealing with primitive societies reveals how differently human life may be patterned in another culture. The student encounters diverse temperaments and images of personal success in the literary works of different ages or even in the literature of a single period. He tends to take these differences for granted, without recognizing the extent to which each work implies a framework of values, mores, and modes of expression particular to some one cultural setting.

Nor are students usually helped to recognize that in any literary work the diverse values of a society are incorporated into the personalities and lives of individual men and women. Mark Twain utilized this insight in *A Connecticut Yankee in King Arthur's Court*. The Yankee embodies the sense of values of one cultural pattern; the Arthurian knights reflect a different pattern. Much of the humor of this book arises from the perspective thus created, so that both cultures are viewed satirically—and, of course, Mark Twain ultimately uses this to question certain values of his own society. Orwell's *1984* is another work that forces readers to ponder the system of values of a whole society and to consider its meaning in terms of individual lives.

Problems in values thrust themselves upon the reader even more urgently in the works of those contemporary novelists, dramatists, and poets who look upon man's life as "absurd." Many young people respond intensely to this image of man born into an indifferent world, shorn of all former external props, and confronting the inevitability of death. Such works as Camus' *The Stranger* or Beckett's *Waiting for Godot* undoubtedly provide a catharsis for many youthful readers. Still, the very sense of alienation may be the beginning of a movement toward positive commitment to society and toward the feeling that man creates himself by his choices. In *The Plague* Camus explores the many different hierarchies of values men affirm through their choices in a crisis. Many contemporary writers, for example, Saul Bellow (*The Dangling Man, Herzog*), Bernard Malamud (*The Fixer*), Ralph Ellison (*Invisible Man*), or John Knowles (*A Separate Peace*), develop such a theme.

Yet surely it is not only in contemporary works that the issue of choices in values imposes itself. As in life itself, questions of values are always implicit in any poem, novel, or play. Characters are faced with the necessity for choice, and by those choices affirm or deny the values of their world; the voice of the *persona* in a poem or narrative, by one clue and another, creates a scale of values by which the reader is asked to measure the mood or the world that has been evoked. Far from the old didacticism is this recognition that all literature affirms or denies values, and that an important part of literary criticism is the clarification of such values. The youth today is confronted by necessity for choice among a vast range of alternatives. Contemporary works relevant to the adolescent's quest for identity will generate receptivity to all that literature, of both the past and the present, has to offer him.

Just as the student will recognize in the literature of the past reflections of dominant drives and emerging alternative attitudes, so he will view contemporary literature as the expression of many minds working, slowly and often at cross purposes, toward the creation of a new and more satisfactory system of common values. Through the experience of literature of the past he will be able also to come into contact with diverse views of the satisfactions to be derived from human life and society. These will serve both as contrast and as commentary on present-day emphases and on any newly offered alternatives for personal and social arrangements. Perhaps such perspective may also lead him to discriminate between works that merely reflect a general mood of disillusionment and those that reveal minds seeking new and positive alternatives.

The introduction of new types of personalities into literature, the picture of new types of relationships, or the assertion of new values in life by the writer will have their repercussions upon the practical social and political life of an age. As George Boas insists, even those works that are in opposition to the dominant attitudes of their time—for instance, the writings of Dickens, Arnold, and Ruskin—are as much a part of their age as the writings that reflect its dogmas. Subtract the works of Dickens and the others from the Victorian Age and it would be something different from that age as we now understand it. The tendency to speak in terms of the social and political "background" of literature is misleading, since it implies that the background existed apart from the literature. This contradicts the view that aspects of any culture tend to act and react upon one another.

Another point requires clarification: Literary works do not inevitably "hold the mirror up to nature." Often the work can best be understood as "a slice of life seen through a temperament." The poem, play, or novel reflects the social philosophy of the author, or it may present a picture of people and situations dictated by the dominant literary conventions of the age in which the author lived. Again, it may be that only the life of a limited group in the society finds any sort of reflection in the literature of a given period. (Typical examples are Restoration comedy or the triangle situations in French novels.) Often, moreover, certain literary trends (for example, the novels of Sir Walter Scott, the great mass of romantic poetry) may represent an attempt to escape from the realities of the society in which the authors live.

Part of a sound equipment for understanding and judging literature is a knowledge of the possible factors, personal obsessions, class bias, political aims, pendulum-swing reactions, that may color the world the writer chooses to create. It would be as absurd for students to think that the novels of futility, such as those of F. Scott Fitzgerald, reflected the whole picture of life in the nineteen-twenties as to believe that Elizabethan drama is a literal transcript of life in England at that time. Learning to sense the angle of vision of the author, the young reader will come to see in contemporary literature the inverted Victorian prudery of some of the clinical descriptions of sex, and to differentiate these from the works seeking to do justice to its central role in a mature life.

The student has to be provided with the tools for weighing the various images of life that he encounters in books. This means that he must often turn from the literary work to other sources of information, whether those be the materials offered by the historian, the literary scholar, the sociologist, the anthropologist, or the psychologist. Both from the point of view of literary criticism and from the point of view of preparation for actual living, he should be stimulated to evaluate the ethical and social implications of the images of life encountered through

literature. To evade this responsibility out of fear of falling into didactic moralism is to narrow the study of literature to a sterile formalism.

The preceding remarks on cultural integration have led
to a transition from general social processes working themselves out in literary history and methods of literary creation to those processes as they are exemplified in the
images of individual lives offered by specific literary
works. Chapter 6 reported the behavioral scientists' emphasis on the concept that the human being is a complex
of qualities and habits which are the end result of a great
many different forces converging upon and interacting
with the individual organism.

Ideas about human growth and development are the
very stuff of literature. The process of cultural conditioning is seen operating in the images of life that the author
places before us. In the course of a year, the student
usually reads works dealing with personalities in a wide
variety of environments, but he is not always led to think
about this. The personal strivings, the ethical problems,
the social conflicts he shares through books, are often part
of social patterns very different from his own. With Macbeth, Jane Eyre, Becky Sharp, Lawrence's Paul Morel,
Dreiser's Clyde Griffiths, Faulkner's Quentin Compson, he
struggles vicariously with social codes reflecting diverse
environments. Because Hardy placed the problem of the
influence of environment in the center of attention, students are often led to associate this question only with his
works. Any writer, particularly any novelist or dramatist,
treats some aspect of this basic process by which the
individual human being lives out his life in terms of the

social structure, the moral code, and even the emotional habits he has acquired through interaction with his specific environment.

As we become more clearly aware of forces that pattern our lives, we acquire a certain power to resist or modify these forces. (See p. 155.) Hence the importance of an understanding of the concept of cultural conditioning. The student may derive this valuable insight from almost any work of literature. To return to *Hamlet* as an illustration: On the one hand, students will perceive in personal terms relevant to life today the nature of Hamlet's problem (such a "modern" interpretation as, for example, that he is a contemplative man caught in a situation demanding action). On the other hand, they should not ignore the fact that Hamlet's problem is bodied forth in specific terms of the code of "eye for eye, tooth for tooth"—a code archaic in Shakespeare's day as well as our own. Obviously, no play about a man of Hamlet's social and intellectual status in our own time would present him as assuming that society expected him personally to kill the murderer of his father.

The fear has been expressed that constant reading of literature of the past might tend to perpetuate the hold of anachronistic images of behavior. Perhaps one way of counteracting this is to make the reader aware that in literary works he submits vicariously to a cultural pattern and code of behavior often different from his own. This may develop some immunity to archaic images and some objectivity toward the cultural situation in which he himself is immersed. If the Jungian concept of an "archetypal pattern" or myth is brought to bear, it will be used with similar objectivity. Thus without inner confusion or maladjustment to contemporary reality, he will be able to profit from the breadth of experience, the flexibility of imaginative insight, and the sensuous enrichment that literature can impart.

THE VARIOUS OTHER CONCEPTS concerning human growth and development sketched in Chapter 6 are also implicit in the great body of literary works. Numerous novels follow the hero or heroine from birth to maturity. Works such as *Tom Jones, Great Expectations, The Way of All Flesh, Of Human Bondage, Sons and Lovers, Portrait of the Artist as a Young Man, The Last Puritan, Pelle the Conqueror, Jean Christophe,* imply the whole developmental approach to personality. As the student shares the life of the hero or heroine, he perceives some of the psychological processes involved in the interaction between the growing human creature and his environment: the child in a world of adults, taking on their behavior and standards, extremely sensitive to their acceptance or rejection of him; the emergence of the child's sense of himself as a separate person, and his struggles to attain some kind of integrated personality; the environmental aids or obstacles to the attainment of this personal and social independence; the necessity for resolving problems and conflicts created by the fact that he is a member of a particular economic and social group; the impact of different religious and ethical systems; the need to make some kind of sexual adjustment; the way all of these factors affect the individual's image of himself and the crystallization of his attitudes toward others; how the individual's sense of the satisfactions worth striving for is formed; the variety of possible attitudes of acceptance or rejection toward the dominant conventions of his environment; the fact that a life viewed from one angle may be a failure, but viewed from another may be highly successful; the element of continuity in any life history.

Such a developmental approach to personality is equally applicable to biography. We have seen how the traditional study of literary history can be given general significance and intellectual motivation. Similar pointedness could be given to the traditional study of writers' lives. Too often, studying an author's biography consists merely in learning the chronology of events. If the personality was in conflict with his environment or maladjusted in any way, as in the case of Shelley or Keats, the student tends to think this a peculiarity of artists. The highly marked personalities of many literary figures, their sensitivity to the world about them, and their articulateness make their biographies particularly vivid material for viewing the complex factors that enter into the crystallization of personality.

A study of various biographies of the same person is another means of making the student conscious of different interpretations of what are the important factors in personality development. Such a point of view would do much to vivify the usual routine and quite irrelevant study of authors' lives—as it would, of course, illuminate the study of any biographies, whether of statesmen, scientists, explorers, or teachers. There has been a revival of interest in biography—all the more reason for helping students to

develop from this reading some general framework of
ideas concerning the growth and development of the
human being.

The province of literature, we have said, is all that man
has thought and felt and created. It would be possible to
multiply examples of how literary works embody one or
another phase of man's social life, or reveal one or another
potentiality of human temperament, or clarify one or another
other process of individual or group development. There
is, for example, the great body of works that express the
broad gamut of social arrangements, temperamental adjustments, conflicts and disillusionments, joys and fulfillments that have grown out of the relations between man
and woman. Literary works whose theme is love, courtship, and marriage may give the adolescent reader not
only an emotional outlet and psychological preparation
but also a historical and cultural perspective.

Suggestions might be offered about how various bodies
of literature throw light on man's life—in, say, the relation
between races, nations, and classes, or between groups
such as the artists and their public. Or how through literature we can apprehend the meaning, for the individual
life, of different religious and philosophic attitudes. What
it means to the individual to live in an agricultural or an
industrial economy, in a rigid or flexible class system; how
variously family relationships can be patterned; what
problems face members of different groups in our own
society today—the artists, the laborers, the sharecroppers,
the Jews, the Negroes, women, youth; what social and
economic philosophies inspire men today—these and in

numerable other questions about man and society are illuminated through literature.

The study of American literature offers the student abundant opportunities for social insights especially relevant to his own problems. He can derive from our literature valuable understanding of the social conditions and processes that are characteristic of our extraordinary history. Our whole literature bears the stamp of a new country only gradually being created out of man's struggle with nature. The works of American authors from Puritan days to the present reveal a cultural heritage drawn from various Old World sources, particularly from England, taking on new overtones, absorbing new values, being slowly merged in a new cultural synthesis. The emphasis throughout this book on the social values and insights implicit in literary experience seems self-evident in relation to American literature. Our writers, almost every one, have in one way or another been conscious of their unique cultural setting and have sought to reflect it, to utter its essential spirit, to castigate its weaknesses, to sing its hopes and aspirations. Even those writers who have seemed to stand aside from the life about them have usually sought to create something of the beauty or the subtlety they found lacking in their environment.

The problem of the American writer has been to utilize everything of value in his literary heritage without letting it screen from him the special qualities of the new way of life about him. Seeking to remain a part of the splendid current of European literary tradition, he has at the same time struggled to grasp and make articulate the nature of the unique American experiment. With varying degrees of success, our writers have sought to use or remold the traditional forms in order to express the energetic spirit of a pioneer society. American literature reveals the convergence of a number of cultural trends produced by the intermingling of many peoples under the conditions imposed by a new land, during a period of economic, social, political, and philosophic readjustment throughout Western civilization. It has been the task of our writers to give utterance to the complex problems of a society in process of creation and yet to place these problems in their larger setting of changing scientific, political, and philosophic thought in the modern world.

The development of programs of "American studies" in undergraduate and graduate institutions has fostered concern with American literature in its cultural setting. Studies of various writers have illuminated different facets of this process of the creation of a new society. Many writers have given sensitive expression to the problems of the immigrant, in his adjustments both to his new environment and to the cultural gap between himself and his Americanized children. Even the great body of regional literature makes vivid the heterogeneous and complex nature of America. Or again, many recent works express the strains and stresses of our society and the plight of minority groups. There is the recurrent theme of aspiration toward an ever more democratic and humane way of life. Works such as these can aid the student in understanding the nature of the past out of which the society has grown and in becoming aware of the forces at work in it today.

Many other areas of human relations could be cited to illustrate this general philosophy of literature study. As the teacher himself comes to view his own literary experiences in this way, he will be able to make the study of any literary work a means for fostering in his students the capacity for such comprehension of man and society.

ESSENTIAL TO THIS APPROACH is the gradual discovery of ideas and insights by the student through actual literary experience and reflection upon it. Hence the focus on general social concepts rather than specific informational topics such as family relations, labor relations, juvenile delinquency, or war. By seeing how certain basic concepts apply throughout the range of his studies, the student will be able to build up an integrated approach to human relations. In this way he will develop fundamental understandings and critical attitudes that he will be able to apply even to those fields or unforeseen situations that his school courses have not covered.

Such recognition of recurrent basic concepts encountered through a variety of approaches to knowledge is probably the soundest kind of "correlation." It is not half so important that the student should acquire history, sociology, and literature simultaneously as it is that he should see exemplified in each of these fields certain unifying concepts concerning human nature and society.

Similarly, outlines of integrated courses are much less important than the teacher's possession of an understanding of how the particular body of knowledge with which he is concerned is related to the rest of man's life. Certainly there is much to be gained from breaking down rigid subject-matter divisions. But the success of any such procedures must depend ultimately on whether or not the teachers themselves have assimilated such an integrated and humanistic point of view.

After all, even in schools and colleges where there are rigidly separate departments, the individual teacher can do much to prevent compartmentalization in the students' minds. The teacher can communicate to his students a sense of his particular subject in its living context. In his class, they can encounter echoes and new incarnations of ideas gained in other classes. They can be made to feel the human implications and overtones of a particular body of knowledge. Learning can be made a process of perceiving wider implications and of relating them to the central core of human values.

As more of his fellow teachers acquire such insight, they will eventually develop external procedures and curriculum arrangements more expressive of their sense of the organic nature of knowledge. Only those integrated courses or "core" curricula that have grown out of such attitudes have much chance of success. If such experiments are sometimes unsatisfactory, the fault is not with the idea of integration or synthesis, but with those who have sought to execute it. Concern about flexible and integrated curricular patterns has tended to obscure the prime essential—flexibility and an organic approach to knowledge in the teacher's own mind.

THE LITERARY EXPERIENCE has been seen to reside in the synthesis of what the reader already knows and feels and desires with what the literary text offers—the patterned sensations, emotions, and ideas through which the author has sought to communicate his sense of life. Our eyes must always be directed toward that dynamic interaction between the work of art and the personality of the reader. The aim will be to increase the student's ability to achieve a full, sound reading of the text, and to broaden the personal context of emotions and ideas into which this response will be incorporated. The development of literary appreciation will depend upon a reciprocal process: An enlargement of the student's understanding of human life leads to increased esthetic sensitivity, and increased esthetic sensitivity makes possible more fruitful human insights from literature. Efforts to heighten the student's appreciation of the formal qualities of the literary work will be organically related to the effort to enrich his sense of human values;

Awareness of the highly personal nature of the literary experience protects against the deadening influence of routine; the student may derive from literature intimate benefits perhaps not visible, yet more precious than anything didactically imposed. Literary works may help him to understand himself and his own problems more completely and may liberate him from his secret self-doubtings and personal anxieties. Literature's revelation of the diverse elements of our complex cultural heritage may free him from the provincialism of his own necessarily limited environment. Books may often provide him with an image of the kind of personality and way of life that he will seek to achieve. A major contribution toward these potential benefits can be to provide him with as broad a gamut of literary experiences as possible. Even more important is the scrupulous effort to avoid any academic procedures that may hinder a spontaneous personal response.

Because the literary experience tends to involve both the intellect and the emotions in a manner that parallels life itself, the insights attained through literature may be assimilated into the matrix of attitudes and ideas which constitute character and govern behavior. Hence the opportunity for the student to develop the habit of reflective thinking within the context of an emotionally colored situation.

THIS BOOK HAS ATTEMPTED to reveal how much the experience and study of literature have to offer that is relevant to the crucial needs of personalities involved in the conflicts and stresses of life in our changing society. Indeed, literary experiences might be made the very core of the kind of educational process needed in a democracy.

If we only do justice to the potentialities inherent in literature itself, we can make a vital social contribution. As the student vicariously shares through literature the emotions and aspirations of other human beings, he can gain heightened sensitivity to the needs and problems of others remote from him in temperament, in space, or in social environment; he can develop a greater imaginative capacity to grasp the meaning of abstract laws or political and social theories for actual human lives. Such sensitivity and imagination are part of the indispensable equipment of the citizen of a democracy.

Moreover, literature may serve the student in the two phases of his development usually neglected by orthodox educational procedures, but essential for successful life in a heterogeneous, democratic society seeking to create more satisfactory ways of life. First, imaginative participation in the wide variety of alternative philosophies and patterns of behavior accessible through literature, and the development of the power to reflect upon them, can liberate the student from anachronistic emotional attitudes.

Second, having freed himself from the tyranny of attitudes and ideas ill-adapted to modern life, the youth should not be left in a state of paralysis of the will. The organic nature of the literary experience provides some assurance that new insights will be assimilated emotionally as well as intellectually. Hence literature can also nourish the impetus toward more fruitful modes of behavior. Literary experiences may help to fasten his emotions upon new and happier types of relationships or upon the images of new and more socially valuable satisfactions to be derived from life. Thus he may acquire the sympathy and insight, the critical attitudes, and the sense of human values needed for his creation of new ideals and new personal goals.

Only as literature teachers actively promote these latent possibilities can they hope to approximate this ideal picture. A preeminent condition for success is that teachers themselves possess a lively sense of all that literature offers. They should avoid inculcating their own assumptions about human beings and social values and should support the student in his efforts to understand himself and the forces that pattern society. He needs to create for himself a humane system of values and the flexibility to apply it under the complex and fluid conditions of contemporary life. One source of such strengths can be literature—the ordered sensuous, emotional, and intellectual perceptions embodied in the literary experience.

Our society needs not only to make possible the creation of great works of art; it needs also to make possible the growth of personalities sufficiently sensitive, rational, and humane to be capable of creative literary experiences. In the pursuit of such ideals, the teaching of literature can become a function worthy of the humane nature of literature itself. Literary experiences will then be a potent force in the growth of critically minded, emotionally liberated individuals who possess the energy and the will to create a happier way of life for themselves and for others.

Coda:
A Performing Art *

THOSE WHO SEEK to praise the riches of literature have
often been well-served by Keats' image of the reader as a
traveler "in the realms of gold" coming upon a great work
like "some watcher of the skies/When a new planet swims
into his ken." But this suggestion of a remote object gazed
upon with awe may reinforce the current, almost hypnoti-
cally repeated, emphasis on "the work itself" as distinct
from author and reader. Fortunately, in another sonnet,
"On Sitting Down To Read *King Lear* Once Again,"
Keats provides a counterbalancing image, which does
justice to the reader's involvement in the literary work:

> . . . once again the fierce dispute
> Betwixt damnation and impassion'd clay,
> *Must I burn through.*

Imaginative literature is indeed something "burned
through," lived through, by the reader. We do not learn
about Lear, we share, we participate in, Lear's stormy
induction into wisdom. In *Huckleberry Finn*, we do not
learn *about* conditions in the pre-Civil War South; we
live in them, we see them through the eyes and personality of Huck. Even while we chuckle at his adventures

* This essay, reprinted from *The English Journal*, November 1966, with
the permission of the National Council of Teachers of English, is added
here to perform the function of the coda in music—a few closing measures introduced at the end of a composition to emphasize the major
chords.

and his idiom, we grow into awareness of the moral dimensions appropriate for viewing that world. Whether it be a lighthearted lyric of Herrick's or a swiftly paced intellectual comedy of Shaw's or a brooding narrative of Hardy's, a reading is of necessity a participation, a personal experience.

The literary work is not primarily a document in the history of language or society. It is not simply a mirror of, or a report on, life. It is not a homily setting forth moral or philosophic or religious precepts. As a work of art, it offers a special kind of experience. It is a mode of living. The poem, the play, the story, is thus an extension, an amplification, of life itself. The reader's primary purpose is to add *this* kind of experience to the other kinds of desirable experience that life may offer.

No ONE ELSE can read a literary work for us. The benefits of literature can emerge only from creative activity on the part of the reader himself. He responds to the little black marks on the page, or to the sounds of the words in his ear, and he "makes something of them." The verbal symbols enable him to draw on his past experiences with what the words point to in life and literature. The text presents these words in a new and unique pattern. Out of these he is enabled actually to mold a new experience, the literary work.

It is this experiential aspect which differentiates the literary work of art from other forms of verbal communication. *Imaginative* literature happens when we focus our attention on what we are sensing, thinking, feeling, structuring, in the act of response to the particular words in their particular order. Even the most modest work—a nursery rhyme, say—demands attention to what the words are calling forth within us. In its highest form, as in Keats' reading of Shakespeare, such absorption in what we are evoking from the text produces feelings of being completely carried out of oneself.

As the reader submits himself to the guidance of the text, he must engage in a most demanding kind of activity. Out of his past experience, he must select appropriate responses to the individual words, he must sense their interplay upon one another, he must respond to clues of tone and attitude and movement. He must focus his attention on what he is structuring through these means. He must try to see it as an organized whole, its parts interrelated as fully as the text and his own capacities permit. From sound and rhythm and image and idea he forges an experience, a synthesis, that he calls the poem or play or novel. Whether for a nursery rhyme or for *King Lear*, such an activity goes on, and its complex nature can only be suggested here. The amazing thing is that critics and theorists have paid so little attention to this synthesizing process itself, contenting themselves usually with the simpler task of classifying the verbal symbols and their various patterns in the text.

In the *teaching* of literature, then, we are basically helping our students to learn to perform in response to a text. In this respect we are perhaps closer to the voice teacher, even the swimming coach, than we are to the teacher of history or botany. The reader performs the poem or the novel, as the violinist performs the sonata. But the instrument on which the reader plays, and from which he evokes the work, is—himself. The final lines of Yeats' "Among School Children" are sometimes used out of context to suggest the fusion of so-called form and substance in the work of art itself.

> O body swayed to music, O brightening glance,
> How can we know the dancer from the dance?

In this image of the dancer, who under the spell of the music makes of his own body the formed substance which is the dance, we can also prefigure the reader: Under the guidance of the text, out of his own thoughts and feelings and sensibilities, the reader makes a new ordering, the formed substance which is for him the literary work of art. The teacher of literature, especially, needs to keep alive this view of the literary work as personal evocation, the product of creative activity carried on by the reader under the guidance of the text.

CRITICAL THEORY during the past few decades has made this emphasis suspect, however. Building on one facet of I. A. Richards' work, the "New Critics" and their sympathizers did much to rescue the poem as a work of art from earlier confusions with the poem either as a biographical document or as a document in intellectual and social history. A mark of much twentieth-century criticism became its avoidance largely of the social and biographical approach to literature. This, moreover, was paralleled by a reaction against impressionist criticism. Walter Pater, for example, became the exemplar of the reader too preoccupied with his own emotions to remain faithful to "the poem itself." The reaction from impressionism fostered the notion of an impersonal or objective criticism, which, avoiding also the historical and social, busied itself with exploitation of the techniques of "close reading." This tended to treat "the poem"—or any literary work—as if it existed as an object, like a machine, whose parts can be

analyzed without reference either to the maker or to the
observer (or reader). Those who have been indoctrinated
with this critical emphasis are especially shocked at insistence on the literary work as experience. They misinterpret this as an invitation to irresponsible emotionalism
and impressionism.

There is, in fact, nothing in the recognition of the personal nature of literature that requires an acceptance of
the notion that every evocation from a text is as good as
every other. We need only think of our successive readings
of the same text, at 15 or 30 or 50, to know that we can
differentiate. Undisciplined, irrelevant, or distorted emotional responses and the lack of relevant experience or
knowledge will, of course, lead to inadequate interpretations of the text. The aim is to help the student toward a
more and more controlled, more and more valid or defensible, response to the text.

This does not imply, however, that there is, as with a
mathematical problem, one single "correct" reading of a
literary text. This raises very complex and thorny problems concerning the criteria of soundness to be applied to
any interpretation. However, this question is much more
difficult to settle in theory than to face in practical interpretation of particular texts. We may not be able to arrive
at a unanimous agreement concerning the best interpretation, say, of *Hamlet* or of "The Second Coming," but we
can arrive at some consensus about interpretations that
are to be rejected as ignoring large elements in the work,
or as introducing irrelevant or exaggerated responses.
Recognition that there is not a single interpretation which
the teacher can impose still leaves room for a very strin-

gent discipline. This can be carried on at the simplest or the highest level.

FIRST, WE CAN always move from our personal responses and interpretations back to the text. What in the text justifies our response? This is what the scientist would call our "control," the means of avoiding arbitrary and irrelevant interpretations.

Second, we can make clear the criteria, the framework of ideas or knowledge, or the standards of evaluation, that we are bringing to bear on our experience. We may sometimes find that differences are due not to a misreading of the work but to very different sets of expectations or bases of judgment.

More is involved than just the need for a reaction from current pseudoscientific "objectivity" or "impersonality." More is implied than merely reinstatement of the social, historical, philosophic, or ethical approaches to literature. We must place in the center of our attention the actual process of literary re-creation. As teachers of literature, our concern should be with the relation between readers and texts. This would change the emphasis in much that we do.

We would not forget, of course, that the text was an event in the life of an author, that he produced it at a particular moment in his life and in the history of his world. But we would not forget, either, that the poem becomes an event in the life of each reader as he re-creates it from the text.

What, then, are some of the implications of this emphasis on the personal nature of literary experience? Above all, our business is to contribute to a continuing process of growth in ability to handle responses—linguistic, emotional, intellectual—to literary texts. This means that our aim is to improve the quality of our students' actual literary experiences. We must seek to bring to our students at each stage of their development sound literary works in which they can indeed become personally involved.

This may seem simply to repeat a cliché of education, that students should be given works suited to their interests and level of maturity. Often, however, the search for appropriate works is perfunctory, and habit or convenience or economy intervenes. Sometimes, the notion of "interest" is oversimplified or superficial, as when works dealing only with teen-age problems are offered to adolescents, or when youngsters are allowed to go on indefinitely following one type of reading—science fiction, say. Nowadays, for the Advanced Placement youngsters especially, the error is to look only at the works, and to be pleased at the number of "great works" or works of high technical complexity being read, rather than at the *quality of the actual reading experiences*. (I hear, alas, of *The Waste Land* in the ninth grade and *The Magic Mountain* in the eleventh. Extreme instances, perhaps, but symptomatic.)

It may be that the youngster reading *National Velvet* or *Johnny Tremain* will have a fuller, more sensitive, more responsible literary experience than the student who is so unready to handle the demands of *The Divine Comedy* or even Henry James that he falls back on criticism of criticism of criticism, and never develops a literary technique of reading and assimilating for himself.

THOSE STRUGGLING TO face the challenge of education for the culturally disadvantaged have been least able to ignore the fact that the reader can read only out of past experience and present interests. Here, however, the danger is

to focus too exclusively on the external life of the reader.
What he brings to the text is not only an external environment and special dialect, but also fundamental human
emotions and relationships. Probably many of the works
which do treat essential human relationships but are considered remote from the interests of the disadvantaged
reader are not so at all; they are made inaccessible by
being expressed in a "standard" dialect which the youngster must learn almost as a second language. Materials
treating the immediate environment and problems of the
slum child have their important uses, but mainly as
bridges, leading the young reader to learn how to enter
through the printed page into the whole culture surrounding him.

When the young reader is confronted with the text—
whether it be *The Pearl* or *The Scarlet Letter* or *Hamlet*
—first of all we should seek to foster his having a personal
experience with it. His efforts and his attention should be
focused on re-creating it sensitively and responsibly. He
should be encouraged to bring to the text whatever in his
past experience is relevant, his sensuous awareness, his
feeling for people and practical circumstances, his ideas
and information, as well as his feeling for the sound and
pace and texture of language. We know that in a reliving
of the work, he does not read coldly, arriving first at
something called "the meaning" or the paraphrasable
sense, and *then* starting to feel or think about it. In an
actually creative reading, all these things may go on either
at the same time or in many different phases: emotional
response, the formulation of ideas, and tentative general
views about the emotional attitudes, the characters or the
situations that the work treats. The young reader needs to

learn how to suspend judgment, to be self-critical, to develop and revise his interpretation as he reads.

To do justice to the text, then, the young reader must be helped to handle his responses to it. Yet the techniques of the usual English classroom tend to hurry past this process of active creation and re-creation of the text. The pupil is, instead, rushed into peripheral concerns. How many times youngsters read poems or stories or plays trying to memorize as many random details as possible because such "facts" will be the teacher's means for testing —in multiple answer questions—whether they have read the work! Or students will read only with half a mind and spirit, knowing that this is sufficient to fill in the requirements of a routine book report: summarize the plot, identify the principal characters, describe the setting, etc. Even the search for meaning is reduced too often to paraphrase that simply dulls and dilutes the impact of the work. The concern with theme often relies too much on high-level abstractions, while the analysis of techniques becomes a preoccupation with recognizing devices—the scanning of verse, the labelling of "types," the listing of symbols, the recognition of recurrent myths.

OUR ASSIGNMENTS, our ways of testing, our questions about the work, our techniques of analysis, should direct attention to, not away from, the work as an esthetic experience. In applying the accepted treatments to the work, we must remember that all the reader has to deal with is whatever he himself lives through in his interchange with the text.

Hence, we should have the courage to admit to our students that the actual business of re-creating a work is difficult and tricky and sometimes frustrating, but always exciting and challenging. Instead of hurrying the youngster into impersonal and so-called objective formulations as quickly as possible, the successful teacher of literature makes the classroom a place for critical sharing of personal responses. Awareness that others have had different experiences with it will lead the reader back to the text for a closer look. The young reader points to what in the text explains his response. He may discover, however, that he has overreacted to some elements and ignored others. Or he may learn that some word or image has triggered a fantasy or awakened some personal preoccupation quite alien to the text. (I. A. Richards, long ago, reported in *Practical Criticism* on the many pitfalls awaiting the reader.) Such exchange of ideas, such scrutiny of the reasons for response, will create awareness of the relevance of critical terminology and will develop ability to handle more and more demanding texts. Discussion of personal responses, of the text-as-lived-through, can thus give rise to a truly inductive study of literature.

The more we teachers understand the linguistic demands of a particular work, the better able we shall be to help the young reader. But we cannot do this by formulas for reading, or by simply requiring the mouthing of the right answers to the right questions. Passive acceptance of the teacher's interpretation can bring only pseudo-understanding, verbalizing about, rather than experience of, the work. Even the skills and knowledge to be imparted can so easily become substitute ends in themselves. The identification of the *persona* of the poem, or the definition of the nature of irony, or the statement of the theme, or the recognition of a mythic pattern—the journey, the Oedipus situation—it is hard to keep in mind that these are not the ends or the justification of our teaching. These are means by which the reader can handle or describe his response to the clues offered by the text. But their value as means lies always in their helping the reader to enter more fully into the total experience by which he organizes, re-creates, the work for himself.

WE MAY NOT ALWAYS be able to look over his shoulder while the student is having a real literary experience, but we can do at least two things. First, we can be very careful to scrutinize all our procedures to be sure that we are not in actuality substituting other aims—things to do *about* literature—for the experience *of* literature. We can ask of every assignment or method or text, no matter what its short-term effectiveness: Does it get in the way of the live sense of literature? Does it make literature something to be regurgitated, analyzed, categorized, or is it a means toward making literature a more personally meaningful and self-disciplined activity? And, second, we can create in our classrooms an atmosphere of give-and-take and mutual challenge; through this, we shall surely find indirect evidences of the real literary experiences, the sources of growth.

A consequence of such an approach is that as the student clarifies his sense of the work, he becomes aware of his own attitudes, his own notions of what is important or desirable; he broadens his awareness of alternatives of

behavior and aspiration. Willy-nilly, the English classroom, if it is a place where literature really resides, becomes the arena for a linkage with the world of the student. What he brings to literature, what he undergoes
through the medium of the literary text, how he is helped
to handle this in the classroom, will affect what he carries
away from it in enhanced sensitivities to language and
to life.

When some remarks of this nature were made not long
ago at a meeting of college teachers of literature, one of
them exclaimed, "Good heavens! You don't propose to
have kids read stories in order to learn that they mustn't
steal cars! Or concentrate on stories about teen-age
dating?"

He was echoing what has been generally a wholesome
reaction against certain kinds of too-literal use of literature: for example, the emphasis on extracting a message or
moral or lesson, or the use of stories as a springboard for
getting youngsters to talk out their problems and release
tensions. This use of literature has probably not been as
widespread as some think, and actually no one denies the
therapeutic potentialities of such use of literature by people trained in such matters. Nor is the reading of poetry as
an art threatened because John Stuart Mill found in
Wordsworth's poetry the experience through which he
overcame a severe mental depression. Yet such didactic or
therapeutic aims should not replace directly literary concerns. The teacher of literature seeks primarily to help students to read so well that they may derive any and all possible benefits from literature. On the other hand, the anti-

septic reaction of the extreme disciples of the so-called purely literary approach, who fear any moral or psychological concern, tends to negate the full nature of the literary work of art.

HERE, THEN, IS another important implication of the emphasis on the essentially personal character of literary experience: It forces us to recognize that in the classroom, if we are to keep literature alive, we cannot completely separate the technical, the esthetic, from the human meanings of the work.

Perhaps a very simple and modest illustration will suffice, drawn from a discussion by a group of verbally not very gifted high school seniors, most of whom were destined for vocational or technical colleges or institutes. One of the girls responded with intense indignation to the story of a man who had left his wife and child and run off to sea. The other pupils objected to her unqualified condemnation. They pointed out the many clues to the father's unhappiness, his boredom with monotonous routine work, the dreary apartment, his nagging wife, and his yearning for the romance of far-off exotic places. Some of these clues were in descriptive details, in items like a picture on the wall which took on symbolic meaning in relation to all the other details. The story was certainly not very complex, but it sufficed to provide the occasion for what amounted to a group process in "close reading." By the time the discussion ended the girl realized that, no matter what her opinions about a husband's responsibilities, she had missed the insights the story offered into personality and the conflicting needs of husband and wife in the situation.

From one point of view, the girl's learning was merely a matter of becoming aware of literary devices and narrative development. From another angle, she had to some slight degree simply acquired a sounder moral stance, in which passing of moral judgment was tempered by understanding of motives and human needs. These are two indivisible facets of the same process of growth in ability to read and respond in a balanced way to the literary work. (Probably none of the youngsters in that group was ready to be amused at the trick ending of the story or to decide on whether it was a sound ending—which again, even for so frail a literary work, would involve the human implications of the story as well as its technical dexterity.) When we are helping students to better techniques of reading through sensitivity to diction, tone, structure, image, symbol, narrative movement, we are also helping them to make the more refined responses that are ultimately the source of human understanding and sensitivity to human values.

WHEN THERE is active participation in literature—the reader living through, reflecting on, and criticizing his own responses to the text—there will be many kinds of benefits. We can call this "growth in ability to share discriminatingly in the possibilities of language as it is used in literature." But this means also the development of the imagination: the ability to escape from the limitations of time and place and environment, the capacity to envisage alternatives in ways of life and in moral and social choices, the sensitivity to thought and feeling and needs of other personalities. The youth will need to grow into the emotional and intellectual and esthetic maturity necessary for appreciating the great works of literature in our own and other languages. As he does this, he grows also into partnership in the wisdom of the past and the aspirations for the future, of our culture and our society. The great abstractions, love, honor, integrity, compassion, individuality, democracy, will take on for him human meaning.

Keats, you recall, ends his sonnet on sitting down to read *King Lear* once again, with the lines:

> But when I am consumèd in the Fire,
> Give me new Phoenix-wings to fly at my desire.

Keats saw himself about to be completely "consumed," absorbed in, the reliving of the play. But he anticipated that he would emerge reborn to even greater freedom and creativity. This is indeed the paradox of the intensely personal nature of the reading of a literary work: It is a kind of experience valuable in and for itself, and yet—or perhaps, therefore—it can also have a liberating and fortifying effect in the ongoing life of the reader.

For Further Reading

IT WOULD BE IMPOSSIBLE to give a complete list of bibliographical sources for this book, since it presents a synthesis developed in the course of many years of teaching. My most obvious debt is to the works of John Dewey and George Santayana.

For the practicing teacher, the journals and other publications of the National Council of Teachers of English (Urbana, Illinois) should be mentioned as sources on teaching methods, selection of literary works, and research in the teaching of literature. The American Library Association (Chicago, Illinois) also publishes helpful book lists.

A section listing a few works on teaching methods is included below. The other sections are offered mainly as an informal supplement to Chapter 6. A sampling of works —some standard, some very recent—has been grouped loosely by fields. My aim is not to be inclusive, but to suggest the kinds of concepts or concerns that might be brought to bear on the literary experience. Almost all the works cited can be found in paperback editions.

I. On Teaching Methods and Education

(Note also items in the Index, e.g., Classroom discussion, Teachers of literature, Teaching methods, Students, etc.)

BLAUG, MARK, ed. *The Economics of Education.* London: Penguin, 1968.

DENNISON, GEORGE. *The Lives of Children.* New York: Random House, 1969.

DEWEY, JOHN. *Experience and Education.* New York: Macmillan, 1938.

DIXON, JOHN. *Growth Through English.* Urbana, Ill.: NCTE, 1967.

FADER, DANIEL, and McNEIL, ELTON. *Hooked on Books*. New York: Berkley, Medallion, 1968.

GULLEY, HALBERT E. *Discussion, Conference, and Group Process*. New York: Holt, Rinehart and Winston, 1968.

HOLT, JOHN. *How Children Learn*. New York: Pitman, 1967.

JUDY, STEPHEN. *Explorations in the Teaching of English: A Source Book for Experimental Teaching*. New York: Dodd, Mead, 1974.

KALLEN, HORACE M. *The Education of Free Men*. New York: Farrar, Straus, 1949.

KOHL, HERBERT. *The Open Classroom*. New York: *New York Review of Books*, 1969.

KOZOL, JONATHAN. *Free Schools*. New York: Houghton Mifflin, 1972.

LOBAN, WALTER D. *Literature and Social Sensitivity*. Champaign, Ill.: NCTE, 1954.

PURVES, ALAN C., and BEACH, RICHARD. *Literature and the Reader: Research in Response to Literature, Reading Interests, and the Teaching of Literature*. Champaign, Ill.: NCTE, 1972.

————. *Literature Education in Ten Countries*. New York: Wiley, 1973.

RICHARDS, I. A. *Practical Criticism*. New York: Harcourt Brace, 1929. Harvest paperback.

SMITH, FRANK. *Understanding Reading*. New York: Holt, Rinehart, and Winston, 1971.

SQUIRE, JAMES R., ed. *Response to Literature*. Urbana, Ill.: NCTE, 1968.

————. *The Responses of Adolescents While Reading Four Short Stories*. Champaign, Ill.: NCTE Research Report No. 7, 1966.

WHITEHEAD, ALFRED NORTH. *The Aims of Education*. New York: Macmillan, 1929.

II. On Values

ALLPORT, GORDON, et al. *The Study of Values*. Boston: Houghton Mifflin, 1960.

BRONOWSKI, JACOB. *Science and Human Values*. Rev. ed. New York: Harper & Row, 1965.

CAMUS, ALBERT. The Myth of Sisyphus. New York: Knopf, 1955.

CANTOR, NATHANIEL. *The Dynamics of Learning*. New York: Agathon Press, 1950.

CRITTENDON, BRIAN. *Form and Content in Moral Education*. Toronto: Ontario Institute for Studies in Education, 1972.

DAHL, ROBERT. *After the Revolution: Authority in a Good Society*. New Haven: Yale University Press, 1970. Yale Fastback Series.

DEWEY, JOHN. *Human Nature and Conduct*. New York: Modern Library, 1930.

————. *The Theory of Valuation*. Chicago: University of Chicago Press, 1939.

MORRIS, CHARLES. *Varieties of Human Value*. Chicago: University of Chicago Press, 1956.

OKUN, ARTHUR M. *Equality and Efficiency: The Big Trade-off*. Washington: The Brookings Institution, 1975.

PETERS, RICHARD S. *Psychology and Ethical Development*. London: Allen and Unwin, 1974.

PIRSIG, ROBERT M. *Zen and the Art of Motorcycle Maintenance*. New York: Bantam Books, 1975.

WARNOCK, MARY. *Ethics Since 1900*. New York: Oxford University Press, 1968.

III. On Some Philosophical Approaches

ABEL, REUBEN. *Man Is the Measure*. New York: Free Press, 1976.

DEWEY, JOHN. *Art as Experience*. New York: Minton, Balch, 1934.

————. *Experience and Nature.* 3rd ed. La Salle, Ill.: Open Court, 1958.

————, and BENTLEY, ARTHUR F. *Knowing and the Known.* Boston: Beacon Press, 1949.

HANSON, NORWOOD R. *Observation and Explanation.* New York: Harper & Row, 1971. Harper Torchbooks.

HOOK, SIDNEY. *The Hero in History.* Boston: Beacon Press, 1955.

KALLEN, HORACE M. *Art and Freedom.* 2 vols. New York: Duell, Sloan, and Pearce, 1942.

————. *Liberty, Laughter and Tears.* De Kalb, Ill.: Northern Illinois University Press, 1968.

KAPLAN, ABRAHAM. *The Conduct of Inquiry.* San Francisco: Chandler Publishing Co., 1964.

KUHN, THOMAS. *The Structure of Scientific Revolutions.* 2nd ed. Chicago: University of Chicago Press, 1970.

NAGEL, ERNEST, and BRANDT, RICHARD R., eds. *Meaning and Knowledge.* New York: Harcourt Brace Jovanovich, 1965.

NATANSON, MAURICE, ed. *Philosophy of the Social Sciences.* New York: Random House, 1963.

OLSON, ROBERT G. *An Introduction to Existentialism.* New York: Dover, 1962.

POLYANI, MICHAEL. *Personal Knowledge.* New York: Harper & Row, 1964.

POPPER, KARL. *The Open Society and Its Enemies.* Princeton: Princeton University Press, 1965.

ROSENBLATT, LOUISE. *L'Idée de l'art pour l'art.* Paris: Champion, 1931.

SANTAYANA, GEORGE. *Reason in Art.* New York: Scribner, 1924.

————. *Three Philosophical Poets.* Cambridge, Mass.: Harvard University Press, 1922.

SEARLE, J. R. *The Philosophy of Language.* New York: Oxford University Press, 1971.

WAISMANN, F. *Principles of Linguistic Philosophy.* New York: St. Martin's, 1965.

IV. On Anthropology

BENEDICT, RUTH. *Patterns of Culture.* Boston: Houghton Mifflin, 1934.

BOAS, FRANZ. *Anthropology and Modern Life.* New York: Norton, 1962.

HERSKOVITS, MELVILLE. *Cultural Anthropology.* New York: Knopf, 1955.

HYMES, DELL. *Language in Culture and Society.* New York: Harper & Row, 1964.

MEAD, MARGARET. *An Anthropologist at Work: Writings of Ruth Benedict.* Boston: Houghton Mifflin, 1959.

————. *Coming of Age in Samoa.* New York: Morrow, 1928.

————. *Continuities in Cultural Evolution.* New Haven, Conn.: Yale University Press, 1964.

————. *Sex and Temperament in Three Primitive Societies.* New York: Morrow, 1935.

NADEL, SIEGFRIED F. *The Foundations of Social Anthropology.* New York: Free Press, 1951.

SAPIR, EDWARD. *Culture, Language and Personality.* Berkeley: University of California Press, 1949.

————. Language: *An Introduction to the Study of Speech.* New York: Harcourt Brace, 1921.

V. On Psychology

ALLPORT, GORDON W. *Pattern and Growth in Personality.* New York: Holt, Rinehart and Winston, 1961.

BATESON, GREGORY. *Steps to an Ecology of Mind.* New York: Ballantine, 1975.

BETTELHEIM, BRUNO. *The Informed Heart.* New York: Free Press, 1960.

BROWN, ROGER. *Social Psychology*. New York: Free Press, 1965.

BRUNER, JEROME. *On Knowing*. Cambridge, Mass.: Harvard University Press, 1962.

CANTRIL, HADLEY. *The Pattern of Human Concerns*. New Brunswick, N.J.: Rutgers University Press, 1965.

DEWEY, JOHN. *How We Think*. Boston: Heath, 1933.

ERIKSON, ERIK H. *Childhood and Society*. Rev. ed. New York: Norton, 1964.

INHELDER, B., and PIAGET, JEAN. Translated by A. Parsons and S. Milgrim. *The Growth of Logical Thinking from Childhood to Adolescence*. New York: Basic Books, 1958.

KAGAN, JEROME, and COLES, ROBERT, eds. *Twelve to Sixteen: Early Adolescence*. New York: Norton, 1972.

PIAGET, JEAN. Translated by M. WORDEN. *The Language and Thought of the Child*. 3rd ed. rev. New York: Humanities Press, 1959.

ROGERS, CARL. *On Becoming a Person*. Boston: Houghton Mifflin, 1970.

SHERIF, MUZAFER, and SHERIF, CAROLYN W., eds. *Problems of Youth: Transition to Adulthood in a Changing World*. Chicago: Aldine, 1965.

VI. On Sociology, Economics and Contemporary Problems

BELL, DANIEL. *The Cultural Contradictions of Capitalism*. New York: Basic Books, 1975.

BOULDING, KENNETH. *The Skills of the Economist*. Cleveland: Howard Allen, 1958.

COLLINS, S. *Conflict Sociology*. New York: Academic Press, 1975.

DE BELL, GARRETT. *The Environmental Handbook*. New York: Ballantine, 1970.

FRANKLIN, JOHN HOPE, ed. *Color and Race*. Boston: Beacon Press, 1969.

GALBRAITH, JOHN K. *Economics and the Public Purpose*. Boston: Houghton Mifflin, 1973.

GOFFMAN, ERVING. *Relations in Public*. New York: Basic Books, 1971.

HANDLIN, OSCAR. *The Uprooted*. Boston: Little, Brown, 1973.

HARRINGTON, MICHAEL. *The Other America*. New York: Macmillan, 1962.

HEILBRONER, ROBERT L. *The Making of Economic Society*. Englewood Cliffs, N.J.: Prentice-Hall, 1962.

LIFTON, ROBERT JAY. *The Woman in America*. Boston: Houghton Mifflin, 1967.

SCHUMACHER, E. F. *Small is Beautiful*. New York: Harper & Row, 1973.

SCHUMPETER, JOSEPH A. *Capitalism, Socialism and Democracy*. New York: Harper & Row, 1962. Harper Torchbooks.

TERKEL, STUDS. *Working*. New York: Pantheon, 1974.

Index